Get Connected

D0084445

FEATURES

Interactive Applications

Case Analysis

expand ▶

key terms

McDonald's Strategy in the Quick-Service Restaurant Industry

Answer the assignment questions for this exercise after reading pages 3–9 in Chapter 1 and Illustration Capsule 1.1 on pages 7 and 8. The illustration capsule is also provided below. The exercise should help you to understand why every company needs a sound strategy to compete successfully, manage the conduct of its business, and strengthen its prospects for long-term success. Furthermore, after reading this chapter, you should be able to develop an awareness of the four most dependable strategic approaches for setting a company apart from rivals and winning a competitive advantage.

In 2010, McDonald's was setting new sales records despite a global economic slowdown and declining consumer confidence in the United States. More than 60 million customers visited one of McDonald's

1 Which of the following strategic actions is a part of McDonald's Plan-to-Win strategy?
c. Actions to gain sales and market share with lower prices based on lower costs (Dollar Me

2 Which of the central strategic questions faced by managers of all types of organizations is addressed by McDonald's Plan-to-Win strategy?
e. How are we going to get there?

3 An important element of McDonald's Plan-to-Win strategy is _____.
d. meeting customer needs more cost effectively than its rivals and attracting a large number

4 Which of the following statements best describes McDonald's action plan for competing successfully and operating profitably?
b. Developing a cost-based advantage while delivering acceptable quality, selection, and con

5 Adding more items to its Dollar Menu was possible because of McDonald's strategic focus on _____.
d. minimizing non-value-adding expenses

6 McDonald's restaurant operations have been improved by

2 Case Analysis

next: submit ▶

Lecture Capture

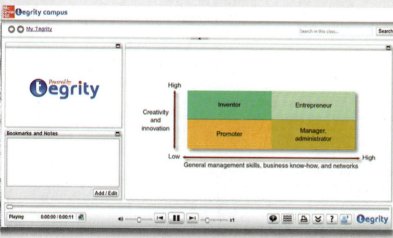

Get Engaged.

Case Exercises

The Connect® platform also includes author-developed case exercises for 14 of the 30 cases in this edition that require students to work through answers to a select number of the assignment questions for the case. These exercises have multiple components and can include calculating assorted financial ratios to assess a company's financial performance and balance sheet strength, identifying a company's strategy, doing five-forces and driving-forces analysis, doing a SWOT analysis, and recommending actions to improve company performance. The content of these case exercises is tailored to match the circumstances presented in each case, calling upon students to do whatever strategic thinking and strategic analysis is called for to arrive at pragmatic, analysis-based action recommendations for improving company performance.

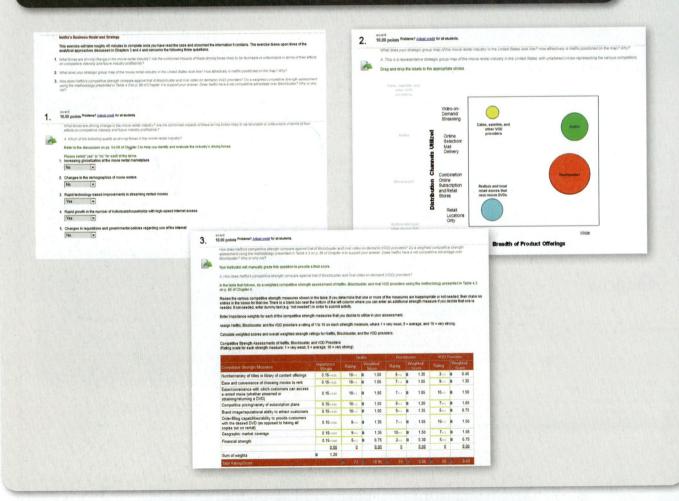

Crafting and Executing Strategy

Concepts and Readings

Crafting and Executing Strategy

Concepts and Readings

NINETEENTH EDITION

Arthur A. Thompson
The University of Alabama

Margaret A. Peteraf
Dartmouth College

John E. Gamble
University of South Alabama

A. J. Strickland III
The University of Alabama

McGraw-Hill Irwin

The McGraw-Hill Companies

McGraw-Hill
Irwin

CRAFTING AND EXECUTING STRATEGY: CONCEPTS AND READINGS, NINETEENTH EDITION

Published by McGraw-Hill/Irwin, a business unit of The McGraw-Hill Companies, Inc., 1221 Avenue of the Americas, New York, NY, 10020. Copyright © 2014 by The McGraw-Hill Companies, Inc. All rights reserved. Printed in the United States of America. Previous editions © 2012, 2010, and 2007. No part of this publication may be reproduced or distributed in any form or by any means, or stored in a database or retrieval system, without the prior written consent of The McGraw-Hill Companies, Inc., including, but not limited to, in any network or other electronic storage or transmission, or broadcast for distance learning.

Some ancillaries, including electronic and print components, may not be available to customers outside the United States.

This book is printed on acid-free paper.

2 3 4 5 6 7 8 9 0 QVS/QVS 1 0 9 8 7 6 5 4 3

ISBN 978-0-07-753707-4
MHID 0-07-753707-6

Senior vice president, products & markets: Kurt L. Strand
Vice president, general manager, products & markets: Brent Gordon
Vice president, content production & technology services: Kimberly Meriwether David
Managing director: Paul Ducham
Executive brand manager: Michael Ablassmeir
Executive director of development: Ann Torbert
Development editor II: Laura Griffin
Marketing manager : Elizabeth Trepkowski
Lead project manager: Harvey Yep

Senior buyer: Michael R. McCormick
Interior designer: Cara Hawthorne, cara david DESIGN
Cover/interior designer: Cara Hawthorne
Content licensing specialist: Joanne Mennemeier
Photo researcher: Bill VanWerden
Manager, content production: Mark Christianson
Senior media project manager: Susan Lombardi
Media project manager: Cathy L. Tepper
Typeface: 10.5/12 Minion Pro
Compositor: Laserwords Private Limited
Printer: Quad/Graphics

All credits appearing on page or at the end of the book are considered to be an extension of the copyright page.

Library of Congress Cataloging-in-Publication Data

Thompson, Arthur A.
  Crafting and executing strategy : the quest for competitive advantage : concepts and readings / Arthur A. Thompson, The University of Alabama, Margaret A. Peteraf, Dartmouth College, John E. Gamble, University of South Alabama, A. J. Strickland III, The University of Alabama.—NINETEENTH EDITION.
    pages cm
  Includes index.
  ISBN 978-0-07-753707-4 (alk. paper)—ISBN 0-07-753707-6 (alk. paper)
  1. Strategic planning. 2. Strategic planning—Case studies. I. Peteraf, Margaret A. II. Gamble, John E. III. Strickland, A. J. IV. Title.
HD30.28.T53 2014
658.4'012—dc23
                                                                                    2012043791

The Internet addresses listed in the text were accurate at the time of publication. The inclusion of a website does not indicate an endorsement by the authors or McGraw-Hill, and McGraw-Hill does not guarantee the accuracy of the information presented at these sites.

www.mhhe.com

To our families and especially our spouses:
Hasseline, Paul, and Kitty.

ABOUT THE AUTHORS

Arthur A. Thompson, Jr., earned his B.S. and Ph.D. degrees in economics from The University of Tennessee, spent three years on the economics faculty at Virginia Tech, and served on the faculty of The University of Alabama's College of Commerce and Business Administration for 24 years. In 1974 and again in 1982, Dr. Thompson spent semester-long sabbaticals as a visiting scholar at the Harvard Business School.

His areas of specialization are business strategy, competition and market analysis, and the economics of business enterprises. In addition to publishing over 30 articles in some 25 different professional and trade publications, he has authored or co-authored five textbooks and six computer-based simulation exercises. His textbooks and strategy simulations have been used at well over 1,000 college and university campuses worldwide.

Dr. Thompson and his wife of 51 years have two daughters, two grandchildren, and a Yorkshire Terrier.

Margaret A. Peteraf is the Leon E. Williams Professor of Management at the Tuck School of Business at Dartmouth College. She is an internationally recognized scholar of strategic management, with a long list of publications in top management journals. She has earned myriad honors and prizes for her contributions, including the 1999 Strategic Management Society Best Paper Award recognizing the deep influence of her work on the field of Strategic Management. Professor Peteraf is on the Board of Directors of the Strategic Management Society and has been elected as a Fellow of the Society. She served previously as a member of the Academy of Management's Board of Governors and as Chair of the Business Policy and Strategy Division of the Academy. She has also served in various editorial roles and is presently on numerous editorial boards, including the *Strategic Management Journal*, the *Academy of Management Review,* and *Organization Science.* She has taught in Executive Education programs in various programs around the world and has won teaching awards at the MBA and Executive level.

Professor Peteraf earned her Ph.D., M.A., and M.Phil. at Yale University and held previous faculty appointments at Northwestern University's Kellogg Graduate School of Management and at the University of Minnesota's Carlson School of Management.

John E. Gamble is currently a Professor of Management in the Mitchell College of Business at the University of South Alabama. His teaching specialty at USA is strategic management and he also conducts a course in strategic management in Germany, which is sponsored by the University of Applied Sciences in Worms.

Dr. Gamble's research interests center on strategic issues in entrepreneurial, health care, and manufacturing settings. His work has been published in various scholarly journals and he is the author or co-author of more than 50 case studies published in an assortment of strategic management and strategic marketing texts. He has done consulting on industry and market analysis for clients in a diverse mix of industries.

Professor Gamble received his Ph.D. in management from The University of Alabama in 1995. Dr. Gamble also has a Bachelor of Science degree and a Master of Arts degree from The University of Alabama.

Dr. A. J. (Lonnie) Strickland is the Thomas R. Miller Professor of Strategic Management at the Culverhouse School of Business at The University of Alabama. He is a native of north Georgia, and attended the University of Georgia, where he received a Bachelor of Science degree in math and physics; Georgia Institute of Technology, where he received a Master of Science in industrial management; and Georgia State University, where he received his Ph.D. in business administration.

Lonnie's experience in consulting and executive development is in the strategic management arena, with a concentration in industry and competitive analysis. He has developed strategic planning systems for numerous firms all over the world. He served as Director of Marketing and Strategy at Bell-South, has taken two companies to the New York Stock Exchange, is one of the founders and directors of American Equity Investment Life Holding (AEL), and serves on numerous boards of directors. He is a very popular speaker in the area of Strategic Management.

Lonnie and his wife, Kitty, have been married for 46 years. They have two children and two grandchildren. Each summer, Lonnie and his wife live on their private game reserve in South Africa where they enjoy taking their friends on safaris.

PREFACE

By offering the most engaging, clearly articulated, and conceptually sound text on strategic management, Crafting and Executing Strategy has been able to maintain its position as the leading textbook in strategic management for close to 30 years. With this latest edition, we build on this strong foundation, maintaining the attributes of the book that have long made it the most teachable text on the market, while updating the content, sharpening its presentation, and providing enlightening new illustrations and examples. The distinguishing mark of the 19th edition is its enriched and enlivened presentation of the material in each of the 12 chapters, providing an as up-to-date and engrossing discussion of the core concepts and analytical tools as you will find anywhere. As with each of our new editions, there is an accompanying collection of new, contemporary readings that amplify important topics in managing a company's strategy-making, strategy-executing process and help drive the chapter lessons home.

While this 19th edition retains the 12-chapter structure of the prior edition, every chapter—indeed every paragraph and every line—has been reexamined, refined, and refreshed. New content has been added to keep the material in line with the latest developments in the theory and practice of strategic management. In other areas, coverage has been trimmed to keep the book at a more manageable size. Scores of new examples have been added, along with 16 new Illustration Capsules, to enrich understanding of the content and to provide students with a ringside view of strategy in action. The result is a text that cuts straight to the chase in terms of what students really need to know and gives instructors a leg up on teaching that material effectively. It remains, as always, solidly mainstream and balanced, mirroring *both* the penetrating insight of academic thought and the pragmatism of real-world strategic management.

A stand-out feature of this text is the tight linkage between the content of the chapters and the selected readings—two new readings for each chapter. The lineup of readings that accompany the 19th edition is outstanding in this respect—a truly appealing mix of strategically relevant and practically oriented readings, certain to engage students and sharpen their thinking on how to apply the concepts and tools of strategic analysis. We are confident you will be impressed with how well the readings work as discussion vehicles and the amount of student interest they will spark.

For some years now, growing numbers of strategy instructors at business schools worldwide have been transitioning from a purely text-readings course structure to a more robust and energizing text-readings-simulation course structure. Incorporating a competition-based strategy simulation has the strong appeal of providing class members with *an immediate and engaging opportunity to apply the concepts and analytical tools covered in the chapters and to become personally involved in crafting and executing a strategy for a virtual company that they have been assigned to manage and that competes head-to-head with companies run by other class members.* Two widely used and pedagogically effective online strategy simulations, *The Business Strategy Game* and *GLO-BUS,* are optional companions for this text. Both simulations were created by Arthur Thompson, one of the text authors, and, like the readings, are closely linked to the content of each chapter in the text. The Exercises for Simulation Participants, found at the end of each chapter, provide clear guidance to class members in applying the concepts and analytical tools covered in the chapters to the issues and decisions that they have to wrestle with in managing their simulation company.

To assist instructors assessing student achievement of program learning objectives, in line with new AACSB requirements, the 19th edition includes a set of Assurance of Learning Exercises at the end of each chapter that link to the specific learning objectives appearing at the beginning of each chapter and highlighted throughout the text. A new feature of the 19th edition is its more closely *integrated* linkage of selected chapter-end Assurance of Learning Exercises to the publisher's web-based assignment and assessment platform called Connect.™ Your students will be able to use the online Connect™ supplement to (1) complete two or three of the Assurance of Learning Exercises appearing at the end of each of the 12 chapters, and (2) complete chapter-end quizzes. All of the Connect™ exercises are automatically graded, thereby enabling you to easily assess the learning that has occurred.

In addition, both of the companion strategy simulations have a built-in Learning Assurance Report that quantifies how well each member of your class performed on nine skills / learning measures *versus tens of thousands of other students worldwide* who completed the simulation in the past 12 months. We believe the chapter-end Assurance of Learning Exercises, the all-new online and automatically graded Connect exercises, and the Learning Assurance Report generated at the conclusion of *The Business Strategy Game* and *GLO-BUS* simulations provide you with easy-to-use, empirical measures of student learning in your course. All can be used in conjunction with other instructor-developed or school-developed scoring rubrics and assessment tools to comprehensively evaluate course or program learning outcomes and measure compliance with AACSB accreditation standards.

Taken together, the various components of the 19th-edition package and the supporting set of instructor resources provide you with enormous course design flexibility and a powerful kit of teaching/learning tools. We've done our very best to ensure that the elements constituting the 19th edition will work well for you in the classroom, help you economize on the time needed to be well prepared for each class, and cause students to conclude that your course is one of the very best they have ever taken—from the standpoint of both enjoyment and learning.

DIFFERENTIATING FEATURES OF THE 19TH EDITION

Six standout features strongly differentiate this text and the accompanying instructional package from others in the field:

1. *Our integrated coverage of the two most popular perspectives on strategic management—positioning theory and resource-based theory—is unsurpassed by any other leading strategy text.* Principles and concepts from both the positioning perspective and the resource-based perspective are prominently and comprehensively integrated into our coverage of crafting both single-business and multibusiness strategies. By highlighting the relationship between a firm's resources and capabilities to the activities it conducts along its value chain, we show explicitly how these two perspectives relate to one another. Moreover, in Chapters 3 through 8 it is emphasized repeatedly that a company's strategy must be matched *not only* to its

external market circumstances *but also* to its internal resources and competitive capabilities.

2. *Our coverage of cooperative strategies and the role that interorganizational activity can play in the pursuit of competitive advantage, is similarly distinguished.* The topics of strategic alliances, licensing, joint ventures, and other types of collaborative relationships are featured prominently in a number of chapters and are integrated into other material throughout the text. We show how strategies of this nature can contribute to the success of single-business companies as well as multibusiness enterprises, whether with respect to firms operating in domestic markets or those operating in the international realm.

3. *With a stand-alone chapter devoted to this topic, our coverage of business ethics, corporate social responsibility, and environmental sustainability goes well beyond that offered by any other leading strategy text.* This chapter, "Ethics, Corporate Social Responsibility, Environmental Sustainability, and Strategy" fulfills the important functions of (1) alerting students to the role and importance of ethical and socially responsible decision making and (2) addressing the accreditation requirement of the AACSB International that business ethics be visibly and thoroughly embedded in the core curriculum. Moreover, discussions of the roles of values and ethics are integrated into portions of other chapters to further reinforce why and how considerations relating to ethics, values, social responsibility, and sustainability should figure prominently into the managerial task of crafting and executing company strategies.

4. *Long known as a valuable accompaniment to this text, the readings collection in the 19th edition is truly unrivaled* from the standpoints of student appeal, teachability, and suitability for sparking discussions of the application of the concepts in Chapters 1 through 12. The 24 readings included in this edition are the very latest, the best, and the most on target that we could find.

5. *The text is now more tightly linked to the publisher's trailblazing web-based assignment and assessment platform called Connect.™* This will enable professors to gauge class members' prowess in accurately completing (a) selected chapter-end exercises and (b) chapter-end quizzes.

6. *Two cutting-edge and widely used strategy simulations—The Business Strategy Game and GLO-BUS—are optional companions to the 19th edition.* These give you an unmatched capability to employ a text-readings-simulation model of course delivery.

ORGANIZATION, CONTENT, AND FEATURES OF THE 19TH-EDITION TEXT CHAPTERS

- Chapter 1 serves as a brief, general introduction to the topic of strategy, focusing on the central questions of *"What is strategy?"* and *"Why is it important?"* As such, it serves as the perfect accompaniment for your opening-day lecture on what the course is all about and why it matters. Using the example of McDonald's to drive home the concepts in this chapter, we introduce students to what we mean by "competitive advantage" and the key features of business-level strategy. Describing strategy-making as a process, we explain why a company's strategy is partly planned and partly reactive and why a strategy tends to co-evolve with its environment over time. We show that a viable business model must provide both an attractive value proposition for the company's customers as well as a formula for making profits for the company, framing this discussion in terms of value, price, and cost. We show how the mark of a winning strategy is its ability to pass three tests: (1) the *fit test* (for internal and external fit), (2) the *competitive advantage test,* and (3) the *performance test.* And we explain why good company performance depends not only upon a sound strategy but upon solid strategy execution as well.

- Chapter 2 presents a more complete overview of the strategic management process, covering topics ranging from the role of vision, mission, and values to what constitutes good corporate governance. It makes a great assignment for the second day of class and provides a smooth transition into the heart of the course. It introduces students to such core concepts as strategic versus financial objectives, the balanced scorecard, strategic intent, and business-level versus corporate-level strategies. It explains why *all managers are on a company's strategy-making, strategy-executing team* and why a company's strategic plan is a collection of strategies devised by different managers at different levels in the organizational hierarchy. The chapter concludes with a section on the role of the board of directors in the strategy-making, strategy-executing process and examines the conditions that led to recent high-profile corporate governance failures.

- The next two chapters introduce students to the two most fundamental perspectives on strategy-making: the positioning view, exemplified by Michael Porter's "five forces model of competition" and the resource-based view. Chapter 3 provides *what has long been the clearest, most straightforward discussion of the five forces framework to be found in any text on strategic management.* It also offers a set of complementary analytical tools for conducting competitive analysis and demonstrates the importance of tailoring strategy to fit the circumstances of a company's industry and competitive environment. What's new in this edition is the inclusion of a framework for conducting competitor analysis that provides a window into a rival's probable moves and countermoves. There is also a more explicit use of the *PESTEL analysis* framework for assessing the *p*olitical, *e*conomic, *s*ocial, *t*echnological, *e*nvironmental, and *l*egal factors in a company's macro-environment.

- Chapter 4 presents the resource-based view of the firm, showing why resource and capability analysis is such a powerful tool for sizing up a company's competitive assets. It offers a simple framework for identifying a company's resources and capabilities and another for determining whether they can provide the company with a sustainable competitive advantage over its competitors. New to this edition is a more explicit reference to the widely used *VRIN framework.* Other topics covered in this chapter include dynamic capabilities, SWOT analysis, value chain analysis, benchmarking, and competitive strength assessments, thus enabling a solid appraisal of a company's relative cost position and customer value proposition vis-à-vis its rivals. *An important feature of this chapter is a table showing how key financial and operating ratios are calculated and how to interpret them.* Students will find this table handy in doing the number crunching needed to evaluate whether a company's strategy is delivering good financial performance.

- Chapter 5 sets forth the basic approaches available for competing and winning in the marketplace in terms of the five generic competitive strategies—low-cost leadership, differentiation, best-cost provider, focused differentiation, and focused low cost. It describes when each of these approaches works best and what pitfalls to avoid. It explains the role of *cost drivers* and *uniqueness drivers* in reducing a company's costs and enhancing its differentiation, respectively.

- Chapter 6 focuses on *other strategic actions* a company can take to complement its competitive approach and maximize the power of its overall strategy. These include a variety of offensive or defensive competitive moves, and their timing, such as blue-ocean strategies and first-mover advantages and disadvantages. It also includes choices concerning the breadth of a company's activities (or its *scope* of operations along an industry's entire value chain), ranging from horizontal mergers and acquisitions, to vertical integration, outsourcing, and strategic alliances. This material serves to segue into that covered in the next two chapters on international and diversification strategies.

- Chapter 7 takes up the topic of how to compete in international markets. It begins with a discussion of why differing market conditions across countries must necessarily influence a company's strategic choices about how to enter and compete in foreign markets. It presents five major strategic options for expanding a company's geographic scope and competing in foreign markets: export strategies, licensing, franchising, establishing a wholly owned subsidiary via acquisition or "greenfield" venture, and alliance strategies. It includes coverage of topics such as Porter's Diamond of National Advantage, profit sanctuaries, and the choice between multidomestic, global, and transnational strategies. This chapter explains the impetus for sharing, transferring, or accessing valuable resources and capabilities across national borders in the quest for competitive advantage, connecting the material to that on the resource-based view from Chapter 4. The chapter concludes with a discussion of the unique characteristics of competing in developing country markets.

- Chapter 8 concerns strategy-making in the multibusiness company, introducing the topic of corporate-level strategy with its special focus on diversification. The first portion of this chapter describes when and why diversification makes good strategic sense, the different means of diversifying a company's business lineup, and the pros and cons of related versus unrelated diversification strategies. The second part of the chapter looks at how to evaluate the attractiveness of a diversified company's business lineup, how to decide whether it has a good diversification strategy, and what the strategic options are for improving a diversified company's future performance. The evaluative technique integrates material concerning both industry analysis and the resource-based view, in that it considers the relative attractiveness of the various industries the company has diversified into, the company's competitive strength in each of its lines of business, and the extent to which its different businesses exhibit both *strategic fit* and *resource fit*.

- Although the topic of ethics and values comes up at various points in this textbook, Chapter 9 brings more direct attention to such issues and may be used as a stand-alone assignment in either the early, middle, or late part of a course. It concerns the themes of ethical standards in business, approaches to ensuring consistent ethical standards for companies with international operations, corporate social responsibility, and environmental sustainability. The contents of this chapter are sure to give students some things to ponder, rouse lively discussion, and help to make students more *ethically aware* and conscious of *why all companies should conduct their business in a socially responsible and sustainable manner.*

- The next three chapters (Chapters 10, 11, and 12) comprise a module on strategy execution that is presented in terms of a 10-step framework. Chapter 10 provides an overview of this framework and then explores the first three of these tasks: (1) staffing the organization with people capable of executing the strategy well, (2) building the organizational capabilities needed for successful strategy execution, and (3) creating an organizational structure supportive of the strategy execution process.

- Chapter 11 discusses five additional managerial actions that advance the cause of good strategy execution: (1) *allocating resources* to enable the strategy execution process, (2) ensuring that *policies and procedures* facilitate rather than impede strategy execution, (3) using *process management tools* and *best practices* to drive continuous improvement in the performance of value chain activities, (4) installing *information and operating systems* that help company personnel carry out their strategic roles, and (5) using *rewards and incentives* to encourage good strategy execution and the achievement of performance targets.

- Chapter 12 completes the framework with a consideration of the roles of corporate culture and leadership in promoting good strategy execution. The recurring theme throughout the final three chapters is that executing strategy involves deciding on the specific actions, behaviors, and conditions needed for a smooth strategy-supportive operation and then following through to get things done and deliver results. The goal here is to ensure that students understand that the strategy-executing phase is a *make-things-happen and make-them-happen-right* kind of managerial exercise—one that is critical for achieving operating excellence and reaching the goal of strong company performance.

In this latest edition, we have put our utmost effort into ensuring that the 12 chapters are consistent with the latest and best thinking of academics and practitioners in the field of strategic management and provide the topical coverage required for both undergraduate and MBA-level strategy courses. The ultimate test of the text, of course, is the positive pedagogical impact it has in the classroom. If this edition sets a more effective stage for your lectures and does a better job of helping you persuade students that the discipline of strategy merits their rapt attention, then it will have fulfilled its purpose.

THE COLLECTION OF READINGS

The 24 readings in this edition are flush with practical examples and valuable lessons for students of the art and science of crafting and executing strategy. There are two readings for each chapter—all chosen with three criteria in mind: relevance, readability, and recency of publication. The *relevance* criterion led us to seek out articles that connected clearly to the material in the text chapters and either extended the chapter coverage or expanded on a topic of strategic importance. The *readability* criterion helped us identify articles that were clearly written, engaging, practically oriented, and relatively short. The *recency* criterion limited our selections to those that appeared in the 2010–2012 period. We endeavored to be highly selective in our choices, deciding that a manageable number of on-target readings was a better fit with the teaching/learning objectives of most senior and MBA courses in strategy than a more sweeping collection of readings. The readings we chose came from recent issues of *Harvard Business Review, MIT Sloan Management Review, McKinsey Quarterly, Business Strategy Review, Business Horizons, Journal of Business Strategy, Ivey Business Journal,* and *IESE Insight,* among others.

The first reading, by Richard Rumelt, "The Perils of Bad Strategy," makes an excellent accompaniment to the introductory chapter with its focus on the question of "What distinguishes good strategy from bad strategy?" It reminds readers that strategy is as much about what NOT to do as it is about what TO do and explains why having a compelling vision, mission, and set of core values is not enough. The second reading, "How to Identify New Business Models," addresses another key topic from Chapter 1. It provides an outstanding discussion of how innovative new business models can enable companies to create value and uncover new opportunities for growth as well.

The third reading, "Strategy Making: The Approach Matters" argues the approach to strategy making is as important as the strategy itself. In practical terms, it focuses on describing how strategy making happens on the continuum of deliberate versus emerging strategy. The fourth reading, "The Real Job of Boards" turns attention to corporate governance issues—the final topic in Chapter 2. It suggests that more leadership on the part of a company's board of directors could help avert many corporate crises in the future and prevent another worldwide financial crisis.

"Which Strategy When?" by Chris Bingham, Kathy Eisenhardt, and Nathan Furr draws attention to the need to match strategy to the changing needs of a company's competitive environment. It suggests that what is right for a company depends on its circumstances as well as its available resources and how those resources are assembled (thus anticipating the topic of Chapter 4 as well). "A Shared Fate," by Ron Adner, uses an ecosystem lens to describe the potential for collaborative advantage. This short piece derives from a framework that can be seen as a valuable extension of, and complement to, the familiar five-forces framework.

Reading 7, entitled "Adaptability: The New Competitive Advantage," suggests that competitive advantage in a changing world stems from the types of organizational capabilities that foster rapid adaptation. Reading 8, by David Teece, continues the theme of the need for adaptive capabilities, but focuses instead on dynamic capabilities, as its title, "Dynamic Capabilities: A Guide for Managers," suggests.

The next two readings provide valuable supplements to the material on generic strategies covered in Chapter 5. The first, "Profiting When Customers Choose Value over Price," contrasts cost-based pricing with value-based pricing, concluding that the latter tends to lead to superior profitability. The second, by David Bryce, Jeff Dyer, and Nile Hatch, focuses on a more challenging pricing issue: how to compete when competitors offer their goods for free (an increasingly prevalent phenomenon).

Clayton Christenson et al.'s article, "The New M&A Playbook," makes a perfect accompaniment to Chapter 6. They argue that to increase the odds of success from acquiring a company, managers need to understand how to select targets, how much to pay for them, and whether and how to integrate them. The next reading, "Adding Value through Offshoring," by Joan Enric Ricart and Pablo Agnese, adds the topic of offshoring to the discussion about outsourcing covered in Chapter 6. They offer insight on modern offshoring practices, showing how companies can not only lower costs through such practices but create value as well.

Reading 13, "Is Your Emerging-Market Strategy Local Enough?" focuses more directly on topical concerns in the area of international strategies. The authors suggest that a one-sized approach for entering emerging markets may not be appropriate for countries like India and China, where market characteristics vary from one locale to another. They advise companies to seize growth opportunities in such environments by targeting more uniform clusters of cities. "Strategic Orchestration" by Don Sull and Alejandro Ruelas-Gossi, continues the theme of how to compete in emerging markets.

They suggest that a management path to success known as "strategic orchestration" is being blazed by companies such as Apple, Ryanair, and Nestlé.

The next two readings complement and extend the material on corporate strategy presented in Chapter 8. Reading 15, "Diversification: Best Practices of the Leading Companies," concerns a central topic in this chapter and describes how successful diversifiers such as GE and MacDonald's manage this aspect of their businesses. "Successful Divestitures Need Proper Cultivation" introduces a topic that supplements those found in Chapter 8, explaining how divestitures, in their many forms, can improve the profitability of both the parent company and the divested unit.

Readings 17 and 18 deal with the core material found in Chapter 9. Rosabeth Kanter's piece entitled "How to Do Well *and* Do Good" argues that achieving both of these goals requires companies to integrate the benefits it offers to society more closely with the mission and strategic objectives of its businesses. "Managing Moral Distress: A Strategy for Resolving Ethical Dilemmas," as its title suggests, takes on the topic of business ethics. It offers a practical framework for assessing and resolving ethical dilemmas in a circumspect and reflective manner.

The next six readings comprise a set of readings that cover various aspects concerning strategy execution. The first of these, "The Role of Perceived Benefits of Training in Generating Affective Commitment and High Value of Firms," concerns how to ensure that training activities will impart needed skills and result in high value for the company. The second, entitled "The Learning Enterprise," describes how firms can incorporate best practices into their knowledge base, encourage innovation, and turn the entire company into a learning team.

Readings 21 and 22 link to the topical material found in Chapter 11. "Why Operational Excellence Matters" explains that small improvements in business processes can become the source of a company's competitive advantage—but only if the company can identify which processes matter and develop the means to manage them well. "Using Knowledge Brokering to Improve Business Processes" continues to develop this theme, focusing on principles that allow companies to enhance their core businesses processes.

The last two readings were chosen to expand upon and complement the central themes of Chapter 12. As its title suggests, "Corporate Culture: Its Value as a Resource for Competitive Advantage" illustrates the potential contribution of a company's culture toward its attaining a competitive advantage over market rivals. "What Matters Now," the closing article by Gary Hamel, is an impassioned plea by this top strategy guru to reinvent management as we know it. Hamel suggests that effective leaders must focus their attention upon five paramount issues, thus providing a strong and inspirational conclusion for a course on strategic management.

THE TWO STRATEGY SIMULATION SUPPLEMENTS: *THE BUSINESS STRATEGY GAME* AND *GLO-BUS*

The Business Strategy Game and *GLO-BUS: Developing Winning Competitive Strategies*—two competition-based strategy simulations that are delivered online and that feature automated processing and grading of performance—are being marketed by the publisher as companion supplements for use with the 19th edition (and other texts in the field).

- *The Business Strategy Game* is the world's most popular strategy simulation, having been used by nearly 2,000 instructors in courses involving approximately 700,000 students on 900 university campuses in 60 countries.
- *GLO-BUS,* a somewhat simpler strategy simulation introduced in 2004, has been used by more than 1,100 instructors at more than 540 university campuses in 40 countries.

How the Strategy Simulations Work

In both *The Business Strategy Game (BSG)* and *GLO-BUS,* class members are divided into teams of one to five persons and assigned to run a company that competes head-to-head against companies run by other class members.

- In *BSG,* team members run an athletic footwear company, producing and marketing both branded and private-label footwear.
- In *GLO-BUS,* team members operate a digital camera company that designs, assembles, and markets entry-level digital cameras and upscale, multifeatured cameras.

In both simulations, companies compete in a global market arena, selling their products in four geographic regions—Europe-Africa, North America, Asia-Pacific, and Latin America. Each management team is called upon to craft a strategy for their company and make decisions relating to plant operations, workforce compensation, pricing and marketing, social responsibility/citizenship, and finance.

Company co-managers are held accountable for their decision making. Each company's performance is scored on the basis of earnings per share, return-on-equity investment, stock price, credit rating, and image rating. Rankings of company performance, along with a wealth of industry and company statistics, are available to company co-managers after each decision round to use in making strategy adjustments and operating decisions for the next competitive round. You can be certain that the market environment, strategic issues, and operating challenges that company co-managers must contend with are *very tightly linked* to what your class members will be reading about in the text chapters. The circumstances that co-managers face in running their simulation company embrace the very concepts, analytical tools, and strategy options they encounter in the text chapters (this is something you can quickly confirm by skimming through some of the Exercises for Simulation Participants that appear at the end of each chapter).

We suggest that you schedule 1 or 2 practice rounds and anywhere from 4 to 10 regular (scored) decision rounds (more rounds are better than fewer rounds). Each decision round represents a year of company operations and will entail roughly two hours of time for company co-managers to complete. In traditional 13-week, semester-long courses, there is merit in scheduling one decision round per week. In courses that run 5 to 10 weeks, it is wise to schedule two decision rounds per week for the last several weeks of the term (sample course schedules are provided for courses of varying length and varying numbers of class meetings).

When the instructor-specified deadline for a decision round arrives, the simulation server automatically accesses the saved decision entries of each company, determines the competitiveness and buyer appeal of each company's product offering relative to the other companies being run by students in your class, and then awards sales and market shares to the competing companies, geographic region by geographic region. The unit sales volumes awarded to each company *are totally governed by:*

- How its prices compare against the prices of rival brands.
- How its product quality compares against the quality of rival brands.
- How its product line breadth and selection compare.
- How its advertising effort compares.
- And so on, for a total of 11 competitive factors that determine unit sales and market shares.

The competitiveness and overall buyer appeal of each company's product offering *in comparison to the product offerings of rival companies* is all-decisive—this algorithmic feature is what makes *BSG* and *GLO-BUS* "competition-based" strategy simulations. Once each company's sales and market shares are awarded based on the competitiveness of its respective overall product offering, the various company and industry reports detailing the outcomes of the decision round are then generated. Company co-managers can access the results of the decision round 15 to 20 minutes after the decision deadline.

The Compelling Case for Incorporating Use of a Strategy Simulation

There are *three exceptionally important benefits* associated with using a competition-based simulation in strategy courses taken by seniors and MBA students:

- *A three-pronged text-readings-simulation course model delivers significantly more teaching-learning power than the traditional text-readings model.* Using *both* readings and a strategy simulation to drill students in thinking strategically and applying what they read in the text chapters is a stronger, more effective means of helping them connect theory with practice and develop better business judgment. But what a competition-based strategy simulation does far better is thrust class members squarely into *an active, hands-on managerial role* where they are totally responsible for assessing market conditions, determining how to respond to the actions of competitors, forging a long-term direction and strategy for their company, and making all kinds of operating decisions. Because they are held fully accountable for their decisions and their company's performance, *co-managers are strongly motivated* to dig deeply into company operations, probe for ways to be more cost-efficient and competitive, and ferret out strategic moves and decisions calculated to boost company performance. *Consequently, incorporating both readings assignments and a strategy simulation to develop the skills of class members in thinking strategically and applying the concepts and tools of strategic analysis turns out to be more pedagogically powerful than relying solely on readings assignments—there's stronger retention of the lessons learned and better achievement of course learning objectives.*

  To provide you with quantitative evidence of the learning that occurs with using *The Business Strategy Game* or *GLO-BUS,* there is a built-in Learning Assurance Report showing how well each class member performs on nine skills / learning measures versus tens of thousands of students worldwide who have completed the simulation in the past 12 months.

- *The competitive nature of a strategy simulation arouses positive energy and steps up the whole tempo of the course by a notch or two.* Nothing sparks class excitement quicker or better than the concerted efforts on the part of class members at each decision round to achieve a high industry ranking and avoid the perilous consequences of being outcompeted by other class members. Students really enjoy taking on the role of a manager, running their own company, crafting strategies, making all kinds of operating decisions, trying to outcompete rival companies, and getting immediate feedback on the resulting company performance. Lots of back-and-forth chatter occurs when the results of the latest simulation round become available and co-managers renew their quest for strategic moves and actions that will strengthen company performance. Co-managers become *emotionally invested* in running their company and figuring out what strategic moves to make to boost their company's performance. Interest levels climb. All this stimulates learning and causes students to see the practical relevance of the subject matter and the benefits of taking your course.

As soon as your students start to say "Wow! Not only is this fun but I am learning a lot," *which they will,* you have won the battle of engaging students in the subject matter and moved the value of taking your course to a much higher plateau in the business school curriculum. This translates into *a livelier, richer learning experience from a student perspective and better instructor-course evaluations.*

- *Use of a fully automated online simulation reduces the time instructors spend on course preparation, course administration, and grading.* Since the simulation exercise involves a 20- to 30-hour workload for student teams (roughly 2 hours per decision round times 10 to 12 rounds, plus optional assignments), simulation adopters often compensate by trimming the number of assigned readings from, say, 10 to 12 to perhaps 4 to 6. Not only does use of a simulation permit assigning fewer readings, but it also permits you to eliminate at least one assignment that entails considerable grading on your part. Grading one less essay exam or other written assignment saves enormous time. With *BSG* and *GLOBUS,* grading is effortless and takes only minutes; once you enter percentage weights for each assignment in your online grade book, a suggested overall grade is calculated for you. You'll be pleasantly surprised—and quite pleased—at how little time it takes to gear up for and administer *The Business Strategy Game* or *GLO-BUS.*

In sum, incorporating use of a strategy simulation turns out to be *a win–win proposition for both students and instructors.* Moreover, a very convincing argument can be made that a competition-based strategy simulation is *the single most effective teaching/learning tool that instructors can employ to teach the discipline of business and competitive strategy, to make learning more enjoyable, and to promote better achievement of course learning objectives.*

A Bird's-Eye View of *The Business Strategy Game*

The setting for *The Business Strategy Game (BSG)* is the global athletic footwear industry (there can be little doubt in today's world that a globally competitive strategy simulation is *vastly superior* to a simulation with a domestic-only setting). Global market demand for footwear grows at the rate of 7 to 9 percent annually for the first five years and 5 to 7 percent annually for the second five years. However, market growth rates vary by geographic region—North America, Latin America, Europe-Africa, and Asia-Pacific.

Companies begin the simulation producing branded and private-label footwear in two plants, one in North America and one in Asia. They have the option to establish production facilities in Latin America and Europe-Africa, either by constructing new plants or by buying previously constructed plants that have been sold by competing companies. Company co-managers exercise control over production costs on the basis of the styling and quality they opt to manufacture, plant location (wages and incentive compensation vary from region to region), the use of best practices and Six Sigma programs to reduce the production of defective footwear and to boost worker productivity, and compensation practices.

All newly produced footwear is shipped in bulk containers to one of four geographic distribution centers. All sales in a geographic region are made from footwear inventories in that region's distribution center. Costs at the four regional distribution centers are a function of inventory storage costs, packing and shipping fees, import tariffs paid on incoming pairs shipped from foreign plants, and exchange rate impacts. At the start of the simulation, import tariffs average $4 per pair in Europe-Africa, $6 per pair in Latin America, and $8 in the Asia-Pacific region. However, the Free Trade Treaty of the Americas allows tariff-free movement of footwear between North America and Latin America. Instructors have the option to alter tariffs as the game progresses.

Companies market their brand of athletic footwear to footwear retailers worldwide and to individuals buying online at the company's website. Each company's sales and market share in the branded footwear segments hinge on its competitiveness on 11 factors: attractive pricing, footwear styling and quality, product line breadth, advertising, use of mail-in rebates, appeal of celebrities endorsing a company's brand, success in convincing footwear retailers to carry its brand, number of weeks it takes to fill retailer orders, effectiveness of a company's online sales effort at its website, and customer loyalty. Sales of private-label footwear hinge solely on being the low-price bidder.

All told, company co-managers make as many as 53 types of decisions each period that cut across production operations (up to 10 decisions per plant, with a maximum of four plants), plant capacity additions/sales/upgrades (up to 6 decisions per plant), worker compensation and training (3 decisions per plant), shipping (up to 8 decisions per plant), pricing and marketing (up to 10 decisions in four geographic regions), bids to sign celebrities (2 decision entries per bid), financing of company operations (up to 8 decisions), and corporate social responsibility and environmental sustainability (up to 6 decisions).

Each time company co-managers make a decision entry, an assortment of on-screen calculations instantly shows the projected effects on unit sales, revenues, market shares, unit costs, profit, earnings per share, ROE, and other operating statistics. The on-screen calculations help team members evaluate the relative merits of one decision entry versus another and put together a promising strategy.

Companies can employ any of the five generic competitive strategy options in selling branded footwear—low-cost leadership, differentiation, best-cost provider, focused low cost, and focused differentiation. They can pursue essentially the same strategy worldwide or craft slightly or very different strategies for the Europe-Africa, Asia-Pacific, Latin America, and North America markets. They can strive for competitive advantage based on more advertising, a wider selection of models, more appealing styling/quality, bigger rebates, and so on.

Any well-conceived, well-executed competitive approach is capable of succeeding, provided it is not overpowered by the strategies of competitors or defeated by the presence of too many copycat strategies that dilute its effectiveness. The challenge for each company's management team is to craft and execute a competitive strategy that produces good performance on five measures: earnings per share, return on equity investment, stock price appreciation, credit rating, and brand image.

All activity for *The Business Strategy Game* takes place at **www.bsg-online.com**.

A Bird's-Eye View of GLO-BUS

The industry setting for *GLO-BUS* is the digital camera industry. Global market demand grows at the rate of 8 to 10 percent annually for the first five years and 4 to 6 percent annually for the second five years. Retail sales of digital cameras are seasonal, with about 20 percent of consumer demand coming in each of the first three quarters of each calendar year and 40 percent coming during the big fourth-quarter retailing season.

Companies produce entry-level and upscale, multifeatured cameras of varying designs and quality in a Taiwan assembly facility and ship assembled cameras directly to retailers in North America, Asia-Pacific, Europe-Africa, and Latin America. All cameras are assembled as retail orders come in and are shipped immediately upon completion of the assembly process—companies maintain no finished-goods inventories, and all parts and components are delivered on a just-in-time basis (which eliminates the need to track inventories and simplifies the accounting for plant operations and costs). Company co-managers exercise control over production costs on the basis of the designs and components they specify for their cameras, workforce compensation and training, the length of warranties offered (which affects warranty costs), the amount spent for technical support provided to buyers of the company's cameras, and their management of the assembly process.

Competition in each of the two product market segments (entry-level and multi-featured digital cameras) is based on 10 factors: price, camera performance and quality, number of quarterly sales promotions, length of promotions in weeks, size of the promotional discounts offered, advertising, number of camera models, size of the retail dealer network, warranty period, and amount/caliber of technical support provided to camera buyers. Low-cost leadership, differentiation strategies, best-cost provider strategies, and focus strategies are all viable competitive options. Rival companies can strive to be the clear market leader in either entry-level cameras or upscale multifeatured cameras or both. They can focus on one or two geographic regions or strive for geographic balance. They can pursue essentially the same strategy worldwide or craft slightly or very different strategies for the Europe-Africa, Asia-Pacific, Latin America, and North America markets. Just as with *The Business Strategy Game,* almost any well-conceived, well-executed competitive approach is capable of succeeding, *provided it is not overpowered by the strategies of competitors or defeated by the presence of too many copycat strategies that dilute its effectiveness.*

Company co-managers make 49 types of decisions each period, ranging from R&D, camera components, and camera performance (10 decisions) to production operations and worker compensation (15 decisions) to pricing and marketing (15 decisions) to the financing of company operations (4 decisions) to corporate social responsibility (5 decisions). *Each time participants make a decision entry, an assortment of on-screen calculations instantly shows the projected effects on unit sales, revenues, market shares, unit costs, profit, earnings per share, ROE, and other operating statistics. These on-screen calculations help team members evaluate the relative merits of one decision entry versus another and stitch the separate decisions into a cohesive and promising strategy.* Company performance is judged on five criteria: earnings per share, return on equity investment, stock price, credit rating, and brand image.

All activity for *GLO-BUS* occurs at **www.glo-bus.com**.

Administration and Operating Features of the Two Simulations

The Internet delivery and user-friendly designs of both *BSG* and *GLO-BUS* make them incredibly easy to administer, even for first-time users. And the menus and controls are so similar that you can readily switch between the two simulations or use one in your undergraduate class and the other in a graduate class. If you have not yet used either of the two simulations, you may find the following of particular interest:

- Setting up the simulation for your course is done online and takes about 10 to 15 minutes. Once setup is completed, no other administrative actions are required beyond those of moving participants to a different team (should the need arise) and monitoring the progress of the simulation (to whatever extent desired).

- Participant's Guides are delivered electronically to class members at the website—students can read the guide on their monitors or print out a copy, as they prefer.

- There are 2- to 4-minute Video Tutorials scattered throughout the software (including each decision screen and each page of each report) that provide on-demand guidance to class members who may be uncertain about how to proceed.

- Complementing the Video Tutorials are detailed and clearly written Help sections explaining "all there is to know" about (a) each decision entry and the relevant cause-effect relationships, (b) the information on each page of the Industry Reports, and (c) the numbers presented in the Company Reports. *The Video Tutorials and the Help screens allow company co-managers to figure things out for themselves, thereby curbing the need for students to ask the instructor "how things work."*

- Team members running the same company who are logged-in simultaneously on different computers at different locations can click a button to enter Collaboration Mode, enabling them to work collaboratively from the same screen in viewing reports and making decision entries, and click a second button to enter Audio Mode letting them talk to one another.
  - When in "Collaboration Mode," each team member sees the same screen at the same time as all other team members who are logged in and have joined Collaboration Mode. If one team member chooses to view a particular decision screen, that same screen appears on the monitors for all team members in Collaboration Mode.
  - Each team member controls their own color-coded mouse pointer (with their first-name appearing in a color-coded box linked to their mouse pointer) and can make a decision entry or move the mouse to point to particular on-screen items.
  - A decision entry change made by one team member is seen by all, in real time, and all team members can immediately view the on-screen calculations that result from the new decision entry.
  - If one team member wishes to view a report page and clicks on the menu link to the desired report, that same report page will immediately appear for the other team members engaged in collaboration.
  - Use of Audio Mode capability requires that each team member work from a computer with a built-in microphone (if they want to be heard by their team members) and speakers (so they may hear their teammates) or else have a headset with a microphone that they can plug into their desktop or laptop. A headset is recommended for best results, but most laptops now are equipped

with a built-in microphone and speakers that will support use of our new voice chat feature.

- ○ Real-time VoIP audio chat capability among team members who have entered both the Audio Mode and the Collaboration Mode is a tremendous boost in functionality that enables team members to go online simultaneously on computers at different locations and conveniently and effectively collaborate in running their simulation company.

- ○ In addition, instructors have the capability to join the online session of any company and speak with team members, thus circumventing the need for team members to arrange for and attend a meeting in the instructor's office. Using the standard menu for administering a particular industry, instructors can connect with the company desirous of assistance. Instructors who wish not only to talk but also enter Collaboration (highly recommended because all attendees are then viewing the same screen) have a red-colored mouse pointer linked to a red box labeled Instructor.

    Without a doubt, the Collaboration and Voice-Chat capabilities are hugely valuable for students enrolled in online and distance-learning courses where meeting face-to-face is impractical or time-consuming. Likewise, the instructors of online and distance-learning courses will appreciate having the capability to join the online meetings of particular company teams when their advice or assistance is requested.

- Both simulations are quite suitable for use in distance-learning or online courses (and are currently being used in such courses on numerous campuses).

- Participants and instructors are notified via e-mail when the results are ready (usually about 15 to 20 minutes after the decision round deadline specified by the instructor/game administrator).

- Following each decision round, participants are provided with a complete set of reports—a six-page Industry Report, a one-page Competitive Intelligence report for each geographic region that includes strategic group maps and bulleted lists of competitive strengths and weaknesses, and a set of Company Reports (income statement, balance sheet, cash flow statement, and assorted production, marketing, and cost statistics).

- Two "open-book" multiple-choice tests of 20 questions are built into each simulation. The quizzes, which you can require or not as you see fit, are taken online and automatically graded, with scores reported instantaneously to participants and automatically recorded in the instructor's electronic grade book. Students are automatically provided with three sample questions for each test.

- Both simulations contain a three-year strategic plan option that you can assign. Scores on the plan are automatically recorded in the instructor's online grade book.

- At the end of the simulation, you can have students complete online peer evaluations (again, the scores are automatically recorded in your online grade book).

- Both simulations have a Company Presentation feature that enables each team of company co-managers to easily prepare PowerPoint slides for use in describing their strategy and summarizing their company's performance in a presentation to either the class, the instructor, or an "outside" board of directors.

- *A Learning Assurance Report provides you with hard data concerning how well your students performed vis-a-vis students playing the simulation worldwide over the past*

12 months. The report is based on nine measures of student proficiency, business know-how, and decision-making skill and can also be used in evaluating the extent to which your school's academic curriculum produces the desired degree of student learning insofar as accreditation standards are concerned.

For more details on either simulation, please consult Section 2 of the Instructor's Manual accompanying this text or register as an instructor at the simulation websites (**www.bsg-online.com** and **www.glo-bus.com**) to access even more comprehensive information. You should also consider signing up for one of the webinars that the simulation authors conduct several times each month (sometimes several times weekly) to demonstrate how the software works, walk you through the various features and menu options, and answer any questions. You have an open invitation to call the senior author of this text at (205) 722-9145 to arrange a personal demonstration or talk about how one of the simulations might work in one of your courses. We think you'll be quite impressed with the cutting-edge capabilities that have been programmed into *The Business Strategy Game* and *GLO-BUS,* the simplicity with which both simulations can be administered, and their exceptionally tight connection to the text chapters, core concepts, and standard analytical tools.

RESOURCES AND SUPPORT MATERIALS FOR THE 19TH EDITION

For Students

Key Points Summaries   At the end of each chapter is a synopsis of the core concepts, analytical tools, and other key points discussed in the chapter. These chapter-end synopses, along with the core concept definitions and margin notes scattered throughout each chapter, help students focus on basic strategy principles, digest the messages of each chapter, and prepare for tests.

Two Sets of Chapter-End Exercises   Each chapter concludes with two sets of exercises. The *Assurance of Learning Exercises* can be used as the basis for class discussion, oral presentation assignments, and short written reports. The *Exercises for Simulation Participants* are designed expressly for use by adopters who have incorporated use of a simulation and want to go a step further in tightly and explicitly connecting the chapter content to the simulation company their students are running. The questions in both sets of exercises (along with those Illustration Capsules that qualify as "mini-cases") can be used to round out the rest of a 75-minute class period should your lecture on a chapter last for only 50 minutes.

A Value-Added Website   The student section of the Online Learning Center (OLC) at website **www.mhhe.com/thompson** contains a number of helpful aids:

- Ten-question self-scoring chapter tests that students can take to measure their grasp of the material presented in each of the 12 chapters.
- PowerPoint slides for each chapter.

The *Connect™ Management* Web-Based Assignment and Assessment Platform

Beginning with the 18th edition, we began taking advantage of the publisher's innovative *Connect™* assignment and assessment platform and created several features that simplify the task of assigning and grading three types of exercises for students:

- There are self-scoring chapter tests consisting of 20 to 25 multiple-choice questions that students can take to measure their grasp of the material presented in each of the 12 chapters.
- There are two author-developed Interactive Application exercises for each of the 12 chapters that drill students in the use and application of the concepts and tools of strategic analysis.
- All of the *Connect™* exercises are automatically graded (with the exception of those exercise components that entail student entry of short answer and/or essay answers), thereby simplifying the task of evaluating each class member's performance and monitoring the learning outcomes. The progress-tracking function built into the *Connect™ Management* system enables you to:
  - View scored work immediately and track individual or group performance with assignment and grade reports.
  - Access an instant view of student or class performance relative to learning objectives.
  - Collect data and generate reports required by many accreditation organizations, such as AACSB.

For Instructors

Online Learning Center (OLC)

In addition to the student resources, the instructor section of www.mhhe.com/thompson includes an Instructor's Manual and other support materials. Your McGraw-Hill representative can arrange delivery of instructor support materials in a format-ready Standard Cartridge for Blackboard, WebCT, and other web-based educational platforms.

Instructor's Manual

The accompanying IM contains:

- A section on suggestions for organizing and structuring your course.
- Sample syllabi and course outlines.
- A set of lecture notes on each chapter.
- Answers to the chapter-end Assurance of Learning Exercises.
- A copy of the test bank.
- Discussion questions and suggested answers for the readings.

Test Bank and EZ Test Online

There is a test bank containing over 900 multiple-choice questions and short-answer/essay questions. It has been tagged with AACSB and Bloom's Taxonomy criteria. All of the test bank questions are also accessible within a computerized test bank powered by McGraw-Hill's flexible electronic testing program EZ Test Online (www.eztestonline.com). Using EZ Test Online allows you to create paper and online tests or quizzes. With EZ Test Online, instructors can select questions from multiple McGraw-Hill test banks or author their own and then either print the test for paper distribution or give it online.

PowerPoint Slides   To facilitate delivery preparation of your lectures and to serve as chapter outlines, you'll have access to approximately 500 colorful and professional-looking slides displaying core concepts, analytical procedures, key points, and all the figures in the text chapters.

The Business Strategy Game and *GLO-BUS Online Simulations*   Using one of the two companion simulations is a powerful and constructive way of emotionally connecting students to the subject matter of the course. We know of no more effective way to arouse the competitive energy of students and prepare them for the challenges of real-world business decision making than to have them match strategic wits with classmates in running a company in head-to-head competition for global market leadership.

ACKNOWLEDGMENTS

A great number of colleagues and students at various universities, business acquaintances, and people at McGraw-Hill provided inspiration, encouragement, and counsel during the course of this project. Like all text authors in the strategy field, we are intellectually indebted to the many academics whose research and writing have blazed new trails and advanced the discipline of strategic management. In addition, we'd like to thank the following reviewers who provided seasoned advice and splendid suggestions over the years for improving the chapters:

Joan H. Bailar, David Blair, Jane Boyland, William J. Donoher, Stephen A. Drew, Jo Anne Duffy, Alan Ellstrand, Susan Fox-Wolfgramm, Rebecca M. Guidice, Mark Hoelscher, Sean D. Jasso, Xin Liang, Paul Mallette, Dan Marlin, Raza Mir, Mansour Moussavi, James D. Spina, Monica A. Zimmerman, Dennis R. Balch, Jeffrey R. Bruehl, Edith C. Busija, Donald A. Drost, Randall Harris, Mark Lewis Hoelscher, Phyllis Holland, James W. Kroeger, Sal Kukalis, Brian W. Kulik, Paul Mallette, Anthony U. Martinez, Lee Pickler, Sabine Reddy, Thomas D. Schramko, V. Seshan, Charles Strain, Sabine Turnley, S. Stephen Vitucci, Andrew Ward, Sibin Wu, Lynne Patten, Nancy E. Landrum, Jim Goes, Jon Kalinowski, Rodney M. Walter, Judith D. Powell, Seyda Deligonul, David Flanagan, Esmerlda Garbi, Mohsin Habib, Kim Hester, Jeffrey E. McGee, Diana J. Wong, F. William Brown, Anthony F. Chelte, Gregory G. Dess, Alan B. Eisner, John George, Carle M. Hunt, Theresa Marron-Grodsky, Sarah Marsh, Joshua D. Martin, William L. Moore, Donald Neubaum, George M. Puia, Amit Shah, Lois M. Shelton, Mark Weber, Steve Barndt, J. Michael Geringer, Ming-Fang Li, Richard Stackman, Stephen Tallman, Gerardo R. Ungson, James Boulgarides, Betty Diener, Daniel F. Jennings, David Kuhn, Kathryn Martell, Wilbur Mouton, Bobby Vaught, Tuck Bounds, Lee Burk, Ralph Catalanello, William Crittenden, Vince Luchsinger, Stan Mendenhall, John Moore, Will Mulvaney, Sandra Richard, Ralph Roberts, Thomas Turk, Gordon Von Stroh, Fred Zimmerman, S. A. Billion, Charles Byles, Gerald L. Geisler, Rose Knotts, Joseph Rosenstein, James B. Thurman, Ivan Able, W. Harvey Hegarty, Roger Evered, Charles B. Saunders, Rhae M. Swisher, Claude I. Shell, R. Thomas Lenz, Michael C. White, Dennis Callahan, R. Duane Ireland, William E. Burr II, C. W. Millard, Richard Mann, Kurt Christensen, Neil W. Jacobs, Louis W. Fry, D. Robley Wood, George J. Gore, and William R. Soukup.

We owe a debt of gratitude to Professors Catherine A. Maritan, Jeffrey A. Martin, Richard S. Shreve, and Anant K. Sundaram for their helpful comments on various chapters. We'd also like to thank the following students of the Tuck School of Business for their assistance with the revisions: Kenneth P. Fraser, John L. Gardner, Dennis L. Huggins, Judith H. Lon, Margaret W. Macauley, Divya A. Mani, Avni V. Patel, Chris Pearson-Smith, Maximilian A. Pinto, Ross M. Templeton, C. David Morgan, Amy E. Florentino, and John R. Moran. And we'd like to acknowledge the help of Dartmouth students Jenna Pfeffer and Xuanyi Chen, as well as Tuck staff member Mary Biathrow. As always, we value your recommendations and thoughts about the book. Your comments regarding coverage and contents will be taken to heart, and we always are grateful for the time you take to call our attention to printing errors, deficiencies, and other shortcomings. Please e-mail us at **athompso@cba.ua.edu**, **margaret.a.peteraf@tuck.dartmouth. edu**, **jgamble@usouthal.edu**, or **astrickl@cba.ua.edu**.

Arthur A. Thompson

Margaret A. Peteraf

John E. Gamble

A. J. Strickland

Chapter Structure and Organization

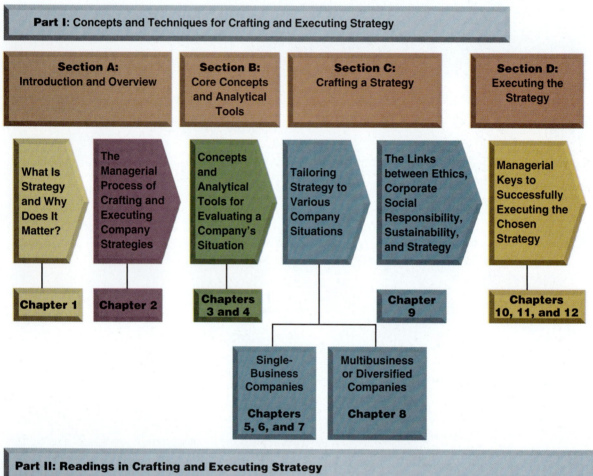

Part I: Concepts and Techniques for Crafting and Executing Strategy

Section A: Introduction and Overview

Section B: Core Concepts and Analytical Tools

Section C: Crafting a Strategy

Section D: Executing the Strategy

What Is Strategy and Why Does It Matter?

The Managerial Process of Crafting and Executing Company Strategies

Concepts and Analytical Tools for Evaluating a Company's Situation

Tailoring Strategy to Various Company Situations

The Links between Ethics, Corporate Social Responsibility, Sustainability, and Strategy

Managerial Keys to Successfully Executing the Chosen Strategy

Chapter 1

Chapter 2

Chapters 3 and 4

Chapter 9

Chapters 10, 11, and 12

Single-Business Companies

Chapters 5, 6, and 7

Multibusiness or Diversified Companies

Chapter 8

Part II: Readings in Crafting and Executing Strategy

Section A: What Is Strategy and How Is the Process of Crafting and Executing Strategy Managed? (4 readings)
Section B: Crafting Strategy in Single-Business Companies (8 readings)
Section C: Crafting Strategy in International and Diversified Companies (4 readings)
Section D: Strategy, Ethics, Social Responsibility, and Sustainability (2 readings)
Section E: Executing Strategy (6 readings)

CHAPTER 1

WHAT IS STRATEGY AND WHY IS IT IMPORTANT?

Learning Objectives

LO 1 Learn what we mean by a company's *strategy*.

LO 2 Grasp the concept of a *sustainable competitive advantage*.

LO 3 Develop an awareness of the four most basic strategic approaches for winning a sustainable competitive advantage.

LO 4 Understand that a company's strategy tends to evolve over time because of changing circumstances and ongoing management efforts to improve the company's strategy.

LO 5 Learn why it is important for a company to have a viable business model that outlines the company's customer value proposition and its profit formula.

LO 6 Learn the three tests of a winning strategy.

> Strategy means making clear-cut choices about how to compete.
>
> Jack Welch – *Former CEO of General Electric*

> One must have strategies to execute dreams.
>
> Azim Premji – *CEO Wipro Technologies and one of the world's richest people*

> If your firm's strategy can be applied to any other firm, you don't have a very good one.
>
> David J. Collis and Michael G. Rukstad – *Consultants and professors*

Learning Objectives are listed at the beginning of each chapter; corresponding numbered indicators in the margins show where learning objectives are covered in the text.

Illustration Capsules appear in boxes throughout each chapter to provide in-depth examples, connect the text presentation to real-world companies, and convincingly demonstrate "strategy in action." Some are appropriate for use as mini-cases.

ILLUSTRATION CAPSULE 9.4

Burt's Bees: A Strategy Based on Corporate Social Responsibility

Burt's Bees is a leading company in natural personal care, offering nearly 200 products including its popular beeswax lip balms and skin-care creams. The brand has enjoyed tremendous success as consumers have begun to embrace all-natural, environmentally friendly products, boosting Burt's Bees' revenues to over $250M by 2012. Much of Burt's Bees' success can be attributed to its skillful use of Corporate Social Responsibility (CSR) as a strategic tool to engage customers and differentiate itself from competitors.

While many companies have embraced Corporate Social Responsibility, few companies have managed to integrate CSR as fully and seamlessly throughout their organizations as Burt's Bees. The company's business model is centered on a principle they refer to as "The Greater Good," which specifies that all company practices must be socially responsible. The execution of this strategy is managed by a special committee dedicated to leading the organization to attain its CSR goals with respect to three primary areas: natural well-being, humanitarian responsibility, and environmental sustainability.

Natural well-being is focused on the ingredients used to create Burt's Bees products. Today, the average Burt's Bees product contains over 99 percent natural ingredients; by 2020, the brand expects to produce only 100 percent natural products.

Burt's Bees' humanitarian focus is centered on its relationships with employees and suppliers. A key part of this effort involves a mandatory employee training program that focuses on four key areas: outreach, wellness, world-class leadership, and the environment. Another is the company's Responsible Sourcing Mission, which lays out a carefully prescribed set of guidelines for sourcing responsible suppliers and managing supplier relationships.

A focus on caring for the environment is clearly interwoven into all aspects of Burt's Bees. By focusing

Burt's Bees faced some consumer backlash when it was purchased recently by The Clorox Company, whose traditional image is viewed in sharp contrast to Burt's Bees values. But while Burt's Bees is still only a small

Margin Notes define core concepts and call attention to important ideas and principles.

efficiently—whatever form it takes—nearly always requires performing value chain activities differently than rivals and building competencies and resource capabilities that are not readily matched. In Illustration Capsule 1.1, it's evident that McDonald's has gained a competitive advantage over its rivals in the fast-food industry through its efforts to minimize costs, ensure fast and consistent delivery of foods with wide appeal, and keep its prices low, thereby driving sales volume. A creative *distinctive* strategy such as that used by McDonald's is a company's most reliable ticket for developing a competitive advantage over its rivals. If a strategy is not distinctive, then there can be no competitive advantage, since no firm would be meeting customer needs better or operating more efficiently than any other.

If a company's competitive edge holds promise for being *sustainable* (as opposed to just temporary), then so much the better for both the strategy and the company's future profitability. What makes a competitive advantage **sustainable** (or durable), as opposed to temporary, are elements of the strategy that give buyers lasting reasons to prefer a company's products or services over those of competitors—*reasons that competitors are unable to nullify or overcome despite their best efforts*. In the case of McDonald's, the company's unparalleled name recognition, reputation for tasty, quick-service food, and formidable volume advantage make it difficult for competitors to weaken or overcome McDonald's competitive advantage. Not only has their strategy provided them with a sustainable competitive advantage, it has made them one of the most admired companies on the planet.

Four of the most frequently used and dependable strategic approaches to setting a company apart from rivals, building strong customer loyalty, and winning a competitive advantage are:

1. *Striving to be the industry's low-cost provider, thereby aiming for a cost-based competitive advantage over rivals.* Walmart and Southwest Airlines have earned strong market positions because of the low-cost advantages they have achieved over their rivals and their consequent ability to underprice competitors. These advantages in meeting customer needs *efficiently* have translated into volume advantages, with Walmart as the world's largest discount retailer and Southwest as the largest U.S. air carrier, based on the number of domestic passengers.[4]

FIGURE 5.2 Cost Drivers: The Keys to Driving Down Company Costs

Sources: Adapted by the authors from M. Porter, *Competitive Advantage: Creating and Sustaining Competitive Advantage* (New York: Free Press, 1985).

Figures scattered throughout the chapters provide conceptual and analytical frameworks.

2. *Taking full advantage of experience and learning-curve effects.* The cost of performing an activity can decline over time as the learning and experience of company personnel build. Learning/experience economies can stem from debugging and mastering newly introduced technologies, using the experiences and suggestions of workers to install more efficient plant layouts and assembly procedures, and the added speed and effectiveness that accrues from repeatedly picking sites for and building new plants, retail outlets, or distribution centers. Well managed low-cost providers pay diligent attention to capturing the benefits of learning and experience and to keeping

Key Points at the end of each chapter provide a handy summary of essential ideas and things to remember.

KEY POINTS

Thinking strategically about a company's external situation involves probing for answers to the following seven questions:

1. *What are the strategically relevant factors in the macro-environment?* Industries differ significantly as to how they are affected by conditions in the broad macro-environment. Identifying which of these factors is strategically relevant is the first step to understanding how a company is situated in its external environment. PESTEL analysis of the political, economic, sociocultural, technological, environmental/ecological, and legal/regulatory factors provides a framework for approaching this issue systematically. Identifying the strategically relevant features of the macro-environment sets the stage for the analysis to come, since they play an important role in determining an industry's potential for attractive profits.

2. *What kinds of competitive forces are industry members facing, and how strong is each force?* The strength of competition is a composite of five forces: (1) competitive pressures stemming from the competitive jockeying among industry rivals, (2) competitive pressures associated with the market inroads being made by the sellers of substitutes, (3) competitive pressures associated with the threat of new entrants into the market, (4) competitive pressures stemming from supplier bargaining power, and (5) competitive pressures stemming from buyer bargaining. The nature and strength of the competitive pressures have to be examined force by force, and their collective strength must be evaluated. One strong force, however, can be sufficient to keep average industry profitability low. Working through the five forces model aids strategy makers in assessing how to insulate the company from the strongest forces, identify attractive arenas for expansion, or alter the

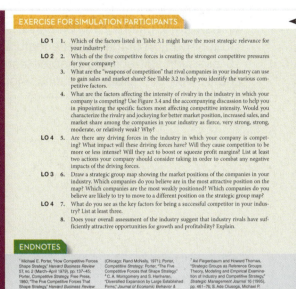

EXERCISE FOR SIMULATION PARTICIPANTS

LO 1 1. Which of the factors listed in Table 3.1 might have the most strategic relevance for your industry?

LO 2 2. Which of the five competitive forces is creating the strongest competitive pressures for your company?

3. What are the "weapons of competition" that rival companies in your industry can use to gain sales and market share? See Table 3.2 to help you identify the various competitive factors.

4. What are the factors affecting the intensity of rivalry in the industry in which your company is competing? Use Figure 3.4 and the accompanying discussion to help you in pinpointing the specific factors most affecting competitive intensity. Would you characterize the rivalry and jockeying for better market position, increased sales, and market share among the companies in your industry as fierce, very strong, strong, moderate, or relatively weak? Why?

LO 4 5. Are there any driving forces in the industry in which your company is competing? What impact will these driving forces have? Will they cause competition to be more or less intense? Will they act to boost or squeeze profit margins? List at least two actions your company should consider taking in order to combat any negative impacts of the driving forces.

LO 3 6. Draw a strategic group map showing the market positions of the companies in your industry. Which companies do you believe are in the most attractive position on the map? Which companies are the most weakly positioned? Which companies do you believe are likely to try to move to a different position on the strategic group map?

LO 4 7. What do you see as the key factors for being a successful competitor in your industry? List at least three.

8. Does your overall assessment of the industry suggest that industry rivals have sufficiently attractive opportunities for growth and profitability? Explain.

The 24 readings in this edition are flush with practical examples and valuable lessons for students of the art and science of crafting and executing strategy. There are two readings for each chapter—all chosen with three criteria in mind: relevance, readability, and recency of publication.

Exercises at the end of each chapter, linked to learning objectives, provide a basis for class discussion, oral presentations, and written assignments. Several chapters have exercises that qualify as mini-cases.

Which Strategy When?

READING 5

Christopher B. Brigham
University of North California

Nathan R. Furr
Brigham Young University

Kathleen M. Eisenhardt
Stanford University

Just when you think you have settled on the right strategy, you may need to change. By understanding the particular circumstances and forces shaping your company's competitive environment, you can choose the most appropriate strategic framework.

Markets are changing, competition is shifting and your business may be suffering or perhaps thriving, at least for now. Whatever the immediate circumstances, managers are forever asking the same questions: Where do we go from here, and which strategy will get us there? Should we fortify our strategic position, move into nearby markets or branch out into radically new territory? To help guide our decisions, most of us have a smorgasbord of strategic frameworks to draw on. But which one is the right one, and when? The strategic plans, market analyses and hefty binders that strategy consulting firms leave behind often jumble strategic lenses: Five-Forces analysis, portfolio review, assessment of core competencies; examination of profit pools, competitive landscape, and so on. But which analyses are most helpful right now?

Most managers recognize that not all strategies work equally well in every setting. So to understand how to choose the right strategy at the right time, we analyzed the logic of the leading strategic frameworks used in business and engineering schools around the world. Then we matched those frameworks with the key strategic choices faced by dozens of industry leaders at different times, during periods of stability as well as change. (See the box "About the Research.") Two surprising insights emerged.

First, we discovered that the logics of the different strategic frameworks break into three archetypes: strategies of position, strategies of leverage, and strategies

of opportunity. What's right for a company depends on its circumstances, its available resources, and how management combines those resources together. (See the chart "Choosing the Right Strategy.")

Second, by observing market leaders employing archetypal strategies, we found that many assumptions about competitive advantage simply don't hold. For example, although strategy gurus talk about strategically valuable resources, sometimes very ordinary resources assembled well are all that's required for competitive advantage. Sometimes it makes good sense to bypass the largest markets and focus instead on where resources fit best. In other circumstances, it may be preferable to ignore existing resources and attack an emergent market. In some situations, basic rules of thumb work better than detailed plans. Surprisingly, these simple strategies can be harder to imitate than complex ones.

HOW TO CHOOSE THE RIGHT STRATEGY

To figure out when it makes sense to pursue strategies of position, leverage, or opportunity, the key is to look first at the immediate circumstances, current

Christopher B. Bingham, Kathleen M. Eisenhardt, and Nathan R. Furr, "Which Strategy When?" *MIT Sloan Management Review*. 53, no. 1 (2011), pp. 71–78.Copyright © 2011 by Massachusetts Institute of Technology. All rights reserved. Distributed by Tribune Media Services.

FOR STUDENTS: An Assortment of Support Materials

Website: www.mhhe.com/thompson The student portion of the website features 10-question self-scoring chapter tests and PowerPoint slides for each chapter.

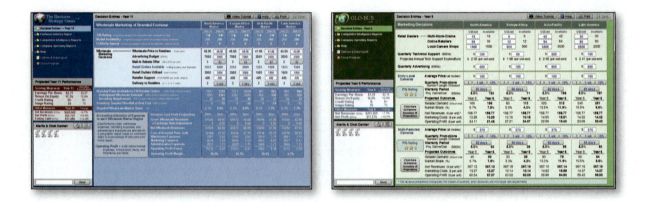

The Business Strategy Game or *GLO-BUS* **Simulation Exercises** Either one of these text supplements involves teams of students managing companies in a head-to-head contest for global market leadership. Company co-managers have to make decisions relating to product quality, production, workforce compensation and training, pricing and marketing, and financing of company operations. The challenge is to craft and execute a strategy that is powerful enough to deliver good financial performance despite the competitive efforts of rival companies. Each company competes in America, Latin America, Europe-Africa, and Asia-Pacific.

BRIEF CONTENTS

CONTENTS

ILLUSTRATION CAPSULE

Section B: Core Concepts and Analytical Tools

ILLUSTRATION CAPSULE

PART TWO   Readings in Crafting and Executing Strategy

Section A: What Is Strategy and How Is the Process of Crafting and Executing Strategy Managed?

Section B: Crafting Strategy in Single-Business Companies

PART 1

Concepts and Techniques for Crafting and Executing Strategy

CHAPTER 1

WHAT IS STRATEGY AND WHY IS IT IMPORTANT?

Learning Objectives

LO 1   Learn what we mean by a company's *strategy*.

LO 2   Grasp the concept of a *sustainable competitive advantage*.

LO 3   Develop an awareness of the four most basic strategic approaches for winning a sustainable competitive advantage.

LO 4   Understand that a company's strategy tends to evolve over time because of changing circumstances and ongoing management efforts to improve the company's strategy.

LO 5   Learn why it is important for a company to have a viable business model that outlines the company's customer value proposition and its profit formula.

LO 6   Learn the three tests of a winning strategy.

Strategy means making clear-cut choices about how to compete.

> Jack Welch – *Former CEO of General Electric*

One must have strategies to execute dreams.

> Azim Premji – *CEO Wipro Technologies and one of the world's richest people*

If your firm's strategy can be applied to any other firm, you don't have a very good one.

> David J. Collis and Michael G. Rukstad – *Consultants and professors*

In any given year, a group of companies will stand out as the top performers, in terms of metrics such as profitability, sales growth, or growth in shareholder value. Some of these companies will find that their star status fades quickly, due to little more than a fortuitous constellation of circumstances, such as being in the right business at the right time. But other companies somehow manage to rise to the top and stay there, year after year, pleasing their customers, shareholders, and other stakeholders alike in the process. Companies such as Apple, Google, Coca-Cola, Procter & Gamble, McDonald's, Berkshire Hathaway, and General Electric come to mind—but long-lived success is not just the province of U.S. companies. Diverse kinds of companies, both large and small, from many different countries have been able to sustain strong performance records, including Singapore Airlines, Sweden's IKEA (in home furnishings), Korea's Hyundai Heavy Industries (in shipbuilding and construction), Mexico's America Movil (in telecommunications), and Japan's Nintendo (in video game systems).

What can explain the ability of companies like these to beat the odds and experience prolonged periods of profitability and growth? Why is it that some companies, like Southwest Airlines and Walmart, continue to do well even when others in their industry are faltering? Why can some companies survive and prosper even through economic downturns and industry turbulence?

Many factors enter into a full explanation of a company's performance, of course. Some come from the external environment; others are internal to the firm. But only one thing can account for the kind of long-lived success records that we see in the world's greatest companies—and that is a cleverly crafted and well executed *strategy*, one that facilitates the capture of emerging opportunities, produces enduringly good performance, is adaptable to changing business conditions, and can withstand the competitive challenges from rival firms.

In this opening chapter, we define the concept of strategy and describe its many facets. We will explain what is meant by a competitive advantage, discuss the relationship between a company's strategy and its business model, and introduce you to the kinds of competitive strategies that can give a company an advantage over rivals in attracting customers and earning above-average profits. We will look at what sets a winning strategy apart from others and why the caliber of a company's strategy determines whether it will enjoy a competitive advantage over other firms or be burdened by competitive disadvantage. By the end of this chapter, you will have a clear idea of why the tasks of crafting and executing strategy are core management functions and why excellent execution of an excellent strategy is the most reliable recipe for turning a company into a standout performer over the long term.

WHAT DO WE MEAN BY *STRATEGY?*

A company's **strategy** is its action plan for outperforming its competitors and achieving superior profitability. In effect, it represents a managerial commitment to an integrated array of considered choices about how to compete.[1] These include choices about:

- *How* to attract and please customers.
- *How* to compete against rivals.
- *How* to position the company in the marketplace.
- *How* best to respond to changing economic and market conditions.
- *How* to capitalize on attractive opportunities to grow the business.
- *How* to achieve the company's performance targets.

The objective of a well-crafted strategy is not merely temporary competitive success and profits in the short run, but rather the sort of lasting success that can support growth and secure the company's future over the long term. In most industries, there are many different avenues for outcompeting rivals and boosting company performance.[2] Consequently, some companies strive to improve their performance by employing strategies aimed at achieving lower costs than rivals, while others pursue strategies aimed at achieving product superiority or personalized customer service or quality dimensions that rivals cannot match. Some companies opt for wide product lines, while others concentrate their energies on a narrow product lineup. Some competitors deliberately confine their operations to local or regional markets; others opt to compete nationally, internationally (several countries), or globally (all or most of the major country markets worldwide).

Strategy Is about Competing Differently   Every strategy needs a distinctive element that attracts customers and produces a competitive edge. But there is no shortage of opportunity to fashion a strategy that both tightly fits a company's own particular situation and is discernibly different from the strategies of rivals. In fact, competitive success requires a company's managers to make strategic choices about the key building blocks of its strategy that differ from the choices made by competitors—not 100 percent different, but at least different in several important respects. A strategy only stands a chance of succeeding when it is predicated on actions, business approaches, and competitive moves aimed at appealing to buyers *in ways that set a company apart from rivals.* Simply trying to mimic the strategies of the industry's successful companies never works. Rather, every company's strategy needs to have some distinctive element that draws in customers and produces a competitive edge. Strategy, at its essence, is about competing differently—doing what rival firms *don't* do or what rival firms *can't* do.[3]

A company's strategy provides direction and guidance, in terms of not only what the company *should* do but also what it *should not* do. Knowing what not to do can be as important as knowing what to do, strategically. At best, making the wrong strategic moves will prove a distraction and a waste of company resources. At worst, it can bring about unintended long-term consequences that put the company's very survival at risk.

Figure 1.1 illustrates the broad types of actions and approaches that often characterize a company's strategy in a particular business or industry. For a more concrete example of the specific actions constituting a firm's strategy, see Illustration Capsule 1.1, describing McDonald's strategy in the quick-service restaurant industry.

Strategy and the Quest for Competitive Advantage

The heart and soul of any strategy are the actions and moves in the marketplace that managers are taking to gain a competitive advantage over rivals. A company achieves a competitive advantage whenever it has some type of edge over rivals in attracting buyers and coping with competitive forces. There are many routes to competitive advantage, but they all involve either giving buyers what they perceive as superior value compared to the offerings of rival sellers or giving buyers the same value as others at a lower cost to the firm. Superior value can mean a good product at a lower price, a superior product that is worth paying more for, or a best-value offering that represents an attractive combination of price, features, quality, service, and other appealing attributes. Delivering superior value or delivering value more

LO 2

Grasp the concept of a *sustainable competitive advantage.*

FIGURE 1.1   Identifying a Company's Strategy—What to Look For

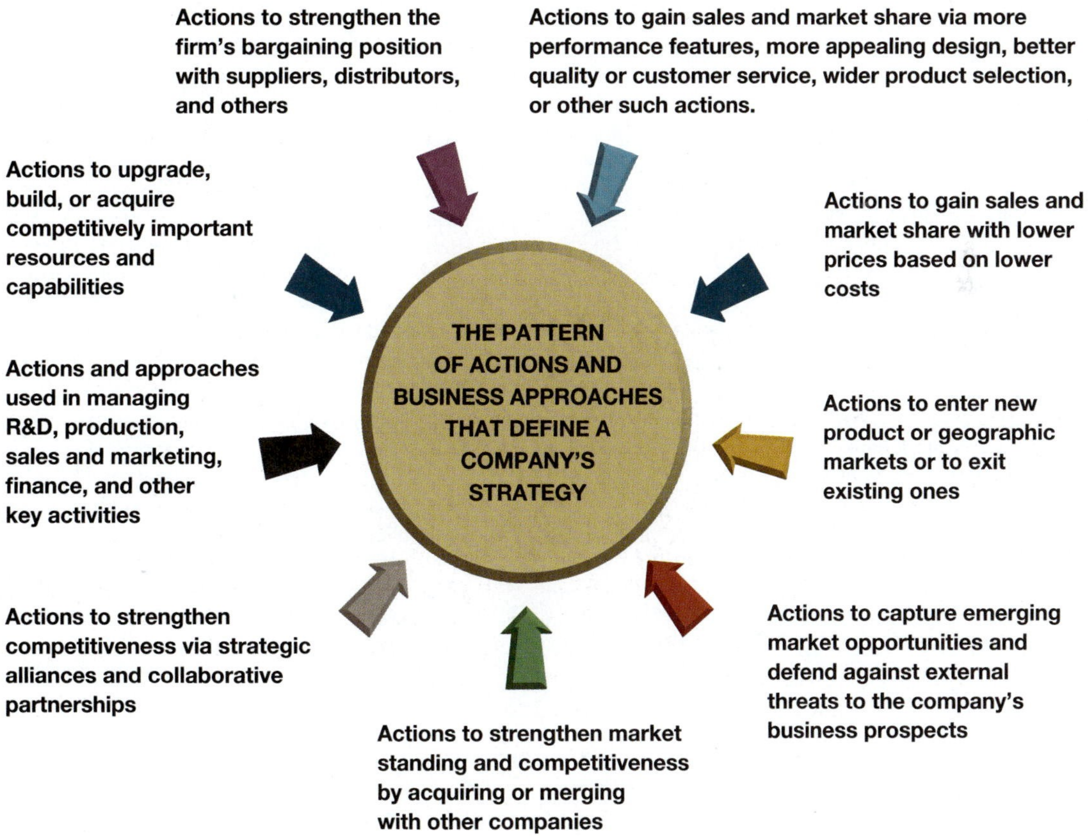

Actions to strengthen the firm's bargaining position with suppliers, distributors, and others

Actions to gain sales and market share via more performance features, more appealing design, better quality or customer service, wider product selection, or other such actions.

Actions to upgrade, build, or acquire competitively important resources and capabilities

Actions to gain sales and market share with lower prices based on lower costs

Actions and approaches used in managing R&D, production, sales and marketing, finance, and other key activities

THE PATTERN OF ACTIONS AND BUSINESS APPROACHES THAT DEFINE A COMPANY'S STRATEGY

Actions to enter new product or geographic markets or to exit existing ones

Actions to strengthen competitiveness via strategic alliances and collaborative partnerships

Actions to capture emerging market opportunities and defend against external threats to the company's business prospects

Actions to strengthen market standing and competitiveness by acquiring or merging with other companies

McDonald's Strategy in the Quick-Service Restaurant Industry

In 2011, McDonald's was setting new sales records despite a global economic slowdown and declining consumer confidence in the United States. More than 64 million customers visited one of McDonald's 33,000 restaurants in 119 countries each day, which allowed the company to record 2011 revenues and earnings of more than $27 billion and $5.5 billion, respectively. McDonald's performance in the marketplace made it the top performing company on the Dow Jones Stock Market Index for 2011, with a 35 percent return to investors. The company's sales were holding up well amid the ongoing economic uncertainty in early 2012, with global sales as measured in constant currencies increasing by more than 4 percent in the first quarter. The company's success was a result of its well-conceived and executed Plan-to-Win strategy that focused on "being better, not just bigger." Key initiatives of the Plan-to-Win strategy included:

- *Improved restaurant operations.* McDonald's global restaurant operations improvement process involved employee training programs ranging from on-the-job training for new crew members to college-level management courses offered at the company's Hamburger University. The company sends nearly 200 high-potential employees annually to its McDonald's Leadership Institute to build leadership skills. The company trains its store managers to closely monitor labor, food, and utility costs. McDonald's excellence earned the company 10th place on *Fortune*'s list of the World's Most Admired Companies in 2011.

- *Affordable pricing.* McDonald's kept its prices low by scrutinizing restaurant operating costs, administrative costs, and other corporate expenses. McDonald's saw the poor economy in the United States as an opportunity to renegotiate its advertising contracts with newspapers and television networks. The company also began to replace its company-owned vehicles with more fuel-efficient models when gasoline prices escalated dramatically. However, McDonald's did not sacrifice product quality in order to offer lower prices. The company implemented extensive supplier monitoring programs to ensure that its suppliers did not change product specifications to lower costs.

- *Wide menu variety and beverage choices.* McDonald's has expanded its menu beyond the popular-selling Big Mac and Quarter Pounder to include new, healthy quick-service items. The company has also added an extensive line of premium coffees that include espressos, cappuccinos, and lattes sold in its McCafé restaurant locations in the United States, Europe, and the Asia/Pacific region.

- *Convenience and expansion of dining opportunities.* The addition of McCafés helped McDonald's increase same store sales by extending traditional dining hours. Customers wanting a midmorning coffee or an afternoon snack helped keep store traffic high after McDonald's had sold its last Egg McMuffin and before the lunch crowd arrived to order Big Macs. The company also extended its drive-thru hours to 24 hours in many cities where consumers tend to eat at all hours of the day and night.

- *Ongoing restaurant reinvestment and international expansion.* With more than 14,000 restaurants in the United States, the focus of McDonald's expansion of units was in rapidly growing emerging markets such as China. The company also intends to refurbish 90 percent of the interiors and 50 percent of the exteriors of its restaurants by the end of 2012 to make its restaurants a pleasant place for both customers and employees.

Developed with Jenna P. Pfeffer. *Sources:* Janet Adamy, "McDonald's Seeks Way to Keep Sizzling," *Wall Street Journal Online,* March 10, 2009; various annual reports; various company press releases.

efficiently—whatever form it takes—nearly always requires performing value chain activities differently than rivals and building competencies and resource capabilities that are not readily matched. In Illustration Capsule 1.1, it's evident that McDonald's has gained a competitive advantage over its rivals in the fast-food industry through its efforts to minimize costs, ensure fast and consistent delivery of foods with wide appeal, and keep its prices low, thereby driving sales volume. A creative *distinctive* strategy such as that used by McDonald's is a company's most reliable ticket for developing a competitive advantage over its rivals. If a strategy is not distinctive, then there can be no competitive advantage, since no firm would be meeting customer needs better or operating more efficiently than any other.

If a company's competitive edge holds promise for being *sustainable* (as opposed to just temporary), then so much the better for both the strategy and the company's future profitability. What makes a competitive advantage **sustainable** (or durable), as opposed to temporary, are elements of the strategy that give buyers lasting reasons to prefer a company's products or services over those of competitors—*reasons that competitors are unable to nullify or overcome despite their best efforts*. In the case of McDonald's, the company's unparalleled name recognition, reputation for tasty, quick-service food, and formidable volume advantage make it difficult for competitors to weaken or overcome McDonald's competitive advantage. Not only has their strategy provided them with a sustainable competitive advantage, it has made them one of the most admired companies on the planet.

Four of the most frequently used and dependable strategic approaches to setting a company apart from rivals, building strong customer loyalty, and winning a competitive advantage are:

1. *Striving to be the industry's low-cost provider, thereby aiming for a cost-based competitive advantage over rivals.* Walmart and Southwest Airlines have earned strong market positions because of the low-cost advantages they have achieved over their rivals and their consequent ability to underprice competitors. These advantages in meeting customer needs *efficiently* have translated into volume advantages, with Walmart as the world's largest discount retailer and Southwest as the largest U.S. air carrier, based on the number of domestic passengers.[4]

2. *Outcompeting rivals on the basis of differentiating features, such as higher quality, wider product selection, added performance, value-added services, more attractive styling, and technological superiority.* Successful adopters of differentiation strategies include Apple (innovative products), Johnson & Johnson in baby products (product reliability), Chanel and Rolex (luxury and prestige), and Mercedes and BMW (engineering design and performance). These companies have achieved a competitive advantage because of their ability to meet customer needs more effectively than rivals can, thus driving up their customers' willingness to pay higher prices. One way to sustain this type of competitive advantage is to be sufficiently innovative to thwart the efforts of clever rivals to copy or closely imitate the product offering.

3. *Developing an advantage based on offering more value for the money.* Giving customers more value for their money by satisfying buyers' expectations on key quality/features/performance/service attributes while beating their price expectations is known as a *best-cost provider strategy*. This approach is a hybrid strategy that blends elements of the previous approaches. Target is an example of a company that is known

---

CORE CONCEPT

A company achieves a **competitive advantage** when it provides buyers with superior value compared to rival sellers or offers the same value at a lower cost to the firm. The advantage is **sustainable** if it persists despite the best efforts of competitors to match or surpass this advantage.

LO 3

Develop an awareness of the four most dependable strategic approaches for setting a company apart from rivals and winning a sustainable competitive advantage.

for its hip product design (a reputation it built by featuring cheap-chic designers such as Isaac Mizrahi), as well as a more appealing shopping ambience for discount store shoppers. It offers the perfect illustration of a best-cost provider strategy.

4. *Focusing on a narrow market niche within an industry.* There are two types of strategies based on focus. The first aims to achieve an advantage through greater efficiency in serving a niche; the goal of the second is greater effectiveness in meeting the niche's special needs. Prominent companies that enjoy competitive success in a specialized market niche include eBay in online auctions, Jiffy Lube International in quick oil changes, McAfee in virus protection software, and The Weather Channel in cable TV.

LO 4

Understand that a company's strategy tends to evolve over time because of changing circumstances and ongoing management efforts to improve the company's strategy.

Winning a *sustainable* competitive edge over rivals with any of the preceding four strategies generally hinges as much on building competitively valuable expertise and capabilities that rivals cannot readily match as it does on having a distinctive product offering. Clever rivals can nearly always copy the attributes of a popular product or service, but for rivals to match the experience, know-how, and specialized capabilities that a company has developed and perfected over a long period of time is substantially harder to do and takes much longer. FedEx, for example, has superior capabilities in next-day delivery of small packages. Apple has demonstrated impressive product innovation capabilities in digital music players, smartphones, and e-readers. Hyundai has become the world's fastest-growing automaker as a result of its advanced manufacturing processes and unparalleled quality control system. Each of these capabilities has proved hard for competitors to imitate or best.

Why a Company's Strategy Evolves over Time

Changing circumstances and ongoing management efforts to improve the strategy cause a company's strategy to evolve over time—a condition that makes the task of crafting strategy *a work in progress,* not a one-time event.

The appeal of a strategy that yields a sustainable competitive advantage is that it offers the potential for an enduring edge over rivals. However, managers of every company must be willing and ready to modify the strategy in response to changing market conditions, advancing technology, unexpected moves by competitors, shifting buyer needs, emerging market opportunities, and mounting evidence that the strategy is not working well. Most of the time, a company's strategy evolves incrementally from management's ongoing efforts to fine-tune the strategy and to adjust certain strategy elements in response to new learning and unfolding events.[5] But in industries where industry and competitive conditions change frequently and in sometimes dramatic ways, the life cycle of a given strategy is short. Industry environments characterized by high-velocity change require companies to repeatedly adapt their strategies.[6] For example, companies in industries with rapid-fire advances in technology like medical equipment, electronics, and wireless devices often find it essential to adjust key elements of their strategies several times a year, sometimes even finding it necessary to "reinvent" their approach to providing value to their customers.

A company's strategy is shaped partly by management analysis and choice and partly by the necessity of adapting and learning by doing.

Regardless of whether a company's strategy changes gradually or swiftly, the important point is that the task of crafting strategy is not a one-time event but always a work in progress. Adapting to new conditions and constantly evaluating what is working well enough to continue and what needs to be improved are normal parts of the strategy-making process, resulting in an *evolving strategy.*[7]

A Company's Strategy Is Partly Proactive and Partly Reactive

The evolving nature of a company's strategy means that the typical company strategy is a blend of (1) *proactive,* planned initiatives to improve the company's financial performance and secure a competitive edge, and (2) *reactive* responses to unanticipated developments and fresh market conditions. The biggest portion of a company's current strategy flows from ongoing actions that have proven themselves in the marketplace and newly launched initiatives aimed at building a larger lead over rivals and further boosting financial performance. This part of management's action plan for running the company is its **deliberate strategy,** consisting of proactive strategy elements that are both planned and realized as planned (while other planned strategy elements may not work out)—see Figure 1.2.[8]

But managers must always be willing to supplement or modify the proactive strategy elements with as-needed reactions to unanticipated conditions. Inevitably, there will be occasions when market and competitive conditions take an unexpected turn that calls for some kind of strategic reaction. Hence, *a portion of a company's strategy is always developed on the fly,* coming as a response to fresh strategic maneuvers on the part of rival firms, unexpected shifts in customer requirements, fast-changing technological developments, newly appearing market opportunities, a changing political or economic climate, or other unanticipated happenings in the surrounding environment. These unplanned, reactive, and adaptive strategy adjustments make up the firm's **emergent strategy.** A company's strategy *in toto* (its **realized strategy**) thus tends to be a *combination* of proactive and reactive elements, with certain strategy elements being *abandoned* because they have become obsolete or ineffective. A company's realized strategy can be observed in the pattern of its actions over time, which is a far better indicator than any of its strategic plans on paper or any public pronouncements about its strategy.

CORE CONCEPT

A company's **deliberate strategy** consists of *proactive* strategy elements that are both planned and realized as planned; its **emergent strategy** consists of *reactive* strategy elements that emerge as changing conditions warrant.

FIGURE 1.2 A Company's Strategy Is a Blend of Proactive Initiatives and Reactive Adjustments

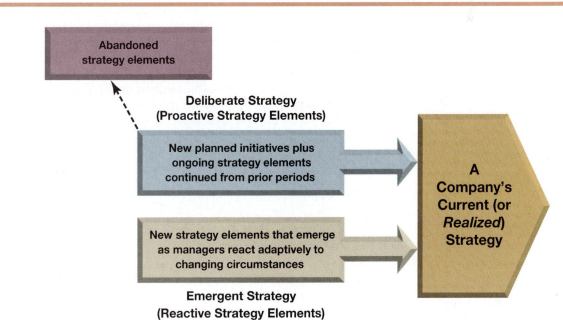

A COMPANY'S STRATEGY AND ITS BUSINESS MODEL

LO 5

Learn why it is important for a company to have a viable business model that outlines the company's customer value proposition and its profit formula.

At the center of a company's strategy is the company's **business model.** A business model is management's blueprint for delivering a valuable product or service to customers in a manner that will generate revenues sufficient to cover costs and yield an attractive profit.[9] The two elements of a company's business model are (1) its *customer value proposition* and (2) its *profit formula.* The customer value proposition lays out the company's approach to satisfying buyer wants and needs at a price customers will consider a good value. Plainly, from a customer perspective, the greater the value delivered *(V)* and the lower the price *(P)*, the more attractive is the company's value proposition. The profit formula describes the company's approach to determining a cost structure that will allow for acceptable profits, given the pricing tied to its customer value proposition. The lower the costs *(C)*, given the customer value proposition *(V – P)*, the greater the ability of the business model to be a moneymaker. Thus the profit formula reveals how efficiently a company can meet customer wants and needs and deliver on the value proposition. The nitty-gritty issue surrounding a company's business model is whether it can execute its customer value proposition profitably. Just because company managers have crafted a strategy for competing and running the business, this does not automatically mean that the strategy will lead to profitability—it may or it may not.

Magazines and newspapers employ a business model keyed to delivering information and entertainment they believe readers will find valuable and a profit formula aimed at securing sufficient revenues from subscriptions and advertising to more than cover the costs of producing and delivering their products to readers. Mobile phone providers, satellite radio companies, and broadband providers also employ a subscription-based business model. The business model of network TV and radio broadcasters entails providing free programming to audiences but charging advertising fees based on audience size. Gillette's business model in razor blades involves selling a "master product"—the razor—at an attractively low price and then making money on repeat purchases of razor blades that can be produced very cheaply and sold at high profit margins. Printer manufacturers like Hewlett-Packard, Lexmark, and Epson pursue much the same business model as Gillette—selling printers at a low (virtually break-even) price and making large profit margins on the repeat purchases of printer supplies, especially ink cartridges. McDonald's invented the business model for fast food—providing value to customers in the form of economical quick-service meals at clean convenient locations. Its profit formula involves such elements as standardized cost-efficient store design, stringent specifications for ingredients, detailed operating procedures for each unit, and heavy reliance on advertising and in-store promotions to drive volume. Illustration Capsule 1.2 describes two contrasting business models in radio broadcasting.

CORE CONCEPT

A company's **business model** sets forth the logic for how its strategy will create value for customers, while at the same time generate revenues sufficient to cover costs and realize a profit.

Sirius XM and Over-the-Air Broadcast Radio: Two Contrasting Business Models

	Sirius XM	Over-the-Air Radio Broadcasters
Customer value proposition	Digital music, news, national and regional weather, traffic reports in limited areas, and talk radio programming provided for a monthly subscription fee. Programming is interrupted only by brief occasional ads.	Free-of-charge music, national and local news, local traffic reports, national and local weather, and talk radio programming. Listeners can expect frequent programming interruption for ads.
Profit formula	***Revenue generation:*** Monthly subscription fees, sales of satellite radio equipment, and advertising revenues. ***Cost structure:*** Fixed costs associated with operating a satellite-based music delivery service. Fixed and variable costs related to programming and content royalties, marketing, and support activities.	***Revenue generation:*** Advertising sales to national and local businesses. ***Cost structure:*** Fixed costs associated with terrestrial broadcasting operations. Fixed and variable costs related to local news reporting, advertising sales operations, network affiliate fees, programming and content royalties, commercial production activities, and support activities.
	Profit margin: Sirius XM's profitability is dependent on attracting a sufficiently large number of subscribers to cover its costs and provide attractive profits.	***Profit margin:*** The profitability of over-the-air radio stations was dependent on generating sufficient advertising revenues to cover costs and provide attractive profits.

WHAT MAKES A STRATEGY A WINNER?

A **winning strategy** must
pass three tests:
1. The Fit Test
2. The Competitive
   Advantage Test
3. The Performance Test

Three tests can be applied to determine whether a strategy is a *winning strategy:*

1. **The Fit Test:** *How well does the strategy fit the company's situation?* To qualify as a winner, a strategy has to be well matched to industry and competitive conditions, a company's best market opportunities, and other pertinent aspects of the business environment in which the company operates. No strategy can work well unless it exhibits good *external fit* and is in sync with prevailing market conditions. At the same time, a winning strategy must be tailored to the company's resources and competitive capabilities and be supported by a complementary set of functional activities (i.e., activities in the realms of supply chain management, operations, sales and marketing, and so on). That is, it must also exhibit *internal fit* and be compatible with a company's ability to execute the strategy in a competent manner. Unless a strategy exhibits good fit with both the external and internal aspects of a company's overall situation, it is likely to be an underperformer and fall short of producing winning results. Winning strategies also exhibit *dynamic fit* in the sense that they evolve over time in a manner that maintains close and effective alignment with the company's situation even as external and internal conditions change.[10]

2. **The Competitive Advantage Test:** *Can the strategy help the company achieve a sustainable competitive advantage?* Strategies that fail to achieve a durable competitive advantage over rivals are unlikely to produce superior performance for more than a brief period of time. Winning strategies enable a company to achieve a competitive advantage over key rivals that is long-lasting. The bigger and more durable the competitive advantage, the more powerful it is.

3. **The Performance Test:** *Is the strategy producing good company performance?* The mark of a winning strategy is strong company performance. Two kinds of performance indicators tell the most about the caliber of a company's strategy: (1) competitive strength and market standing and (2) profitability and financial strength. Above-average financial performance or gains in market share, competitive position, or profitability are signs of a winning strategy.

Strategies that come up short on one or more of the preceding tests are plainly less appealing than strategies passing all three tests with flying colors. Managers should use the same questions when evaluating either proposed or existing strategies. New initiatives that don't seem to match the company's internal and external situations should be scrapped before they come to fruition, while existing strategies must be scrutinized on a regular basis to ensure they have good fit, offer a competitive advantage, and are contributing to above-average performance or performance improvements.

WHY CRAFTING AND EXECUTING STRATEGY ARE IMPORTANT TASKS

Crafting and executing strategy are top-priority managerial tasks for a very big reason. A clear and reasoned strategy is management's prescription for doing business, its road map to competitive advantage, its game plan for pleasing customers, and its formula for improving performance. High-achieving enterprises are nearly always the product of astute, creative, and proactive strategy making. Companies don't get to the top of the industry rankings or stay there with illogical strategies, copy-cat strategies, or timid attempts to try to do better. Only a handful of companies can boast of hitting home runs in the marketplace due to lucky breaks or the good fortune of having stumbled into the right market at the right time with the right product. And even then, unless they subsequently craft a strategy that capitalizes on their luck, building on what's working and discarding the rest, success of this sort will be fleeting. So there can be little argument that a company's strategy matters—and matters a lot.

The chief executive officer of one successful company put it well when he said:

> In the main, our competitors are acquainted with the same fundamental concepts and techniques and approaches that we follow, and they are as free to pursue them as we are. More often than not, the difference between their level of success and ours lies in the relative thoroughness and self-discipline with which we and they develop and execute our strategies for the future.

Good Strategy + Good Strategy Execution = Good Management

Crafting and executing strategy are thus core management functions. Among all the things managers do, nothing affects a company's ultimate success or failure more fundamentally than how well its management team charts the company's direction, develops competitively effective strategic moves and business approaches, and pursues what needs to be done internally to produce good day-in, day-out strategy execution and operating excellence. Indeed, *good strategy and good strategy execution are the most telling signs of good management.* Managers don't deserve a gold star for designing a potentially brilliant strategy but failing to put the organizational means in place to carry it out in high-caliber fashion. Competent execution of a mediocre strategy scarcely merits enthusiastic applause for management's efforts either. The rationale for using the twin standards of good strategy making and good strategy execution to determine whether a company is well managed is therefore compelling: *The better conceived a company's strategy and the more competently it is executed, the more likely the company will be a standout performer in the marketplace.* In stark contrast, a company that lacks clear-cut direction, has a flawed strategy, or can't execute its strategy competently is a company whose financial performance is probably suffering, whose business is at long-term risk, and whose management is sorely lacking.

How well a company performs is directly attributable to the caliber of its strategy and the proficiency with which the strategy is executed.

THE ROAD AHEAD

Throughout the chapters to come and in the accompanying case collection, the spotlight will be trained on the foremost question in running a business enterprise: *What must managers do, and do well, to make a company a winner in the marketplace?* The answer that emerges is that doing a good job of managing inherently requires good strategic thinking and good management of the strategy-making, strategy-executing process.

The mission of this book is to provide a solid overview of what every business student and aspiring manager needs to know about crafting and executing strategy. We will explore what good strategic thinking entails, describe the core concepts and tools of strategic analysis, and examine the ins and outs of crafting and executing strategy. The accompanying cases will help build your skills in both diagnosing how well the strategy-making, strategy-executing task is being performed and prescribing actions for how the strategy in question or its execution can be improved. The strategic management course that you are enrolled in may also include a strategy simulation exercise where you will run a company in head-to-head competition with companies run by your classmates. Your mastery of the strategic management concepts presented in the following chapters will put you in a strong position to craft a winning strategy for your company and figure out how to execute it in a cost-effective and profitable manner. As you progress through the chapters of the text and the activities assigned during the term, we hope to convince you that first-rate capabilities in crafting and executing strategy are essential to good management.

KEY POINTS

1. A company's strategy is its action plan for outperforming its competitors and achieving superior profitability.

2. The central thrust of a company's strategy is undertaking moves to build and strengthen the company's long-term competitive position and financial performance by *competing differently* from rivals and gaining a sustainable competitive advantage over them.

3. A company achieves a **competitive advantage** when it provides buyers with superior value compared to rival sellers or offers the same value at a lower cost to the firm. The advantage is **sustainable** if it persists despite the best efforts of competitors to match or surpass this advantage.

4. A company's strategy typically evolves over time, emerging from a blend of (1) proactive deliberate actions on the part of company managers to improve the strategy, and (2) reactive emergent responses to unanticipated developments and fresh market conditions.

5. A company's business model sets forth the logic for how its strategy will create value for customers, while at the same time generate revenues sufficient to cover costs and realize a profit. Thus, it contains two crucial elements: (1) the *customer value proposition*—a plan for satisfying customer wants and needs at a price customers will consider good value, and (2) the *profit formula*—a plan for a cost structure that will enable the company to deliver the customer value proposition profitably.

6. A winning strategy will pass three tests: (1) *Fit* (external, internal, and dynamic consistency), (2) *Competitive Advantage* (durable competitive advantage), and (3) *Performance* (outstanding financial and market performance).

7. Crafting and executing strategy are core management functions. How well a company performs and the degree of market success it enjoys are directly attributable to the caliber of its strategy and the proficiency with which the strategy is executed.

ASSURANCE OF LEARNING EXERCISES

connect

LO 1, LO 2, LO 3

1. Based on what you know about the quick-service restaurant industry, does McDonald's strategy (as described in Illustration Capsule 1.1) seem to be well-matched to industry and competitive conditions? Does the strategy seem to be keyed to a cost-based advantage, differentiating features, serving the unique needs of a niche, or some combination of these? What is there about McDonald's strategy that can lead to sustainable competitive advantage?

connect

LO 4, LO 6

2. Elements of Walmart's strategy have evolved in meaningful ways since the company's founding in 1962. Prepare a one- to two-page report that discusses how its strategy has evolved after reviewing all of the links at Walmart's About Us page, which can be found at **walmartstores.com/AboutUs/**. Your report should also assess how well Walmart's strategy passes the three tests of a winning strategy.

3. Go to www.nytco.com/investors and check whether *The New York Times'* recent financial reports indicate that its business model is working. Does the company's business model remain sound as more consumers go to the Internet to find general information and stay abreast of current events and news stories? Is its revenue stream from advertisements growing or declining? Are its subscription fees and circulation increasing or declining?

EXERCISE FOR SIMULATION PARTICIPANTS

Three basic questions must be answered by managers of organizations of all sizes as they begin the process of crafting strategy:

- What is our present situation?
- Where do we want to go from here?
- How are we going to get there?

After you have read the Participant's Guide or Player's Manual for the strategy simulation exercise that you will participate in this academic term, you and your co-managers should come up with brief one- or two-paragraph answers to these three questions *prior* to entering your first set of decisions. While your answers to the first of the three questions can be developed from your reading of the manual, the second and third questions will require a collaborative discussion among the members of your company's management team about how you intend to manage the company you have been assigned to run.

1. What is our company's current situation? A substantive answer to this question should cover the following issues:

   - Is your company in a good, average, or weak competitive position vis-à-vis rival companies?
   - Does your company appear to be in a sound financial condition?
   - Does it appear to have a competitive advantage and is it likely to be sustainable?
   - What problems does your company have that need to be addressed?

2. Where do we want to take the company during the time we are in charge? A complete answer to this question should say something about each of the following:

   - What goals or aspirations do you have for your company?
   - What do you want the company to be known for?
   - What market share would you like your company to have after the first five decision rounds?
   - By what amount or percentage would you like to increase total profits of the company by the end of the final decision round?
   - What kinds of performance outcomes will signal that you and your co-managers are managing the company in a successful manner?

3. How are we going to get there? Your answer should cover these issues:

   - Which of the basic strategic and competitive approaches discussed in this chapter do you think makes the most sense to pursue?
   - What kind of competitive advantage over rivals will you try to achieve?

- How would you describe the company's business model?
- What kind of actions will support these objectives?

ENDNOTES

[1] Jan Rivkin, "An Alternative Approach to Making Strategic Choices," Harvard Business School, 9-702-433, 2001.

[2] Michael E. Porter, "What Is Strategy?" *Harvard Business Review* 74, no. 6 (November–December 1996).

[3] Ibid.

[4] Walmartstores.com/download/2230.pdf; Southwest Airlines Fact Sheet, July 16, 2009.

[5] Eric T. Anderson and Duncan Simester, "A Step-by-Step Guide to Smart Business Experiments," *Harvard Business Review* 89, no. 3 (March 2011).

[6] Shona L. Brown and Kathleen M. Eisenhardt, *Competing on the Edge: Strategy as Structured Chaos* (Boston, MA: Harvard Business School Press, 1998).

[7] Cynthia A. Montgomery, "Putting Leadership Back into Strategy," *Harvard Business Review* 86, no. 1 (January 2008).

[8] Henry Mintzberg and J. A. Waters, "Of Strategies, Deliberate and Emergent," *Strategic Management Journal* 6 (1985); Costas Markides, "Strategy as Balance: From 'Either-Or' to 'And,'" *Business Strategy Review* 12, no. 3 (September 2001).

[9] Mark W. Johnson, Clayton M. Christensen, and Henning Kagermann, "Reinventing Your Business Model," *Harvard Business Review* 86, no. 12 (December 2008); Joan Magretta, "Why Business Models Matter," *Harvard Business Review* 80, no. 5 (May 2002).

[10] Jan Rivkin, "An Alternative Approach to Making Strategic Choices."

CHAPTER 2

CHARTING A COMPANY'S DIRECTION: ITS VISION, MISSION, OBJECTIVES, AND STRATEGY

Learning Objectives

LO 1   Grasp why it is critical for company managers to have a clear strategic vision of where a company needs to head and why.

LO 2   Understand the importance of setting both strategic and financial objectives.

LO 3   Understand why the strategic initiatives taken at various organizational levels must be tightly coordinated to achieve companywide performance targets.

LO 4   Become aware of what a company must do to achieve operating excellence and to execute its strategy proficiently.

LO 5   Become aware of the role and responsibility of a company's board of directors in overseeing the strategic management process.

The vision we have . . . determines what we do and the opportunities we see or don't see.

    Charles G. Koch – *CEO of Koch Industries*

I dream for a living.

    Steven Spielberg – *The most financially successful motion picture director in history*

A good goal is like a strenuous exercise—it makes you stretch.

    Mary Kay Ash – *Founder of Mary Kay Cosmetics*

Crafting and executing strategy are the heart and soul of managing a business enterprise. But exactly what is involved in developing a strategy and executing it proficiently? What are the various components of the strategy-making, strategy-executing process and to what extent are company personnel—aside from senior management—involved in the process? In this chapter, we present an overview of the ins and outs of crafting and executing company strategies. Special attention will be given to management's direction-setting responsibilities—charting a strategic course, setting performance targets, and choosing a strategy capable of producing the desired outcomes. We will also explain why strategy making is a task for a company's entire management team and discuss which kinds of strategic decisions tend to be made at which levels of management. The chapter concludes with a look at the roles and responsibilities of a company's board of directors in the strategy-making, strategy-executing process and how good corporate governance protects shareholder interests and promotes good management.

WHAT DOES THE STRATEGY-MAKING, STRATEGY-EXECUTING PROCESS ENTAIL?

The managerial process of crafting and executing a company's strategy consists of five integrated tasks:

1. *Developing a strategic vision* that charts the company's long-term direction, a *mission statement* that describes the company's purpose, and a set of *core values* to guide the pursuit of the vision and mission.
2. *Setting objectives* for measuring the company's performance and tracking its progress in moving in the intended long-term direction.
3. *Crafting a strategy* to move the company along the strategic course that management has charted and achieve the objectives.
4. *Executing the chosen strategy* efficiently and effectively.
5. *Monitoring developments, evaluating performance, and initiating corrective adjustments* in the company's vision and mission statement, objectives, strategy, or approach to strategy execution in light of actual experience, changing conditions, new ideas, and new opportunities.

FIGURE 2.1 The Strategy-Making, Strategy-Executing Process

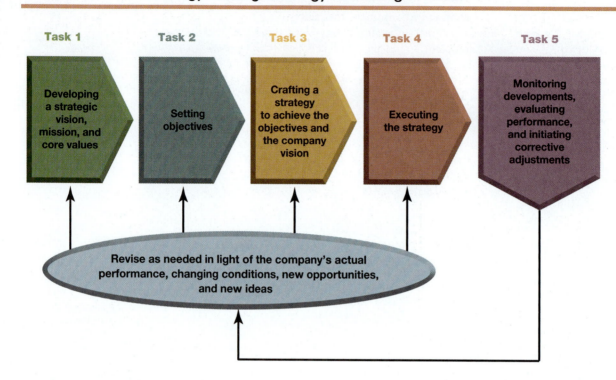

Figure 2.1 displays this five-task process, which we examine next in some detail.

The first three tasks of the strategic management process make up a strategic plan. A **strategic plan** maps out where a company is headed, establishes strategic and financial targets, and outlines the competitive moves and approaches to be used in achieving the desired business results.[1]

A company's **strategic plan** lays out its future direction, performance targets, and strategy.

TASK 1: DEVELOPING A STRATEGIC VISION, A MISSION STATEMENT, AND A SET OF CORE VALUES

LO 1

Grasp why it is critical for company managers to have a clear strategic vision of where a company needs to head and why.

At the outset of the strategy-making process, a company's senior managers must wrestle with the issue of what directional path the company should take. Can the company's prospects be improved by changing its product offerings, or the markets in which it participates, or the customers it aims to serve? Deciding to commit the company to one path versus another pushes managers to draw some carefully reasoned conclusions about whether the company's present strategic course offers attractive opportunities for growth and profitability or whether changes of one kind or another in the company's strategy and long-term direction are needed.

Developing a Strategic Vision

Top management's views and conclusions about the company's long-term direction and what product–market–customer mix seems optimal for the road ahead constitute a **strategic vision** for the company. A strategic vision delineates management's aspirations for the business, providing a panoramic view of "where we are going" and a convincing rationale for why this makes good business sense for the company. A strategic vision thus points an organization in a particular direction, charts a strategic path for it to follow in preparing for the future, and builds commitment to the future course of action. A clearly articulated strategic vision communicates management's aspirations to stakeholders and helps steer the energies of company personnel in a common direction. For instance, Henry Ford's vision of a car in every garage had power because it captured the imagination of others, aided internal efforts to mobilize the Ford Motor Company's resources, and served as a reference point for gauging the merits of the company's strategic actions.

Well-conceived visions are *distinctive* and *specific* to a particular organization; they avoid generic, feel-good statements like "We will become a global leader and the first choice of customers in every market we serve"—which could apply to hundreds of organizations.[2] A surprising number of the vision statements found on company websites and in annual reports are vague and unrevealing, saying very little about the company's future direction. Some could apply to almost any company in any industry. Many read like a public relations statement—high-sounding words that someone came up with because it is fashionable for companies to have an official vision statement.[3] But the real purpose of a vision statement is to serve as a management tool for giving the organization a sense of direction.

For a strategic vision to function as a valuable managerial tool, it must convey what management wants the business to look like and provide managers with a reference point in making strategic decisions and preparing the company for the future. It must say something definitive about how the company's leaders intend to position the company beyond where it is today. Table 2.1 provides some dos and don'ts in composing an effectively worded vision statement. Illustration Capsule 2.1 provides a critique of the strategic visions of several prominent companies.

Communicating the Strategic Vision

A strategic vision has little value to the organization unless it's effectively communicated down the line to lower-level managers and employees. A vision cannot provide direction for middle managers nor can it inspire and energize employees unless everyone in the company is familiar with it and can observe management's commitment to the vision. It is particularly important for executives to provide a compelling rationale for a dramatically *new* strategic vision and company direction. When company personnel don't understand or accept the need for redirecting organizational efforts, they are prone to resist change. Hence, explaining the basis for the new direction, addressing employee concerns head-on, calming fears, lifting spirits, and providing updates and progress reports as events unfold all become part of the task in mobilizing support for the vision and winning commitment to needed actions.

Winning the support of organization members for the vision nearly always means putting "where we are going and why" in writing, distributing the statement organizationwide, and having executives personally explain the vision and its rationale to as

TABLE 2.1   Wording a Vision Statement—the Dos and Don'ts

The Dos	The Don'ts
Be graphic. Paint a clear picture of where the company is headed and the market position(s) the company is striving to stake out.	**Don't be vague or incomplete.** Never skimp on specifics about where the company is headed or how the company intends to prepare for the future.
Be forward-looking and directional. Describe the strategic course that will help the company prepare for the future.	**Don't dwell on the present.** A vision is not about what a company once did or does now; it's about "where we are going."
Keep it focused. Focus on providing managers with guidance in making decisions and allocating resources.	**Don't use overly broad language.** All-inclusive language that gives the company license to pursue any opportunity must be avoided.
Have some wiggle room. Language that allows some flexibility allows the directional course to be adjusted as market–customer–technology circumstances change.	**Don't state the vision in bland or uninspiring terms.** The best vision statements have the power to motivate company personnel and inspire shareholder confidence about the company's future.
Be sure the journey is feasible. The path and direction should be within the realm of what the company can accomplish; over time, a company should be able to demonstrate measurable progress in achieving the vision.	**Don't be generic.** A vision statement that could apply to companies in any of several industries (or to any of several companies in the same industry) is not specific enough to provide any guidance.
Indicate why the directional path makes good business sense. The directional path should be in the long-term interests of stakeholders (especially shareowners, employees, and suppliers).	**Don't rely on superlatives.** Visions that claim the company's strategic course is one of being the "best" or "most successful" usually lack specifics about the path the company is taking to get there.
Make it memorable. To give the organization a sense of direction and purpose, the vision needs to be easily communicated. Ideally, it should be reducible to a few choice lines or a memorable "slogan."	**Don't run on and on.** A vision statement that is not short and to the point will tend to lose its audience.

Sources: John P. Kotter, *Leading Change* (Boston: Harvard Business School Press, 1996), Hugh Davidson, *The Committed Enterprise* (Oxford: Butterworth Heinemann, 2002), and Michel Robert, *Strategy Pure and Simple II* (New York: McGraw-Hill, 1992).

many people as feasible. *A strategic vision can usually be stated adequately in one to two paragraphs, and managers should be able to explain it to company personnel and outsiders in 5 to 10 minutes.* Ideally, executives should present their vision for the company in a manner that reaches out and grabs people. An engaging and convincing strategic vision has enormous motivational value—for the same reason that a stonemason is more inspired by the opportunity to build a great cathedral for the ages. Thus executive ability to paint a convincing and inspiring picture of a company's journey and destination is an important element of effective strategic leadership.

Examples of Strategic Visions—How Well Do They Measure Up?

Vision Statement	Effective Elements	Shortcomings
Coca-Cola Our vision serves as the framework for our Roadmap and guides every aspect of our business by describing what we need to accomplish in order to continue achieving sustainable, quality growth. • People: Be a great place to work where people are inspired to be the best they can be. • Portfolio: Bring to the world a portfolio of quality beverage brands that anticipate and satisfy people's desires and needs. • Partners: Nurture a winning network of customers and suppliers; together we create mutual, enduring value. • Planet: Be a responsible citizen that makes a difference by helping build and support sustainable communities. • Profit: Maximize long-term return to shareowners while being mindful of our overall responsibilities. • Productivity: Be a highly effective, lean, and fast-moving organization.	• Graphic • Focused • Flexible • Makes good business sense	• Long • Not forward-looking
Procter & Gamble We will provide branded products and services of superior quality and value that improve the lives of the world's consumers, now and for generations to come. As a result, consumers will reward us with leadership sales, profit and value creation, allowing our people, our shareholders and the communities in which we live and work to prosper.	• Forward-looking • Flexible • Feasible • Makes good business sense	• Not graphic • Not focused • Not memorable
Heinz We define a compelling, sustainable future and create the path to achieve it.	• Forward-looking • Flexible	• Not graphic • Not focused • Confusing • Not memorable • Not necessarily feasible

Developed with Jenna P. Pfeffer.

Sources: Company documents and websites (accessed June 6, 2010, February 4 and 12, 2012).

Expressing the Essence of the Vision in a Slogan   The task of effectively conveying the vision to company personnel is assisted when management can capture the vision of where to head in a catchy or easily remembered slogan. A number of organizations have summed up their vision in a brief phrase:

- Levi Strauss & Company: "We will clothe the world by marketing the most appealing and widely worn casual clothing in the world."
- Nike: "To bring innovation and inspiration to every athlete in the world."
- Mayo Clinic: "The best care to every patient every day."
- Scotland Yard: "To make London the safest major city in the world."
- Greenpeace: "To halt environmental abuse and promote environmental solutions."

Creating a short slogan to illuminate an organization's direction and purpose and using it repeatedly as a reminder of "where we are headed and why" helps rally organization members to hurdle whatever obstacles lie in the company's path and maintain their focus.

Why a Sound, Well-Communicated Strategic Vision Matters

A well thought-out, forcefully communicated strategic vision pays off in several respects: (1) It crystallizes senior executives' own views about the firm's long-term direction; (2) it reduces the risk of rudderless decision making; (3) it is a tool for winning the support of organization members to help make the vision a reality; (4) it provides a beacon for lower-level managers in setting departmental objectives and crafting departmental strategies that are in sync with the company's overall strategy; and (5) it helps an organization prepare for the future. When management is able to demonstrate significant progress in achieving these five benefits, it can count its efforts to create an effective vision for the company as successful.

Developing a Company Mission Statement

The defining characteristic of a strategic vision is what it says about the company's *future strategic course*—"the direction we are headed and what we want our business to look like in the future." It is aspirational. In contrast, a **mission statement** describes the enterprise's *present business and purpose*—"who we are, what we do, and why we are here." It is purely descriptive. Ideally, a company mission statement (1) identifies the company's products/services, (2) specifies the buyer needs that it seeks to satisfy and the customer groups or markets it serves, and (3) gives the company its own identity. The mission statements that one finds in company annual reports or posted on company websites are typically quite brief; some do a better job than others of conveying what the enterprise is all about.

The following three mission statements provide reasonably informative specifics about "who we are, what we do, and why we are here:"

- Trader Joe's (a specialty grocery chain): "The mission of Trader Joe's is to give our customers the best food and beverage values that they can find anywhere and to provide them with the information required for informed buying decisions. We provide these with a dedication to the highest quality of customer satisfaction delivered with a sense of warmth, friendliness, fun, individual pride, and company spirit.
- Occupational Safety and Health Administration (OSHA): "To assure the safety and health of America's workers by setting and enforcing standards; providing training, outreach, and education; establishing partnerships; and encouraging continual improvement in workplace safety and health."
- Google: "To organize the world's information and make it universally accessible and useful."

The distinction between a strategic vision and a mission statement is fairly clear-cut: A **strategic vision** portrays a company's aspirations for its *future* ("where we are going"), whereas a company's **mission** describes its *purpose* and its *present* business ("who we are, what we do, and why we are here").

An example of a not-so-revealing mission statement is that of Microsoft. "To help people and businesses throughout the world realize their full potential" says nothing about its products or business makeup and could apply to many companies in many different industries. A person unfamiliar with Microsoft could not discern from its mission statement that it is a globally known provider of PC software and a leading maker of video game consoles (the popular Xbox 360). Coca-Cola, which markets nearly 400 beverage brands in over 200 countries, also has an uninformative mission statement: "to benefit and refresh everyone it touches." The usefulness of a mission statement that blurs the essence of a company's business activities and purpose is unclear.

Occasionally, companies couch their mission in terms of making a profit. This, too, is flawed. Profit is more correctly an *objective* and a *result* of what a company does. More-over, earning a profit is the obvious intent of every commercial enterprise. Such compa-nies as BMW, Netflix, Shell Oil, Procter & Gamble, Google, and McDonald's are each striving to earn a profit for shareholders; but plainly the fundamentals of their businesses are substantially different when it comes to "who we are and what we do." It is manage-ment's answer to "make a profit doing what and for whom?" that reveals the substance of a company's true mission and business purpose.

Linking the Vision and Mission with Company Values

The **values** of a company (sometimes called *core values*) are the beliefs, traits, and behavioral norms that management has determined should guide the pursuit of its vision and mission. They relate to such things as fair treatment, integrity, ethical behavior, innovativeness, teamwork, top-notch quality, superior customer service, social responsibility, and community citizenship. Many companies have developed a statement of values to emphasize the expectation that the values be reflected in the conduct of company operations and the behavior of company personnel.

> ### CORE CONCEPT
>
> A company's **values** are the beliefs, traits, and behavioral norms that company per-sonnel are expected to display in conducting the company's business and pursuing its strategic vision and mission.

Most companies have articulated four to eight core values that company person-nel are expected to display and that are supposed to be mirrored in how the company conducts its business. Kodak's core values are respect for the dignity of the individual, uncompromising integrity, unquestioned trust, constant credibility, continual improve-ment and personal renewal, and open celebration of individual and team achievements. At Foster Wheeler, a global engineering and construction firm, the four core values are integrity, accountability, high performance, valuing people, and teamwork. In its quest to be the world's leading home-improvement retail, Home Depot embraces eight values— entrepreneurial spirit, excellent customer service, giving back to the community, respect for all people, doing the right thing, taking care of people, building strong relationships, and creating shareholder value.

Do companies practice what they preach when it comes to their professed values? Sometimes no, sometimes yes—it runs the gamut. At one extreme are companies with window-dressing values; the values are given lip service by top executives but have little discernible impact on either how company personnel behave or how the company oper-ates. Such companies have value statements because they are in vogue and make the company look good. At the other extreme are companies whose executives are commit-ted to grounding company operations on sound values and principled ways of doing business. Executives at these companies deliberately seek to ingrain the designated core values into the corporate culture—the core values thus become an integral part of the company's DNA and what makes it tick. At such values-driven companies, executives "walk the talk" and company personnel are held accountable for embodying the stated values in their behavior.

Zappos Family Mission and Core Values

We've been asked by a lot of people how we've grown so quickly, and the answer is actually really simple. . . . We've aligned the entire organization around one mission: *to provide the best customer service possible.* Internally, we call this our **WOW** philosophy.

These are the ten core values that we live by:

DELIVER WOW THROUGH SERVICE.

At the Zappos Family of Companies, anything worth doing is worth doing with WOW. WOW is such a short, simple word, but it really encompasses a lot of things. To WOW, you must differentiate yourself, which means doing something a little unconventional and innovative. You must do something that's above and beyond what's expected. And whatever you do must have an emotional impact on the receiver. We are not an average company, our service is not average, and we don't want our people to be average. We expect every employee to deliver WOW.

EMBRACE AND DRIVE CHANGE.

Part of being in a growing company is that change is constant. For some people, especially those who come from bigger companies, the constant change can be

somewhat unsettling at first. If you are not prepared to deal with constant change, then you probably are not a good fit for the company.

CREATE FUN AND A LITTLE WEIRDNESS.

At Zappos, We're Always Creating Fun and A Little Weirdness! One of the things that makes our company different from a lot of other companies is that we value being fun and being a little weird. We don't want to become one of those big companies that feels corporate

At companies where the stated values are real rather than cosmetic, managers connect values to the pursuit of the strategic vision and mission in one of two ways. In companies with long-standing values that are deeply entrenched in the corporate culture, senior managers are careful to craft a vision, mission, and strategy that match established values; they also reiterate how the value-based behavioral norms contribute to the company's business success. If the company changes to a different vision or strategy, executives take care to explain how and why the core values continue to be relevant. In new companies, top management has to consider what values, behaviors, and business conduct should characterize the company and then draft a value statement that is circulated among managers and employees for discussion and possible modification. A final value statement that incorporates the desired behaviors and traits and that connects to the vision and mission is then officially adopted. Some companies combine their vision, mission, and values into a single statement or document, circulate it to all organization members, and in many instances post the vision, mission, and values statement on the company's website. Illustration Capsule 2.2 describes how core values drive the company's mission at the Zappos Family of Companies, a widely known and quite successful online shoe and apparel retailer.

and boring. We want to be able to laugh at ourselves. We look for both fun and humor in our daily work.

BE ADVENTUROUS, CREATIVE, AND OPEN MINDED.

We think it's important for people and the company as a whole to be bold and daring (but not reckless). We do not want people to be afraid to take risks and make mistakes. We believe if people aren't making mistakes, then that means they're not taking enough risks. Over time, we want everyone to develop his/her gut about business decisions. We want people to develop and improve their decision-making skills. We encourage people to make mistakes as long as they learn from them.

PURSUE GROWTH AND LEARNING.

We think it's important for employees to grow both personally and professionally. It's important to constantly challenge and stretch yourself and not be stuck in a job where you don't feel like you are growing or learning.

BUILD OPEN AND HONEST RELATIONSHIPS WITH COMMUNICATION.

Fundamentally, we believe that openness and honesty make for the best relationships because that leads to trust and faith. We value strong relationships in all areas: with managers, direct reports, customers (internal and external), vendors, business partners, team members, and co-workers.

BUILD A POSITIVE TEAM AND FAMILY SPIRIT.

At our company, we place a lot of emphasis on our culture because we are both a team and a family. We want to create an environment that is friendly, warm, and exciting. We encourage diversity in ideas, opinions, and points of view.

DO MORE WITH LESS.

The Zappos Family of Companies has always been about being able to do more with less. While we may be casual in our interactions with each other, we are focused and serious about the operations of our business. We believe in working hard and putting in the extra effort to get things done.

BE PASSIONATE AND DETERMINED.

Passion is the fuel that drives us and our company forward. We value passion, determination, perseverance, and the sense of urgency. We are inspired because we believe in what we are doing and where we are going. We don't take "no" or "that'll never work" for an answer because if we had, then our company would have never started in the first place.

BE HUMBLE.

While we have grown quickly in the past, we recognize that there are always challenges ahead to tackle. We believe that no matter what happens we should always be respectful of everyone.

Source: Information posted at **www.zappos.com** (accessed June 6, 2010). Copyright © 2011 **Zappos.com**, Inc.

TASK 2: SETTING OBJECTIVES

LO 2

Understand the importance of setting both strategic and financial objectives.

The managerial purpose of setting **objectives** is to convert the vision and mission into specific performance targets. Objectives reflect management's aspirations for company performance in light of the industry's prevailing economic and competitive conditions and the company's internal capabilities. Well-stated objectives are *quantifiable* or *measurable,* and contain a *deadline for achievement.* As Bill Hewlett, cofounder of Hewlett-Packard, shrewdly observed, "You cannot manage what you cannot measure. . . . And what gets measured gets done."[4] Concrete, measurable objectives are managerially valuable for three reasons: (1) They focus efforts and align actions throughout the organization, (2) they serve as *yardsticks* for tracking a company's performance and progress, and (3) they motivate employees to expend greater effort and perform at a high level.

> **CORE CONCEPT**
>
> **Objectives** are an organization's performance targets—the specific results management wants to achieve.

The Imperative of Setting Stretch Objectives   The experiences of countless companies and managers teach that one of the best ways to promote outstanding company performance is for managers to deliberately set performance targets high enough to *stretch an organization to perform at its full potential and deliver the best possible results.* Challenging company personnel to go all out and deliver "stretch" gains in performance pushes an enterprise to be more inventive, to exhibit more urgency in improving both its financial performance and its business position, and to be more intentional and focused in its actions. Stretch objectives spur exceptional performance and help build a firewall against contentment with modest gains in organizational performance. Manning Selvage & Lee (MS&L), a U.S. public relations firm, used ambitious stretch objectives to triple its revenues in three years. A company exhibits *strategic intent* when it relentlessly pursues an ambitious strategic objective, concentrating the full force of its resources and competitive actions on achieving that objective. MS&L's strategic intent was to become one of the leading global PR firms, which it achieved with the help of its stretch objectives. Honda's long-standing strategic intent of producing an ultra-light jet was finally realized in 2012 when the five-passenger plane dubbed the "Honda Civic of the sky" went into production.

What Kinds of Objectives to Set   Two very distinct types of performance targets are required: those relating to financial performance and those relating to strategic performance. **Financial objectives** communicate management's goals for financial performance. **Strategic objectives** are goals concerning a company's marketing standing and competitive position. A company's set of financial and strategic objectives should include both near-term and longer-term performance targets. Short-term (quarterly or annual) objectives focus attention on delivering performance improvements in the current period and satisfy shareholder expectations for near-term progress. Longer-term targets (three to five years off) force managers to consider what to do *now* to put the company in position to perform better later. Long-term objectives are critical for achieving optimal long-term performance and stand as a barrier to a nearsighted management philosophy and an undue focus on short-term results. When trade-offs have to be made between achieving long-term objectives and achieving short-term objectives, long-term objectives should take precedence (unless the achievement of one or more short-term performance targets has unique importance). Examples of commonly used financial and strategic objectives include the following:

The Need for a Balanced Approach to Objective Setting   The importance of setting and attaining financial objectives is obvious. Without adequate profitability and financial strength, a company's long-term health and ultimate survival are jeopardized. Furthermore, subpar earnings and a weak balance sheet alarm shareholders and creditors and put the jobs of senior executives at risk. However, good financial performance, by itself, is not enough. Of equal or greater importance is a company's strategic performance—outcomes that indicate whether a company's market position and competitiveness are deteriorating, holding steady, or improving. *A stronger market standing and greater competitive vitality is what enables a company to improve its financial performance.*

Moreover, a company's financial performance measures are really *lagging indicators* that reflect the results of past decisions and organizational activities.[5] But a company's past or current financial performance is not a reliable indicator of its future prospects—poor financial performers often turn things around and do better, while good financial

Financial Objectives	Strategic Objectives
<ul><li>An *x* percent increase in annual revenues</li><li>Annual increases in after-tax profits *of x* percent</li><li>Annual increases in earnings per share of *x* percent</li><li>Annual dividend increases of *x* percent</li><li>Profit margins of *x* percent</li><li>An *x* percent return on capital employed (ROCE) or return on shareholders' equity investment (ROE)</li><li>Increased shareholder value—in the form of an upward-trending stock price</li><li>Bond and credit ratings of *x*</li><li>Internal cash flows of *x* dollars to fund new capital investment</li></ul>	<ul><li>Winning an *x* percent market share</li><li>Achieving lower overall costs than rivals</li><li>Overtaking key competitors on product performance or quality or customer service</li><li>Deriving *x* percent of revenues from the sale of new products introduced within the past five years</li><li>Having broader or deeper technological capabilities than rivals</li><li>Having a wider product line than rivals</li><li>Having a better-known or more powerful brand name than rivals</li><li>Having stronger national or global sales and distribution capabilities than rivals</li><li>Consistently getting new or improved products to market ahead of rivals</li></ul>

performers can fall upon hard times. The best and most reliable *leading indicators* of a company's future financial performance and business prospects are strategic outcomes that indicate whether the company's competitiveness and market position are stronger or weaker. The accomplishment of strategic objectives signals that the company is well positioned to sustain or improve its performance. For instance, if a company is achieving ambitious strategic objectives such that its competitive strength and market position are on the rise, then there's reason to expect that its *future* financial performance will be better than its current or past performance. If a company begins to lose competitive strength and fails to achieve important strategic objectives, then its ability to maintain its present profitability is doubtful.

Consequently, it is important to utilize a performance measurement system that strikes a *balance* between financial objectives and strategic objectives.[6] The most widely used framework for balancing financial objectives with strategic objectives is known as the **Balanced Scorecard.**[7] This is a method for linking financial performance objectives to specific strategic objectives that derive from a company's business model. It provides a company's employees with clear guidelines about how their jobs are linked to the overall objectives of the organization, so they can contribute most productively and collaboratively to the achievement of these goals. In 2010, nearly 50 percent of global companies used a balanced-scorecard approach to measuring strategic and financial performance.[8] Examples of organizations that have adopted a balanced-scorecard approach to setting objectives and measuring performance include SAS Institute, UPS, Ann Taylor Stores, Fort Bragg Army Garrison, Caterpillar, Daimler AG, Hilton Hotels, Susan G. Komen for the Cure, and Siemens AG.[9] Illustration Capsule 2.3 provides selected strategic and financial objectives of three prominent companies.

Setting Objectives for Every Organizational Level   Objective setting should not stop with top management's establishing of companywide performance targets. Company objectives need to be broken down into performance targets for each of the organization's separate businesses, product lines, functional departments, and

Business strategy is concerned with building competitive advantage in a single business unit of a diversified company or in a non-diversified single business company. Business strategy is also the responsibility of the CEO and other senior executives, but key business-unit heads may also be influential, especially in strategic decisions affecting the businesses they head.

Functional-area strategies concern the actions and approaches employed in managing particular functions within a business—like R&D, production, sales and marketing, customer service, and finance. A company's marketing strategy, for example, represents the managerial game plan for running the sales and marketing part of the business. A company's product development strategy represents the game plan for keeping the company's product lineup in tune with what buyers are looking for. The primary role of functional strategies is to flesh out the details of a company's business strategy. Lead responsibility for functional strategies within a business is normally delegated to the heads of the respective functions, with the general manager of the business having final approval. Since the different functional-level strategies must be compatible with the overall business strategy and with one another to have beneficial impact, the general business manager may at times exert stronger influence on the content of the functional strategies.

Operating strategies concern the relatively narrow strategic initiatives and approaches for managing key operating units (e.g., plants, distribution centers, purchasing centers) and specific operating activities with strategic significance (e.g., quality control, materials purchasing, brand management, Internet sales). A distribution center manager of a company promising customers speedy delivery must have a strategy to ensure that finished goods are rapidly turned around and shipped out to customers once they are received from the company's manufacturing facilities. Even though operating strategy is at the bottom of the strategy-making hierarchy, its importance should not be downplayed. A major plant that fails in its strategy to achieve production volume, unit cost, and quality targets can damage the company's reputation for quality products and undercut the achievement of company sales and profit objectives. Frontline managers are thus an important part of an organization's strategy-making team.

In single business companies, the uppermost level of the strategy-making hierarchy is the business strategy, so a single-business company has three levels of strategy: business strategy, functional-area strategies, and operating strategies. Proprietorships, partnerships, and owner-managed enterprises may have only one or two strategy-making levels since their strategy-making process can be handled by just a few key people. The larger and more diverse the operations of an enterprise, the more points of strategic initiative it has and the more levels of management that have a significant strategy-making role.

Uniting the Strategy-Making Hierarchy

Ideally, the pieces of a company's strategy up and down the strategy hierarchy should be cohesive and mutually reinforcing, fitting together like a jigsaw puzzle. *Anything less than a unified collection of strategies weakens the overall strategy and is likely to impair company performance.*[11] It is the responsibility of top executives to achieve this unity by clearly communicating the company's vision, objectives, and major strategy components to down-the-line managers and key personnel. Midlevel and frontline managers cannot craft unified strategic moves without first understanding the company's long-term direction and knowing the major components of the corporate and/or business strategies that their strategy-making efforts are supposed to support and enhance.

Thus, as a general rule, strategy-making must start at the top of the organization and then proceed downward from the corporate level to the business level and then from the business level to the associated functional and operating levels.

Furthermore, once strategies up and down the hierarchy have been created, lower-level strategies must be scrutinized for consistency and support of higher-level strategies. Any strategy conflicts must be addressed and resolved, either by modifying the lower-level strategies with conflicting elements or by adapting the higher-level strategy to accommodate what may be more appealing strategy ideas and initiatives bubbling up from below.

A Strategic Vision + Objectives + Strategy = A Strategic Plan

Developing a strategic vision and mission, setting objectives, and crafting a strategy are basic direction-setting tasks. They map out where a company is headed, its purpose, the targeted strategic and financial outcomes, the basic business model, and the competitive moves and internal action approaches to be used in achieving the desired business results. Together, they constitute a **strategic plan** for coping with industry conditions, outcompeting rivals, meeting objectives, and making progress toward the strategic vision.[12] Typically, a strategic plan includes a commitment to allocate resources to the plan and specifies a time period for achieving goals (usually three to five years).

In companies that do regular strategy reviews and develop explicit strategic plans, the strategic plan usually ends up as a written document that is circulated to most managers and perhaps selected employees. A number of companies summarize key elements of their strategic plans in the company's annual report to shareholders, in postings on their websites, or in statements provided to the business media, whereas others, perhaps for reasons of competitive sensitivity, make only vague, general statements about their strategic plans.[13] In small, privately owned companies, it is rare for strategic plans to exist in written form. Small-company strategic plans tend to reside in the thinking and directives of owners/executives, with aspects of the plan being revealed in conversations with company personnel about where to head, what to accomplish, and how to proceed.

> **CORE CONCEPT**
>
> A company's **strategic plan** lays out its future direction and business purpose, performance targets, and strategy.

TASK 4: EXECUTING THE STRATEGY

Managing the implementation of a strategy is easily the most demanding and time-consuming part of the strategy management process. Converting strategic plans into actions and results tests a manager's ability to direct organizational action, motivate people, build and strengthen competitive capabilities, create and nurture a strategy-supportive work climate, and meet or beat performance targets. Initiatives to put the strategy in place and execute it proficiently have to be launched and managed on many organizational fronts.

Management's action agenda for executing the chosen strategy emerges from assessing what the company will have to do to achieve the targeted financial and strategic performance. Each company manager has to think through the answer to "What has to be done in my area to execute my piece of the strategic plan, and what actions should I take to get the process under way?" How much internal change is needed depends on how much of the strategy is new, how far internal practices and competencies deviate from what the strategy requires, and how well the present work culture supports good strategy execution. Depending on the amount of internal change involved, full implementation and proficient execution of the company strategy (or important new pieces thereof) can take several months to several years.

> **LO 4**
>
> Become aware of what a company must do to achieve operating excellence and to execute its strategy proficiently.

In most situations, managing the strategy execution process includes the following principal aspects:

- Staffing the organization to obtain needed skills and expertise.
- Developing and strengthening strategy-supporting resources and capabilities.
- Creating a strategy-supporting structure.
- Allocating ample resources to the activities critical to strategic success.
- Ensuring that policies and procedures facilitate effective strategy execution.
- Organizing the work effort along the lines of best practice.
- Installing information and operating systems that enable company personnel to perform essential activities.
- Motivating people and tying rewards directly to the achievement of performance objectives.
- Creating a company culture and work climate conducive to successful strategy execution.
- Exerting the internal leadership needed to propel implementation forward.

Good strategy execution requires diligent pursuit of operating excellence. It is a job for a company's whole management team. Success hinges on the skills and cooperation of operating managers who can push for needed changes in their organizational units and consistently deliver good results. Management's handling of the strategy implementation process can be considered successful if things go smoothly enough that the company meets or beats its strategic and financial performance targets and shows good progress in achieving management's strategic vision.

TASK 5: EVALUATING PERFORMANCE AND INITIATING CORRECTIVE ADJUSTMENTS

The fifth component of the strategy management process—monitoring new external developments, evaluating the company's progress, and making corrective adjustments—is the trigger point for deciding whether to continue or change the company's vision and mission, objectives, strategy, and/or strategy execution methods.[14] As long as the company's strategy continues to pass the three tests of a winning strategy discussed in Chapter 1 (good fit, competitive advantage, strong performance), company executives may well decide to stay the course. Simply fine-tuning the strategic plan and continuing with efforts to improve strategy execution are sufficient.

But whenever a company encounters disruptive changes in its environment, questions need to be raised about the appropriateness of its direction and strategy. If a company experiences a downturn in its market position or persistent shortfalls in performance, then company managers are obligated to ferret out the causes—Do they relate to poor strategy, poor strategy execution, or both?—and take timely corrective action. A company's direction, objectives, and strategy have to be revisited anytime external or internal conditions warrant.

Likewise, managers are obligated to assess which of the company's operating methods and approaches to strategy execution merit continuation and which need improvement. Proficient strategy execution is always the product of much organizational learning. It is achieved unevenly—coming quickly in some areas and proving nettlesome in others. Consequently, top-notch strategy execution requires a company's

A company's vision and mission, as well as its objectives, strategy, and approach to strategy execution are never final; managing strategy is an ongoing process.

management team to scrutinize the entire strategy execution effort and proactively institute timely and effective adjustments that will move the company closer to operating excellence.

CORPORATE GOVERNANCE: THE ROLE OF THE BOARD OF DIRECTORS IN THE STRATEGY-CRAFTING, STRATEGY-EXECUTING PROCESS

Although senior managers have the *lead responsibility* for crafting and executing a company's strategy, it is the duty of a company's board of directors to exercise strong oversight and see that the five tasks of strategic management are conducted in a manner that is in the best interests of shareholders and other stakeholders.[15] A company's board of directors has four important obligations to fulfill:

1. *Oversee the company's financial accounting and financial reporting practices.* While top executives, particularly the company's CEO and CFO (chief financial officer), are primarily responsible for seeing that the company's financial statements fairly and accurately report the results of the company's operations, board members have a fiduciary duty to protect shareholders by exercising oversight of the company's financial practices. In addition, corporate boards must ensure that generally acceptable accounting principles (GAAP) are properly used in preparing the company's financial statements and determine whether proper financial controls are in place to prevent fraud and misuse of funds. Virtually all boards of directors monitor the financial reporting activities by appointing an audit committee, always composed entirely of *outside directors* (*inside directors* hold management positions in the company and either directly or indirectly report to the CEO). The members of the audit committee have the lead responsibility for overseeing the decisions of the company's financial officers and consulting with both internal and external auditors to ensure that financial reports are accurate and that adequate financial controls are in place. Faulty oversight of corporate accounting and financial reporting practices by audit committees and corporate boards during the early 2000s resulted in the federal investigation of more than 20 major corporations between 2000 and 2002. The investigations of such well-known companies as AOL Time Warner, Enron, Qwest Communications, and WorldCom found that upper management had employed fraudulent or unsound accounting practices to artificially inflate revenues, overstate assets, and reduce expenses. The scandals resulted in the conviction of a number of corporate executives and the passage of the Sarbanes–Oxley Act of 2002, which tightened financial reporting standards and created additional compliance requirements for public boards.

2. *Critically appraise the company's direction, strategy, and business approaches.* Even though board members have a legal obligation to warrant the accuracy of the company's financial reports, directors must set aside time to guide management in choosing a strategic direction and to make independent judgments about the validity and wisdom of management's proposed strategic actions. This aspect of their duties takes on heightened importance when the company's strategy is failing or is plagued with faulty execution, and certainly when there is a precipitous collapse in profitability. But under more normal circumstances, many boards have found that meeting agendas become consumed by compliance matters with little time left to discuss matters of strategic importance. The board of directors and management at Philips Electronics

hold annual two- to three-day retreats devoted exclusively to evaluating the company's long-term direction and various strategic proposals. The company's exit from the semiconductor business and its increased focus on medical technology and home health care resulted from management-board discussions during such retreats.[16]

3. *Evaluate the caliber of senior executives' strategic leadership skills.* The board is always responsible for determining whether the current CEO is doing a good job of strategic leadership.[17] The board must also evaluate the leadership skills of other senior executives, since the board must elect a successor when the incumbent CEO steps down, either going with an insider or deciding that an outsider is needed. Evaluation of senior executives' skills is enhanced when outside directors visit company facilities and talk with company personnel personally to evaluate whether the strategy is on track, how well the strategy is being executed, and how well issues and problems are being addressed. Independent board members at GE visit operating executives at each major business unit once a year to assess the company's talent pool and stay abreast of emerging strategic and operating issues affecting the company's divisions.

4. *Institute a compensation plan for top executives that rewards them for actions and results that serve shareholder interests.* A basic principle of corporate governance is that the owners of a corporation (the shareholders) delegate operating authority and managerial control to top management in return for compensation. In their role as an *agent* of shareholders, top executives have a clear and unequivocal duty to make decisions and operate the company in accord with shareholder interests. (This does not mean disregarding the interests of other stakeholders—employees, suppliers, the communities in which the company operates, and society at large.) Most boards of directors have a compensation committee, composed entirely of directors from *outside* the company, to develop a salary and incentive compensation plan that rewards senior executives for boosting the company's *long-term* performance on behalf of shareholders. The compensation committee's recommendations are presented to the full board for approval. But during the past 10 to 15 years, many boards of directors have done a poor job of ensuring that executive salary increases, bonuses, and stock option awards are tied tightly to performance measures that are truly in the long-term interests of shareholders. Rather, compensation packages at many companies have increasingly rewarded executives for short-term performance improvements—most notably, achieving quarterly and annual earnings targets and boosting the stock price by specified percentages. This has had the perverse effect of causing company managers to become preoccupied with actions to improve a company's near-term performance, often motivating them to take unwise business risks to boost short-term earnings by amounts sufficient to qualify for multimillion dollar compensation packages (that, in the view of many people, were obscenely large). The focus on short-term performance has proved damaging to long-term company performance and shareholder interests— witness the huge loss of shareholder wealth that occurred at many financial institutions in 2008–2009 because of executive risk taking in subprime loans, credit default swaps, and collateralized mortgage securities in 2006–2007. As a consequence, the need to overhaul and reform executive compensation has become a hot topic in both public circles and corporate boardrooms. Illustration Capsule 2.4 discusses how weak governance at the mortgage companies Fannie Mae and Freddie Mac allowed opportunistic senior managers to secure exorbitant bonuses while making decisions that imperiled the futures of the companies they managed.

> Effective corporate governance requires the board of directors to oversee the company's strategic direction, evaluate its senior executives, handle executive compensation, and oversee financial reporting practices.

Every corporation should have a strong independent board of directors that (1) is well informed about the company's performance, (2) guides and judges the CEO and other top executives, (3) has the courage to curb management actions the board

Corporate Governance Failures at Fannie Mae and Freddie Mac

Excessive executive compensation in the financial services industry ranks high among examples of failed corporate governance. Corporate governance at the government-sponsored mortgage giants Fannie Mae and Freddie Mac was particularly weak. The politically appointed boards at both enterprises failed to understand the risks of the subprime loan strategies being employed, did not adequately monitor the decisions of the CEO, did not exercise effective oversight of the accounting principles being employed (which led to inflated earnings), and approved executive compensation systems that allowed management to manipulate earnings to receive lucrative performance bonuses. The audit and compensation committees at Fannie Mae were particularly ineffective in protecting shareholder interests, with the audit committee allowing the company's financial officers to audit reports prepared under their direction and used to determine performance bonuses. Fannie Mae's audit committee also was aware of management's use of questionable accounting practices that reduced losses and recorded one-time gains to achieve financial targets linked to bonuses. In addition, the audit committee failed to investigate formal charges of accounting improprieties filed by a manager in the Office of the Controller.

Fannie Mae's compensation committee was equally ineffective. The committee allowed the company's CEO, Franklin Raines, to select the consultant employed to design the mortgage firm's executive compensation plan and agreed to a tiered bonus plan that would permit Raines and other senior managers to receive maximum bonuses without great difficulty. The compensation plan allowed Raines to earn performance-based bonuses of $52 million and a total compensation of $90 million between 1999 and 2004. Raines was forced to resign in December 2004 when the Office of Federal Housing Enterprise Oversight found that Fannie Mae executives had fraudulently inflated earnings to receive bonuses linked to financial performance. Securities and Exchange Commission investigators also found evidence of improper accounting at Fannie Mae and required the company to restate its earnings between 2002 and 2004 by $6.3 billion.

Poor governance at Freddie Mac allowed its CEO and senior management to manipulate financial data

to receive performance-based compensation as well. Freddie Mac CEO Richard Syron received 2007 compensation of $19.8 million while the mortgage company's share price declined from a high of $70 in 2005 to $25 at year-end 2007. During Syron's tenure as CEO, the company became embroiled in a multibillion-dollar accounting scandal, and Syron personally disregarded internal reports dating to 2004 that cautioned of an impending financial crisis at the company. Forewarnings within Freddie Mac and by federal regulators and outside industry observers proved to be correct, with loan underwriting policies at Freddie Mac and Fannie Mae leading to combined losses at the two firms in 2008 of more than $100 billion. The price of Freddie Mac's shares had fallen to below $1 by the time of Syron's resignation in September 2008.

(continued)

where and how to compete. Attention centers on the broad environmental context, the narrower competitive arena in which a company operates, the drivers of market change, the market positions of rival companies, the moves and countermoves of rivals, and the factors that determine competitive success. In Chapter 4, we explore the methods of evaluating a company's internal circumstances and competitive capabilities. Here we begin with a set of questions that managers should address in analyzing and making strategic sense of their external situation.

QUESTION 1: WHAT ARE THE STRATEGICALLY RELEVANT FACTORS IN THE MACRO-ENVIRONMENT?

Every company operates in a broad **"macro-environment"** that comprises six principal components: political factors, economic conditions in the firm's general environment (local, country, regional, worldwide), sociocultural forces, technological factors, environmental factors (concerning the natural environment), and legal/regulatory conditions. Each of these components has the potential to affect the firm's more immediate industry and competitive environment, although some are likely to have a more important effect than others (see Figure 3.2). An analysis of the impact of these factors is often referred to as **PESTEL analysis**, an acronym that serves as a reminder of the six components involved.

Since macroeconomic factors affect different industries in different ways and to different degrees, it is important for managers to determine which of these represent the most *strategically relevant factors* outside the firm's industry boundaries. By *strategically relevant,* we mean important enough to have a bearing on the decisions the company ultimately makes about its long-term direction, objectives, strategy, and business model. The impact of the outer-ring factors depicted in Figure 3.2 on a company's choice of strategy can range from big to small. But even if those factors change slowly or are likely to have a low impact on the company's business situation, they still merit a watchful eye.

For example, the strategic opportunities of cigarette producers to grow their businesses are greatly reduced by antismoking ordinances, the decisions of governments to impose higher cigarette taxes, and the growing cultural stigma attached to smoking. Motor vehicle companies must adapt their strategies to customer concerns about high gasoline prices and to environmental concerns about carbon emissions. Companies in the food processing, restaurant, sports, and fitness industries have to pay special attention to changes in lifestyles, eating habits, leisure-time preferences, and attitudes toward nutrition and fitness in fashioning their strategies. Table 3.1 provides a brief description of the components of the macro-environment and some examples of the industries or business situations that they might affect.

FIGURE 3.2 The Components of a Company's Macro-Environment

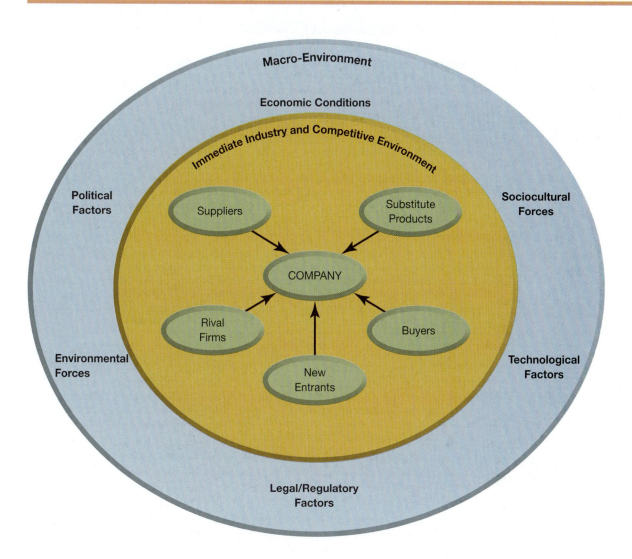

As company managers scan the external environment, they must be alert for potentially important outer-ring developments, assess their impact and influence, and adapt the company's direction and strategy as needed. However, the factors in a company's environment having the *biggest* strategy-shaping impact typically pertain to the company's immediate industry and competitive environment. Consequently, it is on a company's industry and competitive environment that we concentrate the bulk of our attention in this chapter.

TABLE 3.1 The Six Components of the Macro-Environment

Component	Description
Political factors	These factors include political policies and processes, including the extent to which a government intervenes in the economy. They include such matters as tax policy, fiscal policy, tariffs, the political climate, and the strength of institutions such as the federal banking system. Some political factors, such as bailouts, are industry-specific. Others, such as energy policy, affect certain types of industries (energy producers and heavy users of energy) more than others.
Economic conditions	Economic conditions include the general economic climate and specific factors such as interest rates, exchange rates, the inflation rate, and the unemployment rate, the rate of economic growth, trade deficits or surpluses, savings rates, and per capita domestic product. Economic factors also include conditions in the markets for stocks and bonds, which can affect consumer confidence and discretionary income. Some industries, such as construction, are particularly vulnerable to economic downturns but are positively affected by factors such as low interest rates. Others, such as discount retailing, may benefit when general economic conditions weaken, as consumers become more price-conscious.
Sociocultural forces	Sociocultural forces include the societal values, attitudes, cultural factors, and lifestyles that impact businesses, as well as demographic factors such as the population size, growth rate and age distribution. Sociocultural forces vary by locale and change over time. An example is the trend toward healthier lifestyles, which can shift spending toward exercise equipment and health clubs and away from alcohol and snack foods. Population demographics can have large implications for industries such as health care, where costs and service needs vary with demographic factors such as age and income distribution.
Technological factors	Technological factors include the pace of technological change and technical developments that have the potential for wide-ranging effects on society, such as genetic engineering and nanotechnology. They include institutions involved in creating new knowledge and controlling the use of technology, such as R&D consortia, university-sponsored technology incubators, patent and copyright laws, and government control over the Internet. Technological change can encourage the birth of new industries, such as those based on nanotechnology, and disrupt others, such as the recording industry.
Environmental forces	This includes ecological and environmental forces such as weather, climate, climate change, and associated factors like water shortages. These factors can directly impact industries such as insurance, farming, energy production, and tourism. They may have an indirect but substantial effect on other industries such as transportation and utilities.
Legal and regulatory factors	These factors include the regulations and laws with which companies must comply such as consumer laws, labor laws, antitrust laws, and occupational health and safety regulation. Some factors, such as banking deregulation, are industry-specific. Others, such as minimum wage legislation, affect certain types of industries (low-wage, labor-intensive industries) more than others.

ASSESSING THE COMPANY'S INDUSTRY AND COMPETITIVE ENVIRONMENT

Thinking strategically about a company's industry and competitive environment entails using some well-validated concepts and analytical tools to get clear answers to six additional questions:

1. How strong are the industry's competitive forces?
2. What are the driving forces in the industry, and what impact will they have on competitive intensity and industry profitability?

3.   What market positions do industry rivals occupy—who is strongly positioned and who is not?
4.   What strategic moves are rivals likely to make next?
5.   What are the industry's key success factors?
6.   Is the industry outlook conducive to good profitability?

Analysis-based answers to these six questions provide managers with the understanding needed to craft a strategy that fits the company's external situation. The remainder of this chapter is devoted to describing the methods of obtaining solid answers to these questions and explaining how the nature of a company's industry and competitive environment weighs upon the strategic choices of company managers.

QUESTION 2: HOW STRONG ARE THE INDUSTRY'S COMPETITIVE FORCES?

The character and strength of the competitive forces operating in an industry are never the same from one industry to another. Far and away the most powerful and widely used tool for diagnosing the principal competitive pressures in a market is the *five forces model of competition*.[1] This model, depicted in Figure 3.3, holds that competitive pressures on companies within an industry come from five sources. These include (1) competition from *rival sellers*, (2) competition from *potential new entrants* to the industry, (3) competition from producers of *substitute products*, (4) *supplier* bargaining power, and (5) *customer* bargaining power.

In brief, using the five forces model to determine the nature and strength of competitive pressures in a given industry involves three steps:

- *Step 1:* For each of the five forces, identify the different parties involved, along with the specific factors that bring about competitive pressures.
- *Step 2:* Evaluate how strong the pressures stemming from each of the five forces are (strong, moderate, or weak).
- *Step 3:* Determine whether the strength of the five forces, overall, is conducive to earning attractive profits in the industry.

Competitive Pressures Created by the Rivalry among Competing Sellers

The strongest of the five competitive forces is often the rivalry for buyer patronage among competing sellers of a product or service. The intensity of rivalry among competing sellers within an industry depends on a number of identifiable factors. Figure 3.4 summarizes these factors, identifying those that intensify or weaken rivalry among direct competitors in an industry. A brief explanation of why these factors affect the degree of rivalry is in order:

- *Rivalry increases when buyer demand is growing slowly or declining.* Rapidly expanding buyer demand produces enough new business for all industry members to grow without using volume-boosting sales tactics to draw customers away from rival enterprises. But in markets where buyer demand is growing only 1 to 2 percent or is shrinking, companies desperate to gain more business typically employ price discounts, sales promotions, and other tactics to boost their sales volumes, sometimes to the point of igniting a fierce battle for market share.

LO 2

Gain command of the basic concepts and analytical tools widely used to diagnose the competitive conditions in a company's industry.

FIGURE 3.3 The Five Forces Model of Competition: A Key Analytical Tool

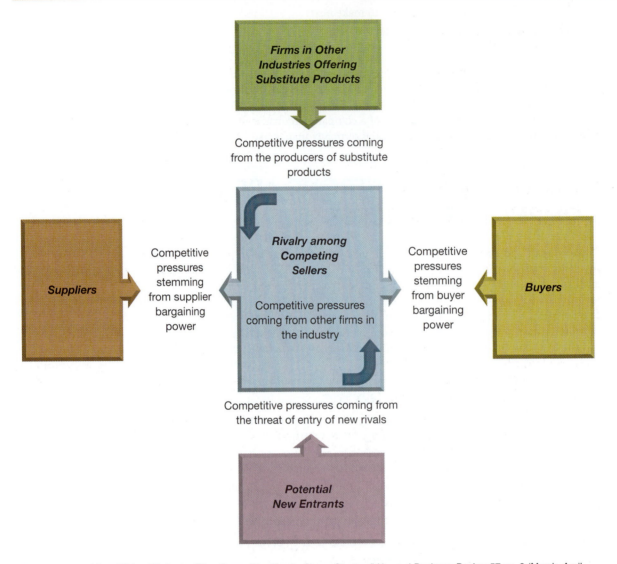

Sources: Adapted from Michael E. Porter, "How Competitive Forces Shape Strategy," *Harvard Business Review* 57, no. 2 (March–April 1979), pp. 137–145, and Michael E. Porter, "The Five Competitive Forces That Shape Strategy," *Harvard Business Review* 86, no. 1 (January 2008), pp. 80–86.

- *Rivalry increases as it becomes less costly for buyers to switch brands.* The less costly it is for buyers to switch their purchases from one seller to another, the easier it is for sellers to steal customers away from rivals. When the cost of switching brands is higher, buyers are less prone to brand switching. Switching costs include not only monetary costs but also the time, inconvenience, and psychological costs involved in switching brands. For example, distributors and retailers may not switch to the brands of rival manufacturers because they are hesitant to sever long-standing supplier relationships, incur any technical support costs or retraining expenses in making the switchover, or go to the trouble of testing the quality and reliability of the rival brand.

FIGURE 3.4 Factors Affecting the Strength of Rivalry

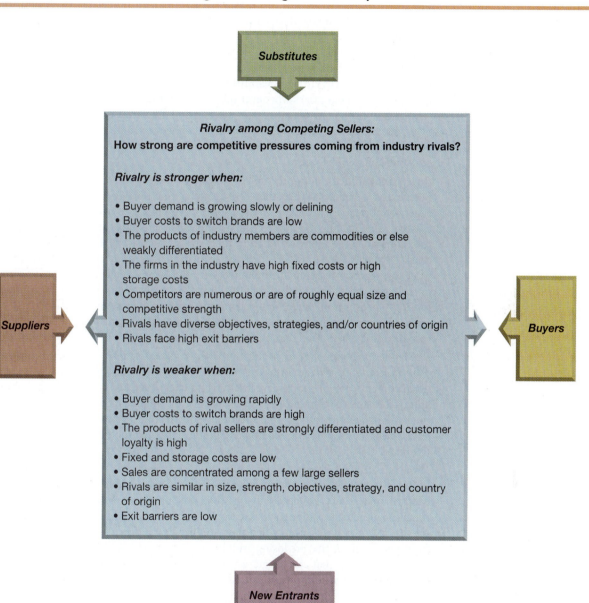

Substitutes

Rivalry among Competing Sellers:
How strong are competitive pressures coming from industry rivals?

Rivalry is stronger when:

• Buyer demand is growing slowly or delining
• Buyer costs to switch brands are low
• The products of industry members are commodities or else weakly differentiated
• The firms in the industry have high fixed costs or high storage costs
• Competitors are numerous or are of roughly equal size and competitive strength
• Rivals have diverse objectives, strategies, and/or countries of origin
• Rivals face high exit barriers

Rivalry is weaker when:

• Buyer demand is growing rapidly
• Buyer costs to switch brands are high
• The products of rival sellers are strongly differentiated and customer loyalty is high
• Fixed and storage costs are low
• Sales are concentrated among a few large sellers
• Rivals are similar in size, strength, objectives, strategy, and country of origin
• Exit barriers are low

Suppliers

Buyers

New Entrants

- *Rivalry increases as the products of rival sellers become less strongly differentiated.* When the offerings of rivals are identical or weakly differentiated, buyers have less reason to be brand-loyal—a condition that makes it easier for rivals to convince buyers to switch to their offerings. Moreover, when the products of different sellers are virtually identical, shoppers will choose on the basis of price, which can result in fierce price competition among sellers. On the other hand, strongly differentiated product offerings among rivals breed high brand loyalty on the part of buyers—because many buyers view the attributes of certain brands as more appealing or better suited to their needs.

- *Rivalry is more intense when there is excess supply or unused production capacity, especially if the industry's product has high fixed costs or high storage costs.* Whenever a market has excess supply, rivalry intensifies as sellers cut prices in a desperate effort to cope with the unsold inventory. A similar effect occurs when a product is perishable or seasonal, since firms often engage in aggressive price cutting to ensure that everything is sold. Likewise, whenever fixed costs account for a large fraction of total cost so that unit costs are significantly lower at full capacity, firms come under significant pressure to cut prices whenever they are operating below full capacity. Unused capacity imposes a significant cost-increasing penalty because there are fewer units over which to spread fixed costs. The pressure of high fixed or high storage costs can push rival firms into price concessions, special discounts, rebates, and other volume-boosting competitive tactics.

- *Rivalry intensifies as the number of competitors increases and they become more equal in size and capability.* When there are many competitors in a market, companies eager to increase their meager market share often engage in price-cutting activities to drive sales, leading to intense rivalry. When there are only three or four competitors, companies are more wary of how their rivals may react to their attempts to take market share away from them. Fear of retaliation and a descent into a damaging price war leads to restrained competitive moves. Moreover, when rivals are of comparable size and competitive strength, they can usually compete on a fairly equal footing—an evenly matched contest tends to be fiercer than a contest in which one or more industry members have commanding market shares and substantially greater resources and capabilities than their much smaller rivals.

- *Rivalry becomes more intense as the diversity of competitors increases in terms of long-term directions, objectives, strategies, and countries of origin.* A diverse group of sellers often contains one or more mavericks willing to try novel or rule-breaking market approaches, thus generating a more volatile and less predictable competitive environment. Globally competitive markets are often more rivalrous, especially when aggressors have lower costs and are intent on gaining a strong foothold in new country markets.

- *Rivalry is stronger when high exit barriers keep unprofitable firms from leaving the industry.* In industries where the assets cannot easily be sold or transferred to other uses, where workers are entitled to job protection, or where owners are committed to remaining in business for personal reasons, failing firms tend to hold on longer than they might otherwise—even when they are bleeding red ink. This increases rivalry in two ways. Firms that are losing ground or in financial trouble often resort to deep price discounting that can trigger a price war and destabilize an otherwise attractive industry. In addition, high exit barriers result in an industry being more overcrowded than it would otherwise be, and this forces the weakest companies to engage in desperate maneuvers to win sufficient sales to stay in business.

Evaluating the strength of rivalry in an industry is a matter of determining whether the factors stated here, taken as a whole, indicate that the rivalry is relatively strong, moderate, or weak. When rivalry is *strong,* the battle for market share is generally so vigorous that the profit margins of most industry members are squeezed to bare-bones levels. When rivalry is *moderate,* a more normal state, the maneuvering among industry members, while lively and healthy, still allows most industry members to earn acceptable profits. When rivalry is *weak,* most companies in the industry are relatively well satisfied with their sales growth and market shares, rarely undertake offensives to steal customers away from one another, and—because of weak competitive forces—earn consistently good profits and returns on investment.

The Choice of Competitive Weapons Competitive contests are ongoing and dynamic. Each competing company endeavors to deploy whatever means it believes will attract and retain buyers, strengthen its market position, and yield good profits. But when one firm makes a strategic move that produces good results, its rivals typically respond with offensive or defensive countermoves of their own. This pattern of action and reaction, move and countermove, produces a continually evolving competitive landscape where the market battle ebbs and flows and produces winners and losers.[2]

Competitive battles among rival sellers can assume many forms that extend well beyond lively price competition. For example, competitors may resort to such marketing tactics as special sales promotions, heavy advertising, rebates, or low-interest-rate financing to drum up additional sales. Rivals may race one another to differentiate their products by offering better performance features or higher quality or improved customer service or a wider product selection. They may also compete through the rapid introduction of next-generation products, the frequent introduction of new or improved products, and efforts to build stronger dealer networks, establish positions in foreign markets, or otherwise expand distribution capabilities and market presence. Table 3.2 provides a sampling of the types of competitive weapons available to rivals, along with their primary effects with respect to the price *(P)*, cost *(C)*, and value *(V)*—the elements of an effective business model, as discussed in Chapter 1.

TABLE 3.2 Common "Weapons" for Competing with Rivals

Types of Competitive Weapons	Primary Effects
Price discounting, clearance sales	Lowers price (*P*), acts to boost total sales volume and market share, lowers profit margins per unit sold when price cuts are big and/or increases in sales volume are relatively small
Couponing, advertising items on sale	Acts to increase unit sales volume and total revenues, lowers price (*P*), increases unit costs (*C*), may lower profit margins per unit sold (*P − C*)
Advertising product or service characteristics, using ads to enhance a company's image	Boosts buyer demand, increases product differentiation and perceived value (*V*), acts to increase total sales volume and market share, may increase unit costs (*C*) and/or lower profit margins per unit sold
Innovating to improve product performance and quality	Acts to increase product differentiation and value (*V*), boosts buyer demand, acts to boost total sales volume, likely to increase unit costs (*C*)
Introducing new or improved features, increasing the number of styles to provide greater product selection	Acts to increase product differentiation and value (*V*), strengthens buyer demand, acts to boost total sales volume and market share, likely to increase unit costs (*C*)
Increasing customization of product or service	Acts to increase product differentiation and value (*V*), increases switching costs, acts to boost total sales volume, often increases unit costs (*C*)
Building a bigger, better dealer network	Broadens access to buyers, acts to boost total sales volume and market share, may increase unit costs (*C*)
Improving warranties, offering low-interest financing	Acts to increase product differentiation and value (*V*), increases unit costs (*C*), increases buyer costs to switch brands, acts to boost total sales volume and market share

Competitive Pressures Associated with the Threat of New Entrants

New entrants to a market bring new production capacity, the desire to establish a secure place in the market, and sometimes substantial resources. Just how serious the competitive threat of entry is in a particular market depends on two classes of factors: the *expected reaction of incumbent firms to new entry* and what are known as *barriers to entry*.

Industry incumbents that are willing and able to launch strong defensive maneuvers to maintain their positions can make it hard for a new entrant to gain a sufficient market foothold to survive and eventually become profitable. Defensive maneuvers against potential entrants may include price discounts (especially to the very customer groups a newcomer is seeking to attract), ramped-up advertising, special sales promotions, new product features (to match or beat the newcomer's product offering), or additional customer services. Such defensive maneuvers on the part of incumbents raise an entrant's costs and risks and have to be considered likely if one or more incumbents have previously tried to strongly contest the entry of new firms into the marketplace.

A barrier to entry exists whenever it is hard for a newcomer to break into the market and/or the economics of the business put a potential entrant at a disadvantage. The most widely encountered barriers that entry candidates must hurdle include the following:[3]

- *Cost advantages enjoyed by industry incumbents.* Existing industry members frequently have costs that are hard for a newcomer to replicate. The cost advantages of industry incumbents can stem from (1) scale economies in production, distribution, advertising, or other activities, (2) the learning-based costs savings that accrue from experience in performing certain activities such as manufacturing or new product development or inventory management, (3) cost-savings accruing from patents or proprietary technology, (4) exclusive partnerships with the best and cheapest suppliers of raw materials and components, (5) favorable locations, and (6) low fixed costs (because they have older facilities that have been mostly depreciated). The bigger the cost advantages of industry incumbents, the riskier it becomes for outsiders to attempt entry (since they will have to accept thinner profit margins or even losses until the cost disadvantages can be overcome).

- *Strong brand preferences and high degrees of customer loyalty.* The stronger the attachment of buyers to established brands, the harder it is for a newcomer to break into the marketplace. In such cases, a new entrant must have the financial resources to spend enough on advertising and sales promotion to overcome customer loyalties and build its own clientele. Establishing brand recognition and building customer loyalty can be a slow and costly process. In addition, if it is difficult or costly for a customer to switch to a new brand, a new entrant may have to offer a discounted price or otherwise persuade buyers that its brand is worth the switching costs. Such barriers discourage new entry because they act to boost financial requirements and lower expected profit margins for new entrants.

- *Strong "network effects" in customer demand.* In industries where buyers are more attracted to a product when there are many other users of the product, there are said to be "network effects," since demand is higher the larger the network of users. Video game systems are an example, since users prefer to have the same systems as their friends so that they can play together on systems they all know and share games. When incumbents have a large existing base of users, new entrants with otherwise comparable products face a serious disadvantage in attracting buyers.

- *High capital requirements.* The larger the total dollar investment needed to enter the market successfully, the more limited the pool of potential entrants. The most obvious capital requirements for new entrants relate to manufacturing facilities and equipment, introductory advertising and sales promotion campaigns, working capital to finance inventories and customer credit, and sufficient cash to cover startup costs.

- *The difficulties of building a network of distributors or dealers and securing adequate space on retailers' shelves.* A potential entrant can face numerous distribution channel challenges. Wholesale distributors may be reluctant to take on a product that lacks buyer recognition. Retailers must be recruited and convinced to give a new brand ample display space and an adequate trial period. When existing sellers have strong, well-functioning distributor–dealer networks, a newcomer has an uphill struggle in squeezing its way into existing distribution channels. Potential entrants sometimes have to "buy" their way into wholesale or retail channels by cutting their prices to provide dealers and distributors with higher markups and profit margins or by giving them big advertising and promotional allowances. As a consequence, a potential entrant's own profits may be squeezed unless and until its product gains enough consumer acceptance that distributors and retailers are anxious to carry it.

- *Restrictive government policies.* Regulated industries like cable TV, telecommunications, electric and gas utilities, radio and television broadcasting, liquor retailing, and railroads entail government-controlled entry. Government agencies can also limit or even bar entry by requiring licenses and permits, such as the medallion required to drive a taxicab in New York City. Government-mandated safety regulations and environmental pollution standards also create entry barriers because they raise entry costs. In international markets, host governments commonly limit foreign entry and must approve all foreign investment applications. National governments commonly use tariffs and trade restrictions (antidumping rules, local content requirements, quotas, and so on) to raise entry barriers for foreign firms and protect domestic producers from outside competition.

Figure 3.5 summarizes the factors that cause the overall competitive threat from potential new entrants to be strong, moderate, or weak. An analysis of these factors can help managers determine whether the threat of entry into their industry is high or low, *in general*. But certain kinds of companies—those with sizable financial resources, proven competitive capabilities, and a respected brand name—may be able to hurdle an industry's entry barriers even when they are high.[4] For example, when Honda opted to enter the U.S. lawnmower market in competition against Toro, Snapper, Craftsman, John Deere, and others, it was easily able to hurdle entry barriers that would have been formidable to other newcomers because it had longstanding expertise in gasoline engines, and a reputation for quality and durability in automobiles that gave it instant credibility with homeowners. As a result, Honda had to spend relatively little on inducing dealers to handle the Honda lawnmower line or attracting customers. Companies already well-established in certain product categories or geographic areas often possess the resources, competencies, and competitive capabilities to hurdle the barriers of entering a different market segment or new geographic area. Thus, *the strongest competitive pressures associated with potential entry frequently come not from outsiders but from current industry participants looking for growth opportunities.*

It is also important to recognize that the threat of entry changes as the industry's prospects grow brighter or dimmer and as entry barriers rise or fall. For example, in the pharmaceutical industry the expiration of a key patent on a widely prescribed drug virtually guarantees that one or more drug makers will enter with generic offerings of their own. Use of the Internet for shopping has made it much easier for e-tailers to enter into competition against some of the best-known retail chains. Moreover, new strategic actions by incumbent firms to increase advertising, strengthen distributor–dealer relations, step up R&D, or improve product quality can erect higher roadblocks to entry.

Whether an industry's entry barriers ought to be considered high or low depends on the resources and capabilities possessed by the pool of potential entrants.

High entry barriers and weak entry threats today do not always translate into high entry barriers and weak entry threats tomorrow.

- *Whether suppliers provide a differentiated input that enhances the performance of the industry's product.* The more valuable a particular input is in terms of enhancing the performance or quality of the products of industry members, the more bargaining leverage suppliers have. On the other hand, the suppliers of commodities are in a weak bargaining position, since industry members have no reason other than price to prefer one supplier over another.

- *Whether it is difficult or costly for industry members to switch their purchases from one supplier to another.* Low switching costs limit supplier bargaining power by enabling industry members to change suppliers if any one supplier attempts to raise prices by more than the costs of switching. Thus, the higher the switching costs of industry members, the stronger the bargaining power of their suppliers.

- *Whether the supplier industry is dominated by a few large companies and whether it is more concentrated than the industry it sells to.* Suppliers with sizable market shares and strong demand for the items they supply generally have sufficient bargaining power to charge high prices and deny requests from industry members for lower prices or other concessions.

- *Whether suppliers provide an item that accounts for a sizable fraction of the costs of the industry's product.* The bigger the cost of a particular part or component, the more industry members will be sensitive to the actions of suppliers to raise or lower their prices. As a result, they will bargain more aggressively.

- *Whether it makes good economic sense for industry members to integrate backward and self-manufacture items they have been buying from suppliers.* As a rule, suppliers are safe from the threat of self-manufacture by their customers until the volume of parts a customer needs becomes large enough for the customer to justify backward integration into self-manufacture of the component. When industry members can threaten credibly to self-manufacture suppliers' goods, their bargaining power over suppliers increases proportionately.

- *Whether there are good substitutes available for the suppliers' products.* The ready availability of substitute inputs lessens the bargaining power of suppliers by reducing the dependence of industry members on the suppliers. The better the price and performance characteristics of the substitute inputs, the weaker the bargaining power of suppliers.

- *Whether industry members are major customers of suppliers.* As a rule, suppliers have less bargaining leverage when their sales to members of the industry constitute a big percentage of their total sales. In such cases, the well-being of suppliers is closely tied to the well-being of their major customers. Suppliers have a big incentive to protect and enhance the competitiveness of their major customers via reasonable prices, exceptional quality, and ongoing advances in the technology of the items supplied.

In identifying the degree of supplier power in an industry, it is important to recognize that different types of suppliers are likely to have different amounts of bargaining power. Thus, the first step is for managers to identify the different types of suppliers, paying particular attention to those that provide the industry with important inputs. The next step is to assess the bargaining power of each type of supplier separately. Figure 3.7 summarizes the conditions that tend to make supplier bargaining power strong or weak.

Competitive Pressures Stemming from Buyer Bargaining Power and Price Sensitivity

Whether buyers are able to exert strong competitive pressures on industry members depends on (1) the degree to which buyers have bargaining power and (2) the extent to which buyers are price-sensitive. Buyers with strong bargaining power can limit industry profitability by demanding price concessions, better payment terms, or additional features and services that increase industry members' costs. Buyer price sensitivity limits the profit potential of industry members by restricting the ability of sellers to raise prices without losing revenue.

The leverage that buyers have in negotiating favorable terms of the sale can range from weak to strong. Individual consumers, for example, rarely have much bargaining power in negotiating price concessions or other favorable terms with sellers. However, their price sensitivity varies by individual and by the type of product they are buying (whether it's a necessity or a discretionary purchase, for example). Business buyers, in contrast, can have considerable bargaining power. Retailers tend to have greater bargaining power over industry sellers if they have influence over the purchase decisions of the end user or if they are critical in providing sellers with access to the end user. For example, large retail chains like Walmart, Best Buy, Staples, and Home Depot typically have considerable negotiating leverage in purchasing products from manufacturers because of manufacturers' need for access to their broad base of customers. Major supermarket chains like Kroger, Safeway, Food Lion, and Publix have sufficient bargaining power to demand promotional allowances and lump-sum payments (called slotting fees) from food products manufacturers in return for stocking certain brands or putting them in the best shelf locations. Motor vehicle manufacturers have strong bargaining power in negotiating to buy original-equipment tires from tire makers not only because they buy in large quantities but also because consumers are more likely to buy replacement tires that match the tire brand on their vehicle at the time of purchase.

Figure 3.8 summarizes the factors determining the strength of buyer power in an industry. As described next, the first six factors are the mirror image of those determining the bargaining power of suppliers.

- *Buyer power increases when buyer demand is weak in relation to industry supply.* Weak or declining demand creates a "buyers' market," in which bargain-hunting buyers are able to press for better deals and special treatment; conversely, strong or rapidly growing demand creates a "sellers' market" and shifts bargaining power to sellers.
- *Buyer power increases when industry goods are standardized or differentiation is weak.* In such circumstances, buyers make their selections on the basis of price, which increases price competition among vendors.
- *Buyers' bargaining power is greater when their costs of switching to competing brands or substitutes are relatively low.* Switching costs put a cap on how much industry producers can raise prices or reduce quality before they will lose the buyer's business.
- *Buyers have more power when they are large and few in number relative to the number of sellers.* The larger the buyer, the more important their business is to the seller and the more sellers will be willing to grant concessions.
- *Buyers gain leverage if they are well informed about sellers' products, prices, and costs.* The more information buyers have, the better bargaining position they are in. The mushrooming availability of product information on the Internet is giving added bargaining power to consumers, since they can use this to find or negotiate for better deals.
- *Buyers' bargaining power is greater when they pose a credible threat of integrating backward into the business of sellers.* Companies like Anheuser-Busch, Coors, and Heinz have partially integrated backward into metal can manufacturing to gain bargaining power in obtaining the balance of their can requirements from otherwise powerful metal can manufacturers.

FIGURE 3.8 Factors Affecting the Bargaining Power of Buyers

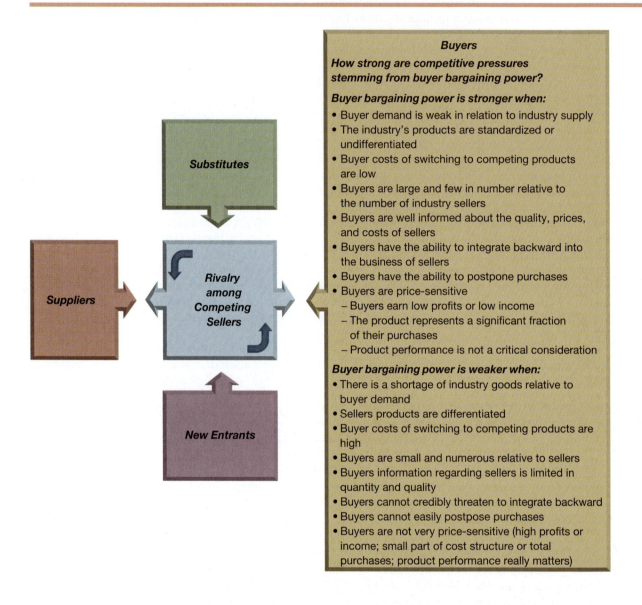

- *Buyer leverage increases if buyers have discretion to delay their purchases or perhaps even not make a purchase at all.* Consumers often have the option to delay purchases of durable goods, such as major appliances, or discretionary goods, such as hot tubs and home entertainment centers, if they are not happy with the prices offered. Business customers may also be able to defer their purchases of certain items, such as plant equipment or maintenance services. This puts pressure on sellers to provide concessions to buyers so that the sellers can keep their sales numbers from dropping off.

- *Buyer price sensitivity increases when buyers are earning low profits or have low income.* Price is a critical factor in the purchase decisions of low-income consumers and companies that are barely scraping by. In such cases, their high price sensitivity limits the ability of sellers to charge high prices.

- *Buyers are more price-sensitive if the product represents a large fraction of their total purchases.* When a purchase eats up a large portion of a buyer's budget or represents a significant part of his or her cost structure, the buyer cares more about price than might otherwise be the case.

The starting point for the analysis of buyers as a competitive force is to identify the different types of buyers along the value chain—then proceed to analyzing the bargaining power and price sensitivity of each type separately. It is important to recognize that *not all buyers of an industry's product have equal degrees of bargaining power with sellers,* and some may be less sensitive than others to price, quality, or service differences. For example, apparel manufacturers confront significant bargaining power when selling to big retailers like Target, Macy's, or L.L. Bean but they can command much better prices selling to small owner-managed apparel boutiques.

Is the Collective Strength of the Five Competitive Forces Conducive to Good Profitability?

Assessing whether each of the five competitive forces gives rise to strong, moderate, or weak competitive pressures sets the stage for evaluating whether, overall, the strength of the five forces is conducive to good profitability. Are some of the competitive forces sufficiently powerful to undermine industry profitability? Can companies in this industry reasonably expect to earn decent profits in light of the prevailing competitive forces?

The most extreme case of a "competitively unattractive" industry occurs when all five forces are producing strong competitive pressures: Rivalry among sellers is vigorous, low entry barriers allow new rivals to gain a market foothold, competition from substitutes is intense, and both suppliers and buyers are able to exercise considerable leverage. Strong competitive pressures coming from all five directions drive industry profitability to unacceptably low levels, frequently producing losses for many industry members and forcing some out of business. But an industry can be competitively unattractive without all five competitive forces being strong. In fact, intense competitive pressures *from just one* of the five forces may suffice to destroy the conditions for good profitability and prompt some companies to exit the business.

As a rule, *the strongest competitive forces determine the extent of the competitive pressure on industry profitability.*[5] Thus, in evaluating the strength of the five forces overall and their effect on industry profitability, managers should look to the strongest forces. Having more than one strong force will not worsen the effect on industry profitability, but it does mean that the industry has multiple competitive challenges with which to cope. In that sense, an industry with three to five strong forces is even more "unattractive" as a place to compete. Especially intense competitive conditions seem to be the norm in tire manufacturing, apparel, and commercial airlines, three industries where profit margins have historically been thin.

In contrast, when the overall impact of the five competitive forces is moderate to weak, an industry is "attractive" in the sense that the *average* industry member can reasonably expect to earn good profits and a nice return on investment. The ideal competitive environment for earning superior profits is one in which both suppliers and customers are in weak bargaining positions, there are no good substitutes, high barriers block further entry, and rivalry among present sellers is muted. Weak competition is the best of all possible worlds for also-ran companies because even they can usually eke out a decent profit—if a company can't make a decent profit when competition is weak, then its business outlook is indeed grim.

CORE CONCEPT

The strongest of the five forces determines the extent of the downward pressure on an industry's profitability.

Matching Company Strategy to Competitive Conditions

Working through the five forces model step by step not only aids strategy makers in assessing whether the intensity of competition allows good profitability but also promotes sound strategic thinking about how to better match company strategy to the specific competitive character of the marketplace. Effectively matching a company's business strategy to prevailing competitive conditions has two aspects:

1. Pursuing avenues that shield the firm from as many of the different competitive pressures as possible.
2. Initiating actions calculated to shift the competitive forces in the company's favor by altering the underlying factors driving the five forces.

But making headway on these two fronts first requires identifying competitive pressures, gauging the relative strength of each of the five competitive forces, and gaining a deep enough understanding of the state of competition in the industry to know which strategy buttons to push.

QUESTION 3: WHAT FACTORS ARE DRIVING INDUSTRY CHANGE, AND WHAT IMPACT WILL THEY HAVE?

While it is critical to understand the nature and intensity of the competitive forces in an industry, it is equally critical to understand that the intensity of these forces is fluid and subject to change. All industries are affected by new developments and ongoing trends that alter industry conditions, some more speedily than others. Any strategies devised by management will therefore play out in a dynamic industry environment, so it's imperative that managers consider the factors driving industry change and how they might affect the industry environment. Moreover, with early notice, managers may be able to influence the direction or scope of environmental change and improve the outlook.

The Concept of Industry Driving Forces

Industry and competitive conditions change because forces are enticing or pressuring certain industry participants (competitors, customers, suppliers) to alter their actions in important ways. The most powerful of the change agents are called **driving forces** because they have the biggest influences in reshaping the industry landscape and altering competitive conditions. Some driving forces originate in the outer ring of the company's macro-environment (see Figure 3.2), but most originate in the company's more immediate industry and competitive environment.

Driving forces analysis has three steps: (1) identifying what the driving forces are, (2) assessing whether the drivers of change are, on the whole, acting to make the industry more or less attractive, and (3) determining what strategy changes are needed to prepare for the impact of the driving forces. All three steps merit further discussion.

Identifying an Industry's Driving Forces

Many developments can affect an industry powerfully enough to qualify as driving forces. Some drivers of change are unique and specific to a particular industry situation, but most drivers of industry and competitive change fall into one of the following categories:

- *Changes in an industry's long-term growth rate.* Shifts in industry growth up or down have the potential to affect the balance between industry supply and buyer demand, entry and exit, and the character and strength of competition. Whether demand is growing or declining is one of the key factors influencing the intensity of rivalry in an industry, as explained earlier. But the strength of this effect will depend on how changes in the industry growth rate affect entry and exit in the industry. If entry barriers are low, then growth in demand will attract new entrants, increasing the number of industry rivals. If exit barriers are low, then shrinking demand will induce exit, resulting in fewer remaining rivals. If demand for the industry's product continues to shrink, the remaining industry members may be forced to close inefficient plants and retrench to a smaller production base. Hence, whether industry growth turns up or down, the outcome is a much-changed competitive landscape.

- *Increasing globalization.* Competition begins to shift from primarily a regional or national focus to an international or global focus when industry members begin seeking out customers in foreign markets or when production activities begin to migrate to countries where costs are lowest. Globalization can also be precipitated by the blossoming of consumer demand in developing countries and by the actions of government officials in many countries to reduce trade barriers or open up once-closed markets to foreign competitors, as is occurring in many parts of Latin America and Asia. Significant differences in labor costs among countries give manufacturers a strong incentive to locate plants for labor-intensive products in low-wage countries and use these plants to supply market demand across the world. Wages in China, India, Singapore, Mexico, and Brazil, for example, are significantly less than those in the United States, Germany, and Japan. The forces of globalization are sometimes such a strong driver that companies find it highly advantageous, if not necessary, to spread their operating reach into more and more country markets. Globalization is very much a driver of industry change in such industries as motor vehicles, steel, petroleum, personal computers, video games, public accounting, and textbook publishing.

- *Emerging new Internet capabilities and applications.* Mushrooming use of high-speed Internet service and Voice-over-Internet-Protocol (VoIP) technology, growing acceptance of Internet shopping, and the exploding popularity of Internet applications ("apps") for cell phones and TVs have been major drivers of change in industry after industry. The ability of companies to reach consumers via the Internet increases the number of rivals a company faces and often escalates rivalry by pitting pure online sellers against brick-and-mortar sellers. Online course offerings, for example, are profoundly affecting higher education. The Internet of the future will feature faster speeds, dazzling applications, and over a billion connected gadgets performing an array of functions, thus driving further industry and competitive changes. But Internet-related impacts vary from industry to industry. The challenges here are to assess precisely how emerging Internet developments are altering a particular industry's landscape and to factor these impacts into the strategy-making equation.

- *Changes in who buys the product and how they use it.* Shifts in buyer demographics and the ways products are used can greatly alter industry and competitive conditions. Longer life expectancies and growing percentages of relatively well-to-do retirees, for example, are driving demand growth in such industries as health care, prescription drugs, recreational living, and vacation travel. Apple's iPod models have transformed how music is bought and listened to—album sales are dropping, downloads of single digital recordings are mushrooming, and iPods have become the device of choice for millions of music listeners. Smart cell phones, with their growing array of features, functions, and downloadable applications, have become multi-use devices that have totally transformed the user experience and attracted altogether new types of buyers.

- *Technological change and manufacturing process innovation.* Advances in technology can cause disruptive change in an industry by introducing substitutes that offer buyers an irresistible price/performance combination. They can also alter the industry landscape by opening up whole new industry frontiers. For instance, high-definition technology has revolutionized TV viewing and broadcasting. Advances in battery technology are beginning to change how motor vehicles are powered. Stem cell research holds promise for finding ways to cure or treat an array of diseases.

- *Product and marketing innovation.* An ongoing stream of product innovations tends to alter the pattern of competition in an industry by attracting more first-time buyers, rejuvenating industry growth, and/or increasing product differentiation, with concomitant effects on rivalry, entry threat, and buyer power. Product innovation has been a key driving force in such industries as digital cameras, golf clubs, video games, toys, and prescription drugs. Similarly, when firms are successful in introducing *new ways* to market their products, they can spark a burst of buyer interest, widen industry demand, increase or lower entry barriers, and increase product differentiation—any or all of which can alter the competitiveness of an industry.

- *Entry or exit of major firms.* The entry of one or more foreign companies into a geographic market once dominated by domestic firms nearly always shakes up competitive conditions. Likewise, when an established domestic firm from another industry attempts entry either by acquisition or by launching its own startup venture, it usually pushes competition in new directions. Entry by a major firm thus often produces a new ball game, not only with new key players but also with new rules for competing. Similarly, exit of a major firm changes the competitive structure by reducing the number of market leaders and increasing the dominance of the leaders who remain.

- *Diffusion of technical know-how across companies and countries.* As knowledge about how to perform a particular activity or execute a particular manufacturing technology spreads, products tend to become more commodity-like. Knowledge diffusion can occur through scientific journals, trade publications, onsite plant tours, word of mouth among suppliers and customers, employee migration, and Internet sources.

- *Changes in cost and efficiency.* Widening or shrinking differences in the costs among key competitors tend to dramatically alter the state of competition. Lower production costs and longer-life products have allowed the makers of super-efficient fluorescent-based spiral light bulbs to cut deeply into the sales of incandescent light bulbs. Lower-cost eBooks are cutting into sales of costlier hardcover books as increasing numbers of consumers opt to buy iPads, Kindles, and other brands of tablets.

- *Reductions in uncertainty and business risk.* Many companies are hesitant to enter industries with uncertain futures or high levels of business risk, and firms already in these industries may be cautious about making aggressive capital investments to expand—often because it is unclear how much time and money it will take to overcome various technological hurdles and achieve acceptable production costs (as is the case in the infant solar power industry). Likewise, firms entering foreign markets where demand is just emerging or where political conditions are volatile may be cautious and limit their downside exposure by using less risky strategies. Over time, however, diminishing risk levels and uncertainty tend to stimulate new entry and capital investments on the part of growth-minded companies seeking new opportunities, thus dramatically altering industry and competitive conditions.

- *Regulatory influences and government policy changes.* Government regulatory actions can often mandate significant changes in industry practices and strategic approaches—as has recently occurred in the world's banking industry. Deregulation has proved to be a potent pro-competitive force in the airline industry. New rules and regulations pertaining to government-sponsored health insurance programs are driving changes in the health care industry. In international markets, host governments can drive competitive changes by opening their domestic markets to foreign participation or closing them to protect domestic companies. Note that this driving force is spawned by forces in a company's macro-environment (Figure 3.2).

- *Changing societal concerns, attitudes, and lifestyles.* Emerging social issues as well as changing attitudes and lifestyles can be powerful instigators of industry change. Growing concerns about climate change have emerged as a major driver of change in the energy industry. Mounting consumer concerns about the use of chemical additives and the nutritional content of food products are driving changes in the restaurant and food industries. Shifting societal concerns, attitudes, and lifestyles alter the pattern of competition, favoring those players that respond with products targeted to the new trends and conditions. As with the preceding driving force, this driving force springs from factors at work in a company's macro-environment.

Table 3.3 lists these 12 most common drivers of change. That there are so many different *potential* drivers of change explains why a full understanding of all types of change drivers is a fundamental part of analyzing industry dynamics. However, for each industry no more than three or four of these drivers are likely to be powerful enough to qualify as the *major determinants* of why and how an industry's competitive conditions are changing. The true analytical task is to evaluate the forces of industry and competitive change carefully enough to separate major factors from minor ones.

TABLE 3.3   The Most Common Drivers of Industry Change

1. Changes in the long-term industry growth rate
2. Increasing globalization
3. Emerging new Internet capabilities and applications
4. Changes in who buys the product and how they use it
5. Technological change and manufacturing process innovation
6. Product and marketing innovation
7. Entry or exit of major firms
8. Diffusion of technical know-how across companies and countries
9. Changes in cost and efficiency
10. Reductions in uncertainty and business risk
11. Regulatory influences and government policy changes
12. Changing societal concerns, attitudes, and lifestyles

Assessing the Impact of the Factors Driving Industry Change

The second step in driving forces analysis is to determine whether the prevailing change drivers, on the whole, are acting to make the industry environment more or less attractive. Answers to three questions are needed:

1. Are the driving forces as a whole causing demand for the industry's product to increase or decrease?
2. Is the collective impact of the driving forces making competition more or less intense?
3. Will the combined impacts of the driving forces lead to higher or lower industry profitability?

Getting a handle on the collective impact of the driving forces requires looking at the likely effects of each factor separately, since the driving forces may not all be pushing change in the same direction. For example, one driving force may be acting to spur demand for the industry's product while another is working to curtail demand. Whether the net effect on industry demand is up or down hinges on which driver of change is the more powerful.

Adjusting Strategy to Prepare for the Impacts of Driving Forces

The third step in the strategic analysis of industry dynamics—where the real payoff for strategy making comes—is for managers to draw some conclusions about *what strategy adjustments will be needed to deal with the impacts of the driving forces.* But taking the "right" kinds of actions to prepare for the industry and competitive changes being wrought by the driving forces first requires accurate diagnosis of the forces driving industry change and the impacts these forces will have on both the industry environment and the company's business. To the extent that managers are unclear about the drivers of industry change and their impacts, or if their views are off-base, the chances of making astute and timely strategy adjustments are slim. So driving-forces analysis is not something to take lightly; it has practical value and is basic to the task of thinking strategically about where the industry is headed and how to prepare for the changes ahead.

QUESTION 4: HOW ARE INDUSTRY RIVALS POSITIONED IN THE MARKET?

Within an industry, companies commonly sell in different price/quality ranges, appeal to different types of buyers, have different geographic coverage, and so on. Some are more attractively positioned than others. Understanding which companies are strongly positioned and which are weakly positioned is an integral part of analyzing an industry's competitive structure. The best technique for revealing the market positions of industry competitors is **strategic group mapping**.

Using Strategic Group Maps to Assess the Market Positions of Key Competitors

A **strategic group** consists of those industry members with similar competitive approaches and positions in the market. Companies in the same strategic group can resemble one another in a variety of ways. For example, they may have comparable product-line breadth, emphasize the same distribution channels, depend on identical technological approaches, or offer buyers essentially the same product attributes or similar services and technical assistance.[6] An industry contains only one strategic group when all sellers pursue essentially identical strategies and have similar market positions. At the other extreme, an industry may contain as many strategic groups as there are competitors when each rival pursues a distinctively different competitive approach and occupies a substantially different market position. The number of strategic groups in an industry and their respective market positions can be displayed on a strategic group map.

> **CORE CONCEPT**
>
> A **strategic group** is a cluster of industry rivals that have similar competitive approaches and market positions.

The procedure for constructing a *strategic group map* is straightforward:

- Identify the competitive characteristics that delineate strategic approaches used in the industry. Typical variables used in creating strategic group maps are price/quality range (high, medium, low), geographic coverage (local, regional, national, global), product-line breadth (wide, narrow), degree of service offered (no frills, limited, full), use of distribution channels (retail, wholesale, Internet, multiple), degree of vertical integration (none, partial, full), and degree of diversification into other industries (none, some, considerable).
- Plot the firms on a two-variable map using pairs of these variables.
- Assign firms occupying about the same map location to the same strategic group.
- Draw circles around each strategic group, making the circles proportional to the size of the group's share of total industry sales revenues.

This produces a two-dimensional diagram like the one for the U.S. beer industry in Illustration Capsule 3.1.

Several guidelines need to be observed in creating strategic group maps. First, the two variables selected as axes for the map should *not* be highly correlated; if they are, the circles on the map will fall along a diagonal and reveal nothing more about the relative positions of competitors than would be revealed by comparing the rivals on just one of the variables. For instance, if companies with broad product lines use multiple distribution channels while companies with narrow lines use a single distribution channel, then looking at the differences in distribution channel approaches adds no new information about positioning. Second, the variables chosen as axes for the map should reflect important differences among rival approaches—when rivals differ on both variables, the locations of the rivals will be scattered, thus showing how they are positioned differently. Third, the variables used as axes don't have to be either quantitative or continuous; rather, they can be discrete variables, defined in terms of distinct classes and combinations. Fourth, drawing the sizes of the circles on the map proportional to the combined sales of the firms in each strategic group allows the map to reflect the relative sizes of each strategic group. Fifth, if more than two good variables can be used as axes for the map, then it is wise to draw several maps to give different exposures to the competitive positioning relationships present in the industry's structure—there is not necessarily one best map for portraying how competing firms are positioned.

Comparative Market Positions of Producers in the U.S. Beer Industry: A Strategic Group Map Example

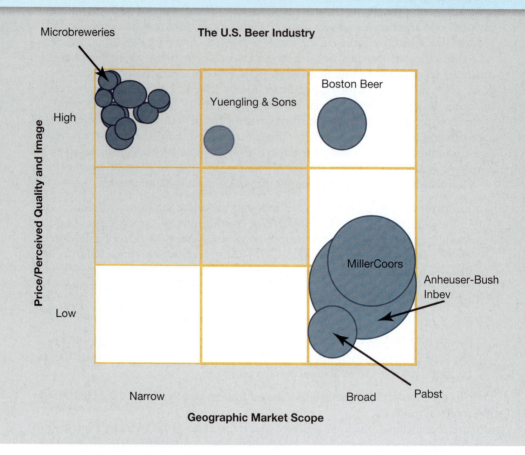

Footnote: Circles are drawn roughly proportional to the sizes of the chains, based on revenues.

The Value of Strategic Group Maps?

Strategic group maps are revealing in several respects. The most important has to do with identifying which industry members are close rivals and which are distant rivals. Firms in the same strategic group are the closest rivals; the next closest rivals are in the immediately adjacent groups. Often, firms in strategic groups that are far apart on the map hardly compete at all. For instance, Walmart's clientele, merchandise selection, and pricing points are much too different to justify calling Walmart a close competitor of Neiman Marcus or Saks Fifth Avenue. For the same reason, Timex is not a meaningful competitive rival of Rolex.

The second thing to be gleaned from strategic group mapping is that *not all positions on the map are equally attractive.*[7] Two reasons account for why some positions can be more attractive than others:

1. *Prevailing competitive pressures from the industry's five forces may cause the profit potential of different strategic groups to vary.* The profit prospects of firms in different

strategic groups can vary from good to poor because of differing degrees of competitive rivalry within strategic groups, differing pressures from potential entrants to each group, differing degrees of exposure to competition from substitute products outside the industry, and differing degrees of supplier or customer bargaining power from group to group. For instance, in the ready-to-eat cereal industry, there are significantly higher entry barriers (capital requirements, brand loyalty, and so on) for the strategic group comprising the large branded-cereal makers than for the group of generic-cereal makers or the group of small natural-cereal producers. Differences in differentiation among the branded rivals versus the generic cereal makers make rivalry stronger within the generic strategic group. In the retail chain industry, the competitive battle between Walmart and Target is more intense (with consequently smaller profit margins) than the rivalry among Versace, Chanel, Fendi, and other high-end fashion retailers.

> Some strategic groups are more favorably positioned than others because they confront weaker competitive forces and/or because they are more favorably impacted by industry driving forces.

2. *Industry driving forces may favor some strategic groups and hurt others.* Likewise, industry driving forces can boost the business outlook for some strategic groups and adversely impact the business prospects of others. In the news industry, for example, Internet news services and cable news networks are gaining ground at the expense of newspapers and networks due to changes in technology and changing social lifestyles. Firms in strategic groups that are being adversely impacted by driving forces may try to shift to a more favorably situated position. If certain firms are known to be trying to change their competitive positions on the map, then attaching arrows to the circles showing the targeted direction helps clarify the picture of competitive maneuvering among rivals.

Thus, part of strategic group map analysis always entails drawing conclusions about where on the map is the "best" place to be and why. Which companies / strategic groups are destined to prosper because of their positions? Which companies / strategic groups seem destined to struggle? What accounts for why some parts of the map are better than others?

QUESTION 5: WHAT STRATEGIC MOVES ARE RIVALS LIKELY TO MAKE NEXT?

Unless a company pays attention to the strategies and situations of competitors and has some inkling of what moves they will be making, it ends up flying blind into competitive battle. As in sports, scouting the opposition is an essential part of game plan development. Having good information about the strategic direction and likely moves of key competitors allows a company to prepare defensive countermoves, to craft its own strategic moves with some confidence about what market maneuvers to expect from rivals in response, and to exploit any openings that arise from competitors' missteps. The question is where to look for such information, since rivals rarely reveal their strategic intentions openly. If information is not directly available, what are the best indicators?

> Studying competitors' past behavior and preferences provides a valuable assist in anticipating what moves rivals are likely to make next and outmaneuvering them in the marketplace.

A FRAMEWORK FOR COMPETITOR ANALYSIS

Michael Porter's **Framework for Competitor Analysis** points to four indicators of a rival's likely strategic moves and countermoves. These include a rival's *current strategy, objectives, capabilities,* and *assumptions* about itself and the industry, as shown in

FIGURE 3.9 A Framework for Competitor Analysis

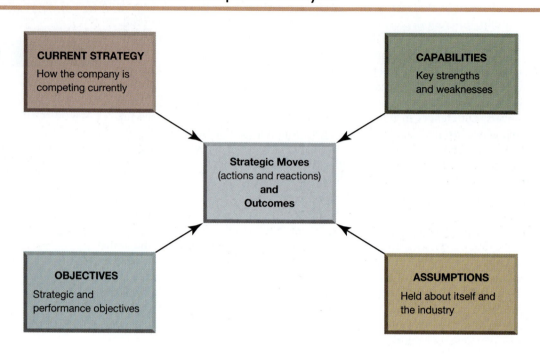

Figure 3.9. A strategic profile of a rival that provides good clues to their behavioral proclivities can be constructed by characterizing the rival along these four dimensions.

Current Strategy   To succeed in predicting a competitor's next moves, company strategists need to have a good understanding of each rival's current strategy, as an indicator of its pattern of behavior and best strategic options. Questions to consider include: How is the competitor positioned in the market? What is the basis for its competitive advantage (if any)? What kinds of investments is it making (as an indicator of its growth trajectory)?

Objectives   An appraisal of a rival's objectives should include not only its financial performance objectives, but strategic ones as well (such as those concerning market share). What is even more important is to consider the extent to which they are meeting these objectives and whether they are under pressure to improve. Rivals with good financial performance are likely to continue their present strategy with only minor fine-tuning. Poorly performing rivals are virtually certain to make fresh strategic moves.

Capabilities   A rival's strategic moves and countermoves are both enabled and constrained by the set of capabilities they have at hand. Thus a rival's capabilities (and efforts to acquire new capabilities) serve as a strong signal of future strategic actions (and reactions to your company's moves). Assessing a rival's capabilities involves sizing up not only their strengths in this respect, but their weaknesses as well.

Those who gather competitive intelligence on rivals can sometimes cross the fine line between honest inquiry and unethical or even illegal behavior. For example, calling rivals to get information about prices, the dates of new product introductions, or wage and salary levels is legal, but misrepresenting one's company affiliation during such calls is unethical. Pumping rivals' representatives at trade shows is ethical only if one wears a name tag with accurate company affiliation indicated.

Avon Products at one point secured information about its biggest rival, Mary Kay Cosmetics (MKC), by having its personnel search through the garbage bins outside MKC's headquarters. When MKC officials learned

of the action and sued, Avon claimed it did nothing illegal, since a 1988 Supreme Court case had ruled that trash left on public property (in this case, a sidewalk) was anyone's for the taking. Avon even produced a videotape of its removal of the trash at the MKC site. Avon won the lawsuit—but Avon's action, while legal, scarcely qualifies as ethical.

Assumptions How a rival's top managers think about their strategic situation can have a big impact on how they behave. Banks that believe they are "too big to fail," for example, may take on more risk than is financially prudent. Assessing a rival's assumptions entails considering their assumptions about itself as well as the industry it participates in.

Information regarding these four analytical components can often be gleaned from company press releases, information posted on the company's website (especially the presentations management has recently made to securities analysts), and such public documents as annual reports and 10-K filings. Many companies also have a competitive intelligence unit that sifts through the available information to construct up-to-date strategic profiles of rivals. (See Illustration Capsule 3.2 for a discussion of the ethical limits to gathering competitive intelligence.)[8]

Doing the necessary detective work can be time-consuming, but scouting competitors well enough to anticipate their next moves allows managers to prepare effective countermoves (perhaps even beat a rival to the punch) and to take rivals' probable actions into account in crafting their own best course of action.

QUESTION 6: WHAT ARE THE INDUSTRY'S KEY FACTORS?

An industry's **key success factors (KSFs)** are those competitive factors that most affect industry members' ability to survive and prosper in the marketplace—the particular strategy elements, product attributes, operational approaches, resources, and competitive capabilities that spell the difference between being a strong competitor and a weak competitor—and between profit and loss. KSFs by their very nature are so important to competitive success that *all firms* in the industry must pay close attention to them or risk becoming an industry laggard or failure. To indicate the significance of KSFs another way, how well the elements of a company's strategy measure up against an industry's KSFs determines whether it can meet the basic criteria for surviving and thriving in the industry. Identifying KSFs, in light of the prevailing and anticipated industry and competitive conditions, is therefore always a top priority in analytical and strategy-making considerations. Company strategists need to understand the industry landscape well enough to separate the factors most important to competitive success from those that are less important.

Key success factors vary from industry to industry, and even from time to time within the same industry, as drivers of change and competitive conditions change. But regardless of the circumstances, an industry's key success factors can always be deduced by asking the same three questions:

1. On what basis do buyers of the industry's product choose between the competing brands of sellers? That is, what product attributes and service characteristics are crucial?
2. Given the nature of competitive rivalry prevailing in the marketplace, what resources and competitive capabilities must a company have to be competitively successful?
3. What shortcomings are almost certain to put a company at a significant competitive disadvantage?

Only rarely are there more than five key factors for competitive success. And even among these, two or three usually outrank the others in importance. Managers should therefore bear in mind the purpose of identifying key success factors—to determine which factors are most important to competitive success—and resist the temptation to label a factor that has only minor importance as a KSF. Compiling a list of every factor that matters even a little bit defeats the purpose of concentrating management attention on the factors truly critical to long-term competitive success.

In the beer industry, for example, although there are many types of buyers (wholesale, retail, end consumer), it is most important to understand the preferences and buying behavior of the beer drinkers. Their purchase decisions are driven by price, taste, convenient access, and marketing. Thus the KSFs include a *strong network of wholesale distributors* (to get the company's brand stocked and favorably displayed in retail outlets, bars, restaurants, and stadiums, where beer is sold) and *clever advertising* (to induce beer drinkers to buy the company's brand and thereby pull beer sales through the established wholesale/retail channels). Because there is a potential for strong buyer power on the part of large distributors and retail chains, competitive success depends on some mechanism to offset that power, of which advertising (to create demand pull) is one. Thus the KSFs also include *superior product differentiation* (as in microbrews) or *superior firm size and branding capabilities* (as in national brands). The KSFs also include *full utilization of brewing capacity* (to keep manufacturing costs low and offset the high advertising, branding, and product differentiation costs).

Correctly diagnosing an industry's KSFs raises a company's chances of crafting a sound strategy. The key success factors of an industry point to those things that every firm in the industry needs to attend to in order to retain customers and weather the competition. If the company's strategy cannot deliver on the key success factors of its industry, it is unlikely to earn enough profits to remain a viable business. The goal of strategists, however, should be to do more than just meet the KSFs, since all firms in the industry need to clear this bar to survive. The goal of company strategists should be to design a strategy that allows it to compare favorably vis-à-vis rivals on each and every one of the industry's KSFs and that aims at being *distinctively better* than rivals on one (or possibly two) of the KSFs.

QUESTION 7: IS THE INDUSTRY OUTLOOK CONDUCIVE TO GOOD PROFITABILITY?

Each of the frameworks presented in this chapter—PESTEL, five forces analysis, driving forces, strategy groups, competitor analysis, and key success factors—provides a useful perspective on an industry's outlook for future profitability. Putting them all together provides an even richer and more nuanced picture. Thus, the final step in evaluating the industry and competitive environment is to use the results of the analyses performed in answering Questions 1 to 6 to determine whether the industry presents the company with strong prospects for competitive success and attractive profits. The important factors on which to base a conclusion include:

LO 4

Learn how to use multiple frameworks to determine whether an industry's outlook presents a company with sufficiently attractive opportunities for growth and profitability.

- How the company is being impacted by the state of the macro-environment.
- Whether strong competitive forces are squeezing industry profitability to subpar levels.
- Whether industry profitability will be favorably or unfavorably affected by the prevailing driving forces.
- Whether the company occupies a stronger market position than rivals.
- Whether this is likely to change in the course of competitive interactions.
- How well the company's strategy delivers on the industry key success factors.

As a general proposition, *the anticipated industry environment is fundamentally attractive if it presents a company with good opportunity for above-average profitability; the industry outlook is fundamentally unattractive if a company's profit prospects are unappealingly low.*

However, it is a mistake to think of a particular industry as being equally attractive or unattractive to all industry participants and all potential entrants.[9] Attractiveness is relative, not absolute, and conclusions one way or the other have to be drawn from the perspective of a particular company. For instance, a favorably positioned competitor may see ample opportunity to capitalize on the vulnerabilities of weaker rivals even though industry conditions are otherwise somewhat dismal. At the same time, industries attractive to insiders may be unattractive to outsiders because of the difficulty of challenging current market leaders or because they have more attractive opportunities elsewhere.

The degree to which an industry is attractive or unattractive is not the same for all industry participants and all potential entrants.

When a company decides an industry is fundamentally attractive and presents good opportunities, a strong case can be made that it should invest aggressively to capture the opportunities it sees and to improve its long-term competitive position in the business. When a strong competitor concludes an industry is becoming less attractive, it may elect to simply protect its present position, investing cautiously—if at all—and looking for opportunities in other industries. A competitively weak company in an unattractive industry may see its best option as finding a buyer, perhaps a rival, to acquire its business.

The Four Tests of a Resource's Competitive Power

The competitive power of a resource or capability is measured by how many of the following four tests it can pass.[5] These tests are often referred to as the **VRIN tests for sustainable competitive advantage**—a short-hand reminder standing for *Valuable, Rare, Inimitable,* and *Non-substitutable.* The first two tests determine whether a resource or capability can support a competitive advantage. The last two determine whether the competitive advantage can be sustained in the face of active competition.

1. *Is the resource (or capability) competitively **Valuable**?* To be competitively valuable, a resource or capability must be directly relevant to the company's strategy, making the company a more effective competitor, able to exploit market opportunities and ward off external threats. Unless the resource contributes to the effectiveness of the company's strategy, it cannot pass this first test. An indicator of its effectiveness is whether the resource enables the company to strengthen its business model through a better customer value proposition and/or profit formula. Companies have to guard against contending that something they do well is necessarily competitively valuable. Apple's operating system for its PCs is by most accounts a world beater (compared to Windows Vista and Windows 7), but Apple has failed miserably in converting its strength in operating system design into competitive success in the global PC market—it is an also-ran with a only a 5 percent market share worldwide. Thus, although Apple has many competitively valuable resources (its design capabilities, for example), its operating system is not among them.

2. *Is the resource **Rare**—is it something rivals lack?* Resources and capabilities that are common among firms and widely available cannot be a source of competitive advantage. All makers of branded cereals have valuable marketing capabilities and brands, since the key success factors in the ready-to-eat cereal industry demand this. They are not rare. The brand strength of Cheerios, however, is uncommon and has provided General Mills with greater market share as well as the opportunity to benefit from brand extensions like Honey Nut Cheerios. A resource or capability is considered rare if it is held by only a small number of firms in an industry or specific competitive domain. Thus, while general management capabilities are not rare in an absolute sense, they are relatively rare in some of the less developed regions of the world and in some business domains.

3. *Is the resource hard to copy **(Inimitable)**?* If a resource or capability is both valuable and rare, it will be competitively superior to comparable resources of rival firms. As such, it is a source of competitive advantage for the company. The more difficult and more costly it is for competitors to imitate, the more likely that it can also provide a *sustainable* competitive advantage. Resources tend to be difficult to copy when they are unique (a fantastic real estate location, patent-protected technology, an unusually talented and motivated labor force), when they must be built over time in ways that are difficult to imitate (a well-known brand name, mastery of a complex process technology, years of cumulative experience and learning), and when they entail financial outlays or large-scale operations that few industry members can undertake (a global network of dealers and distributors). Imitation is also difficult for resources that reflect a high level of *social complexity* (company culture, interpersonal relationships among the managers or R&D teams, trust-based relations with customers or suppliers) and *causal ambiguity,* a term that signifies the hard-to-disentangle nature of the complex resources, such as a web of intricate processes enabling new drug discovery. Hard-to-copy resources and capabilities are important competitive assets, contributing to the longevity of a company's market position and offering the potential for sustained profitability.

4. *Is the resource invulnerable to the threat of substitution from different types of resources and capabilities (**Non-substitutable**)?* Even resources and capabilities that are valuable, rare, and hard to copy can lose much of their competitive power if rivals have other types of resources and capabilities that are of equal or greater competitive power. A company may have the most technologically advanced and sophisticated plants in its industry, but any efficiency advantage it enjoys may be nullified if rivals are able to produce equally good products at lower cost by locating their plants in countries where wage rates are relatively low and a labor force with adequate skills is available.

The vast majority of companies are not well endowed with standout resources or capabilities, capable of passing all four tests with high marks. Most firms have a mixed bag of resources—one or two quite valuable, some good, many satisfactory to mediocre. Resources and capabilities that are valuable pass the first of the four tests. As key contributors to the effectiveness of the strategy, they are relevant to the firm's competitiveness but are no guarantee of competitive advantage. They may offer no more than competitive parity with competing firms.

Passing both of the first two tests requires more—it requires resources and capabilities that are not only valuable but also rare. This is a much higher hurdle that can be cleared only by resources and capabilities that are *competitively superior*. Resources and capabilities that are competitively superior are the company's true strategic assets. They provide the company with a competitive advantage over its competitors, if only in the short run.

To pass the last two tests, a resource must be able to maintain its competitive superiority in the face of competition. It must be resistant to imitative attempts and efforts by competitors to find equally valuable substitute resources. Assessing the availability of substitutes is the most difficult of all the tests since substitutes are harder to recognize, but the key is to look for resources or capabilities held by other firms that *can serve the same function* as the company's core resources and capabilities.[6]

Very few firms have resources and capabilities that can pass all four tests, but those that do enjoy a sustainable competitive advantage with far greater profit potential. Walmart is a notable example, with capabilities in logistics and supply chain management that have surpassed those of its competitors for over 30 years. Lincoln Electric Company, less well known but no less notable in its achievements, has been the world leader in welding products for over 100 years as a result of its unique piecework incentive system for compensating production workers and the unsurpassed worker productivity and product quality that this system has fostered.

A Company's Resources and Capabilities Must Be Managed Dynamically

Even companies like Walmart and Lincoln Electric cannot afford to rest on their laurels. Rivals that are initially unable to replicate a key resource may develop better and better substitutes over time. Resources and capabilities can depreciate like other assets if they are managed with benign neglect. Disruptive changes in technology, customer preferences, distribution channels, or other competitive factors can also destroy the value of key strategic assets, turning resources and capabilities "from diamonds to rust."[7]

Resources and capabilities must be continually strengthened and nurtured to sustain their competitive power and, at times, may need to be broadened and deepened to allow the company to position itself to pursue emerging market opportunities.[8] Organizational resources and capabilities that grow stale can impair competitiveness unless they are refreshed, modified, or even phased out and replaced in response

A company requires a dynamically evolving portfolio of resources and capabilities to sustain its competitiveness and help drive improvements in its performance.

to ongoing market changes and shifts in company strategy. Management's challenge in managing the firm's resources and capabilities dynamically has two elements: (1) attending to the ongoing modification of existing competitive assets and (2) casting a watchful eye for opportunities to develop totally new kinds of capabilities.

The Role of Dynamic Capabilities   Companies that know the importance of recalibrating and upgrading their most valuable resources and capabilities ensure that these activities are done on a continual basis. By incorporating these activities into their routine managerial functions, they gain the experience necessary to be able to do them consistently well. At that point, their ability to freshen and renew their competitive assets becomes a capability in itself—a **dynamic capability.** A dynamic capability is the ability to modify, deepen, or augment the company's existing resources and capabilities.[9] This includes the capacity to improve existing resources and capabilities incrementally, in the way that 3M continually upgrades the R&D resources driving its product innovation strategy. It also includes the capacity to add new resources and capabilities to the company's competitive asset portfolio. An example is Pfizer's acquisition capabilities, which have enabled it to replace degraded resources such as expiring patents with newly acquired capabilities in biotechnology.

QUESTION 3: IS THE COMPANY ABLE TO SEIZE MARKET OPPORTUNITIES AND NULLIFY EXTERNAL THREATS?

In evaluating a company's overall situation, a key question is whether the company is in a position to pursue attractive market opportunities and defend against external threats to its future well-being. The simplest and most easily applied tool for conducting this examination is widely known as *SWOT analysis,* so named because it zeros in on a company's internal **S**trengths and **W**eaknesses, market **O**pportunities, and external **T**hreats. A first-rate SWOT analysis provides the basis for crafting a strategy that capitalizes on the company's strengths, overcomes its weaknesses, aims squarely at capturing the company's best opportunities, and defends against competitive and environmental threats.

Identifying a Company's Internal Strengths

A *strength* is something a company is good at doing or an attribute that enhances its competitiveness in the marketplace. A company's strengths depend on the quality of its resources and capabilities. Resource and capability analysis provides a way for managers to assess the quality objectively. While resources and capabilities that pass the VRIN tests of sustainable competitive advantage are among the company's greatest strengths, other types can be counted among the company's strengths as well. A capability that is not potent enough to produce a sustainable advantage over rivals may yet enable a series of temporary advantages if used as a basis for entry into a new market or market segment. A resource bundle that fails to match those of top-tier competitors may still allow a company to compete successfully against the second tier.

Assessing a Company's Competencies—What Activities Does It Perform Well?

One way to appraise the degree of a company's strengths has to do with the company's skill level in performing key pieces of its business—such as supply chain management, R&D, production, distribution, sales and marketing, and customer service. A company's skill or proficiency in performing different facets of its operations can range from one of minimal ability to perform an activity (perhaps having just struggled to do it the first time) to the other extreme of being able to perform the activity better than any other company in the industry.

When a company's proficiency rises from that of mere ability to perform an activity to the point of being able to perform it consistently well and at acceptable cost, it is said to have a **competence**—a true *capability,* in other words. A **core competence** is a proficiently performed internal activity that is *central* to a company's strategy and competitiveness. A core competence is a more competitively valuable strength than a competence because of the activity's key role in the company's strategy and the contribution it makes to the company's market success and profitability. Often, core competencies can be leveraged to create new markets or new product demand, as the engine behind a company's growth. 3M Corporation has a core competence in product innovation—its record of introducing new products goes back several decades and new product introduction is central to 3M's strategy of growing its business.

A **distinctive competence** is a competitively valuable activity that a company *performs better than its rivals.* A distinctive competence thus signifies greater proficiency than a core competence. Because a distinctive competence represents a level of proficiency that rivals do not have, it qualifies as a *competitively superior strength* with competitive advantage potential. This is particularly true when the distinctive competence enables a company to deliver standout value to customers (in the form of lower prices, better product performance, or superior service). For instance, Walt Disney has a distinctive competence in feature film animation.

The conceptual differences between a competence, a core competence, and a distinctive competence draw attention to the fact that a company's strengths and competitive assets are not all equal.[10] All competencies have some value. But mere ability to perform an activity well does not necessarily give a company competitive clout. Some competencies merely enable market survival because most rivals also have them—indeed, not having a competence that rivals have can result in competitive disadvantage. An apparel manufacturer cannot survive without the capability to produce its apparel items very cost-efficiently, given the intensely price-competitive nature of the apparel industry. A maker of cell phones cannot survive without good product design and product innovation capabilities.

Identifying Company Weaknesses and Competitive Deficiencies

A **weakness**, or *competitive deficiency,* is something a company lacks or does poorly (in comparison to others) or a condition that puts it at a disadvantage in the marketplace. A company's internal weaknesses can relate to (1) inferior or unproven skills, expertise, or intellectual capital in competitively important areas of the business; (2) deficiencies in competitively important physical, organizational, or intangible assets; or (3) missing or competitively inferior capabilities in key areas. *Company weaknesses*

Basing a company's strategy on its most competitively valuable strengths gives the company its best chance for market success.

CORE CONCEPT

A **competence** is an activity that a company has learned to perform with proficiency—a capability, in other words.

CORE CONCEPT

A **core competence** is an activity that a company performs proficiently that is also central to its strategy and competitive success.

CORE CONCEPT

A **distinctive competence** is a competitively important activity that a company performs better than its rivals—it thus represents *a competitively superior internal strength.*

CORE CONCEPT

A company's **strengths** represent its competitive assets; its **weaknesses** are shortcomings that constitute competitive liabilities.

are thus internal shortcomings that constitute competitive liabilities. Nearly all companies have competitive liabilities of one kind or another. Whether a company's internal weaknesses make it competitively vulnerable depends on how much they matter in the marketplace and whether they are offset by the company's strengths.

Table 4.3 lists many of the things to consider in compiling a company's strengths and weaknesses. Sizing up a company's complement of strengths and deficiencies is akin to constructing a *strategic balance sheet,* where strengths represent *competitive assets* and weaknesses represent *competitive liabilities.* Obviously, the ideal condition is for the company's competitive assets to outweigh its competitive liabilities by an ample margin—a 50-50 balance is definitely not the desired condition!

Identifying a Company's Market Opportunities

Market opportunity is a big factor in shaping a company's strategy. Indeed, managers can't properly tailor strategy to the company's situation without first identifying its market opportunities and appraising the growth and profit potential each one holds. Depending on the prevailing circumstances, a company's opportunities can be plentiful or scarce, fleeting or lasting, and can range from wildly attractive (an absolute "must" to pursue) to marginally interesting (because of the high risks or questionable profit potentials) to unsuitable (because the company's strengths are ill-suited to successfully capitalizing on the opportunities). A sampling of potential market opportunities is shown in Table 4.3.

Newly emerging and fast-changing markets sometimes present stunningly big or "golden" opportunities, but it is typically hard for managers at one company to peer into "the fog of the future" and spot them much ahead of managers at other companies.[11] But as the fog begins to clear, golden opportunities are nearly always seized rapidly—and the companies that seize them are usually those that have been actively waiting, staying alert with diligent market reconnaissance, and preparing themselves to capitalize on shifting market conditions by patiently assembling an arsenal of competitively valuable resources—talented personnel, technical know-how, strategic partnerships, and a war chest of cash to finance aggressive action when the time comes. In mature markets, unusually attractive market opportunities emerge sporadically, often after long periods of relative calm—but future market conditions may be more predictable, making emerging opportunities easier for industry members to detect.

In evaluating a company's market opportunities and ranking their attractiveness, managers have to guard against viewing every *industry* opportunity as a *company* opportunity. Rarely does a company have the resource depth to pursue all available market opportunities simultaneously without spreading itself too thin. Some companies have resources and capabilities that are better-suited for pursuing some opportunities, and a few companies may be hopelessly outclassed in competing for any of an industry's attractive opportunities. *The market opportunities most relevant to a company are those that match up well with the company's competitive assets, offer the best prospects for growth and profitability, and present the most potential for competitive advantage.*

A company is well advised to pass on a particular market opportunity unless it has or can acquire the resources and competencies needed to capture it.

Identifying the Threats to a Company's Future Profitability

Often, certain factors in a company's external environment pose *threats* to its profitability and competitive well-being. Threats can stem from the emergence of cheaper or better technologies, the entry of lower-cost foreign competitors into a company's market stronghold,

TABLE 4.3   What to Look for in Identifying a Company's Strengths, Weaknesses, Opportunities, and Threats

Potential Strengths and Competitive Assets	Potential Weaknesses and Competitive Deficiencies
• Competencies that are well matched to industry key success factors • Ample financial resources to grow the business • Strong brand-name image/company reputation • Economies of scale and/or learning and experience curve advantages over rivals • Other cost advantages over rivals • Attractive customer base • Proprietary technology, superior technological skills, important patents • Strong bargaining power over suppliers or buyers • Resources and capabilities that are valuable and rare • Resources and capabilities that are hard to copy and for which there are no good substitutes • Superior product quality • Wide geographic coverage and/or strong global distribution capability • Alliances / joint ventures that provide access to valuable technology, competencies, and/or attractive geographic markets	• No clear strategic vision • No well-developed or proven core competencies • No distinctive competencies or competitively superior resources • Lack of attention to customer needs • A product/service with features and attributes that are inferior to those of rivals • Weak balance sheet, short on financial resources to grow the firm, too much debt • Higher overall unit costs relative to those of key competitors • Too narrow a product line relative to rivals • Weak brand image or reputation • Weaker dealer network than key rivals and/or lack of adequate distribution capability • Lack of management depth • Plagued with internal operating problems or obsolete facilities • Too much underutilized plant capacity • Resources that are readily copied or for which there are good substitutes
Potential Market Opportunities	**Potential External Threats to a Company's Future Profitability**
• Sharply rising buyer demand for the industry's product • Serving additional customer groups or market segments • Expanding into new geographic markets • Expanding the company's product line to meet a broader range of customer needs • Utilizing existing company skills or technological know-how to enter new product lines or new businesses • Falling trade barriers in attractive foreign markets • Acquiring rival firms or companies with attractive technological expertise or capabilities • Entering into alliances or joint ventures to expand the firm's market coverage or boost its competitive capability	• Increasing intensity of competition among industry rivals—may squeeze profit margins • Slowdowns in market growth • Likely entry of potent new competitors • Growing bargaining power of customers or suppliers • A shift in buyer needs and tastes away from the industry's product • Adverse demographic changes that threaten to curtail demand for the industry's product • Adverse economic conditions that threaten critical suppliers or distributers • Changes in technology—particularly disruptive technology that can undermine the company's distinctive competencies • Restrictive foreign trade policies • Costly new regulatory requirements • Tight credit conditions • Rising prices on energy or other key inputs

new regulations that are more burdensome to a company than to its competitors, unfavorable demographic shifts, political upheaval in a foreign country where the company has facilities, and the like. A list of potential threats to a company's future profitability and market position is shown in Table 4.3.

Simply making lists of a company's strengths, weaknesses, opportunities, and threats is not enough; the payoff from SWOT analysis comes from the conclusions about a company's situation and the implications for strategy improvement that flow from the four lists.

External threats may pose no more than a moderate degree of adversity (all companies confront some threatening elements in the course of doing business), or they may be so imposing as to make a company's situation look quite tenuous. On rare occasions, market shocks can give birth to a *sudden-death* threat that throws a company into an immediate crisis and a battle to survive. Many of the world's major financial institutions were plunged into unprecedented crisis in 2008–2009 by the aftereffects of high-risk mortgage lending, inflated credit ratings on subprime mortgage securities, the collapse of housing prices, and a market flooded with mortgage-related investments (collateralized debt obligations) whose values suddenly evaporated. It is management's job to identify the threats to the company's future prospects and to evaluate what strategic actions can be taken to neutralize or lessen their impact.

What Do the SWOT Listings Reveal?

SWOT analysis involves more than making four lists. The two most important parts of SWOT analysis are *drawing conclusions* from the SWOT listings about the company's overall situation and *translating these conclusions into strategic actions* to better match the company's strategy to its internal strengths and market opportunities, to correct important weaknesses, and to defend against external threats. Figure 4.2 shows the steps involved in gleaning insights from SWOT analysis.

Just what story the SWOT listings tell about the company's overall situation is often revealed in the answers to the following set of questions:

- What are the attractive aspects of the company's situation?
- What aspects are of the most concern?
- Are the company's internal strengths and competitive assets sufficiently strong to enable it to compete successfully?
- Are the company's weaknesses and competitive deficiencies of small consequence and readily correctable, or could they prove fatal if not remedied soon?
- Do the company's strengths outweigh its weaknesses by an attractive margin?
- Does the company have attractive market opportunities that are well suited to its internal strengths? Does the company lack the competitive assets to pursue the most attractive opportunities?
- All things considered, where on a scale of 1 to 10 (where 1 is alarmingly weak and 10 is exceptionally strong) do the company's overall situation and future prospects rank?

The final piece of SWOT analysis is to translate the diagnosis of the company's situation into actions for improving the company's strategy and business prospects. *A company's internal strengths should always serve as the basis of its strategy—placing heavy reliance on a company's best competitive assets is the soundest route to attracting customers and competing successfully against rivals.*[12] As a rule, strategies that place heavy demands on areas where the company is weakest or has unproven competencies should be avoided. Plainly, managers must look toward correcting competitive weaknesses that make the company vulnerable, hold down profitability, or disqualify it from pursuing an attractive opportunity. Furthermore, a company's strategy should be aimed squarely at capturing those market opportunities that are most attractive and suited to the company's collection

FIGURE 4.2 The Steps Involved in SWOT Analysis: Identify the Four Components of SWOT, Draw Conclusions, Translate Implications into Strategic Actions

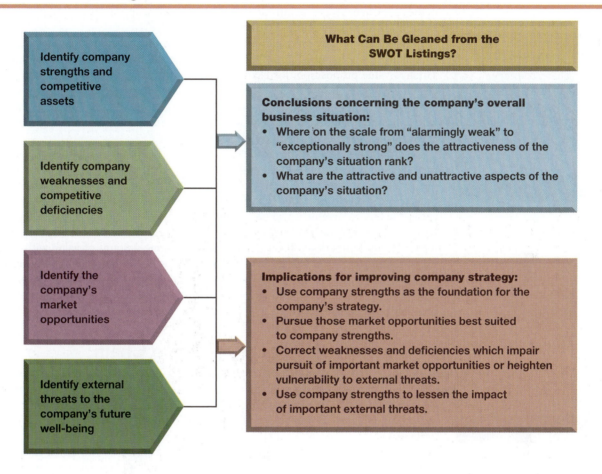

of capabilities. How much attention to devote to defending against external threats to the company's future performance hinges on how vulnerable the company is, whether defensive moves can be taken to lessen their impact, and whether the costs of undertaking such moves represent the best use of company resources.

QUESTION 4: ARE THE COMPANY'S COST STRUCTURE AND CUSTOMER VALUE PROPOSITION COMPETITIVE?

LO 4

Grasp how a company's value chain activities can affect the company's cost structure and customer value proposition.

Company managers are often stunned when a competitor cuts its prices to "unbelievably low" levels or when a new market entrant comes on strong with a great new product offered at a surprisingly low price. Such competitors may not, however, be buying market positions with prices that are below costs. They may simply have substantially lower costs and therefore are able to offer prices that result in more appealing customer value propositions.

While less common, new entrants can also storm the market with a product that ratchets the quality level up so high that customers will abandon competing sellers even if they have to pay more for the new product. With its vastly greater storage capacity and lightweight, cool design, Apple's iPod left other makers of portable digital music players in the dust when it was first introduced. Apple's new iPad appears to be doing the same in the market for e-readers and tablet PCs.

Regardless of where on the quality spectrum a company competes, it must remain competitive in terms of its customer value proposition in order to stay in the game. Tiffany's value proposition, for example, remains attractive to customers who want customer service, the assurance of quality, and a high-status brand despite the availability of cut-rate diamond jewelry online. Target's customer value proposition has withstood the Walmart low-price juggernaut by attention to product design, image, and attractive store layouts in addition to efficiency.

The value provided to the customer depends on how well a customer's needs are met for the price paid. How well customer needs are met depends on the perceived quality of a product or service as well as other, more tangible attributes. The greater the amount of customer value that the company can offer profitably compared to its rivals, the less vulnerable it will be to competitive attack. For managers, the key is to keep close track of how *cost effectively* the company can deliver value to customers relative to its competitors. If they can deliver the same amount of value with lower expenditures (or more value at the same cost), they will maintain a competitive edge.

Two analytical tools are particularly useful in determining whether a company's costs and customer value proposition are competitive: value chain analysis and benchmarking.

> The higher a company's costs are above those of close rivals, the more competitively vulnerable it becomes.

> The greater the amount of customer value that a company can offer profitably relative to close rivals, the less competitively vulnerable it becomes.

The Concept of a Company Value Chain

Every company's business consists of a collection of activities undertaken in the course of producing, delivering, and supporting its product or service. All the various activities that a company performs internally combine to form a **value chain**—so-called because the underlying intent of a company's activities is to do things that ultimately *create value for buyers*.

> **CORE CONCEPT**
>
> A company's **value chain** identifies the primary activities and related support activities that create customer value.

As shown in Figure 4.3, a company's value chain consists of two broad categories of activities: the *primary activities* that are foremost in creating value for customers and the requisite *support activities* that facilitate and enhance the performance of the primary activities.[13] The exact natures of the primary and secondary activities that make up a company's value chain vary according to the specifics of a company's business; hence, the listing of the primary and support activities in Figure 4.3 is illustrative rather than definitive. For example, the primary activities at a hotel chain like Sheraton are mainly comprised of site selection and construction, reservations, and hotel operations (check-in and check-out, maintenance and housekeeping, dining and room service, and conventions and meetings); principal support activities that drive costs and impact customer value include hiring and training hotel staff, and general administration. Supply chain management is a crucial activity for Nissan and Amazon.com but is not a value chain component at Google or a radio broadcasting company. Sales and marketing are dominant activities at Procter & Gamble and Sony but have minor roles at oil drilling companies and natural gas pipeline companies.

With its focus on value-creating activities, the value chain is an ideal tool for examining how a company delivers on its customer value proposition. It permits a deep look at the company's cost structure and ability to offer low prices. It reveals the emphasis that a company places on activities that enhance differentiation and support higher

FIGURE 4.3 A Representative Company Value Chain

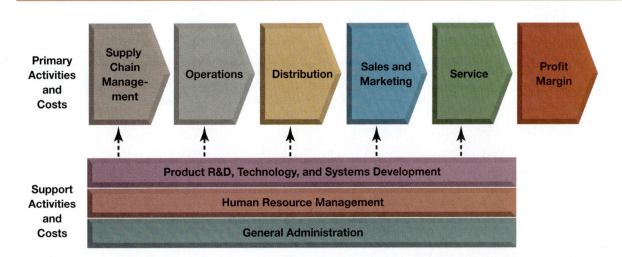

PRIMARY ACTIVITIES

- **Supply Chain Management**—Activities, costs, and assets associated with purchasing fuel, energy, raw materials, parts and components, merchandise, and consumable items from vendors; receiving, storing, and disseminating inputs from suppliers; inspection; and inventory management.

- **Operations**—Activities, costs, and assets associated with converting inputs into final product form (production, assembly, packaging, equipment maintenance, facilities, operations, quality assurance, environmental protection).

- **Distribution**—Activities, costs, and assets dealing with physically distributing the product to buyers (finished goods warehousing, order processing, order picking and packing, shipping, delivery vehicle operations, establishing and maintaining a network of dealers and distributors).

- **Sales and Marketing**—Activities, costs, and assets related to sales force efforts, advertising and promotion, market research and planning, and dealer/distributor support.

- **Service**—Activities, costs, and assets associated with providing assistance to buyers, such as installation, spare parts delivery, maintenance and repair, technical assistance, buyer inquiries, and complaints.

SUPPORT ACTIVITIES

- **Product R&D, Technology, and Systems Development**—Activities, costs, and assets relating to product R&D, process R&D, process design improvement, equipment design, computer software development, telecommunications systems, computer-assisted design and engineering, database capabilities, and development of computerized support systems.

- **Human Resources Management**—Activities, costs, and assets associated with the recruitment, hiring, training, development, and compensation of all types of personnel; labor relations activities; and development of knowledge-based skills and core competencies.

- **General Administration**—Activities, costs, and assets relating to general management, accounting and finance, legal and regulatory affairs, safety and security, management information systems, forming strategic alliances and collaborating with strategic partners, and other "overhead" functions.

Source: Based on the discussion in Michael E. Porter, *Competitive Advantage* (New York: Free Press, 1985), pp. 37–43.

The Value Chain for KP MacLane, a Producer of Polo Shirts

Value Chain Activities and Costs in Producing and Selling a Women's Polo Shirt	
1. Cotton-blend fabric from France	$ 6.80
2. Fabric for placket and vent	$ 0.99
3. 4 buttons, including 1 extra	$ 0.12
4. Thread	$ 0.09
5. Labels	$ 1.10
6. Hang tag	$ 0.40
7. Waste fabric	$ 0.85
8. Labor	$ 11.05
9. Packing materials	$ 0.17
10. Shipping materials to factory; shirt to store	$ 5.00
11. Hand-embroidered linen bag	$ 3.00
12. Total company costs	$ 29.57
13. Wholesale markup over company costs (company operating profit)	$ 35.43
14. Wholesale price	$ 65.00
15. Retailer's markup	$ 90.00
16. Retail price	$155.00

Source: Christina Binkley, "What Goes Into a $155 Price Tag?" *The Wall St. Journal,* U.S Home Edition, On Style, 2/2/2012, Accessed 2/3/12 online at http://online.wsj .com/article_email/SB10001424052970204652904577195252388913754-lMyQjAxMTAyMDAwMzEwNDMyWj.html?mod=wsj_share_email.

prices, such as service and marketing. Note that there is also a profit margin component to the value chain; this is because profits are necessary to compensate the company's owners/shareholders and investors, who bear risks and provide capital. Tracking the profit margin along with the value-creating activities is critical because unless an enterprise succeeds in delivering customer value profitably (with a sufficient return on invested capital), it can't survive for long. Attention to a company's profit formula in addition to its customer value proposition is the essence of a sound business model, as described in Chapter 1.

Illustration Capsule 4.1 shows representative costs for various activities performed by KP MacLane, a maker of upscale polo shirts.

Comparing the Value Chains of Rival Companies   The primary purpose of value chain analysis is to facilitate a comparison, activity-by-activity, of how effectively and efficiently a company delivers value to its customers, relative to its competitors. Segregating the company's operations into different types of primary and secondary activities is the first step in this comparison. The next is to do the same for the company's most significant competitors.

Even rivals in the same industry may differ significantly in terms of the activities they perform. For instance, the "operations" component of the value chain for a manufacturer that makes all of its own parts and components and assembles them into a finished product differs from the "operations" of a rival producer that buys the needed parts and components from outside suppliers and only performs assembly operations. How each activity is performed may affect a company's relative cost position as well as its capacity for differentiation. Thus, even a simple comparison of how the activities of rivals' value chains differ can be revealing of competitive differences.

A Company's Primary and Secondary Activities Identify the Major Components of Its Internal Cost Structure   The
combined costs of all the various primary and support activities comprising a company's value chain define its internal cost structure. Further, the cost of each activity contributes to whether the company's overall cost position relative to rivals is favorable or unfavorable. Key purposes of value chain analysis and benchmarking are to develop the data for comparing a company's costs activity by activity against the costs of key rivals and to learn which internal activities are a source of cost advantage or disadvantage.

Evaluating a company's cost-competitiveness involves using what accountants call *activity-based costing* to determine the costs of performing each value chain activity (and the assets required, including working capital).[14] The degree to which a company's total costs should be broken down into costs for specific activities depends on how valuable it is to know the costs of very specific activities versus broadly defined activities. At the very least, cost estimates are needed for each broad category of primary and support activities, but cost estimates for more specific activities within each broad category may be needed if a company discovers that it has a cost disadvantage vis-à-vis rivals and wants to pin down the exact source or activity causing the cost disadvantage. However, a company's own *internal costs* may be insufficient to assess whether its product offering and customer value proposition are competitive with those of rivals. Cost and price differences among competing companies can have their origins in activities performed by suppliers or by distribution allies involved in getting the product to the final customer or end user of the product, in which case the company's entire *value chain system* becomes relevant.

> A company's cost competitiveness depends not only on the costs of internally performed activities (its own value chain) but also on costs in the value chains of its suppliers and distribution channel allies.

The Value Chain System

A company's value chain is embedded in a larger system of activities that includes the value chains of its suppliers and the value chains of whatever wholesale distributors and retailers it utilizes in getting its product or service to end users. This *value chain system* has implications that extend far beyond the company's costs. It can affect attributes like product quality that enhance differentiation and have importance for the company's customer value proposition, as well as its profitability.[15] Suppliers' value chains are relevant because suppliers perform activities and incur costs in creating and delivering the purchased inputs utilized in a company's own value-creating activities. The costs, performance features, and quality of these inputs influence a company's own costs and product differentiation capabilities. Anything a company can do to help its suppliers' drive down the costs of their value chain activities or improve the quality and performance of the items being supplied can enhance its own competitiveness—a powerful reason for working collaboratively with suppliers in managing supply chain activities.[16]

Similarly, the value chains of a company's distribution channel partners are relevant because (1) the costs and margins of a company's distributors and retail dealers are part of the price the ultimate consumer pays and (2) the activities that distribution allies perform affect sales volumes and customer satisfaction. For these reasons, companies normally work closely with their distribution allies (who are their direct customers) to perform value chain activities in mutually beneficial ways. For instance, motor vehicle manufacturers have a competitive interest in working closely with their automobile dealers to promote higher sales volumes and better customer satisfaction with dealers' repair and maintenance services. Producers of kitchen cabinets are heavily dependent on the sales and promotional activities of their distributors and building supply retailers and on whether distributors/retailers operate cost-effectively enough to be able to sell at prices that lead to attractive sales volumes.

As a consequence, *accurately assessing a company's competitiveness entails scrutinizing the nature and costs of value chain activities throughout the entire value chain system for delivering its products or services to end-use customers.* A typical value chain system that incorporates the value chains of suppliers and forward channel allies (if any) is shown in Figure 4.4. As was the case with company value chains, the specific activities constituting value chain systems vary significantly from industry to industry. The primary value chain system activities in the pulp and paper industry (timber farming, logging, pulp mills, and papermaking) differ from the primary value chain system activities in the home appliance industry (parts and components manufacture, assembly, wholesale distribution, retail sales). The value chain system in the soft-drink industry (syrup manufacture, bottling, wholesale distribution, advertising, and retail merchandising) differs from that in the computer software industry (programming, disk loading, marketing, distribution).

FIGURE 4.4 A Representative Value Chain System

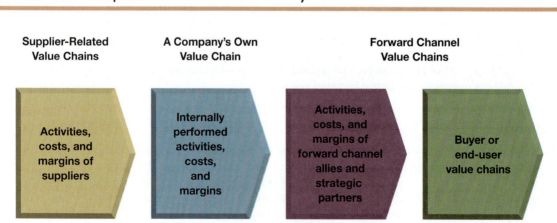

Supplier-Related Value Chains	A Company's Own Value Chain	Forward Channel Value Chains	
Activities, costs, and margins of suppliers	Internally performed activities, costs, and margins	Activities, costs, and margins of forward channel allies and strategic partners	Buyer or end-user value chains

Source: Based in part on the single-industry value chain displayed in Michael E. Porter, *Competitive Advantage* (New York: Free Press, 1985), p. 35.

Benchmarking: A Tool for Assessing Whether the Costs and Effectiveness of a Company's Value Chain Activities Are in Line

Once a company has developed good estimates for the costs and effectiveness of each of the major activities in its own value chain and has sufficient data relating to the value chain activities of suppliers and distribution allies, then it is ready to explore how it compares on these dimensions with key rivals. This is where benchmarking comes in. **Benchmarking** entails comparing how different companies perform various value chain activities—how materials are purchased, how inventories are managed, how products are assembled, how fast the company can get new products to market, how customer orders are filled and shipped—and then making cross-company comparisons of the costs and effectiveness of these activities.[17] The objectives of benchmarking are to identify the best practices in performing an activity and to emulate those best practices when they are possessed by others.

> **CORE CONCEPT**
>
> **Benchmarking** is a potent tool for improving a company's own internal activities that is based on learning how other companies perform them and borrowing their "best practices."

Xerox led the way in the use of benchmarking to become more cost-competitive, quickly deciding not to restrict its benchmarking efforts to its office equipment rivals but to extend them to any company regarded as "world class" in performing *any activity* relevant to Xerox's business. Other companies quickly picked up on Xerox's approach. Toyota managers got their idea for just-in-time inventory deliveries by studying how U.S. supermarkets replenished their shelves. Southwest Airlines reduced the turnaround time of its aircraft at each scheduled stop by studying pit crews on the auto racing circuit. Over 80 percent of Fortune 500 companies reportedly use benchmarking for comparing themselves against rivals on cost and other competitively important measures.

The tough part of benchmarking is not whether to do it but rather how to gain access to information about other companies' practices and costs. Sometimes benchmarking can be accomplished by collecting information from published reports, trade groups, and industry research firms or by talking to knowledgeable industry analysts, customers, and suppliers. Sometimes field trips to the facilities of competing or noncompeting companies can be arranged to observe how things are done, compare practices and processes, and perhaps exchange data on productivity and other cost components. However, such companies, even if they agree to host facilities tours and answer questions, are unlikely to share competitively sensitive cost information. Furthermore, comparing two companies' costs may not involve comparing apples to apples if the two companies employ different cost accounting principles to calculate the costs of particular activities.

However, a third and fairly reliable source of benchmarking information has emerged. The explosive interest of companies in benchmarking costs and identifying best practices has prompted consulting organizations (e.g., Accenture, A. T. Kearney, Benchnet—The Benchmarking Exchange, and Best Practices, LLC) and several associations (e.g., the Qualserve Benchmarking Clearinghouse, and the Strategic Planning Institute's Council on Benchmarking) to gather benchmarking data, distribute information about best practices, and provide comparative cost data without identifying the names of particular companies. Having an independent group gather the information and report it in a manner that disguises the names of individual companies protects competitively sensitive data and lessens the potential for unethical behavior on the part of company personnel in gathering their own data about competitors. Illustration Capsule 4.2 presents a widely recommended code of conduct for engaging in benchmarking.

> Benchmarking the costs of company activities against rivals provides hard evidence of whether a company is cost-competitive.

Benchmarking and Ethical Conduct

Because discussions between benchmarking partners can involve competitively sensitive data, conceivably raising questions about possible restraint of trade or improper business conduct, many benchmarking organizations urge all individuals and organizations involved in benchmarking to abide by a code of conduct grounded in ethical business behavior. One of the most widely used codes of conduct is the one developed by APQC (formerly the American Productivity and Quality Center) and advocated by the Qualserve Benchmarking Clearinghouse; it is based on the following principles and guidelines:

- Avoid discussions or actions that could lead to or imply an interest in restraint of trade, market and/or customer allocation schemes, price fixing, dealing arrangements, bid rigging, or bribery. Don't discuss costs with competitors if costs are an element of pricing.

- Refrain from the acquisition of trade secrets from another by any means that could be interpreted as improper, including the breach of any duty to maintain secrecy. Do not disclose or use any trade secret that may have been obtained through improper means or that was disclosed by another in violation of duty to maintain its secrecy or limit its use.

- Be willing to provide to your benchmarking partner the same type and level of information that you request from that partner.

- Communicate fully and early in the relationship to clarify expectations, avoid misunderstanding, and establish mutual interest in the benchmarking exchange.

- Be honest and complete with the information submitted.

- The use or communication of a benchmarking partner's name with the data obtained or practices observed requires the prior permission of the benchmarking partner.

- Honor the wishes of benchmarking partners regarding how the information that is provided will be handled and used.

- In benchmarking with competitors, establish specific ground rules up front. For example, "We don't want to talk about things that will give either of us a competitive advantage, but rather we want to see where we both can mutually improve or gain benefit."

- Check with legal counsel if any information-gathering procedure is in doubt. If uncomfortable, do not proceed. Alternatively, negotiate and sign a specific non-disclosure agreement that will satisfy the attorneys representing each partner.

- Do not ask competitors for sensitive data or cause benchmarking partners to feel they must provide data to continue the process.

- Use an ethical third party to assemble and "blind" competitive data, with inputs from legal counsel in direct competitor sharing. (Note: When cost is closely linked to price, sharing cost data can be considered to be the same as sharing price data.)

- Any information obtained from a benchmarking partner should be treated as internal, privileged communications. If "confidential" or proprietary material is to be exchanged, then a specific agreement should be executed to specify the content of the material that needs to be protected, the duration of the period of protection, the conditions for permitting access to the material, and the specific handling requirements necessary for that material.

Sources: APQC, **www.apqc.org**; Qualserve Benchmarking Clearinghouse, **www.awwa.org** (accessed October 8, 2010).

Strategic Options for Remedying a Cost or Value Disadvantage

The results of value chain analysis and benchmarking may disclose cost or value disadvantages relative to key rivals. Such information is vital in crafting strategic actions to eliminate any such disadvantages and improve profitability. Information of this nature can also help a company to recognize and reinforce activities in which it has a comparative advantage and to find new avenues for enhancing its competitiveness through lower costs or a more attractive customer value proposition. There are three main areas in a company's total value chain system where company managers can try to improve its efficiency and effectiveness in delivering customer value: (1) a company's own internal activities, (2) suppliers' part of the value chain system, and (3) the forward channel portion of the value chain system.

Improving Internally Performed Value Chain Activities

Managers can pursue any of several strategic approaches to reduce the costs of internally performed value chain activities and improve a company's cost competitiveness:

- *Implement the use of best practices* throughout the company, particularly for high-cost activities.

- *Eliminate some cost-producing activities altogether* by revamping the value chain. Many retailers have found that donating returned items to charitable organizations and taking the appropriate tax deduction results in a smaller loss than incurring the costs of the value chain activities involved in reverse logistics.

- *Relocate high-cost activities* (such as manufacturing) to geographic areas like China, Latin America, or Eastern Europe where they can be performed more cheaply.

- *Outsource activities* from vendors or contractors if they can perform them more cheaply than can be done in-house.

- *Invest in productivity enhancing, cost-saving technological improvements* (robotics, flexible manufacturing techniques, state-of-the-art electronic networking).

- *Find ways to detour around the activities or items where costs are high*—computer chip makers regularly design around the patents held by others to avoid paying royalties; automakers have substituted lower-cost plastic for metal at many exterior body locations.

- Redesign the product and/or some of its components to facilitate speedier and more economical manufacture or assembly.

How successfully a company competes depends on more than low costs. It also depends on how effectively it delivers value to the customer and on its ability to differentiate itself from rivals. To improve the effectiveness of its customer value proposition and enhance differentiation, there are several approaches a manager can take:

- Implement the use of best practices for quality throughout the company, particularly for high-value activities (those that are important for creating value for the customer).

- Adopt best practices and technologies that spur innovation, improve design, and enhance creativity.

- Implement the use of best practices in providing customer service.

- Reallocate resources to activities that address buyers' most important purchase criteria, which will have the biggest impact on the value delivered to the customer.

- For intermediate buyers (distributors or retailers, for example), gain an understanding of how the activities the company performs impact the buyer's value chain and improve those that have the greatest impact.

- Adopt best practices for marketing, brand management, and enhancing customer perceptions.

Improving Supplier-Related Value Chain Activities   Improving suppliers' performance of value chain activities can also remedy company disadvantages concerning costs and customer value. On the cost side, a company can gain savings in the suppliers' part of the overall value chain by pressuring those suppliers for lower prices, switching to lower-priced substitute inputs, and collaborating closely with suppliers to identify mutual cost-saving opportunities.[18] For example, just-in-time deliveries from suppliers can lower a company's inventory and internal logistics costs and may also allow suppliers to economize on their warehousing, shipping, and production scheduling costs—a win–win outcome for both. In a few instances, companies may find that it is cheaper to integrate backward into the business of high-cost suppliers and make the item in-house instead of buying it from outsiders.

Similarly, a company can enhance its customer value proposition by working with or through its suppliers to do so. Some methods include selecting and retaining suppliers who meet higher-quality standards, coordinating with suppliers to enhance design or other features desired by customers, providing incentives to encourage suppliers to meet higher-quality standards, and assisting suppliers in their efforts to improve. Fewer defects in parts from suppliers not only improve quality and enhance differentiation throughout the value chain system but can lower costs as well since there is less waste and disruption to the production processes.

Improving Value Chain Activities of Forward Channel Allies   Any of three means can be used to achieve better cost competitiveness in the forward portion of the industry value chain: (1) pressure distributors, dealers, and other forward channel allies to reduce their costs and markups; (2) collaborate with forward channel allies to identify win–win opportunities to reduce costs—a chocolate manufacturer, for example, learned that by shipping its bulk chocolate in liquid form in tank cars instead of as 10-pound molded bars, it could not only save its candy bar manufacturing customers the costs associated with unpacking and melting but also eliminate its own costs of molding bars and packing them; and (3) change to a more economical distribution strategy, including switching to cheaper distribution channels (perhaps direct sales via the Internet) or perhaps integrating forward into company-owned retail outlets. Dell Computer's direct sales model eliminated all costs associated with distributors, dealers, and retailers by allowing buyers to purchase customized PCs directly from Dell.

The means to enhance differentiation through activities at the forward end of the value chain system include (1) engaging in cooperative advertising and promotions with forward allies (dealers, distributors, retailers, and so on), (2) creating exclusive arrangements with downstream sellers or other mechanisms that increase their incentives to enhance delivered customer value, and (3) creating and enforcing standards for downstream activities and assisting in training channel partners in business practices. Harley-Davidson, for example, enhances the shopping experience and perceptions of buyers by selling through retailers that sell Harley-Davidson motorcycles exclusively and meet Harley-Davidson standards.

Translating Proficient Performance of Value Chain Activities into Competitive Advantage

Value chain analysis and benchmarking are not only useful for identifying and remedying competitive disadvantages; they can also be used to uncover and strengthen competitive advantages. A company's value-creating activities can offer a competitive advantage in one of two ways: (1) They can contribute to greater efficiency and lower costs relative to competitors, or (2) they can provide a basis for differentiation, so customers are willing to pay relatively more for the company's goods and services. A company that does a *first-rate job* of managing its value chain activities *relative to competitors* stands a good chance of profiting from its competitive advantage.

Achieving a cost-based competitive advantage requires determined management efforts to be cost-efficient in performing value chain activities. Such efforts have to be ongoing and persistent, and they have to involve each and every value chain activity. The goal must be continuous cost reduction, not a one-time or on-again–off-again effort. Companies like Dollar General, Nucor Steel, Irish airline Ryanair, Greyhound Lines, and

French discount retailer Carrefour have been highly successful in managing their value chain in a low-cost manner.

Ongoing and persistent efforts are also required for a competitive advantage based on differentiation. Superior reputations and brands are built up slowly over time, through continuous investment and activities that deliver consistent, reinforcing messages. Differentiation based on quality requires vigilant management of activities for quality assurance throughout the value chain. While the basis for differentiation (e.g., status, design, innovation, customer service, reliability, image) may vary widely among companies pursuing a differentiation advantage, companies that succeed do so on the basis of a commitment to coordinated value chain activities aimed purposefully at this objective. Examples include Grey Goose Vodka (status), IKEA (design), FedEx (reliability), 3M (innovation), and Nordstrom (customer service).

How Activities Relate to Resources and Capabilities   There is a close relationship between the value-creating activities that a company performs and its resources and capabilities. An organizational capability or competence implies a *capacity* for action; in contrast, a value-creating activity *initiates* the action. With respect to resources and capabilities, activities are "where the rubber hits the road." When companies engage in a value-creating activity, they do so by drawing on specific company resources and capabilities that underlie and enable the activity. For example, brand-building activities depend on human resources, such as experienced brand managers (including their knowledge and expertise in this arena), as well as organizational capabilities in advertising and marketing. Cost-cutting activities may derive from organizational capabilities in inventory management, for example, and resources such as inventory tracking systems.

Because of this correspondence between activities and supporting resources and capabilities, value chain analysis can complement resource and capability analysis as another tool for assessing a company's competitive advantage. Resources and capabilities that are *both valuable and rare* provide a company with *what it takes* for competitive advantage. For a company with competitive assets of this sort, the potential is there. When these assets are deployed in the form of a value-creating activity, that potential is realized due to their competitive superiority. Resource analysis is one tool for identifying competitively superior resources and capabilities. But their value and the competitive superiority of that value can only be assessed objectively *after* they are deployed. Value chain analysis and benchmarking provide the type of data needed to make that objective assessment.

There is also a dynamic relationship between a company's activities and its resources and capabilities. Value-creating activities are more than just the embodiment of a resource's or capability's potential. They also contribute to the formation and development of capabilities. The road to competitive advantage begins with management efforts to build organizational expertise in performing certain competitively important value chain activities. With consistent practice and continuous investment of company resources, these activities rise to the level of a reliable organizational capability or a competence. To the extent that top management makes the growing capability a cornerstone of the company's strategy, this capability becomes a core competence for the company. Later, with further organizational learning and gains in proficiency, the core competence may evolve into a distinctive competence, giving the company superiority over rivals in performing an important value chain activity. Such superiority, if it gives the company significant competitive clout in the marketplace, can produce an attractive competitive edge over rivals. Whether the resulting competitive advantage is on the cost side or on the differentiation side (or both) will depend on the company's choice of which types of competence-building activities to engage in over this time period, as shown in Figure 4.5.

Performing value chain activities with capabilities that permit the company to either outmatch rivals on differentiation or beat them on costs will give the company a competitive advantage.

FIGURE 4.5 Translating Company Performance of Value Chain Activities into Competitive Advantage

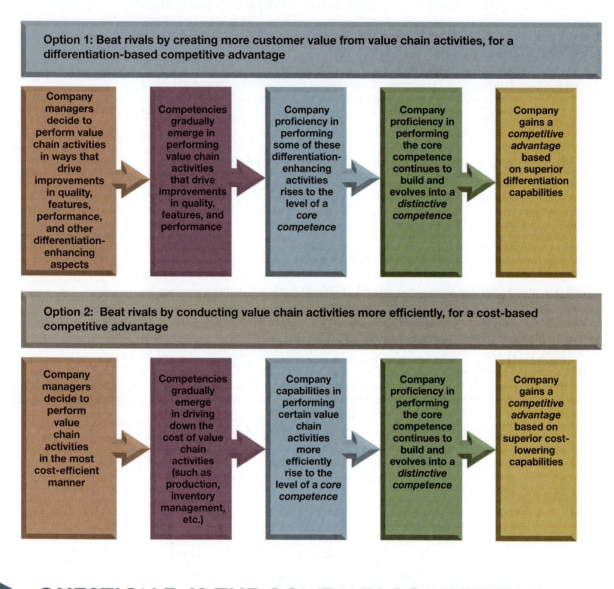

QUESTION 5: IS THE COMPANY COMPETITIVELY STRONGER OR WEAKER THAN KEY RIVALS?

Using resource analysis, value chain analysis, and benchmarking to determine a company's competitiveness on value and cost is necessary but not sufficient. A more comprehensive assessment needs to be made of the company's *overall* competitive strength. The answers to two questions are of particular interest: First, how does the company rank relative to competitors on each of the important factors that determine market success? Second, all things considered, does the company have a *net* competitive advantage or disadvantage versus major competitors?

An easy-to-use method for answering these two questions involves developing quantitative strength ratings for the company and its key competitors on each industry key success factor and each competitively pivotal resource, capability, and value chain activity. Much of the information needed for doing a competitive strength assessment comes from previous analyses. Industry and competitive analyses reveal the key success factors and competitive forces that separate industry winners from losers. Benchmarking data and scouting key competitors provide a basis for judging the competitive strength of rivals on such factors as cost, key product attributes, customer service, image and reputation, financial strength, technological skills, distribution capability, and other factors. Resource and capability analysis reveals which of these are competitively important, given the external situation, and whether the company's competitive advantages are sustainable. SWOT analysis provides a more comprehensive and forward-looking picture of the company's overall situation.

Step 1 in doing a competitive strength assessment is to make a list of the industry's key success factors and other telling measures of competitive strength or weakness (6 to 10 measures usually suffice). Step 2 is to assign weights to each of the measures of competitive strength based on their perceived importance. (The sum of the weights for each measure must add up to 1.0.) Step 3 is to calculate weighted strength ratings by scoring each competitor on each strength measure (using a 1 to 10 rating scale where 1 is very weak and 10 is very strong) and multiplying the assigned rating by the assigned weight. Step 4 is to sum the weighted strength ratings on each factor to get an overall measure of competitive strength for each company being rated. Step 5 is to use the overall strength ratings to draw conclusions about the size and extent of the company's net competitive advantage or disadvantage and to take specific note of areas of strength and weakness.

Table 4.4 provides an example of competitive strength assessment in which a hypothetical company (ABC Company) competes against two rivals. In the example, relative cost is the most telling measure of competitive strength, and the other strength measures are of lesser importance. The company with the highest rating on a given measure has an implied competitive edge on that measure, with the size of its edge reflected in the difference between its weighted rating and rivals' weighted ratings. For instance, Rival 1's 3.00 weighted strength rating on relative cost signals a considerable cost advantage versus ABC Company (with a 1.50 weighted score on relative cost) and an even bigger cost advantage against Rival 2 (with a weighted score of 0.30). The measure-by-measure ratings reveal the competitive areas where a company is strongest and weakest, and against whom.

The overall competitive strength scores indicate how all the different strength measures add up—whether the company is at a net overall competitive advantage or disadvantage against each rival. The higher a company's *overall weighted strength rating,* the stronger its *overall competitiveness* versus rivals. The bigger the difference between a company's overall weighted rating and the scores of *lower-rated* rivals, the greater is its implied *net competitive advantage.* Thus, Rival 1's overall weighted score of 7.70 indicates a greater net competitive advantage over Rival 2 (with a score of 2.10) than over ABC Company (with a score of 5.95). Conversely, the bigger the difference between a company's overall rating and the scores of *higher-rated* rivals, the greater its implied *net competitive disadvantage.* Rival 2's score of 2.10 gives it a smaller net competitive disadvantage against ABC Company (with an overall score of 5.95) than against Rival 1 (with an overall score of 7.70).

Strategic Implications of Competitive Strength Assessments

In addition to showing how competitively strong or weak a company is relative to rivals, the strength ratings provide guidelines for designing wise offensive and defensive strategies. For example, if ABC Co. wants to go on the offensive to win additional sales and market share,

LO 5

Understand how a comprehensive evaluation of a company's competitive situation can assist managers in making critical decisions about their next strategic moves.

High-weighted competitive strength ratings signal a strong competitive position and possession of competitive advantage; low ratings signal a weak position and competitive disadvantage.

TABLE 4.4 A Representative Weighted Competitive Strength Assessment

Key Success Factor / Strength Measure	Importance Weight	ABC Co.		Rival 1		Rival 2	
		Strength Rating	Weighted Score	Strength Rating	Weighted Score	Strength Rating	Weighted Score
Quality/product performance	0.10	8	0.80	5	0.50	1	0.10
Reputation/image	0.10	8	0.80	7	0.70	1	0.10
Manufacturing capability	0.10	2	0.20	10	1.00	5	0.50
Technological skills	0.05	10	0.50	1	0.05	3	0.15
Dealer network / distribution capability	0.05	9	0.45	4	0.20	5	0.25
New product innovation capability	0.05	9	0.45	4	0.20	5	0.25
Financial resources	0.10	5	0.50	10	1.00	3	0.30
Relative cost position	0.30	5	1.50	10	3.00	1	0.30
Customer service capabilities	0.15	5	0.75	7	1.05	1	0.15
Sum of importance weights	**1.00**						
Overall weighted competitive strength rating			**5.95**		**7.70**		**2.10**

Competitive Strength Assessment

(Rating scale: 1 = very weak; 10 = very strong)

A company's competitive strength scores pinpoint its strengths and weaknesses against rivals and point directly to the kinds of offensive/defensive actions it can use to exploit its competitive strengths and reduce its competitive vulnerabilities.

such an offensive probably needs to be aimed directly at winning customers away from Rival 2 (which has a lower overall strength score) rather than Rival 1 (which has a higher overall strength score). Moreover, while ABC has high ratings for technological skills (a 10 rating), dealer network / distribution capability (a 9 rating), new product innovation capability (a 9 rating), quality/product performance (an 8 rating), and reputation/image (an 8 rating), these strength measures have low importance weights—meaning that ABC has strengths in areas that don't translate into much competitive clout in the marketplace. Even so, it outclasses Rival 2 in all five areas, plus it enjoys substantially lower costs than Rival 2 (ABC has a 5 rating on relative cost position versus a 1 rating for Rival 2)—and relative cost position carries the highest importance weight of all the strength measures. ABC also has greater competitive strength than Rival 3 as concerns customer service capabilities (which carries the second-highest importance weight). Hence, because ABC's strengths are in the very areas where Rival 2 is weak, ABC is in a good position to attack Rival 2. Indeed, ABC may well be able to persuade a number of Rival 2's customers to switch their purchases over to its product.

But ABC should be cautious about cutting price aggressively to win customers away from Rival 2, because Rival 1 could interpret that as an attack by ABC to win away Rival 1's customers as well. And Rival 1 is in far and away the best position to compete on the basis of low price, given its high rating on relative cost in an industry where low costs are competitively important (relative cost carries an importance weight of 0.30).

Rival 1's very strong relative cost position vis-à-vis both ABC and Rival 2 arms it with the ability to use its lower-cost advantage to thwart any price cutting on ABC's part. Clearly ABC is vulnerable to any retaliatory price cuts by Rival 1—Rival 1 can easily defeat both ABC and Rival 2 in a price-based battle for sales and market share. If ABC wants to defend against its vulnerability to potential price cutting by Rival 1, then it needs to aim a portion of its strategy at lowering its costs.

The point here is that a competitively astute company should utilize the strength scores in deciding what strategic moves to make. When a company has important competitive strengths in areas where one or more rivals are weak, it makes sense to consider offensive moves to exploit rivals' competitive weaknesses. When a company has important competitive weaknesses in areas where one or more rivals are strong, it makes sense to consider defensive moves to curtail its vulnerability.

QUESTION 6: WHAT STRATEGIC ISSUES AND PROBLEMS MERIT FRONT-BURNER MANAGERIAL ATTENTION?

The final and most important analytical step is to zero in on exactly what strategic issues company managers need to address—and resolve—for the company to be more financially and competitively successful in the years ahead. This step involves drawing on the results of both industry analysis and the evaluations of the company's own competitiveness. The task here is to get a clear fix on exactly what strategic and competitive challenges confront the company, which of the company's competitive shortcomings need fixing, and what specific problems merit front-burner attention by company managers. *Pinpointing the precise things that management needs to worry about sets the agenda for deciding what actions to take next to improve the company's performance and business outlook.*

The "worry list" of issues and problems that have to be wrestled with can include such things as *how* to stave off market challenges from new foreign competitors, *how* to combat the price discounting of rivals, *how* to reduce the company's high costs, *how* to sustain the company's present rate of growth in light of slowing buyer demand, *whether* to correct the company's competitive deficiencies by acquiring a rival company with the missing strengths, *whether* to expand into foreign markets, *whether* to reposition the company and move to a different strategic group, *what to do* about growing buyer interest in substitute products, and *what to do* to combat the aging demographics of the company's customer base. The worry list thus always centers on such concerns as "how to . . .," "what to do about . . .," and "whether to . . ."—the purpose of the worry list is to identify the specific issues/problems that management needs to address, not to figure out what specific actions to take. Deciding what to do—which strategic actions to take and which strategic moves to make—comes later (when it is time to craft the strategy and choose among the various strategic alternatives).

If the items on the worry list are relatively minor—which suggests that the company's strategy is mostly on track and reasonably well matched to the company's overall situation—company managers seldom need to go much beyond fine-tuning the present strategy. If, however, the problems confronting the company are serious and indicate the present strategy is not well suited for the road ahead, the task of crafting a better strategy needs to be at the top of management's action agenda.

> Zeroing in on the strategic issues a company faces and compiling a list of problems and roadblocks creates a strategic agenda of problems that merit prompt managerial attention.

> A good strategy must contain ways to deal with all the strategic issues and obstacles that stand in the way of the company's financial and competitive success in the years ahead.

FIGURE 5.1 The Five Generic Competitive Strategies

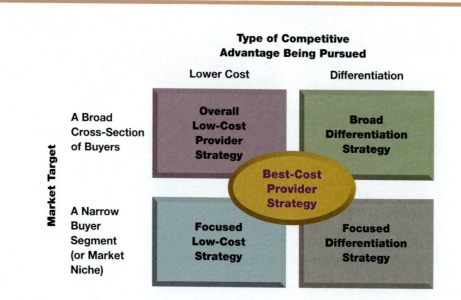

Source: This is an author-expanded version of a three-strategy classification discussed in Michael E. Porter, *Competitive Strategy* (New York: Free Press, 1980).

3. *A focused low-cost strategy*—concentrating on a narrow buyer segment (or market niche) and outcompeting rivals on costs, thus being able to serve niche members at a lower price.

4. *A focused differentiation strategy*—concentrating on a narrow buyer segment (or market niche) and outcompeting rivals with a product offering that meets the specific tastes and requirements of niche members better than the product offerings of rivals.

5. *A best-cost provider strategy*—giving customers *more value for their money* by satisfying buyers' expectations on key quality/features/performance/service attributes while beating their price expectations. This option is a *hybrid* strategy that blends elements of differentiation and low-cost strategies; the aim is to have the lowest (best) costs and prices among sellers offering products with comparable differentiating attributes.

The remainder of this chapter explores the ins and outs of these five generic competitive strategies and how they differ.

LOW-COST PROVIDER STRATEGIES

Striving to be the industry's overall low-cost provider is a powerful competitive approach in markets with many price-sensitive buyers. A company achieves **low-cost leadership** when it becomes the industry's lowest-cost provider rather than just being one of perhaps several competitors with comparatively low costs. Successful low-cost providers boast meaningfully lower costs than rivals—but not necessarily the absolutely lowest possible cost. In striving for a cost advantage over rivals, company managers must take care to incorporate features and services that buyers consider essential. A product offering that is too frills-free can be viewed by consumers as offering little value even, regardless of its pricing.

A company has two options for translating a low-cost advantage over rivals into attractive profit performance. Option 1 is to use the lower-cost edge to underprice competitors and attract price-sensitive buyers in great enough numbers to increase total profits. Option 2 is to maintain the present price, be content with the present market share, and use the lower-cost edge to earn a higher profit margin on each unit sold, thereby raising the firm's total profits and overall return on investment.

While many companies are inclined to exploit a low-cost advantage by using option 1 (attacking rivals with lower prices), this strategy can backfire if rivals respond with retaliatory price cuts of their own (in order to protect their customer base) and the aggressor's price cuts fail to produce sales gains that are big enough to offset the profit erosion associated with charging a lower price. The bigger the risk that rivals will respond with matching price cuts, the more appealing it becomes to employ the second option for using a low-cost advantage to achieve higher profitability.

The Two Major Avenues for Achieving a Cost Advantage

To achieve a low-cost edge over rivals, a firm's cumulative costs across its overall value chain must be lower than competitors' cumulative costs. There are two ways to accomplish this:[2]

1. Perform value chain activities more cost-effectively than rivals.
2. Revamp the firm's overall value chain to eliminate or bypass some cost-producing activities.

Cost-Efficient Management of Value Chain Activities

For a company to do a more cost-efficient job of managing its value chain than rivals, managers must launch a concerted, ongoing effort to ferret out cost-saving opportunities in every part of the value chain. No activity can escape cost-saving scrutiny, and all company personnel must be expected to use their talents and ingenuity to come up with innovative and effective ways to keep costs down. Particular attention, however, needs to be paid to a set of factors known as **cost drivers**, which have an especially strong effect on a company's costs and which managers can use as levers to push costs down. (Figure 5.2 provides a list of important cost drivers.) Cost-cutting methods that demonstrate an effective use of the cost drivers include:

1. *Striving to capture all available economies of scale.* Economies of scale stem from an ability to lower unit costs by increasing the scale of operation. Many occasions arise when a large plant or distribution center is more economical to operate than a small one. In global industries, selling a mostly standard product worldwide tends to lower unit costs as opposed to making separate products for each country market where costs are typically higher due to an inability to reach the most economic scale of production for each country. There are economies of scale in advertising as well. For example, Anheuser-Busch could afford to pay the $3.5 million cost of a 30-second Super Bowl ad in 2012 because the cost could be spread out over the hundreds of millions of units of Budweiser that they sell.

LO 2

Gain command of the major avenues for achieving a competitive advantage based on lower costs.

CORE CONCEPT

A **low-cost provider's** basis for competitive advantage is lower overall costs than competitors. Successful **low-cost leaders,** who have the lowest industry costs, are exceptionally good at finding ways to drive costs out of their businesses and still provide a product or service that buyers find acceptable.

A low-cost advantage over rivals can translate into better profitability than rivals attain.

CORE CONCEPT

A **cost driver** is a factor that has a strong influence on a company's costs.

FIGURE 5.2 Cost Drivers: The Keys to Driving Down Company Costs

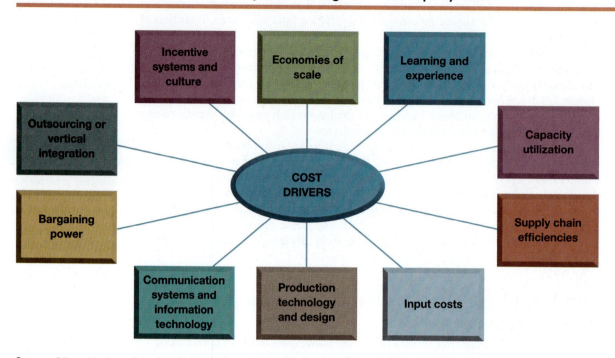

Sources: Adapted by the authors from M. Porter, *Competitive Advantage: Creating and Sustaining Competitive Advantage* (New York: Free Press, 1985).

2. *Taking full advantage of experience and learning-curve effects.* The cost of performing an activity can decline over time as the learning and experience of company personnel build. Learning/experience economies can stem from debugging and mastering newly introduced technologies, using the experiences and suggestions of workers to install more efficient plant layouts and assembly procedures, and the added speed and effectiveness that accrues from repeatedly picking sites for and building new plants, retail outlets, or distribution centers. Well managed low-cost providers pay diligent attention to capturing the benefits of learning and experience and to keeping these benefits proprietary to whatever extent possible.

3. *Trying to operate facilities at full capacity.* Whether a company is able to operate at or near full capacity has a big impact on units costs when its value chain contains activities associated with substantial fixed costs. Higher rates of capacity utilization allow depreciation and other fixed costs to be spread over a larger unit volume, thereby lowering fixed costs per unit. The more capital-intensive the business and the higher the fixed costs as a percentage of total costs, the greater the unit-cost penalty for operating at less than full capacity.

4. *Improving supply chain efficiency.* Partnering with suppliers to streamline the ordering and purchasing process, to reduce inventory carrying costs via just-in-time inventory practices, to economize on shipping and materials handling, and to ferret out other cost-saving opportunities is a much-used approach to cost reduction. A company with a distinctive competence in cost-efficient supply chain management, such as BASF (the world's leading chemical company), can sometimes achieve a sizable cost advantage over less adept rivals.

5. *Using lower cost inputs wherever doing so will not entail too great a sacrifice in quality.* Some examples include lower-cost raw materials or component parts, nonunion labor "inputs," and lower rental fees due to differences in location. If the costs of certain factors are "too high," a company may even design the high-cost inputs out of the product altogether.

6. *Using the company's bargaining power vis-à-vis suppliers or others in the value chain system to gain concessions.* Home Depot, for example, has sufficient bargaining clout with suppliers to win price discounts on large-volume purchases. PepsiCo similarly uses its bargaining power to win concessions from supermarkets, mass merchandisers, and other forward channel allies.

7. *Using communication systems and information technology to achieve operating efficiencies.* For example, sharing data and production schedules with suppliers, coupled with the use of enterprise resource planning (ERP) and manufacturing execution system (MES) software, can reduce parts inventories, trim production times, and lower labor requirements.

8. *Employing advanced production technology and process design to improve overall efficiency.* Often production costs can be cut by utilizing design for manufacture (DFM) procedures and computer-assisted design (CAD) techniques that enable more integrated and efficient production methods, investing in highly automated robotic production technology, and shifting to a production. Dell's highly automated PC assembly plant in Austin, Texas, is a prime example of the use of advanced product and process technologies. Many companies are ardent users of total quality management systems, business process reengineering, six sigma methodology, and other business process management techniques that aim at boosting efficiency and reducing costs.

9. *Being alert to the cost advantages of outsourcing or vertical integration.* Outsourcing the performance of certain value chain activities can be more economical than performing them in-house if outside specialists, by virtue of their expertise and volume, can perform the activities at lower cost. On the other hand, there can be times when integrating into the activities of either suppliers or distribution channel allies can lower costs through greater production efficiencies, reduced transaction costs, or a better bargaining position.

10. *Motivating employees through incentives and company culture.* A company's incentive system can encourage not only greater worker productivity but also cost-saving innovations that come from worker suggestions. The culture of a company can also spur worker pride in productivity and continuous improvement. Companies that are well known for their cost-reducing incentive systems and culture include Nucor Steel, which characterizes itself as a company of "11,900 teammates," Southwest Airlines, and Walmart.

Revamping the Value Chain System to Lower Costs
Dramatic cost advantages can often emerge from redesigning the company's value chain system in ways that eliminate costly work steps and entirely bypass certain cost-producing value chain activities. Such value chain revamping can include:

- *Selling direct to consumers and bypassing the activities and costs of distributors and dealers.* To circumvent the need for distributors–dealers, a company can (1) create its own direct sales force (which adds the costs of maintaining and supporting a sales force but which may well be cheaper than utilizing independent distributors and dealers to

Differentiation enhances profitability whenever a company's product can command a sufficiently higher price or produce sufficiently bigger unit sales *to more than cover the added costs of achieving the differentiation*. Company differentiation strategies fail when buyers don't value the brand's uniqueness sufficiently and/or when a company's approach to differentiation is easily matched by its rivals.

Companies can pursue differentiation from many angles: a unique taste (Red Bull, Listerine); multiple features (Microsoft Office, Apple iPad); wide selection and one-stop shopping (Home Depot, Amazon.com); superior service (Ritz-Carlton, Nordstrom); engineering design and performance (Mercedes, BMW); luxury and prestige (Rolex, Gucci); product reliability (Whirlpool and Bosch in large home appliances); quality manufacture (Michelin, Honda); technological leadership (3M Corporation in bonding and coating products); a full range of services (Charles Schwab); and wide product selection (Campbell's soups, Frito-Lay snack foods).

Managing the Value Chain to Create the Differentiating Attributes

Differentiation is not something hatched in marketing and advertising departments, nor is it limited to the catchalls of quality and service. Differentiation opportunities can exist in activities all along an industry's value chain. The most systematic approach that managers can take, however, involves focusing on the **uniqueness drivers**, a set of factors—analogous to cost drivers—that are particularly effective in creating differentiation. Figure 5.3 contains a list of important uniqueness drivers. Ways that managers can enhance differentiation based on these drivers include the following:

FIGURE 5.3 Uniqueness Drivers: The Keys to Creating a Differentiation Advantage

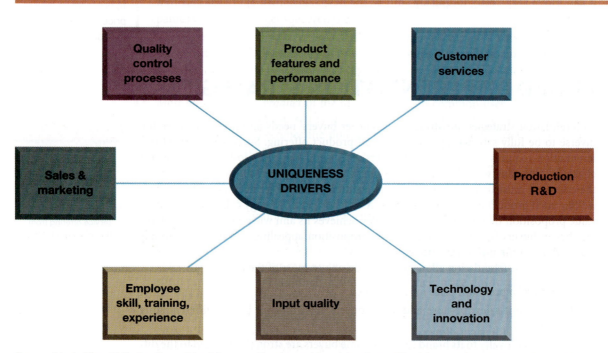

Source: Adapted from M. Porter, *Competitive Advantage: Creating and Sustaining Competitive Advantage* (New York: Free Press, 1985).

1. *Striving to create superior product features, design, and performance.* This applies to the physical as well as functional attributes of a product, including features such as expanded end uses and applications, added user safety, greater recycling capability, or enhanced environmental protection. Design features can be important in enhancing the aesthetic appeal of a product. Ducati's motorcycles, for example, are prized for their designs and have been exhibited in the Guggenheim art museum in New York City.[4]

> **CORE CONCEPT**
>
> A **uniqueness driver** is a factor that can have a strong differentiating effect.

2. *Improving customer service or adding additional services.* Better customer services, in areas such as delivery, returns, and repair, can be as important in creating differentiation as superior product features. Examples include superior technical assistance to buyers, higher-quality maintenance services, more and better product information provided to customers, more and better training materials for end users, better credit terms, quicker order processing, or greater customer convenience.

3. *Pursuing production R&D activities.* Engaging in production R&D may permit custom-order manufacture at an efficient cost, provide wider product variety and selection through product "versioning," improve product quality, or make production methods safer for the environment. Many manufacturers have developed flexible manufacturing systems that allow different models and product versions to be made on the same assembly line. Being able to provide buyers with made-to-order products can be a potent differentiating capability.

4. *Striving for innovation and technological advances.* Successful innovation is the route to more frequent first-on-the-market victories and is a powerful differentiator. If the innovation proves hard to replicate, through patent protection or other means, it can provide a company with a first mover advantage that is sustainable.

5. *Pursuing continuous quality improvement.* Quality control processes can be applied throughout the value chain, including postsale customer service activities. They can reduce product defects, prevent premature product failure, extend product life, make it economical to offer longer warranty coverage, improve economy of use, result in more end-user convenience, or enhance product appearance. Companies whose quality management systems meet certification standards, such as the ISO 9001 standards, can enhance their reputation for quality with customers.

6. *Increasing emphasis on marketing and brand-building activities.* Marketing and advertising can have a tremendous effect on the value perceived by buyers and therefore their willingness to pay more for the company's offerings. They can create differentiation even when little tangible differentiation exists otherwise. For example, blind taste tests show that even the most loyal Pepsi or Coke drinkers have trouble telling one cola drink from another.[5] Brands create customer loyalty, which increases the perceived "cost" of switching to another product.

7. *Seeking out high-quality inputs.* Input quality can ultimately spill over to affect the performance or quality of the company's end product. Starbucks, for example, gets high ratings on its coffees partly because it has very strict specifications on the coffee beans purchased from suppliers.

8. *Emphasizing human resource management activities that improve the skills, expertise, and knowledge of company personnel.* A company with high-caliber intellectual capital often has the capacity to generate the kinds of ideas that drive product innovation, technological advances, better product design and product performance, improved production techniques, and higher product quality. Well-designed incentive compensation systems can often unleash the efforts of talented personnel to develop and implement new and effective differentiating attributes.

Revamping the Value Chain System to Increase Differentiation   Just as pursuing a cost advantage can involve the entire value chain system, the same is true for a differentiation advantage. Activities performed upstream by suppliers or downstream by distributors and retailers can have a meaningful effect on customers' perceptions of a company's offerings and its value proposition. Approaches to enhancing differentiation through changes in the value chain system include:

- *Coordinating with channel allies to enhance customer perceptions of value.* Coordinating with downstream partners such as distributors, dealers, brokers, and retailers can contribute to differentiation in a variety of ways. Methods that companies use to influence the value chain activities of their channel allies include setting standards for downstream partners to follow, providing them with templates to standardize the selling environment or practices, training channel personnel, or cosponsoring promotions and advertising campaigns. Coordinating with retailers is important for enhancing the buying experience and building a company's image. Coordinating with distributors or shippers can mean quicker delivery to customers, more accurate order filling, and/or lower shipping costs. The Coca-Cola Company considers coordination with its bottler/distributors so important that it has at times taken over a troubled bottler for the purpose of improving its management and upgrading its plant and equipment before releasing it again.[6]
- *Coordinating with suppliers to better address customer needs.* Collaborating with suppliers can also be a powerful route to a more effective differentiation strategy. Coordinating and collaborating with suppliers can improve many dimensions affecting product features and quality. This is particularly true for companies that only engage in assembly operations, such as Dell in PCs and Ducati in motorcycles. Close coordination with suppliers can also enhance differentiation by speeding up new product development cycles or speeding delivery to end customers. Strong relationships with suppliers can also mean that the company's supply requirements are prioritized when industry supply is insufficient to meet overall demand.

Delivering Superior Value via a Broad Differentiation Strategy

Differentiation strategies depend on meeting customer needs in unique ways or creating new needs, through activities such as innovation or persuasive advertising. The objective is to offer customers something that rivals can't—at least in terms of the level of satisfaction. There are four basic routes to achieving this aim.

The first route is to incorporate product attributes and user features that *lower the buyer's overall costs* of using the company's product. This is the least obvious and most overlooked route to a differentiation advantage. It is a differentiating factor since it can help business buyers be more competitive in their markets and more profitable. Producers of materials and components often win orders for their products by reducing a buyer's raw-material waste (providing cut-to-size components), reducing a buyer's inventory requirements (providing just-in-time deliveries), using online systems to reduce a buyer's procurement and order processing costs, and providing free technical support. This route to differentiation can also appeal to individual consumers who are looking to economize on their overall costs of consumption. Making a company's product more economical for a buyer to use can be done by incorporating energy-efficient features (energy-saving appliances and lightbulbs help cut buyers' utility bills; fuel-efficient vehicles cut buyer costs for gasoline) and/or by increasing maintenance intervals and product reliability so as to lower buyer costs for maintenance and repairs.

A second route is to incorporate *tangible* features that increase customer satisfaction with the product, such as product specifications, functions, and styling. This can be accomplished by including attributes that add functionality, enhance the design, save time for the user, are more reliable, or make the product cleaner, safer, quieter, simpler to use, more portable, more convenient, or longer-lasting than rival brands. Cell phone manufacturers are in a race to introduce next-generation devices capable of being used for more purposes and having simpler menu functionality.

A third route to a differentiation-based competitive advantage is to incorporate *intangible* features that enhance buyer satisfaction in noneconomic ways. Toyota's Prius appeals to environmentally conscious motorists not only because these drivers want to help reduce global carbon dioxide emissions but also because they identify with the image conveyed. Rolls-Royce, Ralph Lauren, Tiffany, Bugatti, and Prada have differentiation-based competitive advantages linked to buyer desires for status, image, prestige, upscale fashion, superior craftsmanship, and the finer things in life. Intangibles that contribute to differentiation can extend beyond product attributes to the reputation of the company and to customer relations or trust.

The fourth route is to *signal the value* of the company's product offering to buyers. Typical signals of value include a high price (in instances where high price implies high quality and performance), more appealing or fancier packaging than competing products, ad content that emphasizes a product's standout attributes, the quality of brochures and sales presentations, and the luxuriousness and ambience of a seller's facilities (important for high-end retailers and for offices or other facilities frequented by customers). They make potential buyers aware of the professionalism, appearance, and personalities of the seller's employees and/or make potential buyers realize that a company has prestigious customers. Signaling value is particularly important (1) when the nature of differentiation is based on intangible features and is therefore subjective or hard to quantify, (2) when buyers are making a first-time purchase and are unsure what their experience with the product will be, and (3) when repurchase is infrequent, and (4) when buyers are unsophisticated.

> Differentiation can be based on *tangible* or *intangible* attributes.

Regardless of the approach taken, achieving a successful differentiation strategy requires, first, that the company have capabilities in areas such as customer service, marketing, brand management, and technology that can create and support differentiation. That is, the resources, competencies, and value chain activities of the company must be well matched to the requirements of the strategy. For the strategy to result in competitive advantage, the company's competencies must also be sufficiently unique in delivering value to buyers that they help set its product offering apart from those of rivals. They must be competitively superior. There are numerous examples of companies that have differentiated themselves on the basis of distinctive capabilities. When a major new event occurs, many people turn to Fox News and CNN because they have the capability to devote more airtime to breaking news stories and get reporters on the scene very quickly. Avon and Mary Kay Cosmetics have differentiated themselves from other cosmetics and personal care companies by assembling a sales force numbering in the hundreds of thousands that gives them a direct sales capability—their sales associates personally demonstrate products to interested buyers, take their orders on the spot, and deliver the items to buyers' homes.

The most successful approaches to differentiation are those that are difficult for rivals to duplicate. Indeed, this is the route to a sustainable differentiation advantage. While resourceful competitors can, in time, clone almost any tangible product attribute, socially complex intangible attributes, such as company reputation, long-standing relationships with buyers, and image are much harder to imitate. Differentiation that creates switching costs that lock in buyers also provides a route to sustainable advantage. For example, if a buyer makes a substantial investment in learning to use one type of system, that buyer is less likely to switch to a competitor's system. (This has kept many users from switching away from Microsoft Office products, despite the fact that there are other applications with superior features.) As a rule, differentiation yields a longer-lasting and more profitable competitive edge when it is based on a well-established brand image, patent-protected product innovation, complex technical superiority, a reputation for superior product quality and reliability, relationship-based customer service, and unique competitive capabilities.

When a Differentiation Strategy Works Best

Differentiation strategies tend to work best in market circumstances where:

- *Buyer needs and uses of the product are diverse.* Diverse buyer preferences present competitors with a bigger window of opportunity to do things differently and set themselves apart with product attributes that appeal to particular buyers. For instance, the diversity of consumer preferences for menu selection, ambience, pricing, and customer service gives restaurants exceptionally wide latitude in creating a differentiated product offering. Other industries with diverse buyer needs include magazine publishing, automobile manufacturing, footwear, and kitchen appliances.

- *There are many ways to differentiate the product or service that have value to buyers.* Industries that offer opportunities for competitors to add features to products and services are well suited to differentiation strategies. For example, hotel chains can differentiate on such features as location, size of room, range of guest services, in-hotel dining, and the quality and luxuriousness of bedding and furnishings. Similarly, cosmetics producers are able to differentiate based upon prestige and image, formulations that fight the signs of aging, UV light protection, exclusivity of retail locations, the inclusion of antioxidants and natural ingredients, or prohibitions against animal testing. Basic commodities, such as chemicals, mineral deposits, and agricultural products, provide few opportunities for differentiation.

- *Few rival firms are following a similar differentiation approach.* The best differentiation approaches involve trying to appeal to buyers on the basis of attributes that rivals are not emphasizing. A differentiator encounters less head-to-head rivalry when it goes its own separate way in creating uniqueness and does not try to outdifferentiate rivals on the very same attributes. When many rivals base their differentiation efforts on the same attributes, the most likely result is weak brand differentiation and "strategy overcrowding"—competitors end up chasing much the same buyers with much the same product offerings.

- *Technological change is fast-paced and competition revolves around rapidly evolving product features.* Rapid product innovation and frequent introductions of next-version products heighten buyer interest and provide space for companies to pursue distinct differentiating paths. In video game hardware and video games, golf equipment, mobile phones, and big-screen TVs, competitors are locked into an ongoing battle to set themselves apart by introducing the best next-generation products. Companies that fail to come up with new and improved products and distinctive performance features quickly lose out in the marketplace.

Pitfalls to Avoid in Pursuing a Differentiation Strategy

Differentiation strategies can fail for any of several reasons. *A differentiation strategy keyed to product or service attributes that are easily and quickly copied is always doomed.* Rapid imitation means that no rival achieves differentiation, since whenever one firm introduces, some aspect of uniqueness that strikes the fancy of buyers, fast-following copycats quickly reestablish parity. This is why a firm must seek out sources of uniqueness that are time-consuming or burdensome for rivals to match if it hopes to use differentiation to win a sustainable competitive edge.

A second pitfall is that the company's attempt at differentiation produces an unenthusiastic response on the part of buyers. Thus even if a company succeeds in setting its product apart from those of rivals, its strategy can result in disappointing sales and profits if buyers find other brands more appealing. Any time many potential buyers look at a company's differentiated product offering with indifference, the company's differentiation strategy is in deep trouble.

The third big pitfall is overspending on efforts to differentiate the company's product offering, thus eroding profitability. Company efforts to achieve differentiation nearly always raise costs—often substantially, since marketing and R&D are expensive undertakings. The key to profitable differentiation is either to keep the unit cost of achieving differentiation below the price premium that the differentiating attributes can command (thus increasing the profit margin per unit sold) or to offset thinner profit margins per unit by selling enough additional units to increase total profits. If a company goes overboard in pursuing costly differentiation, it could be saddled with unacceptably thin profit margins or even losses.

Other common mistakes in crafting a differentiation strategy include:

- *Offering only trivial improvements in quality, service, or performance features vis-à-vis the products of rivals.* Tiny differences between rivals' product offerings may not be visible or important to buyers. If a company wants to generate the fiercely loyal customer following needed to earn superior profits and open up a differentiation-based competitive advantage over rivals, then its strategy must result in *strong rather than weak product differentiation.* In markets where differentiators do no better than achieve weak product differentiation, customer loyalty is weak, the costs of brand switching are low, and no one company has enough of a market edge to command a price premium over rival brands.

- *Adding so many frills and extra features that the product exceeds the needs and use patterns of most buyers.* A dazzling array of features and options not only drives up product price but also runs the risk that many buyers will conclude that a less deluxe and lower-priced brand is a better value, since they have little occasion to use the deluxe attributes.

- *Charging too high a price premium.* While buyers may be intrigued by a product's deluxe features, they may nonetheless see it as being overpriced relative to the value delivered by the differentiating attributes. A company must guard against turning off would-be buyers with what is perceived as "price gouging." Normally, the bigger the price premium for the differentiating extras, the harder it is to keep buyers from switching to the lower-priced offerings of competitors.

> Overdifferentiating and overcharging are fatal strategy mistakes.

A low-cost provider strategy can defeat a differentiation strategy when buyers are satisfied with a basic product and don't think "extra" attributes are worth a higher price.

FOCUSED (OR MARKET NICHE) STRATEGIES

What sets focused strategies apart from low-cost provider and broad differentiation strategies is concentrated attention on a narrow piece of the total market. The target segment, or niche, can be defined by geographic uniqueness, by specialized requirements in using the product, or by special product attributes that appeal only to niche members.

Community Coffee, the largest family-owned specialty coffee retailer in the United States, has a geographic focus on the state of Louisiana and communities across the Gulf of Mexico. Community holds only a 1.1 percent share of the national coffee market but has recorded sales in excess of $100 million and has won a 50 percent share of the coffee business in the 11-state region where it is distributed. Examples of firms that concentrate on a well-defined market niche keyed to a particular product or buyer segment include Animal Planet and the History Channel (in cable TV), Cartier (in high-end jewelry), Ferrari (in sports cars), and CGA, Inc. (a specialist in providing insurance to cover the cost of lucrative hole-in-one prizes at golf tournaments). Microbreweries, local bakeries, bed-and-breakfast inns, and local owner-managed retail boutiques are all good examples of enterprises that have scaled their operations to serve narrow or local customer segments.

A Focused Low-Cost Strategy

A focused strategy based on low cost aims at securing a competitive advantage by serving buyers in the target market niche at a lower cost and lower price than those of rival competitors. This strategy has considerable attraction when a firm can lower costs significantly by limiting its customer base to a well-defined buyer segment. The avenues to achieving a cost advantage over rivals also serving the target market niche are the same as those for low-cost leadership—outmanage rivals in keeping the costs of value chain activities contained to a bare minimum and search for innovative ways to bypass nonessential activities. The only real difference between a low-cost provider strategy and a focused low-cost strategy is the size of the buyer group to which a company is appealing—the former involves a product offering that appeals broadly to almost all buyer groups and market segments, whereas the latter aims at just meeting the needs of buyers in a narrow market segment.

Focused low-cost strategies are fairly common. Producers of private-label goods are able to achieve low costs in product development, marketing, distribution, and advertising by concentrating on making generic items imitative of name-brand merchandise and selling directly to retail chains wanting a low-priced store brand. The Perrigo Company has become a leading manufacturer of over-the-counter health care products, with 2011 sales of more than $2.7 billion, by focusing on producing private-label brands for retailers such as Walmart, CVS, Walgreens, Rite-Aid, and Safeway. Budget motel chains, like Motel 6, Sleep Inn, and Super 8, cater to price-conscious travelers who just want to pay for a clean, no-frills place to spend the night. Illustration Capsule 5.2 describes how Aravind's focus on lowering the costs of cataract removal allowed it to address the needs of the "bottom of the pyramid" in India's population where blindness due to cataracts is an endemic problem.

A Focused Differentiation Strategy

Focused differentiation strategies are keyed to offering products or services designed to appeal to the unique preferences and needs of a narrow, well-defined group of buyers. Successful use of a focused differentiation strategy depends on the existence of a buyer segment that is looking for special product attributes or seller capabilities and on a firm's ability to stand apart from rivals competing in the same target market niche.

Companies like Godiva Chocolates, Rolls-Royce, Louis Vuitton, and W. L. Gore (the maker of GORE-TEX) employ successful differentiation-based focused strategies targeted at upscale buyers wanting products and services with world-class attributes. Indeed, most markets contain a buyer segment willing to pay a big price premium for the very finest items available, thus opening the strategic window for some competitors to

Aravind Eye Care System's Focused Low-Cost Strategy

Cataracts, the largest cause of preventable blindness, can be treated with a quick surgical procedure that restores sight; however, poverty and limited access to care prevent millions worldwide from obtaining surgery. The Aravind Eye Care System has found a way to address this problem, with a *focused low-cost strategy* that has made cataract surgery not only affordable for more people in India, but free for the very poorest. On the basis of this strategy, Aravind has achieved world renown and become the largest provider of eye care in the world.

High volume and high efficiency are at the cornerstone of Aravind's strategy. The Aravind network with its five eye hospitals in India has become one of the most productive systems in the world, conducting about 300,000 surgeries a year in addition to seeing over 2.6 million outpatients each year. Using the unique model of screening eye camps all over the country, Aravind reaches a broader cross-section of the market for surgical treatment. Additionally, Aravind attains very high staff productivity with each surgeon performing more than 2,500 surgeries annually, compared to 125 for a comparable American surgeon.

What enabled this level of productivity (with no loss in quality of care) was the development of a standardized system of surgical treatment, capitalizing on the fact that cataract removal was already a fairly routine process. Aravind streamlined as much of the process as possible, reducing discretionary elements to a minimum, and tracking outcomes to ensure continuous process improvement. At Aravind's hospitals, there is no wasted

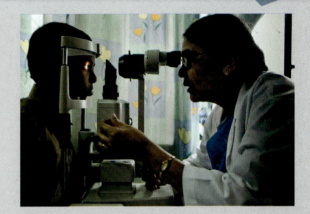

time between surgeries as different teams of support-staff prepare patients for surgery and bring them to the operating theater so that surgeons simply need to turn from one table to another to perform surgery on the next prepared patient. Aravind also drove costs down through the creation of its own manufacturing division, Aurolab, to produce intraocular lenses, suture needles, pharmaceuticals, and surgical blades in India.

Aravind's low costs allow them to keep their prices for cataract surgery very low at Rs. 500.00 ($10) per patient, compared to an average cost of $1500 for surgery in the US. Nevertheless, the system provides surgical outcomes and quality comparable to clinics in the United States. As a result of its unique fee system and effective management, Aravind is also able to provide free eye care to 60 percent of its patients from the revenue generated from paying.

Developed with Avni V. Patel.

Sources: G. Natchiar, A. L. Robin, R. Thulasiraj, et al., "Attacking the Backlog of India's Curable Blind; The Aravind Eye Hospital Model," *Arch Ophthalmol* (1994) 112:987–93; D. F. Chang, "Tackling the Greatest Challenge in Cataract Surgery," *Br J Ophthalmol.,* (2005) 89:1073–7; "Driving Down the Cost of High Quality Care," *McKinsey Health International,* December 2011.

pursue differentiation-based focused strategies aimed at the very top of the market pyramid. Another successful focused differentiator is "fashion food retailer" Trader Joe's, a 369-store, 33-state chain that is a combination gourmet deli and food warehouse. Customers shop Trader Joe's as much for entertainment as for conventional grocery items—the store stocks out-of-the-ordinary culinary treats like raspberry salsa, salmon burgers, and jasmine fried rice, as well as the standard goods normally found in supermarkets. What sets Trader Joe's apart is not just its unique combination of food novelties and competitively priced grocery items but also its capability to turn an otherwise mundane grocery excursion into a whimsical treasure hunt that is just plain fun. Illustration Capsule 5.3 describes how Popchips has been grabbing market share with a focused differentiation strategy.

Popchips's Focused Differentiation Strategy

Potato chips are big business: Americans consume $7B worth annually. But the industry is a hard one to break into since it's a mature, slow-growth industry, dominated by a few large competitors. Frito-Lay alone (maker of Lays and Ruffles) has a commanding 60 percent market share. These characteristics are enough to dissuade most potential entrants, but not Popchips, a small potato chip startup. Despite difficult odds, Popchips has made impressive inroads into the industry over the last five years, with the help of a *focused differentiation strategy*.

Popchips was founded in 2007 by Keith Belling, a serial entrepreneur, and Pat Turpin, a former Costco snack executive. Their idea was simple: take advantage of high-income purchasers' growing desire for tasty, low-fat snacks. Using an innovative cooking method, they found a way to halve the fat content in potato chips while preserving flavor. Popchips has a differentiated product. But its real point of differentiation is in its brand and distribution strategy. Most potato chips have mass distribution and a broad buyer base. Belling and Turpin decided from the outset to narrow their distribution and narrow their targeted buyers. They hoped that focusing on a market niche would allow their product to stand out from the bags of *Lays* and cans of *Pringles* in aisles all over America. Popchips's target: upper income, health-conscious urban and suburban consumers.

To that end, the firm has signed distribution deals with Whole Foods, Target, and, reflecting Turpin's roots, Costco. Popchips's marketing emphasizes social marketing and word of mouth recommendations. The company sends out samples to key tastemakers who tweet, blog, or recommend the product in traditional media. Ashton Kutcher, MTV's former Punk'd host, was so impressed with the chips that he volunteered to promote them. Like Punk'd, Popchips's advertising is similarly irreverent, with taglines like, "love. without the handles."

Popchips's differentiation strategy is succeeding. Between 2009–2011, the company's sales accounted for

nearly all potato chip sales growth at natural supermarket stores, like Whole Foods. Popchips now has nearly 15 percent market share in this niche distribution channel. The company's 2010 sales were $45.7M, over double the 2009 figure. That's particularly impressive given that the industry growth rate has been a paltry 4 percent. In 2011, Forbes put Popchips on its list of America's Most Promising Companies.

Developed with Dennis L. Huggins.

Sources: Molly Maier, "Chips, Pretzels and Corn Snacks - US - January 2012," *Mintel,* January 2012, www.oxygen.mintel.com (accessed on February 1, 2012); Lindsay Blakely and Caitlin Elsaesser, "One Snacker at a Time: How Popchips Grew Without Losing Its Character," *CBS News,* January 2011, (accessed at www.cbsnews.com on February 1, 2012); Laura Petrecca, "Popchips CEO Keith Belling is 'Pop-timist' on Healthy Snacks," *USA Today,* March 2010 (accessed at www.usatoday.com on February 13, 2012); http://www.forbes.com/, accessed February 28, 2012; Popchips website.

When a Focused Low-Cost or Focused Differentiation Strategy Is Attractive

A focused strategy aimed at securing a competitive edge based either on low cost or differentiation becomes increasingly attractive as more of the following conditions are met:

- The target market niche is big enough to be profitable and offers good growth potential.
- Industry leaders have chosen not to compete in the niche—in which case focusers can avoid battling head to head against the industry's biggest and strongest competitors.
- It is costly or difficult for multisegment competitors to meet the specialized needs of niche buyers and at the same time satisfy the expectations of their mainstream customers.
- The industry has many different niches and segments, thereby allowing a focuser to pick the niche best suited to its resources and capabilities. Also, with more niches there is more room for focusers to avoid each other in competing for the same customers.
- Few if any rivals are attempting to specialize in the same target segment—a condition that reduces the risk of segment overcrowding.

The advantages of focusing a company's entire competitive effort on a single market niche are considerable, especially for smaller and medium-sized companies that may lack the breadth and depth of resources to tackle going after a broad customer base with a "something for everyone" lineup of models, styles, and product selection. YouTube has become a household name by concentrating on short video clips posted online. Papa John's and Domino's Pizza have created impressive businesses by focusing on the home delivery segment.

The Risks of a Focused Low-Cost or Focused Differentiation Strategy

Focusing carries several risks. One is the chance that competitors will find effective ways to match the focused firm's capabilities in serving the target niche—perhaps by coming up with products or brands specifically designed to appeal to buyers in the target niche or by developing expertise and capabilities that offset the focuser's strengths. In the lodging business, large chains like Marriott have launched multibrand strategies that allow them to compete effectively in several lodging segments simultaneously. Marriott has flagship J.W. Marriot and Ritz-Carlton hotels with deluxe accommodations for business travelers and resort vacationers. Its Courtyard by Marriott and SpringHill Suites brands cater to business travelers looking for moderately priced lodging, while Marriott Residence Inns and TownePlace Suites are designed as a "home away from home" for travelers staying five or more nights, and the 670 Fairfield Inn & Suite locations are intended to appeal to travelers looking for quality lodging at an "affordable" price. Multibrand strategies are attractive to large companies like Marriott precisely because they enable a company to enter a market niche and siphon business away from companies that employ a focused strategy.

A second risk of employing a focused strategy is the potential for the preferences and needs of niche members to shift over time toward the product attributes desired by the majority of buyers. An erosion of the differences across buyer segments lowers entry barriers into a focuser's market niche and provides an open invitation for rivals in adjacent segments to begin competing for the focuser's customers. A third risk is that the segment may become so attractive that it is soon inundated with competitors, intensifying rivalry and splintering segment profits. And there is always the risk for segment growth to slow to such a small rate that a focusers' prospects for future sales and profit gains become unacceptably dim.

BEST-COST PROVIDER STRATEGIES

As Figure 5.1 indicates, **best-cost provider strategies** stake out a middle ground between pursuing a low-cost advantage and a differentiation advantage, and between appealing to the broad market as a whole and a narrow market niche. Companies pursuing best-cost strategies aim squarely at the sometimes great mass of value-conscious buyers looking for a good-to-very-good product or service at an economical price. Value-conscious buyers frequently shy away from both cheap low-end products and expensive high-end products, but they are quite willing to pay a "fair" price for extra features and functionality they find appealing and useful. The essence of a best-cost provider strategy is giving customers more *value for the money* by satisfying buyer desires for appealing features/performance/quality/service and charging a lower price for these attributes compared to rivals with similar caliber product offerings.[7] From a competitive-positioning standpoint, best-cost strategies are thus a *hybrid,* balancing a strategic emphasis on low cost against a strategic emphasis on differentiation (desirable features delivered at a relatively low price).

To profitably employ a best-cost provider strategy, a company *must have the resources and capabilities to incorporate attractive or upscale attributes into its product offering at a lower cost than rivals.* When a company can incorporate appealing features, good to excellent product performance or quality, or more satisfying customer service into its product offering *at a lower cost than rivals,* then it enjoys "best-cost" status—it is the low-cost provider of a product or service with *upscale attributes.* A best-cost provider can use its low-cost advantage to underprice rivals whose products or services have similarly upscale attributes and still earn attractive profits.

Being a best-cost provider is different from being a low-cost provider because the additional attractive attributes entail additional costs (which a low-cost provider can avoid by offering buyers a basic product with few frills). Moreover, the two strategies aim at a distinguishably different market target. *The target market for a best-cost provider is value-conscious buyers*—buyers who are looking for appealing extras and functionality at a comparatively low price. Value-hunting buyers (as distinct from *price-conscious buyers* looking for a basic product at a bargain-basement price) often constitute a very sizable part of the overall market for a product or service.

When a Best-Cost Provider Strategy Works Best

A best-cost provider strategy works best in markets where product differentiation is the norm and an attractively large number of value-conscious buyers can be induced to purchase midrange products rather than cheap, basic products or expensive top-of-the-line products. A best-cost provider needs to position itself near the middle of the market with either a medium-quality product at a below-average price or a high-quality product at an average or slightly higher price. Best-cost provider strategies also work well in recessionary times when great masses of buyers become value-conscious and are attracted to economically priced products and services with appealing attributes. But unless a

Toyota's Best-Cost Provider Strategy for Its Lexus Line

Toyota Motor Company is widely regarded as a low-cost producer among the world's motor vehicle manufacturers. Despite its emphasis on product quality, Toyota has achieved low-cost leadership because it has developed considerable skills in efficient supply chain management and low-cost assembly capabilities and because its models are positioned in the low-to-medium end of the price spectrum, where high production volumes are conducive to low unit costs. But when Toyota decided to introduce its new Lexus models to compete in the luxury-car market segment, it employed a classic best-cost provider strategy. Toyota took the following four steps in crafting and implementing its Lexus strategy:

- Designing an array of high-performance characteristics and upscale features into the Lexus models to make them comparable in performance and luxury to other high-end models and attractive to Mercedes, BMW, Audi, Jaguar, Cadillac, and Lincoln buyers.

- Transferring its capabilities in making high-quality Toyota models at low cost to making premium-quality Lexus models at costs below other luxury-car makers. Toyota's supply chain capabilities and low-cost assembly know-how allowed it to incorporate high-tech performance features and upscale quality into Lexus models at substantially less cost than comparable Mercedes and BMW models.

- Using its relatively lower manufacturing costs to underprice comparable Mercedes and BMW models. With its cost advantage, Toyota could price attractively equipped Lexus cars low enough to draw price-conscious buyers away from comparable high-end brands. Toyota's pricing policy also allowed it to induce Honda, Ford, or GM owners desiring more luxury to switch to a Lexus. Lexus's pricing advantage over Mercedes and BMW was sometimes quite significant. For example, in 2012 the Lexus RX 350, a mid-sized SUV, carried a sticker price in the $39,000–$54,000 range (depending on how it was equipped), whereas variously equipped Mercedes ML 350 SUVs had price tags from $48,000 to over $92,000 and a BMW X5 SUV could range anywhere from $46,000 to $94,000, depending on the optional equipment chosen.

- Establishing a new network of Lexus dealers, separate from Toyota dealers, dedicated to providing a level of personalized, attentive customer service unmatched in the industry.

Toyota's best-cost strategy for its Lexus line succeeded in making Lexus the best-selling luxury car brand worldwide from 1999 through 2010.

company has the resources, know-how, and capabilities to incorporate upscale product or service attributes at a lower cost than rivals, adopting a best-cost strategy is ill-advised—*a winning strategy must always be matched to a company's resources and capabilities.*

Illustration Capsule 5.4 describes how Toyota has applied the principles of the best-cost provider strategy in producing and marketing its Lexus brand.

The Big Risk of a Best-Cost Provider Strategy

A company's biggest vulnerability in employing a best-cost provider strategy is getting squeezed between the strategies of firms using low-cost and high-end differentiation strategies. Low-cost providers may be able to siphon customers away with the appeal of a lower price (despite less appealing product attributes). High-end differentiators may be able to steal customers away with the appeal of better product attributes (even though their products carry a higher price tag). Thus, to be successful, a best-cost provider has to achieve significantly lower costs in providing upscale features so it can outcompete high-end differentiators on the basis of a *significantly* lower price. Likewise, it must offer buyers *significantly* better product attributes in order to justify a price above what low-cost leaders are charging.

THE CONTRASTING FEATURES OF THE FIVE GENERIC COMPETITIVE STRATEGIES: A SUMMARY

Deciding which generic competitive strategy should serve as the framework on which to hang the rest of the company's strategy is not a trivial matter. Each of the five generic competitive strategies *positions* the company differently in its market and competitive environment. Each establishes a central theme for how the company will endeavor to out-compete rivals. Each creates some boundaries or guidelines for maneuvering as market circumstances unfold and as ideas for improving the strategy are debated. Each entails differences in terms of product line, production emphasis, marketing emphasis, and means of maintaining the strategy, as shown in Table 5.1.

Thus a choice of which generic strategy to employ spills over to affect many aspects of how the business will be operated and the manner in which value chain activities must

TABLE 5.1   Distinguishing Features of the Five Generic Competitive Strategies

	Low-Cost Provider	Broad Differentiation	Focused Low-Cost Provider	Focused Differentiation	Best-Cost Provider
Strategic target	• A broad cross-section of the market.	• A broad cross-section of the market.	• A narrow market niche where buyer needs and preferences are distinctively different.	• A narrow market niche where buyer needs and preferences are distinctively different.	• Value-conscious buyers. • A middle market range.
Basis of competitive strategy	• Lower overall costs than competitors.	• Ability to offer buyers something attractively different from competitors' offerings.	• Lower overall cost than rivals in serving niche members.	• Attributes that appeal specifically to niche members.	• Ability to offer better goods at attractive prices.
Product line	• A good basic product with few frills (acceptable quality and limited selection).	• Many product variations, wide selection; emphasis on differentiating features.	• Features and attributes tailored to the tastes and requirements of niche members.	• Features and attributes tailored to the tastes and requirements of niche members.	• Items with appealing attributes; assorted features; better quality, not best.
Production emphasis	• A continuous search for cost reduction without sacrificing acceptable quality and essential features.	• Build in whatever differentiating features buyers are willing to pay for; strive for product superiority.	• A continuous search for cost reduction for products that meet basic needs of niche members.	• Small-scale production or custom-made products that match the tastes and requirements of niche members.	• Build in appealing features and better quality at lower cost than rivals.

(Continued)

TABLE 5.1   *(Concluded)*

	Low-Cost Provider	Broad Differentiation	Focused Low-Cost Provider	Focused Differentiation	Best-Cost Provider
Marketing emphasis	• Low prices, good value. • Try to make a virtue out of product features that lead to low cost.	• Tout differentiating features. • Charge a premium price to cover the extra costs of differentiating features.	• Communicate attractive features of a budget-priced product offering that fits niche buyers' expectations.	• Communicate how product offering does the best job of meeting niche buyers' expectations.	• Tout delivery of *best* value. • Either deliver comparable features at a lower price than rivals or else match rivals on prices and provide better features.
Keys to maintaining the strategy	• Economical prices, good value. • Strive to manage costs down, year after year, in every area of the business.	• Stress constant innovation to stay ahead of imitative competitors. • Concentrate on a few key differentiating features.	• Stay committed to serving the niche at the lowest overall cost; don't blur the firm's image by entering other market segments or adding other products to widen market appeal.	• Stay committed to serving the niche better than rivals; don't blur the firm's image by entering other market segments or adding other products to widen market appeal.	• Unique expertise in simultaneously managing costs down while incorporating upscale features and attributes.
Resources and capabilities required	• Capabilities for driving costs out of the value chain system. • *Examples:* large-scale automated plants, an efficiency-oriented culture, bargaining power.	• Capabilities concerning quality, design, intangibles, and innovation. • *Examples:* marketing capabilities, R&D teams, technology.	• Capabilities to lower costs on niche goods. • *Examples:* lower input costs for the specific product desired by the niche, batch production capabilities.	• Capabilities to meet the highly specific needs of niche members. • *Examples:* custom production, close customer relations.	• Capabilities to simultaneously deliver lower cost and higher-quality/differentiated features. • *Examples:* TQM practices, mass customization.

be managed. Deciding which generic strategy to employ is perhaps the most important strategic commitment a company makes—it tends to drive the rest of the strategic actions a company decides to undertake.

Successful Competitive Strategies Are Resource-Based

For a company's competitive strategy to succeed in delivering good performance and the intended competitive edge over rivals, it has to be well-matched to a company's internal situation and underpinned by an appropriate set of resources, know-how, and competitive capabilities. To succeed in employing a low-cost provider strategy, a company must have the resources and capabilities to keep its costs below those of its competitors.

How would you characterize Stihl's competitive strategy? Should it be classified as a low-cost provider strategy? A differentiation strategy? A best-cost strategy? Also, has the company chosen to focus on a narrow piece of the market or does it appear to pursue a broad market approach? Explain your answer.

connect

LO1, LO3, LO4

4. Explore BMW's website at **www.bmwgroup.com** and see if you can identify at least three ways in which the company seeks to differentiate itself from rival automakers. Is there reason to believe that BMW's differentiation strategy has been successful in producing a competitive advantage? Why or why not?

EXERCISE FOR SIMULATION PARTICIPANTS

LO 1, LO 2, LO 3, LO 4

1. Which one of the five generic competitive strategies best characterize your company's strategic approach to competing successfully?
2. Which rival companies appear to be employing a low-cost provider strategy?
3. Which rival companies appear to be employing a broad differentiation strategy?
4. Which rival companies appear to be employing a best-cost provider strategy?
5. Which rival companies appear to be employing some type of focused strategy?
6. What is your company's action plan to achieve a sustainable competitive advantage over rival companies? List at least three (preferably more than three) specific kinds of decision entries on specific decision screens that your company has made or intends to make to win this kind of competitive edge over rivals.

ENDNOTES

[1]Michael E. Porter, *Competitive Strategy: Techniques for Analyzing Industries and Competitors* (New York: Free Press, 1980), Chapter 2; Michael E. Porter, "What Is Strategy?" *Harvard Business Review* 74, no. 6 (November–December 1996).
[2]M. Porter, *Competitive Advantage: Creating and Sustaining Superior Performance* (New York: Free Press, 1985).

[3]Richard L. Priem, "A Consumer Perspective on Value Creation," *Academy of Management Review* 32, no. 1 (2007), pp. 219–35.
[4]G. Gavetti, "Ducati," Harvard Business School case 9-701-132, rev. March 8, 2002.
[5]http://jrscience.wcp.muohio.edu/nsfall01/FinalArticles/Final-IsitWorthitBrandsan.html.
[6]D. Yoffie, "Cola Wars Continue: Coke and Pepsi in 2006," Harvard Business School case 9-706-447.

[7]Peter J. Williamson and Ming Zeng, "Value-for-Money Strategies for Recessionary Times," *Harvard Business Review* 87, no. 3 (March 2009), pp. 66–74.

A company's co
strategy should
matched to its i
situation and pr
on leveraging it
of competitively
resources and

CHAPTER 6

STRENGTHENING A COMPANY'S COMPETITIVE POSITION

Strategic Moves, Timing, and Scope of Operations

Learning Objectives

LO 1   Learn whether and when to pursue offensive or defensive strategic moves to improve a company's market position.

LO 2   Recognize when being a first mover or a fast follower or a late mover is most advantageous.

LO 3   Become aware of the strategic benefits and risks of expanding a company's horizontal scope through mergers and acquisitions.

LO 4   Learn the advantages and disadvantages of extending the company's scope of operations via vertical integration.

LO 5   Become aware of the conditions that favor farming out certain value chain activities to outside parties.

LO 6   Understand when and how strategic alliances can substitute for horizontal mergers and acquisitions or vertical integration and how they can facilitate outsourcing.

> Competing in the marketplace is like war. You have injuries and casualties, and the best strategy wins.
>
> John Collins – *NHL executive*

> In the virtual economy, collaboration is a new competitive imperative.
>
> Michael Dell – *CEO of Dell Inc.*

> Our success has really been based on partnerships from the very beginning.
>
> Bill Gates – *Founder and CEO of Microsoft*

> Don't form an alliance to correct a weakness . . . The only result from a marriage of weaknesses is the creation of even more weaknesses.
>
> Michel Robert – *Author and consultant*

Once a company has settled on which of the five generic competitive strategies to employ, attention turns to what *other strategic actions* it can take to complement its competitive approach and maximize the power of its overall strategy. The first set of decisions concerns whether to undertake offensive or defensive competitive moves, and the timing of such moves. The second set concerns the breadth of a company's activities (or its *scope* of operations along an industry's entire value chain). All in all, the following measures to strengthen a company's competitive position must be considered:

- Whether to go on the offensive and initiate aggressive strategic moves to improve the company's market position.
- Whether to employ defensive strategies to protect the company's market position.
- When to undertake strategic moves—whether advantage or disadvantage lies in being a first mover, a fast follower, or a late mover.
- Whether to bolster the company's market position by merging with or acquiring another company in the same industry.
- Whether to integrate backward or forward into more stages of the industry value chain system.
- Which value chain activities, if any, should be outsourced.
- Whether to enter into strategic alliances or partnership arrangements with other enterprises.

This chapter presents the pros and cons of each of these measures.

GOING ON THE OFFENSIVE—STRATEGIC OPTIONS TO IMPROVE A COMPANY'S MARKET POSITION

LO 1

Learn whether and when to pursue offensive or defensive strategic moves to improve a company's market position.

No matter which of the five generic competitive strategies a firm employs, there are times when it makes sense for the company to *go on the offensive* to improve its market position and business performance. Strategic offensives are called for when a company spots opportunities to gain profitable market share at the expense of rivals or when a company has no choice but to try to whittle away at a strong rival's competitive advantage. Companies like Exxon Mobil, Amazon, Walmart, and Microsoft play hardball, aggressively pursuing competitive advantage and trying to reap the benefits a competitive edge offers—a leading market share, excellent profit margins, and rapid growth.[1] The best offensives tend to incorporate several principles: (1) focusing relentlessly on building competitive advantage and then striving to convert it into a sustainable advantage, (2) applying resources where rivals are least able to defend themselves, (3) employing the element of surprise as opposed to doing what rivals expect and are prepared for, and (4) displaying a strong bias for swift, decisive, and overwhelming actions to overpower rivals.[2]

Sometimes a company's best strategic option is to seize the initiative, go on the attack, and launch a strategic offensive to improve its market position.

Choosing the Basis for Competitive Attack

Challenging rivals on competitive grounds where they are strong is an uphill struggle.[3] Offensive initiatives that exploit competitor weaknesses stand a better chance of succeeding than do those that challenge competitor strengths, especially if the weaknesses represent important vulnerabilities and weak rivals can be caught by surprise with no ready defense.

Strategic offensives should, as a general rule, be based on a company's strongest competitive assets—its most valuable resources and capabilities such as a better-known brand name, a more efficient production or distribution system, greater technological capability, or a superior reputation for quality. But a consideration of the company's strengths should not be made without also considering the rival's strengths and weaknesses. A strategic offensive should be based on those areas of strength where the company has its greatest competitive advantage over the targeted rivals. If a company has especially good customer service capabilities, it can make special sales pitches to the customers of those rivals that provide subpar customer service. Likewise, it may be attractive to pay special attention to buyer segments that a rival is neglecting or is weakly equipped to serve.

The best offensives use a company's most powerful resources and capabilities to attack rivals in the areas where they are weakest.

Ignoring the need to tie a strategic offensive to a company's competitive strengths and what it does best is like going to war with a popgun—the prospects for success are dim. For instance, it is foolish for a company with relatively high costs to employ a price-cutting offensive. Price-cutting offensives are best left to financially strong companies whose costs are relatively low in comparison to those of the companies being attacked.

The principal offensive strategy options include the following:

1. *Offering an equally good or better product at a lower price.* Lower prices can produce market share gains if competitors don't respond with price cuts of their own and if the challenger convinces buyers that its product is just as good or better. However, such a strategy increases total profits only if the gains in additional unit sales are enough to offset the impact of lower prices and thinner margins per unit sold. Price-cutting offensives are best initiated by companies that have *first achieved a cost advantage.*[4] Irish airline Ryanair used this strategy successfully against rivals such

as British Air and Aer Lingus, by first cutting costs to the bone and then targeting leisure passengers who care more about low price than in-flight amenities and service.[5]

2. *Leapfrogging competitors by being first to market with next-generation products.* In technology-based industries, the opportune time to overtake an entrenched competitor is when there is a shift to the next generation of the technology. Microsoft got its next-generation Xbox 360 to market a full 12 months ahead of Sony's PlayStation 3 and Nintendo's Wii, helping it build a sizeable market share and develop a reputation for cutting-edge innovation in the video game industry.

3. *Pursuing continuous product innovation to draw sales and market share away from less innovative rivals.* Ongoing introductions of new and improved products can put rivals under tremendous competitive pressure, especially when rivals' new product development capabilities are weak. But such offensives can be sustained only if a company can keep its pipeline full and maintain buyer enthusiasm for its new and better product offerings.

4. *Adopting and improving on the good ideas of other companies (rivals or otherwise).* The idea of warehouse-type home improvement centers did not originate with Home Depot cofounders Arthur Blank and Bernie Marcus; they got the "big-box" concept from their former employer Handy Dan Home Improvement. But they were quick to improve on Handy Dan's business model and take Home Depot to the next plateau in terms of product line breadth and customer service. Offense-minded companies are often quick to adopt any good idea (not nailed down by a patent or other legal protection) and build upon it to create competitive advantage for themselves.

5. *Using hit-and-run or guerrilla warfare tactics to grab market share from complacent or distracted rivals.* Options for "guerrilla offensives" include occasional lowballing on price (to win a big order or steal a key account from a rival), surprising rivals with sporadic but intense bursts of promotional activity (offering a special trial offer to draw customers away from rival brands), or undertaking special campaigns to attract the customers of rivals plagued with a strike or problems in meeting buyer demand.[6] Guerrilla offensives are particularly well suited to small challengers that have neither the resources nor the market visibility to mount a full-fledged attack on industry leaders.

6. *Launching a preemptive strike to secure an advantageous position that rivals are prevented or discouraged from duplicating.*[7] What makes a move preemptive is its one-of-a-kind nature—whoever strikes first stands to acquire competitive assets that rivals can't readily match. Examples of preemptive moves include (1) securing the best distributors in a particular geographic region or country, (2) moving to obtain the most favorable site at a new interchange or intersection, in a new shopping mall, and so on, (3) tying up the most reliable, high-quality suppliers via exclusive partnerships, long-term contracts, or acquisition, and (4) moving swiftly to acquire the assets of distressed rivals at bargain prices. To be successful, a preemptive move doesn't have to totally block rivals from following; it merely needs to give a firm a prime position that is not easily circumvented.

How long it takes for an offensive to yield good results varies with the competitive circumstances.[8] It can be short if buyers respond immediately (as can occur with a dramatic cost-based price cut, an imaginative ad campaign, or an especially appealing new product). Securing a competitive edge can take much longer if winning consumer acceptance of an innovative product will take some time or if the firm may need several years to debug a new technology or put a new production capacity in place. But how long it takes for an offensive move to improve a company's market standing (and whether it can do so) also depends on whether market rivals recognize the threat and begin a counterresponse. And whether rivals will respond depends on whether they are capable of making an effective response and if they believe that a counterattack is worth the expense and the distraction.[9]

Choosing Which Rivals to Attack

Offensive-minded firms need to analyze which of their rivals to challenge as well as how to mount the challenge. The following are the best targets for offensive attacks:[10]

- *Market leaders that are vulnerable.* Offensive attacks make good sense when a company that leads in terms of market share is not a true leader in terms of serving the market well. Signs of leader vulnerability include unhappy buyers, an inferior product line, a weak competitive strategy with regard to low-cost leadership or differentiation, aging technology or outdated plants and equipment, a preoccupation with diversification into other industries, and financial problems. Toyota's massive product recalls in 2009 and 2010 due to safety concerns presented other car companies with a prime opportunity to attack a vulnerable and distracted market leader. GM and Ford used incentives and low-financing offers aimed at winning over Toyota buyers to increase their market share during this period.
- *Runner-up firms with weaknesses in areas where the challenger is strong.* Runner-up firms are an especially attractive target when a challenger's resources and capabilities are well suited to exploiting their weaknesses.
- *Struggling enterprises that are on the verge of going under.* Challenging a hard-pressed rival in ways that further sap its financial strength and competitive position can weaken its resolve and hasten its exit from the market. In this type of situation, it makes sense to attack the rival in the market segments where it makes the most profits, since this will threaten its survival the most.
- *Small local and regional firms with limited capabilities.* Because small firms typically have limited expertise and resources, a challenger with broader and/or deeper capabilities is well positioned to raid their biggest and best customers—particularly those that are growing rapidly, have increasingly sophisticated requirements, and may already be thinking about switching to a supplier with a more full-service capability.

CORE CONCEPT

A **blue-ocean strategy** offers growth in revenues and profits by discovering or inventing new industry segments that create altogether new demand.

Blue-Ocean Strategy—A Special Kind of Offensive

A **blue-ocean strategy** seeks to gain a dramatic and durable competitive advantage by abandoning efforts to beat out competitors in existing markets and, instead, *inventing a new industry or distinctive market segment that renders existing competitors largely irrelevant and allows a company to create and capture altogether new demand.*[11] This strategy views the business universe as consisting of two distinct types of market space. One is where industry boundaries are defined and accepted, the competitive rules of the game are well understood by all industry members, and companies try to outperform rivals by capturing a bigger share of existing demand. In such markets, lively competition constrains a company's prospects for rapid growth and superior profitability since rivals move quickly to either imitate or counter the successes of competitors. The second type of market space is a "blue ocean," where the industry does not really exist yet, is untainted by competition, and offers wide-open opportunity for profitable and rapid growth if a company can create new demand with a new type of product offering.

A terrific example of such wide-open or blue-ocean market space is the online auction industry that eBay created and now dominates. Other examples of companies that

Gilt Groupe's Blue-Ocean Strategy in the U.S. Flash Sale Industry

Luxury fashion flash sales exploded onto the U.S. e-commerce scene when Gilt Groupe launched its business in 2007. Flash sales offer limited quantities of high-end designer brands at steep discounts to site members over a very narrow timeframe: the opportunity to snap up an incredible bargain is over in a "flash." The concept of online time-limited, designer-brand sale events, available to members only, had been invented six years earlier by the French company, Vente Privée. But since Vente Privée operated in Europe and the UK, the U.S. market represented a wide-open, blue ocean of uncontested opportunity. Gilt Groupe's only rival was Ideeli, another U.S. startup that had launched in the same year.

Gilt Groupe thrived and grew rapidly in the calm waters of the early days of the U.S. industry. Its tremendous growth stemmed from its recognition of an underserved segment of the population—the web-savvy, value-conscious fashionista—and also from fortuitous timing. The Great Recession hit the U.S. in December 2007, causing a sharp decline in consumer buying and leaving designers with unforeseen quantities of luxury items they could not sell. The fledgling flash sale industry was the perfect channel to offload some of the excess inventory since it still maintained the cachet of exclusivity, with members-only sales and limited-time availability.

Gilt's revenue grew exponentially from $25 million in 2008 to upwards of $600 million by 2011. But their success prompted an influx of fast followers into the luxury flash sale industry, including Hautelook and RueLaLa, who were able to enter the market in December 2007 and April 2008, respectively. The new rivals not only competed for online customers, who could switch costlessly from site to site (since memberships were free), but they also competed for unsold designer inventory. As the U.S. economy came out of the recession, much less of this type of inventory was available. Larger players had also begun to enter the flash sales market in the U.S., with Nordstrom's acquisition of Hautelook, eBay's

purchase of RueLaLa, and Amazon's 2011 acquisition of MyHabit.com. In late 2011, Vente Privée announced the launch of their U.S. online site, via a joint venture with American Express.

As the competitive waters have begun to roil and turn increasingly red, Gilt Groupe has been looking for new ways to compete, expanding into a variety of online luxury product and services niches and venturing overseas. They have been successful in getting new rounds of venture capital, but as of early 2012 had not yet become profitable. Can they survive and prosper in a more crowded competitive space? Only time will tell.

Developed with Judith H. Lin.

Sources: Matthew Carroll, "The Rise of Gilt Groupe," *Forbes.com*, January 2012; Mark Brohan, "The Top 500 Guide," *Internet Retailer,* June 2011; Colleen Debaise, "Launching Gilt Groupe, A Fashionable Enterprise," *The Wall Street Journal,* October 2010 (all accessed at www.wsj.com on February 26, 2012); and http://about.americanexpress.com/news/pr/2011/vente_usa.aspx, accessed March 3, 2012.

have achieved competitive advantages by creating blue-ocean market spaces include Starbucks in the coffee shop industry, The Weather Channel in cable TV, FedEx in overnight package delivery, and Cirque du Soleil in live entertainment. Cirque du Soleil "reinvented the circus" by pulling in a whole new group of customers—adults and corporate clients—who not only were noncustomers of traditional circuses (like Ringling Brothers), but were also willing to pay several times more than the price of a conventional circus ticket to have a "sophisticated entertainment experience" featuring stunning visuals and star-quality acrobatic acts. Zipcar Inc. is presently using a blue-ocean strategy to compete against entrenched rivals in the rental-car industry. It rents cars by the hour or day (rather than by the week) to members who pay a yearly fee for access to cars parked in designated spaces located conveniently throughout large cities. By allowing drivers under 25 years of age to rent cars and by targeting city dwellers who need to supplement their use of public transportation with short-term car rentals, Zipcar entered uncharted waters in the rental-car industry, growing rapidly in the process.

Blue-ocean strategies provide a company with a great opportunity in the short run. But they don't guarantee a company's long-term success, which depends more on whether a company can protect the market position they opened up and sustain their early advantage. See Illustration Capsule 6.1 for an example of a company that opened up new competitive space in online luxury retailing only to see their blue ocean waters ultimately turn red.

> Good defensive strategies can help protect a competitive advantage but rarely are the basis for creating one.

DEFENSIVE STRATEGIES—PROTECTING MARKET POSITION AND COMPETITIVE ADVANTAGE

In a competitive market, all firms are subject to offensive challenges from rivals. The purposes of defensive strategies are to lower the risk of being attacked, weaken the impact of any attack that occurs, and influence challengers to aim their efforts at other rivals. While defensive strategies usually don't enhance a firm's competitive advantage, they can definitely help fortify the firm's competitive position, protect its most valuable resources and capabilities from imitation, and defend whatever competitive advantage it might have. Defensive strategies can take either of two forms: actions to block challengers and actions to signal the likelihood of strong retaliation.

Blocking the Avenues Open to Challengers

The most frequently employed approach to defending a company's present position involves actions that restrict a challenger's options for initiating a competitive attack. There are any number of obstacles that can be put in the path of would-be challengers. A defender can introduce new features, add new models, or broaden its product line to close off gaps and vacant niches to opportunity-seeking challengers. It can thwart the efforts of rivals to attack with a lower price by maintaining economy-priced options of its own. It can try to discourage buyers from trying competitors' brands by lengthening warranties, offering free training and support services, and providing coupons and sample giveaways to buyers most prone to experiment. It can make early announcements about impending new products or price changes to induce potential buyers to postpone switching. It can challenge the quality or safety of rivals' products. Finally, a defender can grant volume discounts or better financing terms to dealers and distributors to discourage them from experimenting with other suppliers, or it can convince them to handle its product line *exclusively* and force competitors to use other distribution outlets.

> There are many ways to throw obstacles in the path of would-be challengers.

Signaling Challengers that Retaliation Is Likely

The goal of signaling challengers that strong retaliation is likely in the event of an attack is either to dissuade challengers from attacking at all or to divert them to less threatening options. Either goal can be achieved by letting challengers know the battle will cost more than it is worth. Signals to would-be challengers can be given by:

- Publicly announcing management's commitment to maintain the firm's present market share.
- Publicly committing the company to a policy of matching competitors' terms or prices.
- Maintaining a war chest of cash and marketable securities.
- Making an occasional strong counterresponse to the moves of weak competitors to enhance the firm's image as a tough defender.

Signaling is most likely to be an effective defensive strategy if the signal is accompanied by a credible commitment to follow through.

TIMING A COMPANY'S OFFENSIVE AND DEFENSIVE STRATEGIC MOVES

When to make a strategic move is often as crucial as *what* move to make. Timing is especially important when **first-mover advantages** or **disadvantages** exist. Under certain conditions, being first to initiate a strategic move can have a high payoff in the form of a competitive advantage that later movers can't dislodge. Moving first is no guarantee of success, however, since first movers also face some significant disadvantages. Indeed, there are circumstances in which it is more advantageous to be a fast follower or even a late mover. Because the timing of strategic moves can be consequential, it is important for company strategists to be aware of the nature of first-mover advantages and disadvantages and the conditions favoring each type.[12]

> **CORE CONCEPT**
>
> Because of **first-mover advantages** and **disadvantages,** competitive advantage can spring from *when* a move is made as well as from *what* move is made.

The Potential for First-Mover Advantages

Market pioneers and other types of first movers typically bear greater risks and greater development costs than firms that move later. If the market responds well to its initial move, the pioneer will benefit from a monopoly position (by virtue of being first to market) that enables it to recover its investment costs and make an attractive profit. If the firm's pioneering move gives it a competitive advantage that can be sustained even after other firms enter the market space, its first-mover advantage will be greater still. The extent of this type of advantage, however, will depend on whether and how fast follower firms can piggyback on the pioneer's success and either imitate or improve on its move.

> **LO 2**
>
> Recognize when being a first mover or a fast follower or a late mover is most advantageous.

The conditions that favor first-mover advantages, then, are those that slow the moves of follower firms or prevent them from imitating the success of the first mover. There are six such conditions in which first-mover advantages are most likely to arise:

1. *When pioneering helps build a firm's reputation and creates strong brand loyalty.* Customer loyalty to an early mover's brand can create a tie that binds, limiting the success of later entrants' attempts to poach from the early mover's customer base and steal market share.

2. *When a first-mover's customers will thereafter face significant switching costs.* Switching costs can protect first movers when consumers make large investments in learning how to use a specific company's product or in complementary products that are also brand-specific. Switching costs can also arise from loyalty programs or long-term contracts that give customers incentives to remain with an initial provider.

3. *When property rights protections thwart rapid imitation of the initial move.* In certain types of industries, property rights protections in the form of patents, copyrights, and trademarks prevent the ready imitation of an early mover's initial moves. First-mover advantages in pharmaceuticals, for example, are heavily dependent on patent protections, and patent races in this industry are common. In other industries, however, patents provide limited protection and can frequently be circumvented. Property rights protections also vary among nations, since they are dependent on a country's legal institutions and enforcement mechanisms.

4. *When an early lead enables the first mover to move down the learning curve ahead of rivals.* When there is a steep learning curve and when learning can be kept proprietary, a first mover can benefit from volume-based cost advantages that grow ever larger as its experience accumulates and its scale of operations increases. This type of first-mover advantage is self-reinforcing and, as such, can preserve a first-mover's competitive advantage over long periods of time. Honda's advantage in small multi-use motorcycles has been attributed to such an effect.

5. *When a first mover can set the technical standard for the industry.* In many technology-based industries, the market will converge around a single technical standard. By establishing the industry standard, a first mover can gain a powerful advantage that, like experienced-based advantages, builds over time. The lure of such an advantage, however, can result in standard wars among early movers, as each strives to set the industry standard. The key to winning such wars is to enter early on the basis of strong fast-cycle product development capabilities, gain the support of key customers and suppliers, employ penetration pricing, and make allies of the producers of complementary products.

Illustration Capsule 6.2 describes how **Amazon.com** achieved a first-mover advantage in online retailing.

The Potential for Late-Mover Advantages or First-Mover Disadvantages

There are instances when there are advantages *to being an adept follower* rather than a first mover. Late-mover advantages (or *first-mover disadvantages*) arise in four instances:

- When pioneering is more costly than imitative following, and only negligible learning-curve benefits accrue to the leader—a condition that allows a follower to end up with lower costs than the first-mover.

- When the products of an innovator are somewhat primitive and do not live up to buyer expectations, thus allowing a follower with better-performing products to win disenchanted buyers away from the leader.

- When rapid market evolution (due to fast-paced changes in either technology or buyer needs) gives second-movers the opening to leapfrog a first-mover's products with more attractive next-version products.

- When market uncertainties make it difficult to ascertain what will eventually succeed, allowing late movers to wait until these needs are clarified.

Amazon.com's First-Mover Advantage in Online Retailing

Amazon.com's path to becoming the world's largest online retailer began in 1994 when Jeff Bezos, a Manhattan hedge fund analyst at the time, noticed that the number of Internet users was increasing by 2,300 percent annually. Bezos saw the tremendous growth as an opportunity to sell products online that would be demanded by a large number of Internet users and could be easily shipped. Bezos launched the online bookseller Amazon.com in 1995. The startup's revenues soared to $148 million in 1997, $610 million in 1998, and $1.6 billion in 1999. Bezos's business plan—hatched while on a cross-country trip with his wife in 1994—made him *Time* magazine's Person of the Year in 1999.

The volume-based and reputational benefits of Amazon.com's early entry into online retailing had delivered a first-mover advantage, but between 2000 and 2011 Bezos undertook a series of additional strategic initiatives to solidify the company's number-one ranking in the industry. Bezos undertook a massive building program in the late-1990s that added five new warehouses and fulfillment centers totaling $300 million. The additional warehouse capacity was added years before it was needed, but Bezos wanted to move preemptively against potential rivals and ensure that, as demand continued to grow, the company could continue to offer its customers the best selection, the lowest prices, and the cheapest and most convenient delivery. The company also expanded its product line to include sporting goods, tools, toys, grocery items, electronics, and digital music downloads, giving it another means of maintaining its experience and scale-based

advantages. Amazon.com's 2010 revenues of $34.2 billion made it the world's largest Internet retailer and Jeff Bezos's shares in Amazon.com made him the 12th wealthiest person in the United States with an estimated net worth of $12.6 billion.

Moving down the learning curve in Internet retailing was not an entirely straightforward process for Amazon.com. Bezos commented in a *Fortune* article profiling the company, "We were investors in every bankrupt, 1999-vintage e-commerce startup. Pets.com, living.com, kozmo.com. We invested in a lot of high-profile flameouts." He went on to specify that although the ventures were a "waste of money," they "didn't take us off our own mission." Bezos also suggested that gaining advantage as a first mover is "taking a million tiny steps—and learning quickly from your missteps."

Sources: Mark Brohan, "The Top 500 Guide," *Internet Retailer,* June 2009 (accessed at www.internetretailer.com on June 17, 2009); Josh Quittner, "How Jeff Bezos Rules the Retail Space," *Fortune,* May 5, 2008, pp. 126–34; company website.

To Be a First Mover or Not

In weighing the pros and cons of being a first mover versus a fast follower versus a late mover, it matters whether the race to market leadership in a particular industry is a marathon or a sprint. In marathons, a slow mover is not unduly penalized—first-mover advantages can be fleeting, and there's ample time for fast followers and sometimes even late movers to catch up.[13] Thus the speed at which the pioneering innovation is likely to catch on matters considerably as companies struggle with whether to pursue an emerging market opportunity aggressively (as a first mover or fast follower) or cautiously (as a late mover). For instance, it took 5.5 years for worldwide mobile phone use to grow from 10 million to 100 million worldwide and close to 10 years for the number of at-home broadband subscribers to grow to 100 million worldwide. The lesson here is that there is a market penetration curve for every emerging opportunity. Typically, the curve has an inflection point at which all the pieces of the business model fall into place, buyer demand explodes, and the market takes off. The inflection point can come early on a fast-rising curve (like the use of e-mail) or farther on up a slow-rising curve (like the use of broadband). Any company that seeks competitive advantage by being a first mover thus needs to ask some hard questions:

- Does market takeoff depend on the development of complementary products or services that currently are not available?
- Is new infrastructure required before buyer demand can surge?
- Will buyers need to learn new skills or adopt new behaviors?
- Will buyers encounter high switching costs in moving to the newly introduced product or service?
- Are there influential competitors in a position to delay or derail the efforts of a first mover?

When the answers to any of these questions are yes, then a company must be careful not to pour too many resources into getting ahead of the market opportunity—the race is likely going to be more of a 10-year marathon than a 2-year sprint.[14] On the other hand, if the market is a winner-take-all type of market, where powerful first-mover advantages insulate early entrants from competition and prevent later movers from making any headway, then it may be best to move quickly despite the risks.

STRENGTHENING A COMPANY'S MARKET POSITION VIA ITS SCOPE OF OPERATIONS

CORE CONCEPT

The **scope of the firm** refers to the range of activities which the firm performs internally, the breadth of its product and service offerings, the extent of its geographic market presence, and its mix of businesses.

Apart from considerations of competitive moves and their timing, there is another set of managerial decisions that can affect the strength of a company's market position. These decisions concern the scope of a company's operations—the breadth of its activities and the extent of its market reach. Decisions regarding the **scope of the firm** focus on which activities a firm will perform internally and which it will not. For example, should Panera Bread Company produce the fresh dough that its company-owned and franchised bakery-cafés use in making baguettes, pastries, bagels, and other types of bread, or should it obtain its dough from outside suppliers? Scope decisions also concern which segments of the market to serve—decisions that can include geographic market segments as well as product and service segments. Should Panera expand its menu to include light dinner entrees? Should it offer delivery or drive-through service? Should it expand into all 50 states or concentrate on strengthening its market presence regionally?

Decisions such as these, in essence, determine where the boundaries of a firm lie and the degree to which the operations within those boundaries cohere. They also have much to do with the direction and extent of a business's growth. In this chapter, we introduce the topic of company scope and discuss different types of scope decisions in relation to a company's business-level strategy. In the next two chapters, we develop two additional dimensions of a firm's scope. Chapter 7 focuses on international expansion—a matter of extending the company's geographic scope into foreign markets. Chapter 8 takes up the topic of corporate strategy, which concerns diversifying into a mix of different businesses. Scope issues are at the very heart of corporate-level strategy.

Several dimensions of firm scope have relevance for business-level strategy in terms of their capacity to strengthen a company's position in a given market. These include the firm's **horizontal scope,** which is the range of product and service segments that the firm serves within its product or service market. Mergers and acquisitions involving other market participants provide a means for a company to expand its horizontal scope. Expanding the firm's vertical scope by means of vertical integration can also affect the success of its market strategy. **Vertical scope** is the extent to which the firm engages in the various activities that make up the industry's entire value chain system, from initial activities such as raw-material production all the way to retailing and after-sales service activities. Outsourcing decisions concern another dimension of scope since they involve narrowing the firm's boundaries with respect to its participation in value chain activities. We discuss the pros and cons of each of these options in the sections that follow. Since strategic alliances and partnerships provide an alternative to vertical integration and acquisition strategies and are sometimes used to facilitate outsourcing, we conclude this chapter with a discussion of the benefits and challenges associated with cooperative arrangements of this nature.

> **CORE CONCEPT**
>
> **Horizontal scope** is the range of product and service segments that a firm serves within its focal market.

> **CORE CONCEPT**
>
> **Vertical scope** is the extent to which a firm's internal activities encompass one, some, many, or all of the activities that make up an industry's entire value chain system, ranging from raw-material production to final sales and service activities.

HORIZONTAL MERGER AND ACQUISITION STRATEGIES

Mergers and acquisitions are much-used strategic options to strengthen a company's market position. A *merger* is the combining of two or more companies into a single corporate entity, with the newly created company often taking on a new name. An *acquisition* is a combination in which one company, the acquirer, purchases and absorbs the operations of another, the acquired. The difference between a merger and an acquisition relates more to the details of ownership, management control, and financial arrangements than to strategy and competitive advantage. The resources and competitive capabilities of the newly created enterprise end up much the same whether the combination is the result of an acquisition or merger.

Horizontal mergers and acquisitions, which involve combining the operations of firms within the same product or service market, provide an effective means for firms to rapidly increase the scale and horizontal scope of their core business. For example, Microsoft has used an aggressive acquisition strategy to extend its software business into new segments and strengthen its technological capabilities in this domain. Mergers between airlines, such as the recent United–Continental merger, have increased their scale of operations and extended their reach geographically.

Merger and acquisition strategies typically set sights on achieving any of five objectives:[15]

> **LO 3**
>
> Become aware of the strategic benefits and risks of expanding a company's horizontal scope through mergers and acquisitions.

1. *Creating a more cost-efficient operation out of the combined companies.* Many mergers and acquisitions are undertaken with the objective of transforming two or more high-cost companies into one lean competitor with significantly lower costs. When a company acquires another company in the same industry, there's usually enough

overlap in operations that less efficient plants can be closed or distribution and sales activities partly combined and downsized. Likewise, it is usually feasible to squeeze out cost savings in administrative activities, again by combining and downsizing such administrative activities as finance and accounting, information technology, human resources, and so on. The combined companies may also be able to reduce supply chain costs because of greater bargaining power over common suppliers and closer collaboration with supply chain partners. By helping to consolidate the industry and remove excess capacity, such combinations can also reduce industry rivalry and improve industry profitability.

2. *Expanding a company's geographic coverage.* One of the best and quickest ways to expand a company's geographic coverage is to acquire rivals with operations in the desired locations. Since a company's size increases with its geographic scope, another benefit is increased bargaining power with the company's suppliers or buyers. Greater geographic coverage can also contribute to product differentiation by enhancing a company's name recognition and brand awareness. Banks like Wells Fargo and Bank of America have used acquisition strategies to establish a market presence and gain name recognition in an ever-growing number of states and localities.

3. *Extending the company's business into new product categories.* Many times a company has gaps in its product line that need to be filled in order to offer customers a more effective product bundle or the benefits of one-stop-shopping. For example, customers might prefer to acquire a suite of software applications from a single vendor that can offer more integrated solutions to the company's problems. Acquisition can be a quicker and more potent way to broaden a company's product line than going through the exercise of introducing a company's own new product to fill the gap. Coca-Cola has increased the effectiveness of the product bundle it provides to retailers by acquiring beverage makers Minute Maid, Odwalla, Hi-C, and Glaceau.

4. *Gaining quick access to new technologies or complementary resources and capabilities.* Making acquisitions to bolster a company's technological know-how or to expand its skills and capabilities allows a company to bypass a time-consuming and expensive internal effort to build desirable new resources and capabilities. From 2000 through April 2011, Cisco Systems purchased 97 companies to give it more technological reach and product breadth, thereby enhancing its standing as the world's largest provider of hardware, software, and services for building and operating Internet networks.

5. *Leading the convergence of industries whose boundaries are being blurred by changing technologies and new market opportunities.* In fast-cycle industries or industries whose boundaries are changing, companies can use acquisition strategies to hedge their bets about the direction that an industry will take, to increase their capacity to meet changing demands, and to respond flexibly to changing buyer needs and technological demands. News Corporation has prepared for the convergence of media services with the purchase of satellite TV companies to complement its media holdings in TV broadcasting (the Fox network and TV stations in various countries), cable TV (Fox News, Fox Sports, and FX), filmed entertainment (Twentieth Century Fox and Fox studios), newspapers, magazines, and book publishing.

Numerous companies have employed a horizontal acquisition strategy to catapult themselves from the ranks of the unknown into positions of market leadership. Wells Fargo began as a small regional bank and grew via acquisition, transforming itself into a nationwide bank with global presence. By 2011, it still lagged behind the largest banks in terms of assets, but far outclassed them in terms of efficiency, profitability, and market value.[16] Moreover, it was also listed by *Fortune* magazine in 2011 as among the world's "Most Admired Companies."

Bristol-Myers Squibb's "String-of-Pearls" Horizontal Acquisition Strategy

Back in 2007, the pharmaceutical company Bristol-Myers Squibb had a problem: its top-selling drugs, Plavix and Abilify, would go off patent by 2012 and its drug pipeline was nearly empty. Together these drugs (the first for heart attacks, the second for depression) accounted for nearly half of the company's sales. Not surprisingly, the company's stock price had stagnated and was underperforming that of its peers.

Developing new drugs is difficult: new drugs must be identified, tested in increasingly sophisticated trials and approved by the Food and Drug Administration. On average, this process takes 13 years and costs $2B. The success rate is low: only one drug in eight manages to pass through clinical testing. In 2007, Bristol-Myers Squibb had only six new drugs at the clinical testing stage.

At the time, many drug companies were diversifying into new markets like over-the-counter drugs to better manage drug development risk. Bristol-Myers Squibb's management pursued a different strategy: product diversification through horizontal acquisitions. Bristol-Myers Squibb targeted small companies in new treatment areas, with the objective of reducing new product development risk by betting on pre-identified drugs. The small companies it targeted, with one or two drugs in development, needed cash; Bristol-Myers Squibb needed new drugs. The firm's management called this its "string-of-pearls" strategy.

To implement its approach and obtain the cash it needed, Bristol-Myers Squibb sold its stake in Mead

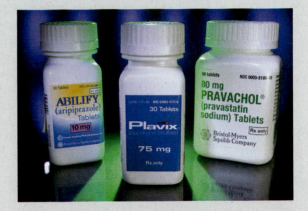

Johnson, a nutritional supplement manufacturer. Then, it went on a shopping spree. Starting in 2007, the company spent over $8B on 18 transactions, including 12 horizontal acquisitions. In the process, the company acquired many promising new drug candidates for common diseases such as cancer, cardiovascular disease, rheumatoid arthritis, and Hepatitis C.

By early 2012, the company's string-of-pearls acquisitions were estimated to have added over $4B of new revenue to the company's coffers. Analysts reported that Bristol-Myers Squibb had one of the best pipelines among drug makers. Investors agreed: between 2007 and 2012, the company's stock price climbed 20 percent, substantially outperforming that of its peers.

Developed with Dennis L. Huggins.

Sources: D. Armstrong and M. Tirrell, "Bristol's Buy of Inhibitex for Hepatitis Drug Won't Be Last," *Bloomberg Businessweek,* January 2012 (accessed at www.bloomberg.com on January 30, 2012); S. M. Paul, et al., "How to Improve R&D Productivity: the Pharmaceutical Industry's Grand Challenge," *Nature Reviews,* March 2010, pp. 203–214; Bristol-Myers Squibb 2007 and 2011 Annual Reports.

Illustration Capsule 6.3 describes how Bristol-Myers Squibb developed its "string-of-pearls" horizontal acquisition strategy to fill in its pharmaceutical product development gaps.

Why Mergers and Acquisitions Sometimes Fail to Produce Anticipated Results

Despite many successes, mergers and acquisitions do not always produce the hoped-for outcomes.[17] Cost savings may prove smaller than expected. Gains in competitive capabilities may take substantially longer to realize or, worse, may never materialize at all. Efforts to mesh the corporate cultures can stall due to formidable resistance from organization members. Key employees at the acquired company can quickly become disenchanted and leave; the morale of company personnel who remain can drop to disturbingly low levels because they disagree with newly instituted changes. Differences in management styles and operating procedures can prove hard to resolve. In addition, the managers appointed to oversee the integration of a newly acquired company can make mistakes in deciding which activities to leave alone and which activities to meld into their own operations and systems.

A number of mergers/acquisitions have been notably unsuccessful. eBay's $2.6 billion acquisition of Skype in 2005 proved to be a mistake—eBay wrote off $900 million of its Skype investment in 2007 and sold 70 percent of its ownership in Skype in September 2009 to a group of investors. While the company finally found a white knight in Microsoft in 2011, the jury is out as to whether or not Microsoft can make this acquisition work. A number of recent mergers and acquisitions have yet to live up to expectations—prominent examples include Oracle's acquisition of Sun Microsystems, the Fiat–Chrysler deal, and Bank of America's acquisition of Countrywide Financial.

VERTICAL INTEGRATION STRATEGIES

LO 4

Learn the advantages and disadvantages of extending the company's scope of operations via vertical integration.

Expanding the firm's vertical scope by means of a vertical integration strategy provides another way to strengthen the company's position in its core market. A **vertically integrated firm** is one that participates in multiple segments or stages of an industry's value chain system. A good example of a vertically integrated firm is Maple Leaf Foods, a major Canadian producer of fresh and processed meats whose best-selling brands include Maple Leaf and Schneiders. Maple Leaf Foods participates in hog and poultry production, with company-owned hog and poultry farms; it has its own meat-processing and rendering facilities; it packages its products and distributes them from company-owned distribution centers; and it conducts marketing, sales, and customer service activities for its wholesale and retail buyers but does not otherwise participate in the final stage of the meat processing vertical chain—the retailing stage.

CORE CONCEPT

A **vertically integrated firm** is one that performs value chain activities along more than one stage of an industry's value chain system.

A vertical integration strategy can expand the firm's range of activities *backward* into sources of supply and/or *forward* toward end users. When Tiffany & Co, a manufacturer and retailer of fine jewelry, began sourcing, cutting, and polishing its own diamonds, it integrated backward along the diamond supply chain. Mining giant De Beers Group and Canadian miner Aber Diamond integrated forward when they entered the diamond retailing business.

A firm can pursue vertical integration by starting its own operations in other stages of the vertical activity chain or by acquiring a company already performing the activities it wants to bring in-house. Vertical integration strategies can aim at *full integration* (participating in all stages of the vertical chain) or *partial integration* (building positions in selected stages of the vertical chain). Firms can also engage in *tapered integration* strategies, which involve a mix of in-house and outsourced activity in any given stage of the vertical chain. Oil companies, for instance, supply their refineries with oil from their own wells as well as with oil that they purchase from other producers—they engage in tapered backward integration. Boston Beer Company, the maker of Samuel Adams, engages in tapered forward integration, since it operates brew-pubs, but sells the majority of its products through third-party distributors.

The Advantages of a Vertical Integration Strategy

Under the right conditions, a vertical integration strategy can add materially to a company's technological capabilities, strengthen the firm's competitive position, and boost its profitability.[18] But it is important to keep in mind that vertical integration has no real payoff strategywise or profitwise unless the extra investment can be justified by compensating improvements in company costs, differentiation, or competitive strength.

Integrating Backward to Achieve Greater Competitiveness

It is harder than one might think to generate cost savings or improve profitability by integrating backward into activities such as parts and components manufacture (which could otherwise be purchased from suppliers with specialized expertise in making these parts and components). For **backward integration** to be a cost-saving and profitable strategy, a company must be able to (1) achieve the same scale economies as outside suppliers and (2) match or beat suppliers' production efficiency with no drop-off in quality. Neither outcome is a slam dunk. To begin with, a company's in-house requirements are often too small to reach the optimum size for low-cost operation. Furthermore, matching the production efficiency of suppliers is fraught with problems when suppliers have considerable production experience of their own, when the technology they employ has elements that are hard to master, and/or when substantial R&D expertise is required to develop next-version components or keep pace with advancing technology in components production.

> **CORE CONCEPT**
>
> **Backward integration** involves entry into activities previously performed by suppliers or other enterprises positioned along earlier stages of the industry value chain system; **forward integration** involves entry into value chain system activities closer to the end user.

That said, occasions still arise when a company can improve its cost position and competitiveness by performing a broader range of industry value chain activities in-house rather than having such activities performed by outside suppliers. When suppliers have outsized profit margins or when there is a sole supplier, vertical integration can lower costs by limiting supplier power. Vertical integration can also lower costs by facilitating the coordination of production flows and avoiding bottleneck problems. Furthermore, when a company has proprietary know-how that it wants to keep from rivals, then in-house performance of value-adding activities related to this know-how is beneficial even if such activities could be performed by outsiders. Apple recently decided to integrate backward into producing its own chips for iPhones, chiefly because chips are a major cost component, they have big profit margins, and in-house production would help coordinate design tasks and protect Apple's proprietary iPhone technology. International Paper Company backward integrates into pulp mills that it sets up near its paper mills (outside suppliers are generally unwilling to make a site-specific investment for a buyer) and reaps the benefits of coordinated production flows, energy savings, and transportation economies.

Backward vertical integration can produce a differentiation-based competitive advantage when performing activities internally contributes to a better quality product/service offering, improves the caliber of customer service, or in other ways enhances the performance of the final product. On occasion, integrating into more stages along the industry value chain system can add to a company's differentiation capabilities by allowing it to build or strengthen its core competencies, better master key skills or strategy-critical technologies, or add features that deliver greater customer value. Spanish clothing maker Inditex has backward integrated into fabric making, as well as garment design and manufacture, for its successful Zara brand. By tightly controlling the process and postponing dyeing until later stages, Zara can respond quickly to changes in fashion trends and supply its customers with the hottest items. NewsCorp backward integrated into film studios (Twentieth Century Fox) and TV program production to ensure access to high-quality content for its TV stations (and to limit supplier power).

Integrating Forward to Enhance Competitiveness   Like backward integration, **forward integration** can lower costs by increasing efficiency and bargaining power. In addition, it can allow manufacturers to gain better access to

end users, improve market visibility, and include the end user's purchasing experience as a differentiating feature. For example, Ducati and Harley motorcycles both have company-owned retail stores that are essentially little museums, filled with iconography, that provide an environment conducive to selling not only motorcycles and gear but also memorabilia, clothing, and other items featuring the brand. Insurance companies and brokerages have the ability to make consumers' interactions with local agents and office personnel a differentiating feature by focusing on building relationships.

In many industries, independent sales agents, wholesalers, and retailers handle competing brands of the same product and have no allegiance to any one company's brand—they tend to push whatever offers the biggest profits. An independent insurance agency, for example, represents a number of different insurance companies. Under this arrangement, there's plenty of opportunity for independent agents to promote the policies of favored insurers over others. An insurance company may conclude, therefore, that it is better off integrating forward and setting up its own local offices, as State Farm and Allstate have done. Likewise, it can be advantageous for a manufacturer to integrate forward into wholesaling or retailing rather than depend on the sales efforts of independent distributors/retailers that stock multiple brands and steer customers to the brands on which they earn the highest profit margins. To avoid dependence on distributors/dealers with divided loyalties, Goodyear has integrated forward into company-owned and franchised retail tire stores. Consumer-goods companies like Bath & Body Works, Tommy Hilfiger, Chico's, and Polo Ralph Lauren have integrated forward into retailing and operate their own branded stores in factory outlet malls, enabling them to move overstocked items, slow-selling items, and seconds.

Some producers have opted to integrate forward by selling directly to customers at the company's website. Bypassing regular wholesale/retail channels in favor of direct sales and Internet retailing can have appeal if it reinforces the brand and enhances consumer satisfaction or if it lowers distribution costs, produces a relative cost advantage over certain rivals, and results in lower selling prices to end users. In addition, sellers are compelled to include the Internet as a retail channel when a sufficiently large number of buyers in an industry prefer to make purchases online. However, a company that is vigorously pursuing online sales to consumers at the same time that it is also heavily promoting sales to consumers through its network of wholesalers and retailers is *competing directly against its distribution allies.* Such actions constitute *channel conflict* and create a tricky route to negotiate. A company that is actively trying to expand online sales to consumers is signaling a weak strategic commitment to its dealers *and* a willingness to cannibalize dealers' sales and growth potential. The likely result is angry dealers and loss of dealer goodwill. Quite possibly, a company may stand to lose more sales by offending its dealers than it gains from its own online sales effort. Consequently, in industries where the strong support and goodwill of dealer networks is essential, companies may conclude that it is important to avoid channel conflict and that *their websites should be designed to partner with dealers rather than compete against them.*

The Disadvantages of a Vertical Integration Strategy

Vertical integration has some substantial drawbacks beyond the potential for channel conflict.[19] The most serious drawbacks to vertical integration include the following concerns:

- Vertical integration raises a firm's capital investment in the industry, thereby *increasing business risk.*

- Vertically integrated companies are often *slow to embrace technological advances* or more efficient production methods when they are saddled with older technology or facilities. A company that obtains parts and components from outside suppliers can always shop the market for the newest, best, and cheapest parts, whereas a vertically integrated firm saddled with older technology or facilities may choose to continue making suboptimal parts rather than face the high costs of premature abandonment.

- Vertical integration can result in *less flexibility in accommodating shifting buyer preferences* when a new product design doesn't include parts and components that the company makes in-house. It is one thing to design out a component made by a supplier and another to design out a component being made in-house (which can mean laying off employees and writing off the associated investment in equipment and facilities). Integrating forward or backward locks a firm into relying on its own in-house activities and sources of supply.

- Vertical integration *may not enable a company to realize economies of scale* if its production levels are below the minimum efficient scale. Small companies in particular are likely to suffer a cost disadvantage by producing in-house when suppliers that serve many small companies can realize scale economies that a small company cannot attain on its own.

- Vertical integration poses all kinds of *capacity matching problems.* In motor vehicle manufacturing, for example, the most efficient scale of operation for making axles is different from the most economic volume for radiators, and different yet again for both engines and transmissions. Consequently, integrating across several production stages in ways that achieve the lowest feasible costs can be a monumental challenge.

- Integration forward or backward often *calls for developing different types of resources and capabilities.* Parts and components manufacturing, assembly operations, wholesale distribution and retailing, and direct sales via the Internet represent different kinds of businesses, operating in different types of industries, with different key success factors. Many manufacturers learn the hard way that company-owned wholesale/retail networks present many headaches, fit poorly with what they do best, and don't always add the kind of value to their core business they thought they would.

In today's world of close working relationships with suppliers and efficient supply chain management systems, *very few businesses can make a case for integrating backward into the business of suppliers* to ensure a reliable supply of materials and components or to reduce production costs. The best materials and components suppliers stay abreast of advancing technology and are adept in improving their efficiency and keeping their costs and prices as low as possible. A company that pursues a vertical integration strategy and tries to produce many parts and components in-house is likely to find itself very hard-pressed to keep up with technological advances and cutting-edge production practices for each part and component used in making its product.

Weighing the Pros and Cons of Vertical Integration

All in all, therefore, a strategy of vertical integration can have both important strengths and weaknesses. The tip of the scales depends on (1) whether vertical integration can enhance the performance of strategy-critical activities in ways that lower cost, build expertise, protect proprietary know-how, or increase differentiation, (2) the impact of vertical integration on investment costs, flexibility, and response times, (3) the administrative costs of coordinating operations across more vertical chain activities, and (4) how difficult it will be for the company to acquire the set of skills and capabilities needed to operate in another stage of the vertical chain. *Vertical integration strategies have merit*

The Drawbacks of Strategic Alliances and Partnerships

While strategic alliances provide a way of obtaining the benefits of vertical integration, mergers and acquisitions, and outsourcing, they also suffer from some of the same drawbacks. Anticipated gains may fail to materialize due to an overly optimistic view of the synergies or a poor fit in terms of the combination of resources and capabilities. When outsourcing is conducted via alliances, there is no less risk of becoming dependent on other companies for essential expertise and capabilities—indeed, this may be the Achilles' heel of such alliances. Moreover, there are additional pitfalls to collaborative arrangements. The greatest danger is that a partner will gain access to a company's proprietary knowledge base, technologies, or trade secrets, enabling the partner to match the company's core strengths and costing the company its hard-won competitive advantage. This risk is greatest when the alliance is among industry rivals or when the alliance is for the purpose of collaborative R&D, since this type of partnership requires an extensive exchange of closely held information.

The question for managers is when to engage in a strategic alliance and when to choose an alternative means of meeting their objectives. The answer to this question depends on the relative advantages of each method and the circumstances under which each type of organizational arrangement is favored.

The principle advantages of strategic alliances over vertical integration or horizontal mergers/acquisitons are threefold:

1. They lower investment costs and risks for each partner by facilitating resource pooling and risk sharing. This can be particularly important when investment needs and uncertainty are high, such as when a dominant technology standard has not yet emerged.

2. They are more flexible organizational forms and allow for a more adaptive response to changing conditions. Flexibility is essential when environmental conditions or technologies are changing rapidly. Moreover, strategic alliances under such circumstances may enable the development of each partner's dynamic capabilities.

3. They are more rapidly deployed—a critical factor when speed is of the essence. Speed is of the essence when there is a winner-take-all type of competitive situation, such as the race for a dominant technological design or a race down a steep experience curve, where there is a large first-mover advantage.

The key advantages of using strategic alliances rather than arm's-length transactions to manage outsourcing are (1) the increased ability to exercise control over the partners' activities and (2) a greater willingness for the partners to make relationship-specific investments. Arm's-length transactions discourage such investments since they imply less commitment and do not build trust.

On the other hand, there are circumstances when other organizational mechanisms are preferable to alliances and partnering. Mergers and acquisitions are especially suited for situations in which strategic alliances or partnerships do not go far enough in providing a company with access to needed resources and capabilities. Ownership ties are more permanent than partnership ties, allowing the operations of the merger/acquisition participants to be tightly integrated and creating more in-house control and autonomy. Other organizational mechanisms are also preferable to alliances when there is limited property rights protection for valuable know-how and when companies fear being taken advantage of by opportunistic partners.

While it is important for managers to understand when strategic alliances and partnerships are most likely (and least likely) to prove useful, it is also important to know how to manage them.

How to Make Strategic Alliances Work

A surprisingly large number of alliances never live up to expectations. Even though the number of strategic alliances increases by about 25 percent annually, about 60 to 70 percent of alliances continue to fail each year. The success of an alliance depends on how well the partners work together, their capacity to respond and adapt to changing internal and external conditions, and their willingness to renegotiate the bargain if circumstances so warrant. A successful alliance requires real in-the-trenches collaboration, not merely an arm's-length exchange of ideas. Unless partners place a high value on the skills, resources, and contributions each brings to the alliance and the cooperative arrangement results in valuable win–win outcomes, it is doomed to fail.

While the track record for strategic alliances is poor on average, many companies have learned how to manage strategic alliances successfully and routinely defy these averages. Samsung Group, which includes Samsung Electronics, successfully manages an ecosystem of over 1,300 partnerships that enable productive activities from global procurement to local marketing to collaborative R&D. Companies that have greater success in managing their strategic alliances and partnerships often credit the following factors:

- *They create a system for managing their alliances.* Companies need to manage their alliances in a systematic fashion, just as they manage other functions. This means setting up a process for managing the different aspects of alliance management from partner selection to alliance termination procedures. To ensure that the system is followed on a routine basis by all company managers, many companies create a set of explicit procedures, process templates, manuals, or the like.
- *They build relationships with their partners and establish trust.* Establishing strong interpersonal relationships is a critical factor in making strategic alliances work since they facilitate opening up channels of communication, coordinating activity, aligning interests, and building trust.
- *They protect themselves from the threat of opportunism by setting up safeguards.* There are a number of means for preventing a company from being taken advantage of by an untrustworthy partner or unwittingly losing control over key assets. Cisco Systems, for example, does not divulge the source code for its designs to its alliance partners, thereby controlling the initiation of all improvements and safeguarding its innovations from imitation. Contractual safeguards, including noncompete clauses, can provide other forms of protection.
- *They make commitments to their partners and see that their partners do the same.* When partners make credible commitments to a joint enterprise, they have stronger incentives for making it work and are less likely to "free-ride" on the efforts of other partners. Because of this, equity-based alliances tend to be more successful than nonequity alliances.[28]
- *They make learning a routine part of the management process.* There are always opportunities for learning from a partner, but organizational learning does not take place automatically. Whatever learning occurs cannot add to a company's knowledge base unless the learning is incorporated systematically into the company's routines and practices.

FIGURE 7.1   The Diamond of National Competitive Advantage

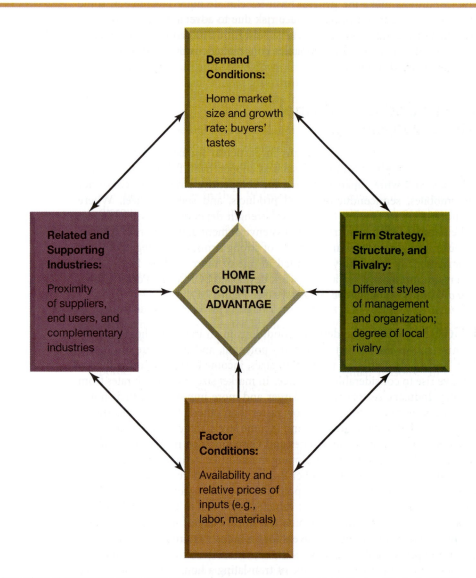

Source: Adapted from M. Porter, "The Competitive Advantage of Nations," *Harvard Business Review,* March–April 1990, pp. 73–93.

Related and Supporting Industries   Robust industries often develop as part of a cluster of related industries, including suppliers of components and capital equipment, end users, and the makers of complementary products, including those that are technologically related. The sports car makers Ferrari and Maserati, for example, are located in an area of Italy known as the "engine technological district" that includes other firms involved in racing, such as Ducati Motorcycles, along with hundreds of small suppliers. The advantage to firms that develop as part of a related-industry cluster comes from the close collaboration with key suppliers and the greater knowledge sharing throughout the cluster, resulting in greater efficiency and innovativeness.

Firm Strategy, Structure, and Rivalry   Different country environments foster the development of different styles of management, organization, and strategy. For example, strategic alliances are a more common strategy for firms from Asian or Latin American countries, which emphasize trust and cooperation in their organizations, than for firms from North America, where individualism is more influential. In addition, countries vary in terms of the competitive rivalry of their industries. Fierce rivalry in home markets tends to hone domestic firms' competitive capabilities and ready them for competing internationally.

For an industry in a particular country to become competitively strong, all four factors must be favorable for that industry. When they are, the industry is likely to contain firms that are capable of competing successfully in the international arena. Thus the diamond framework can be used to reveal the answers to several questions that are important for competing on an international basis. First, it can help predict where foreign entrants into an industry are most likely to come from. This can help managers prepare to cope with new foreign competitors, since the framework also reveals something about the basis of the new rivals' strengths. Second, it can reveal the countries in which foreign rivals are likely to be weakest and thus help managers decide which foreign markets to enter first. And third, because it focuses on the attributes of a country's business environment that allow firms to flourish, it reveals something about the advantages of conducting particular business activities in that country. Thus the diamond framework is an aid to deciding where to locate different value chain activities most beneficially—a topic that we address next.

Locating Value Chain Activities Advantageously

Increasingly, companies are locating different value chain activities in different parts of the world to exploit location-based advantages that vary from country to country. This is particularly evident with respect to the location of manufacturing activities. Differences in wage rates, worker productivity, energy costs and the like, create sizable variations in manufacturing costs from country to country. By locating its plants in certain countries, firms in some industries can reap major manufacturing cost advantages because of lower input costs (especially labor), relaxed government regulations, the proximity of suppliers and technologically related industries, or unique natural resources. In such cases, the low-cost countries become principal production sites, with most of the output being exported to markets in other parts of the world. Companies that build production facilities in low-cost countries (or that source their products from contract manufacturers in these countries) gain a competitive advantage over rivals with plants in countries where costs are higher. The competitive role of low manufacturing costs is most evident in low-wage countries like China, India, Pakistan, Cambodia, Vietnam, Mexico, Brazil, Guatemala, the Philippines, and several countries in Africa and eastern Europe that have become production havens for manufactured goods with high labor content (especially textiles and apparel). Hourly compensation for manufacturing workers in 2009 averaged about $1.36 in China, $1.50 in the Philippines, $5.38 in Mexico, $5.96 in Brazil, $7.76 in Taiwan, $8.62 in Hungary, $11.95 in Portugal, $14.20 in South Korea, $30.36 in Japan, $33.53 in the U.S., $29.60 in Canada, $46.52 in Germany, and $53.89 in Norway.[6] Not surprisingly, China has emerged as the manufacturing capital of the world—virtually all of the world's major manufacturing companies now have facilities in China.

For other types of value chain activities, input quality or availability are more important considerations. Tiffany entered the mining industry in Canada to access diamonds that could be certified as "conflict free" and not associated with either the funding of African wars or unethical mining conditions. Many U.S. companies locate call centers in countries such as India and Ireland, where English is spoken and the workforce is well educated. Other companies locate R&D activities in countries where there are prestigious research institutions and well-trained scientists and engineers. Likewise, concerns about short delivery times and low shipping costs make some countries better locations than others for establishing distribution centers.

The Impact of Government Policies and Economic Conditions in Host Countries

Cross-country variations in government policies and economic conditions affect both the opportunities available to a foreign entrant and the risks of operating within that country. The governments of some countries are anxious to attract foreign investments and go all out to create a business climate that outsiders will view as favorable. Governments anxious to spur economic growth, create more jobs, and raise living standards for their citizens usually enact policies aimed at stimulating business innovation and capital investment. They may provide such incentives as reduced taxes, low-cost loans, site location and site development assistance, and government-sponsored training for workers to encourage companies to construct production and distribution facilities. When new business-related issues or developments arise, pro-business governments make a practice of seeking advice and counsel from business leaders. When tougher business-related regulations are deemed appropriate, they endeavor to make the transition to more costly and stringent regulations somewhat business-friendly rather than adversarial.

On the other hand, governments sometimes enact policies that, from a business perspective, make locating facilities within a country's borders less attractive. For example, the nature of a company's operations may make it particularly costly to achieve compliance with a country's environmental regulations. Some governments, desirous of discouraging foreign imports, provide subsidies and low-interest loans to domestic companies (to enable them to better compete against foreign companies), enact deliberately burdensome procedures and requirements for imported goods to pass customs inspection (to make it harder for imported goods to compete against the products of local businesses), and impose tariffs or quotas on the imports of certain goods (also to help protect local businesses from foreign competition). Additionally, they may specify that a certain percentage of the parts and components used in manufacturing a product be obtained from local suppliers, require prior approval of capital spending projects, limit withdrawal of funds from the country, and require minority (sometimes majority) ownership of foreign company operations by local companies or investors. There are times when a government may place restrictions on exports to ensure adequate local supplies and regulate the prices of imported and locally produced goods. Such government actions make a country's business climate less attractive and in some cases may be sufficiently onerous as to discourage a company from locating production or distribution facilities in that country or maybe even selling its products in that country.

A country's business climate is also a function of the political and economic risks associated with operating within its borders. **Political risks** have to do with the instability of weak governments, the likelihood of new onerous legislation or regulations on foreign-owned businesses, and the potential for future elections to produce corrupt or tyrannical government leaders. In industries that a government deems critical to the national welfare, there is sometimes a risk that the government will nationalize the industry and expropriate the assets of foreign companies. In 2010, for example, Ecuador threatened to expropriate the holdings of all foreign oil companies that refused to sign new contracts giving the state control of all production. Other political risks include the loss of investments due to war or political unrest, regulatory changes that create operating uncertainties, security risks due to terrorism, and corruption. **Economic risks** have to do with the stability of a country's economy—whether inflation rates might skyrocket or whether uncontrolled deficit-spending on the part of government could lead to a breakdown of the country's monetary system and prolonged economic distress. The threat of piracy and lack of protection for intellectual property are also sources of economic risk. Another is fluctuations in the value of different currencies—a factor that we discuss in more detail next.

The Risks of Adverse Exchange Rate Shifts

When companies produce and market their products and services in many different countries, they are subject to the impacts of sometimes favorable and sometimes unfavorable changes in currency exchange rates. The rates of exchange between different currencies can vary by as much as 20 to 40 percent annually, with the changes occurring sometimes gradually and sometimes swiftly. Sizable shifts in exchange rates, which tend to be hard to predict because of the variety of factors involved and the uncertainties surrounding when and by how much these factors will change, shuffle the global cards of which countries represent the low-cost manufacturing locations and which rivals have the upper hand in the marketplace.

To understand the economic risks associated with fluctuating exchange rates, consider the case of a U.S. company that has located manufacturing facilities in Brazil (where the currency is *reals*—pronounced "ray-alls") and that exports most of the Brazilian-made goods to markets in the European Union (where the currency is euros). To keep the numbers simple, assume that the exchange rate is 4 Brazilian reals for 1 euro and that the product being made in Brazil has a manufacturing cost of 4 Brazilian reals (or 1 euro). Now suppose that for some reason the exchange rate shifts from 4 reals per euro to 5 reals per euro (meaning that the real has declined in value and that the euro is stronger). Making the product in Brazil is now more cost-competitive because a Brazilian good costing 4 reals to produce has fallen to only 0.8 euro at the new exchange rate (4 reals divided by 5 reals per euro = 0.8 euro) and this clearly puts the producer of the Brazilian-made good *in a better position to compete* against the European makers of the same good. On the other hand, should the value of the Brazilian real grow stronger in relation to the euro—resulting in an exchange rate of 3 reals to 1 euro—the same Brazilian-made good formerly costing 4 reals (or 1 euro) to produce now has a cost of 1.33 euros (4 reals divided by 3 reals per euro = 1.33 euros) and this puts the producer of the Brazilian-made good in a weaker competitive position vis-à-vis European producers of the same good. Clearly, the attraction of manufacturing a good in Brazil and selling it in Europe is far greater when the euro is strong (an exchange rate of 1 euro for 5 Brazilian reals) than when the euro is weak and exchanges for only 3 Brazilian reals.

But there is one more piece to the story. When the exchange rate changes from 4 reals per euro to 5 reals per euro, not only is the cost competitiveness of the Brazilian manufacturer stronger relative to European manufacturers of the same item but the Brazilian-made good that formerly cost 1 euro and now costs only 0.8 euros can also be sold to consumers in the European Union for a lower euro price than before. In other words, the combination of a stronger euro and a weaker real acts to *lower the price of Brazilian-made goods* in all the countries that are members of the European Union, and this is likely to *spur sales of the Brazilian-made good in Europe and boost Brazilian exports to Europe.* Conversely, should the exchange rate shift from 4 reals per euro to 3 reals per euro—which makes the Brazilian manufacturer less cost competitive with European manufacturers of the same item—the Brazilian-made good that formerly cost 1 euro and now costs 1.33 euros will sell for a higher price in euros than before, thus weakening the demand of European consumers for Brazilian-made goods and acting to reduce Brazilian exports to Europe. Thus Brazilian exporters are likely to experience (1) rising demand for their goods in Europe whenever the Brazilian real grows weaker relative to the euro and (2) falling demand for their goods in Europe whenever the real grows stronger relative to the euro. Consequently, from the standpoint of a company with Brazilian manufacturing plants, *a weaker Brazilian real is a favorable exchange rate shift* and *a stronger Brazilian real is an unfavorable exchange rate shift.*

It follows from the previous discussion that shifting exchange rates have a big impact on the ability of domestic manufacturers to compete with foreign rivals. For example, U.S.-based manufacturers locked in a fierce competitive battle with low-cost foreign imports benefit from a *weaker* U.S. dollar. There are several reasons why this is so:

- Declines in the value of the U.S. dollar against foreign currencies have the effect of raising the U.S. dollar–costs of goods manufactured by foreign rivals at plants located in the countries whose currencies have grown stronger relative to the U.S. dollar. A weaker dollar acts to reduce or eliminate whatever cost advantage foreign manufacturers may have had over U.S. manufacturers (and helps protect the manufacturing jobs of U.S. workers).

- A *weaker* dollar makes foreign-made goods more expensive in dollar terms to U.S. consumers—this acts to curtail U.S. buyer demand for foreign-made goods, stimulate greater demand on the part of U.S. consumers for U.S.-made goods, and reduce U.S. imports of foreign-made goods.

- A *weaker* U.S. dollar has the effect of enabling the U.S.-made goods to be sold at lower prices to consumers in those countries whose currencies have grown stronger relative to the U.S. dollar—such lower prices boost foreign buyer demand for the now relatively cheaper U.S.-made goods, thereby stimulating exports of U.S.-made goods to foreign countries and perhaps creating more jobs in U.S.-based manufacturing plants.

- A *weaker* dollar has the effect of increasing the dollar value of profits a company earns in those foreign country markets where the local currency is stronger relative to the dollar. For example, if a U.S.-based manufacturer earns a profit of €10 million on its sales in Europe, those €10 million convert to a larger number of dollars when the dollar grows weaker against the euro.

Fluctuating exchange rates pose significant economic risks to a company's competitiveness in foreign markets. Exporters are disadvantaged when the currency of the country where goods are being manufactured grows stronger relative to the currency of the importing country.

A weaker U.S. dollar is therefore an economically favorable exchange rate shift for manufacturing plants based in the United States. A decline in the value of the U.S. dollar strengthens the cost-competitiveness of U.S.-based manufacturing plants and boosts buyer demand for U.S.-made goods. When the value of the U.S. dollar is expected to remain weak for some time to come, foreign companies have an incentive to build manufacturing facilities in the U.S. to make goods for U.S. consumers rather than export the same goods to the U.S. from foreign plants where production costs in dollar terms have been driven up by the decline in the value of the dollar. Conversely, a *stronger* U.S. dollar is an *unfavorable exchange rate shift* for U.S.-based manufacturing plants because it makes such plants less cost-competitive with foreign plants and weakens foreign demand for U.S.-made goods. A strong dollar also weakens the incentive of foreign companies to locate manufacturing facilities in the U.S. to make goods for U.S. consumers. The same reasoning applies to companies who have plants in countries in the European Union where euros are the local currency. A weak euro versus other currencies enhances the cost-competitiveness of companies manufacturing goods in Europe vis-à-vis foreign rivals with plants in countries whose currencies have grown stronger relative to the euro; a strong euro versus other currencies weakens the cost-competitiveness of companies with plants in the European Union.

Insofar as U.S.-based manufacturers are concerned, declines in the value of the U.S. dollar against foreign currencies act to reduce or eliminate whatever cost advantage foreign manufacturers might have over U.S. manufacturers and can even prompt foreign companies to establish production plants in the United States. Likewise, a weak euro versus other currencies enhances the cost competitiveness of companies manufacturing goods in Europe for export to foreign markets; a strong euro versus other currencies weakens the cost competitiveness of European plants that manufacture goods for export. The growing strength of the euro relative to the U.S. dollar has encouraged a number of European manufacturers such as Volkswagen, Fiat, and Airbus to shift production from European factories to new facilities in the United States. Also, the weakening dollar caused Chrysler to discontinue its contract manufacturing agreement with an Austrian firm for assembly of minivans and Jeeps sold in Europe. Beginning in 2008, Chrysler's vehicles sold in Europe were exported from its factories in Illinois and Missouri. The weak dollar was also a factor in Ford's and GM's recent decisions to begin exporting U.S.-made vehicles to China and Latin America.

> Domestic companies facing competitive pressure from lower-cost imports benefit when their government's currency grows *weaker* in relation to the currencies of the countries where the lower-cost imports are being made.

It is important to note that *currency exchange rates are rather unpredictable,* swinging first one way and then another way, so the competitiveness of any company's facilities in any country is partly dependent on whether exchange rate changes over time have a favorable or unfavorable cost impact. Companies producing goods in one country for export abroad always improve their cost competitiveness when the country's currency grows weaker relative to currencies of the countries where the goods are being exported to, and they find their cost competitiveness eroded when the local currency grows stronger. On the other hand, domestic companies that are under pressure from lower-cost imported goods become more cost competitive when their currency grows weaker in relation to the currencies of the countries where the imported goods are made—in other words, a U.S. manufacturer views a weaker U.S. dollar as a *favorable exchange rate shift* because such shifts help make its costs more competitive than those of foreign rivals.

Cross-Country Differences in Demographic, Cultural, and Market Conditions

Buyer tastes for a particular product or service sometimes differ substantially from country to country. In France, consumers prefer top-loading washing machines, while in most other European countries consumers prefer front-loading machines. Soups that appeal to Swedish consumers are not popular in Malaysia. Italian coffee drinkers prefer espressos, but in North America the preference is for mild-roasted coffees. Sometimes, product designs suitable in one country are inappropriate in another because of differing local standards—for example, in the United States electrical devices run on 110-volt electric systems, but in some European countries the standard is a 240-volt electric system, necessitating the use of different electrical designs and components. Cultural influences can also affect consumer demand for a product. For instance, in South Korea, many parents are reluctant to purchase PCs even when they can afford them because of concerns that their children will be distracted from their schoolwork by surfing the Web, playing PC-based video games, and becoming Internet "addicts."[7]

Consequently, companies operating in an international marketplace have to wrestle with *whether and how much to customize their offerings in each different country market to match the tastes and preferences of local buyers or whether to pursue a strategy of offering a mostly standardized product worldwide.* While making products that are closely matched to local tastes makes them more appealing to local buyers, customizing a company's products country by country may have the effect of raising production and distribution costs due to the greater variety of designs and components, shorter production runs, and the complications of added inventory handling and distribution logistics. Greater standardization of a multinational company's product offering, on the other hand, can lead to scale economies and learning curve effects, thus contributing to the achievement of a low-cost advantage. *The tension between the market pressures to localize a company's product offerings country by country and the competitive pressures to lower costs is one of the big strategic issues that participants in foreign markets have to resolve.*

STRATEGIC OPTIONS FOR ENTERING AND COMPETING IN INTERNATIONAL MARKETS

Once a company decides to expand beyond its domestic borders, it must consider the question of how to enter foreign markets. There are six primary strategic options for doing so:

1. Maintain a national (one-country) production base and export goods to foreign markets.
2. License foreign firms to produce and distribute the company's products abroad.
3. Employ a franchising strategy.
4. Establish a subsidiary in a foreign market via acquisition or internal development.
5. Rely on strategic alliances or joint ventures with foreign companies.

Which option to employ depends on a variety of factors, including the nature of the firm's strategic objectives, whether the firm has the full range of resources and capabilities needed to operate abroad, country-specific factors such as trade barriers, and the transaction costs involved (the costs of contracting with a partner and monitoring its compliance with the terms of the contract, for example). The options vary considerably regarding the level of investment required and the associated risks, but higher levels of investment and risk generally provide the firm with the benefits of greater ownership and control.

Export Strategies

Using domestic plants as a production base for exporting goods to foreign markets is an excellent initial strategy for pursuing international sales. It is a conservative way to test the international waters. The amount of capital needed to begin exporting is often quite minimal; existing production capacity may well be sufficient to make goods for export. With an export-bases entry strategy, a manufacturer can limit its involvement in foreign markets by contracting with foreign wholesalers experienced in importing to handle the entire distribution and marketing function in their countries or regions of the world. If it is more advantageous to maintain control over these functions, however, a manufacturer can establish its own distribution and sales organizations in some or all of the target foreign markets. Either way, a home-based production and export strategy helps the firm minimize its direct investments in foreign countries.

Whether an export strategy can be pursued successfully over the long run hinges on whether its advantages for the company continue to outweigh its disadvantages. This depends in part on the relative cost competitiveness of the home-country production base. In some industries, firms gain additional scale economies and learning curve benefits from centralizing production in one or several giant plants whose output capability exceeds demand in any one country market; exporting is one obvious way to capture such economies. However, an export strategy is vulnerable when (1) manufacturing costs in the home country are substantially higher than in foreign countries where rivals have plants, (2) the costs of shipping the product to distant foreign markets are relatively high, (3) adverse shifts occur in currency exchange rates, and (4) importing countries impose tariffs or erect other trade barriers. Unless an exporter can both keep its production and shipping costs competitive with rivals, secure adequate local distribution and marketing support of its products, and successfully hedge against unfavorable changes in currency exchange rates, its success will be limited.

Licensing Strategies

Licensing as an entry strategy makes sense when a firm with valuable technical know-how, an appealing brand, or a unique patented product has neither the internal organizational capability nor the resources to enter foreign markets. Licensing also has the advantage of avoiding the risks of committing resources to country markets that are unfamiliar, politically volatile, economically unstable, or otherwise risky. By licensing the technology, trademark, or production rights to foreign-based firms, the firm does not have to bear the costs and risks of entering foreign markets on its own, yet it is able to generate income from royalties. The big disadvantage of licensing is the risk of providing valuable technological know-how to foreign companies and thereby losing some degree of control over its use. Monitoring licensees and safeguarding the company's proprietary know-how can prove quite difficult in some circumstances. But if the royalty potential is considerable and the companies to whom the licenses are being granted are trustworthy and reputable, then licensing can be a very attractive option. Many software and pharmaceutical companies use licensing strategies to compete in foreign markets.

Franchising Strategies

While licensing works well for manufacturers and owners of proprietary technology, franchising is often better suited to the international expansion efforts of service and retailing enterprises. McDonald's, Yum! Brands (the parent of A&W, Pizza Hut, KFC, Long John Silver's, and Taco Bell), the UPS Store, Roto-Rooter, 7-Eleven, and Hilton Hotels have all used franchising to build a presence in foreign markets. Franchising has much the same advantages as licensing. The franchisee bears most of the costs and risks of establishing foreign locations; a franchisor has to expend only the resources to recruit, train, support, and monitor franchisees. The big problem a franchisor faces is maintaining quality control; foreign franchisees do not always exhibit strong commitment to consistency and standardization, especially when the local culture does not stress the same kinds of quality concerns. Another problem that can arise is whether to allow foreign franchisees to make modifications in the franchisor's product offering so as to better satisfy the tastes and expectations of local buyers. Should McDonald's give franchisees in each nation some leeway in what products they put on their menus? Should the franchised KFC units in China be permitted to substitute spices that appeal to Chinese consumers? Or should the same menu offerings be rigorously and unvaryingly required of all franchisees worldwide?

Foreign Subsidiary Strategies

While exporting, licensing, and franchising rely upon the resources and capabilities of allies in international markets to deliver goods or services to buyers, companies pursuing international expansion may elect to take responsibility for the performance of all essential value chain activities in foreign markets. Companies that prefer direct control over all aspects of operating in a foreign market can establish a wholly owned subsidiary, either by acquiring a foreign company or by establishing operations from the ground up via internal development. A subsidiary business that is established by setting up the entire operation from the ground up is called a **greenfield venture**.

> **CORE CONCEPT**
>
> A **greenfield venture** is a subsidiary business that is established by setting up the entire operation from the ground up.

Acquisition is the quicker of the two options, and it may be the least risky and cost-efficient means of hurdling such entry barriers as gaining access to local distribution channels, building supplier relationships, and establishing working relationships with key government officials and other constituencies. Buying an ongoing operation allows the acquirer to move directly to the task of transferring resources and personnel to the newly acquired business, integrating and redirecting the activities of the acquired business into its own operation, putting its own strategy into place, and accelerating efforts to build a strong market position.[8]

The big issue an acquisition-minded firm must consider is whether to pay a premium price for a successful local company or to buy a struggling competitor at a bargain price. If the buying firm has little knowledge of the local market but ample capital, it is often better off purchasing a capable, strongly positioned firm—unless the acquisition price is prohibitive. However, when the acquirer sees promising ways to transform a weak firm into a strong one and has the resources and managerial know-how to do it, a struggling company can be the better long-term investment.

Entering a new foreign country via a greenfield venture strategy makes sense when a company already operates in a number of countries, has experience in getting new subsidiaries up and running and overseeing their operations, and has a sufficiently large pool of resources and competencies to rapidly equip a new subsidiary with the personnel and capabilities it needs to compete successfully and profitably. Four other conditions make an internal startup strategy appealing:

- When creating an internal startup is cheaper than making an acquisition.
- When adding new production capacity will not adversely impact the supply–demand balance in the local market.
- When a startup subsidiary has the ability to gain good distribution access (perhaps because of the company's recognized brand name).
- When a startup subsidiary will have the size, cost structure, and resource strengths to compete head-to-head against local rivals.

Greenfield ventures in foreign markets can also pose problems, just as other entry strategies do. They represent a costly capital investment, subject to a high level of risk. They require numerous other company resources as well, diverting them from other uses. They do not work well in countries without strong, well-functioning markets and institutions that protect the rights of foreign investors and provide other legal protections. Moreover, an important disadvantage of greenfield ventures relative to other means of international expansion is that they are the slowest entry route—particularly if the objective is to achieve a sizable market share. On the other hand, successful greenfield ventures may offer higher returns to compensate for their high risk and slower path.

Alliance and Joint Venture Strategies

Strategic alliances, joint ventures, and other cooperative agreements with foreign companies are a widely used means of entering foreign markets.[9] A company can benefit immensely from a foreign partner's familiarity with local government regulations, its knowledge of the buying habits and product preferences of consumers, its distribution channel relationships, and so on.[10] Both Japanese and American companies are actively forming alliances with European companies to better compete in the 27-nation European Union and to capitalize on emerging opportunities in the countries of Eastern Europe. Many U.S. and European companies are allying with Asian companies in their efforts to enter markets in China, India, Thailand, Indonesia, and other Asian countries. Many foreign companies, of course, are particularly interested in strategic partnerships that will strengthen their ability to gain a foothold in the U.S. market.

Collaborative strategies involving alliances or joint ventures with foreign partners are a popular way for companies to edge their way into the markets of foreign countries.

A second big appeal of cross-border alliances is to capture economies of scale in production and/or marketing. By joining forces in producing components, assembling models, and marketing their products, companies can realize cost savings not achievable with their own small volumes. A third motivation for entering into a cross-border alliance is to fill gaps in technical expertise and/or knowledge of local markets (buying habits and product preferences of consumers, local customs, and so on). Allies learn much from one another in performing joint research, sharing technological know-how, studying one another's manufacturing methods, and understanding how to tailor sales and marketing approaches to fit local cultures and traditions. Indeed, one of the win–win benefits of an alliance is to learn from the skills, technological know-how, and capabilities of alliance partners and implant the knowledge and know-how of these partners in personnel throughout the company.

> Cross-border alliances enable a growth-minded company to widen its geographic coverage and strengthen its competitiveness in foreign markets; at the same time, they offer flexibility and allow a company to retain some degree of autonomy and operating control.

A fourth motivation for cross-border alliances is to share distribution facilities and dealer networks, and to mutually strengthen each partner's access to buyers. A fifth benefit is that cross-border allies can direct their competitive energies more toward mutual rivals and less toward one another; teaming up may help them close the gap on leading companies. A sixth driver of cross-border alliances comes into play when companies wanting to enter a new foreign market conclude that alliances with local companies are an effective way to establish working relationships with key officials in the host-country government.[11] And, finally, alliances can be a particularly useful way for companies across the world to gain agreement on important technical standards—they have been used to arrive at standards for assorted PC devices, Internet-related technologies, high-definition televisions, and mobile phones.

What makes cross-border alliances an attractive strategic means of gaining the aforementioned types of benefits (as compared to acquiring or merging with foreign-based companies) is that entering into alliances and strategic partnerships allows a company to preserve its independence and avoid using perhaps scarce financial resources to fund acquisitions. Furthermore, an alliance offers the flexibility to readily disengage once its purpose has been served or if the benefits prove elusive, whereas an acquisition is a more permanent sort of arrangement.[12]

Illustration Capsule 7.1 shows how California-based Solazyme, a maker of biofuels and other green products, has used cross-border strategic alliances to fuel its growth.

The Risks of Strategic Alliances with Foreign Partners
Alliances and joint ventures with foreign partners have their pitfalls, however. Sometimes the knowledge and expertise of local partners turns out to be less valuable than expected (because their knowledge is rendered obsolete by fast-changing market conditions or because their operating practices are archaic). Cross-border allies typically must overcome language and cultural barriers and figure out how to deal with diverse (or perhaps conflicting) operating practices. The transaction costs of working out a mutually agreeable arrangement and monitoring partner compliance with the terms of the arrangement can be high. The communication, trust building, and coordination costs are not trivial in terms of management time.[13] Often, partners soon discover they have conflicting objectives and strategies and/or deep differences of opinion about how to proceed, and/or important differences in corporate values and ethical standards. It is not unusual for there to be little personal chemistry among some of the key people on whom success or failure of the alliance depends—the rapport such personnel need to work well together may never emerge. And even if allies are able to develop productive personal relationships, they can still have trouble reaching mutually agreeable ways to deal with key issues or resolve differences. Occasionally, the egos of corporate executives can clash. An alliance between Northwest Airlines and KLM Royal Dutch Airlines resulted in a bitter feud among both companies' top officials (who, according to some reports, refused

Solazyme's Cross-Border Alliances with Unilever, Sephora, Qantas, and Roquette

Solazyme, a California-based company that produces oils for nutritional, cosmetic, and biofuel products from algae, was named "America's Fastest-Growing Manufacturing Company" by *Inc. Magazine* in 2011. The company has fueled its rapid growth through a variety of cross-border strategic alliances with much larger partners. These partnerships have not only facilitated Solazyme's entry into new markets, they have also created value through resource sharing and risk spreading.

Its partnership with Unilever, a British–Dutch consumer goods company, has focused on collaborative R&D. Projects underway are aimed at meeting the growing demand for completely renewable, natural, and sustainable personal care products through the use of algal oils. By further developing Solazyme's technology platform, the partnership will enable the production of Solazyme's oils and other biomaterials efficiently and at large scale.

Solazyme has entered into a variety of marketing and distribution agreements with French cosmetics company Sephora (now part of LVMH). In March 2011, Solazyme launched its luxury skin care brand, Algenist, with Sephora's help. Sephora has also agreed to distribute Solazyme's anti-aging skincare line, making it available in Sephora stores and at Sephora.com.

In 2011, Solazyme also signed a contract with Australian airline Qantas to supply, test, and refine Solazyme's jet fuel product, SolaJet. Solazyme stands to gain valuable input on how to design and distribute its product while receiving media attention and the marketing advantage of a well-known customer. On the other hand, Qantas hopes to better understand how it will achieve its sustainability goals while building its reputation as a sustainability leader in the airline industry.

Because its algae require sugar to produce oil, Solazyme has an interest in securing a stable supply of this feedstock. For this purpose, Solazyme created a 50/50 joint venture with French starch processor Roquette to develop, produce, and market food products globally. By working with Roquette to source feedstock and manufacture final food products, Solazyme lowered its exposure to sugar price fluctuations while taking advantage of Roquette's manufacturing infrastructure and expertise. In return, Roquette gained access to Solazyme's innovative technological resources.

Developed with John L. Gardner.

Sources: Company website; http://gigaom.com/; http://www.businessgreen.com/; http://www.reuters.com/; http://www.foodnavigator-usa.com/ (all accessed March 4, 2012).

to speak to each other).[14] Plus there is the thorny problem of getting alliance partners to sort through issues and reach decisions fast enough to stay abreast of rapid advances in technology or fast-changing market conditions.

One worrisome problem with alliances or joint ventures is that a firm may risk losing some of its competitive advantage if an alliance partner is given full access to its proprietary technological expertise or other unique and competitively valuable capabilities.

There is a natural tendency for allies to struggle to collaborate effectively in competitively sensitive areas, thus spawning suspicions on both sides about forthright exchanges of information and expertise. It requires many meetings of many people working in good faith over a period of time to iron out what is to be shared, what is to remain proprietary, and how the cooperative arrangements will work.

Even if a collaborative arrangement proves to be a win–win proposition for both parties, a company must guard against becoming overly dependent on foreign partners for essential expertise and competitive capabilities. Companies aiming for global market leadership often need to develop their own resource capabilities in order to be masters of their destiny. Frequently, experienced multinational companies operating in 50 or more countries across the world find less need for entering into cross-border alliances than do companies in the early stages of globalizing their operations.[15] Companies with global operations make it a point to develop senior managers who understand how "the system" works in different countries, plus they can avail themselves of local managerial talent and know-how by simply hiring experienced local managers and thereby detouring the hazards of collaborative alliances with local companies. One of the lessons about cross-border partnerships is that they are more effective in helping a company establish a beachhead of new opportunity in world markets than they are in enabling a company to achieve and sustain global market leadership.

COMPETING INTERNATIONALLY: THE THREE MAIN STRATEGIC APPROACHES

Broadly speaking, a firm's **international strategy** is simply its strategy for competing in two or more countries simultaneously. Typically, a company will start to compete internationally by entering just one or perhaps a select few foreign markets—selling its products or services in countries where there is a ready market for them. But as it expands further internationally, it will have to confront head-on the conflicting pressures of local responsiveness versus efficiency gains from standardizing its product offering globally. Deciding upon the degree to vary its competitive approach to fit the specific market conditions and buyer preferences in each host country is perhaps the foremost strategic issue that must be addressed when operating in two or more foreign markets.[16] Figure 7.2 shows a company's three options for resolving this issue: choosing a *multidomestic, global,* or *transnational* strategy.

Multidomestic Strategy—Think Local, Act Local

A **multidomestic strategy** is one in which a company varies its product offering and competitive approach from country to country in an effort to meet differing buyer needs and to address divergent local market conditions. It involves having plants produce different product versions for different local markets and adapting marketing and distribution to fit local customs, cultures, regulations, and market requirements. The strength of employing a multidomestic strategy is that the company's actions and business approaches are deliberately crafted to appeal to the tastes and expectations of buyers in each country and to stake out the most attractive market positions vis-à-vis local competitors.[17] Castrol, a specialist in oil lubricants, produces over 3,000 different formulas of lubricants to meet the requirements of different climates, vehicle types and uses, and equipment applications that characterize different country markets. In the food products industry, it is common for companies to vary the ingredients in their products and sell

against one another, due to the fear of a retaliatory response that might escalate the battle into a cross-border competitive war. **Mutual restraint** of this sort tends to stabilize the competitive position of multimarket rivals against one another. And while it may prevent each firm from making any major market share gains at the expense of its rival, it also protects against costly competitive battles that would be likely to erode the profitability of both companies without any compensating gain.

STRATEGIES FOR COMPETING IN THE MARKETS OF DEVELOPING COUNTRIES

LO 6

Gain an understanding of the unique characteristics of competing in developing-country markets.

Companies racing for global leadership have to consider competing in developing-economy markets like China, India, Brazil, Indonesia, Thailand, and Russia—countries where the business risks are considerable but where the opportunities for growth are huge, especially as their economies develop and living standards climb toward levels in the industrialized world.[20] With the world now comprising nearly 7 billion people—fully 40 percent of whom live in India and China, and hundreds of millions more live in other, less developed countries in Asia and Latin America—a company that aspires to world market leadership (or to sustained rapid growth) cannot ignore the market opportunities or the base of technical and managerial talent such countries offer. For example, in 2010 China was the world's second-largest economy (behind the United States), as measured by purchasing power. Its population of 1.4 billion people now consumes a quarter of the world's luxury products, due to the rapid growth of a wealthy class.[21] China is also the world's largest consumer of many commodities. China's growth in demand for consumer goods had made it the world's largest market for vehicles by 2009 and put it on track to become the world's largest market for luxury goods by 2014.[22] Thus, no company that aspires to global market leadership can afford to ignore the strategic importance of establishing competitive market positions in the so-called BRIC countries (Brazil, Russia, India, and China), as well as in other parts of the Asia-Pacific region, Latin America, and Eastern Europe. Illustration Capsule 7.2 describes Yum! Brands's strategy to increase its sales and market share in China.

Tailoring products to fit market conditions in developing countries, however, often involves more than making minor product changes and becoming more familiar with local cultures. Ford's attempt to sell a Ford Escort in India at a price of $21,000—a luxury-car price, given that India's best-selling Maruti-Suzuki model sold at the time for $10,000 or less and that fewer than 10 percent of Indian households had an annual purchasing power greater than $20,000—met with a less-than-enthusiastic market response. Kellogg has struggled to introduce its cereals successfully because consumers in many less developed countries do not eat cereal for breakfast. Single-serving packages of detergents, shampoos, pickles, cough syrup, and cooking oils are very popular in India because they allow buyers to conserve cash by purchasing only what they need immediately. Thus, many companies find that trying to employ a strategy akin to that used in the markets of developed countries is hazardous.[23] Experimenting with some, perhaps many, local twists is usually necessary to find a strategy combination that works.

Strategy Options for Competing in Developing-Country Markets

There are several options for tailoring a company's strategy to fit the sometimes unusual or challenging circumstances presented in developing-country markets:

Yum! Brands's Strategy for Becoming the Leading Food Service Brand in China

In 2012, Yum! Brands operated more than 37,000 restaurants in more than 117 countries. Its best-known brands were KFC, Taco Bell, Pizza Hut, A&W, and Long John Silver's. In 2011, its fastest growth in revenues came from its 4,500 restaurants in China, which recorded operating profits of $908 million during the year. KFC was the largest quick-service chain in China, with 3,700 units in 2011, while Pizza Hut was the largest casual-dining chain, with 630 units. Yum! Brands planned to open at least 500 new restaurant locations annually in China, including new Pizza Hut home delivery units and East Dawning units, which had a menu offering traditional Chinese food. All of Yum! Brands's menu items for China were developed in its R&D facility in Shanghai.

In addition to adapting its menu to local tastes and adding new units at a rapid pace, Yum! Brands also adapted the restaurant ambience and decor to appeal to local consumer preferences and behavior. The company changed its KFC store formats to provide educational displays that supported parents' priorities for their children and to make KFC a fun place for children to visit. The typical KFC outlet in China averaged two birthday parties per day.

In 2011, Yum! Brands operated 60 KFC, Taco Bell, Pizza Hut, A&W, and Long John Silver's restaurants for every 1 million Americans. The company's more than 4,500 units in China represented only three restaurants per 1 million Chinese. Yum! Brands management believed that its strategy keyed to continued expansion in the number of units in China, and additional menu refinements would allow its operating profits from restaurants located in China to account for 40 percent of systemwide operating profits by 2017.

Sources: http://www.brandchannel.com/home/post/2011/01/13/International-Expansion-Looks-Yummy-for-Yum!-Brands-Inc.aspx and other information posted at www.yum.com, accessed March 28, 2012.

- *Prepare to compete on the basis of low price.* Consumers in developing markets are often highly focused on price, which can give low-cost local competitors the edge unless a company can find ways to attract buyers with bargain prices as well as better products. For example, in order to enter the market for laundry detergents in India, Unilever had to develop a low-cost detergent (named Wheel), construct new low-cost production facilities, package the detergent in single-use amounts so that it could be sold at a very low unit price, distribute the product to local merchants by handcarts, and craft an economical marketing campaign that included painted signs on buildings and demonstrations near stores. The new brand quickly captured $100 million in sales and was the number-one detergent brand in India based on 2011 dollar sales. Unilever later replicated the strategy in India with low-priced packets of shampoos and deodorants and in South America with a detergent brand named Ala.

- *Modify aspects of the company's business model to accommodate local circumstances (but not to such an extent that the company loses the advantage of global scale and branding).* For instance, when Dell entered China, it discovered that individuals and businesses were not accustomed to placing orders through the Internet. To adapt,

Dell modified its direct sales model to rely more heavily on phone and fax orders and decided to be patient in getting Chinese customers to place Internet orders. Further, because numerous Chinese government departments and state-owned enterprises insisted that hardware vendors make their bids through distributors and systems integrators (as opposed to dealing directly with Dell salespeople), Dell opted to use third parties in marketing its products to this buyer segment. But Dell was careful not to abandon the parts of its business model that gave it a competitive edge over rivals. Similarly, when McDonald's moved into Russia in the 1990s, it was forced to alter its practice of obtaining supplies from outside vendors because capable local suppliers were not available. In order to supply its Russian outlets and stay true to its core principle of serving consistent-quality fast food, McDonald's set up its own vertically integrated supply chain—cattle were imported from Holland and russet potatoes were imported from the United States. McDonald's management also worked with a select number of Russian bakers for its bread, brought in agricultural specialists from Canada and Europe to improve the management practices of Russian farmers, built its own 100,000-square-foot McComplex to produce hamburgers, French fries, ketchup, mustard, and Big Mac sauce, and set up a trucking fleet to move supplies to restaurants.

- *Try to change the local market to better match the way the company does business elsewhere.* A multinational company often has enough market clout to drive major changes in the way a local country market operates. When Hong Kong–based STAR launched its first satellite TV channel in 1991, it generated profound impacts on the TV marketplace in India. The Indian government lost its monopoly on TV broadcasts, several other satellite TV channels aimed at Indian audiences quickly emerged, and the excitement of additional TV channels in India triggered a boom in TV manufacturing in India. When Japan's Suzuki entered India, it triggered a quality revolution among Indian auto parts manufacturers. Local component suppliers teamed up with Suzuki's vendors in Japan and worked with Japanese experts to produce higher-quality products. Over the next two decades, Indian companies became proficient in making top-notch components for vehicles, won more prizes for quality than companies in any country other than Japan, and broke into the global market as suppliers to many automakers in Asia and other parts of the world. Mahindra and Mahindra, one of India's premier automobile manufacturers, has been recognized by a number of organizations for its product quality.

- *Stay away from developing markets where it is impractical or uneconomic to modify the company's business model to accommodate local circumstances.* Home Depot expanded into Mexico in 2001 and China in 2006, but it has avoided entry into other developing countries because its value proposition of good quality, low prices, and attentive customer service relies on (1) good highways and logistical systems to minimize store inventory costs, (2) employee stock ownership to help motivate store personnel to provide good customer service, and (3) high labor costs for housing construction and home repairs that encourage homeowners to engage in do-it-yourself projects. Relying on these factors in the U.S. and Canadian markets has worked spectacularly for Home Depot, but the company has found that it cannot count on these factors in nearby Latin America.

> Profitability in developing markets rarely comes quickly or easily—new entrants have to adapt their business models to local conditions and be patient in earning a profit.

Company experiences in entering developing markets like Argentina, Vietnam, Malaysia, and Brazil indicate that profitability seldom comes quickly or easily. Building a market for the company's products can often turn into a long-term process that involves re-education of consumers, sizable investments in advertising to alter tastes and buying habits, and upgrades of the local infrastructure (transportation systems, distribution channels, etc.). In such cases, a company must be patient, work within the system to improve the infrastructure, and lay the foundation for generating sizable revenues and profits once conditions are ripe for market takeoff.

DEFENDING AGAINST GLOBAL GIANTS: STRATEGIES FOR LOCAL COMPANIES IN DEVELOPING COUNTRIES

If opportunity-seeking, resource-rich multinational companies are looking to enter developing-country markets, what strategy options can local companies use to survive? As it turns out, the prospects for local companies facing global giants are by no means grim. Studies of local companies in developing markets have disclosed five strategies that have proved themselves in defending against globally competitive companies.[24] Illustration Capsule 7.3 discusses how a travel agency in China used a combination of these strategies to become that country's largest travel consolidator and online travel agent.

1. *Develop business models that exploit shortcomings in local distribution networks or infrastructure.* In many instances, the extensive collection of resources possessed by the global giants is of little help in building a presence in developing markets. The lack of well-established wholesaler and distributor networks, telecommunication systems, consumer banking, or media necessary for advertising makes it difficult for large internationals to migrate business models proved in developed markets to emerging markets. Such markets sometimes favor local companies whose managers are familiar with the local language and culture and are skilled in selecting large numbers of conscientious employees to carry out labor-intensive tasks. Shanda, a Chinese producer of massively multiplayer online role-playing games (MMORPG), has overcome China's lack of an established credit card network by selling prepaid access cards through local merchants. The company's focus on online games also addresses shortcomings in China's software piracy laws. An India-based electronics company has been able to carve out a market niche for itself by developing an all-in-one business machine designed especially for India's 1.2 million small shopkeepers that tolerates the frequent power outages in that country.[25]

2. *Utilize keen understanding of local customer needs and preferences to create customized products or services.* When developing-country markets are largely made up of customers with strong local needs, a good strategy option is to concentrate on customers who prefer a local touch and to accept the loss of the customers attracted to global brands.[26] A local company may be able to astutely exploit its local orientation—its familiarity with local preferences, its expertise in traditional products, its long-standing customer relationships. A small Middle Eastern cell phone manufacturer competes successfully against industry giants Nokia, Samsung, and Motorola by selling a model designed especially for Muslims—it is loaded with the Koran, alerts people at prayer times, and is equipped with a compass that points them toward Mecca. Shenzhen-based Tencent has become the leader in instant messaging in China through its unique understanding of Chinese behavior and culture.

3. *Take advantage of aspects of the local workforce with which large multinational companies may be unfamiliar.* Local companies that lack the technological capabilities of foreign entrants may be able to rely on their better understanding of the local labor force

How Ctrip Successfully Defended against International Rivals to Become China's Largest Online Travel Agency

Ctrip has utilized a business model tailored to the Chinese travel market, its access to low-cost labor, and its unique understanding of customer preferences and buying habits to build scale rapidly and defeat foreign rivals such as Expedia and Travelocity in becoming the largest travel agency in China. The company was founded in 1999 with a focus on business travelers, since corporate travel accounts for the majority of China's travel bookings. The company also placed little emphasis on online transactions, since at the time there was no national ticketing system in China, most hotels did not belong to a national or international chain, and most consumers preferred paper tickets to electronic tickets. To overcome this infrastructure shortcoming, the company established its own central database of 5,600 hotels located throughout China and flight information for all major airlines operating in China. Ctrip set up a call center of 3,000 representatives that could use its proprietary database to provide travel information for up to 100,000 customers per day. Because most of its transactions were not done over the Internet, the company hired couriers in all major cities in China to ride by bicycle or scooter to collect payments and deliver tickets to Ctrip's corporate customers. Ctrip also initiated a loyalty program that provided gifts and incentives to the administrative personnel who arranged travel for business executives. By 2011, Ctrip.com held 60 percent of China's online travel market, having grown 40 percent every year since 1999. As of March 2012, its market cap reached $3.1 billion and was creeping up rapidly on Expedia's market cap of over $4 billion.

Sources: Arindam K. Bhattacharya and David C. Michael, "How Local Companies Keep Multinationals at Bay," *Harvard Business Review* 86, no. 3 (March 2008), pp. 85–95; http://www.thatsmags.com/shanghai/article/detail/480/a-journey-with-ctrip; http://money.cnn.com/quote/quote.html?symb=EXPE, accessed March 28, 2012.

to offset any disadvantage. Focus Media is China's largest outdoor advertising firm and has relied on low-cost labor to update its 130,000 LCD displays and billboards in 90 cities in a low-tech manner, while multinational companies operating in China use electronically networked screens that allow messages to be changed remotely. Focus uses an army of employees who ride to each display by bicycle to change advertisements with programming contained on a USB flash drive or DVD. Indian information technology firms such as Infosys Technologies and Satyam Computer Services have been able to keep their personnel costs lower than those of international competitors EDS and Accenture because of their familiarity with local labor markets. While the large internationals have focused recruiting efforts in urban centers like Bangalore and Delhi, driving up engineering and computer science salaries in such cities, local companies have shifted recruiting efforts to second-tier cities that are unfamiliar to foreign firms.

4. *Use acquisition and rapid-growth strategies to better defend against expansion-minded internationals.* With the growth potential of developing markets such as China, Indonesia, and Brazil obvious to the world, local companies must attempt to develop scale and upgrade their competitive capabilities as quickly as possible to defend against the stronger international's arsenal of resources. Most successful companies

in developing markets have pursued mergers and acquisitions at a rapid-fire pace to build first a nationwide and then an international presence. Hindalco, India's largest aluminum producer, has followed just such a path to achieve its ambitions for global dominance. By acquiring companies in India first, it gained enough experience and confidence to eventually acquire much larger foreign companies with world-class capabilities.[27] When China began to liberalize its foreign trade policies, Lenovo (the Chinese PC maker) realized that its long-held position of market dominance in China could not withstand the onslaught of new international entrants such as Dell and HP. Its acquisition of IBM's PC business allowed Lenovo to gain rapid access to IBM's globally recognized PC brand, its R&D capability, and its existing distribution in developed countries. This has allowed Lenovo not only to hold its own against the incursion of global giants into its home market but to expand into new markets around the world.[28]

5. *Transfer company expertise to cross-border markets and initiate actions to contend on an international level.* When a company from a developing country has resources and capabilities suitable for competing in other country markets, launching initiatives to transfer its expertise to foreign markets becomes a viable strategic option. Televisa, Mexico's largest media company, used its expertise in Spanish culture and linguistics to become the world's most prolific producer of Spanish-language soap operas. By continuing to upgrade its capabilities and learn from its experience in foreign markets, a company can sometimes transform itself into one capable of competing on a worldwide basis, as an emerging global giant. Sundaram Fasteners of India began its foray into foreign markets as a supplier of radiator caps to GM—an opportunity it pursued when GM first decided to outsource the production of this part. As a participant in GM's supplier network, the company learned about emerging technical standards, built its capabilities, and became one of the first Indian companies to achieve QS 9000 quality certification. With the expertise it gained and its recognition for meeting quality standards, Sundaram was then able to pursue opportunities to supply automotive parts in Japan and Europe.

KEY POINTS

1. Competing in international markets allows companies to (1) gain access to new customers, (2) achieve lower costs through greater scale economies, learning curve effects, or purchasing power, (3) leverage core competencies developed domestically in additional country markets, (4) gain access to resources and capabilities located outside a company's domestic market, and (5) spread business risk across a wider market base.

2. Strategy making is more complex for five reasons: (1) different countries have *home-country advantages* in different industries; (2) there exist location-based advantages to performing different value chain activities in different parts of the world; (3) varying political and economic risks make the business climate of some countries more favorable than others; (4) companies face the risk of adverse shifts in exchange rates when operating in foreign countries; and (5) differences in buyer tastes and preferences present a conundrum concerning the trade-off between customizing and standardizing products and services.

3. The strategies of firms that expand internationally are usually grounded in home-country advantages concerning demand conditions, factor conditions, related and supporting industries, and firm strategy, structure, and rivalry, as described by the Diamond of National Competitive Advantage framework.

LO 5, LO 6 4. Using your university library's subscription to Lexis-Nexis, EBSCO, or a similar database, identify and discuss three key strategies that Volkswagen is using to compete in China.

EXERCISES FOR SIMULATION PARTICIPANTS

The following questions are for simulation participants whose companies operate in an international market arena. If your company competes only in a single country, then skip the questions in this section.

LO 2 1. To what extent, if any, have you and your co-managers adapted your company's strategy to take shifting exchange rates into account? In other words, have you undertaken any actions to try to minimize the impact of adverse shifts in exchange rates?

LO 2 2. To what extent, if any, have you and your co-managers adapted your company's strategy to take geographic differences in import tariffs or import duties into account?

LO 4 3. Which one of the following best describes the strategic approach your company is taking in trying to compete successfully on an international basis?

- Multidomestic or think local, act local approach
- Global or think global, act local approach
- Transnational or think global, act global approach

Explain your answer and indicate two or three chief elements of your company's strategy for competing in two or more different geographic regions.

ENDNOTES

[1] Sidney G. Winter and Gabriel Szulanski, "Replication as Strategy," *Organization Science* 12, no. 6 (November–December 2001), pp. 730–43; Sidney G. Winter and Gabriel Szulanski, "Getting It Right the Second Time," *Harvard Business Review* 80, no. 1 (January 2002), pp. 62–69.
[2] A. C. Inkpen and A. Dinur, "Knowledge Management Processes and International Joint Ventures," *Organization Science* 9, no. 4 (July–August 1998), pp. 454–68; P. Dussauge, B. Garrette, and W. Mitchell, "Learning from Competing Partners: Outcomes and Durations of Scale and Link Alliances in Europe, North America and Asia," *Strategic Management Journal* 21, no. 2 (February 2000), pp. 99–126; C. Dhanaraj, M. A. Lyles, H. K. Steensma, et al., "Managing Tacit and Explicit Knowledge Transfer in IJVs: The Role of Relational Embeddedness and the Impact on Performance," *Journal of International Business Studies* 35, no. 5 (September 2004), pp. 428–42; K. W. Glaister and P. J. Buckley, "Strategic Motives for International Alliance Formation," *Journal of Management Studies* 33, no. 3 (May 1996), pp. 301–32.
[3] J. Anand and B. Kogut, "Technological Capabilities of Countries, Firm Rivalry

and Foreign Direct Investment," *Journal of International Business Studies* 28, no. 3 (1997), pp. 445–65; J. Anand and A. Delios, "Absolute and Relative Resources as Determinants of International Acquisitions," *Strategic Management Journal* 23, no. 2 (February 2002), pp. 119–35; A. Seth, K. Song, and A. Pettit, "Value Creation and Destruction in Cross-Border Acquisitions: An Empirical Analysis of Foreign Acquisitions of U.S. Firms," *Strategic Management Journal* 23, no. 10 (October 2002), pp. 921–40; J. Anand, L. Capron, and W. Mitchell, "Using Acquisitions to Access Multinational Diversity: Thinking beyond the Domestic versus Cross-Border M&A Comparison," *Industrial & Corporate Change* 14, no. 2 (April 2005), pp. 191–224.
[4] M. Porter, "The Competitive Advantage of Nations," *Harvard Business Review,* March–April 1990, pp. 73–93.
[5] "China Car Sales 'Overtook the US' in 2009," *BBC News,* January 11, 2010, http://news.bbc.co.uk/2/hi/8451887.stm.
[6] New release by U.S. Department of Labor, Bureau of Labor Statistics, "International Comparisons of Hourly Compensation Costs in Manufacturing, 2009," March 8, 2011, pp. 3–6.

[7] Sangwon Yoon, "South Korea Targets Internet Addicts; 2 Million Hooked," *Valley News,* April 25, 2010, p. C2.
[8] E. Pablo, "Determinants of Cross-Border M&As in Latin America," *Journal of Business Research* 62, no. 9 (2009); R. Olie, "Shades of Culture and Institutions in International Mergers," *Organization Studies* 15, no. 3 (1994); K. E. Meyer, M. Wright, and S. Pruthi, "Institutions, Resources, and Entry Strategies in Emerging Economies," *Strategic Management Journal* 30, no. 5 (2009).
[9] Yves L. Doz and Gary Hamel, *Alliance Advantage* (Boston: Harvard Business School Press, 1998); Joel Bleeke and David Ernst, "The Way to Win in Cross-Border Alliances," *Harvard Business Review* 69, no. 6 (November –December 1991), pp. 127–33; Gary Hamel, Yves L. Doz, and C. K. Prahalad, "Collaborate with Your Competitors— and Win," *Harvard Business Review* 67, no. 1 (January–February 1989), pp. 134–35.
[10] K. W. Glaister and P. J. Buckley, "Strategic Motives for International Alliance Formation," *Journal of Management Studies* 33, no. 3 (May 1996), pp. 301–32.
[11] H. Kurt Christensen, "Corporate Strategy: Managing a Set of Businesses," in *The*

Portable MBA in Strategy, ed. Liam Fahey and Robert M. Randall (New York: Wiley, 2001).

[12] Jeffrey H. Dyer, Prashant Kale, and Harbir Singh, "When to Ally and When to Acquire," *Harvard Business Review* 82, no. 7/8 (July–August 2004).

[13] Doz and Hamel, *Alliance Advantage,* chaps. 2–7; Rosabeth Moss Kanter, "Collaborative Advantage: The Art of the Alliance," *Harvard Business Review* 72, no. 4 (July–August 1994), pp. 96–108.

[14] Shawn Tully, "The Alliance from Hell," *Fortune,* June 24, 1996, pp. 64–72.

[15] C. K. Prahalad and Kenneth Lieberthal, "The End of Corporate Imperialism," *Harvard Business Review* 76, no. 4 (July–August, 2004), p. 77.

[16] Pankaj Ghemawat, "Managing Differences: The Central Challenge of Global Strategy," *Harvard Business Review* 85, no. 3 (March 2007).

[17] C. A. Bartlett and S. Ghoshal, *Managing Across Borders: The Transnational Solution,* 2nd ed. (Boston: Harvard Business School Press, 1998).

[18] Lynn S. Paine, "The China Rules," *Harvard Business Review* 88, no. 6 (June 2010) pp. 103–8.

[19] C. K. Prahalad and Yves L. Doz, *The Multinational Mission* (New York: Free Press).

[20] David J. Arnold and John A. Quelch, "New Strategies in Emerging Markets," *Sloan Management Review* 40, no. 1 (Fall 1998), pp. 7–20; C. K. Prahalad, *The Fortune at the Bottom of the Pyramid: Eradicating Poverty through Profits* (Upper Saddle River, NJ: Wharton, 2005).

[21] "Is a Luxury Good Consumption Tax Useful?" *Beijing Review.com.cn,* June 18, 2010, www.bjreview.com.cn/print/txt/2010-06/18/content_280191.htm; "GM's First-Half China Sales Surge Past the U.S.," *Bloomberg Businessweek,* July 2, 2010, http://businessweek.com/news/2010-07-02/gm-s-first-half-china-sales-surge-past-the-u-s-.html.

[22] Joanne Muller, "Can China Save GM?" *Forbes.com,* May 10, 2010, www.forbes.com/forbes/2010/0510/global-2000-10-automobiles-china-detroit-whitacre-save-gm.html.

[23] Tarun Khanna, Krishna G. Palepu, and Jayant Sinha, "Strategies That Fit Emerging Markets," *Harvard Business Review* 83, no. 6 (June 2005), p. 63; Arindam K. Bhattacharya and David C. Michael, "How Local Companies Keep Multinationals at Bay,"

Harvard Business Review 86, no. 3 (March 2008), pp. 94–95.

[24] Tarun Khanna and Krishna G. Palepu, "Emerging Giants: Building World-Class Companies in Developing Countries," *Harvard Business Review* 84, no. 10 (October 2006), pp. 60–69.

[25] Steve Hamm, "Tech's Future," *BusinessWeek,* September 27, 2004, p. 88.

[26] Niroj Dawar and Tony Frost, "Competing with Giants: Survival Strategies for Local Companies in Emerging Markets," *Harvard Business Review* 77, no. 1 (January–February 1999), p. 122; Guitz Ger, "Localizing in the Global Village: Local Firms Competing in Global Markets," *California Management Review* 41, no. 4 (Summer 1999), pp. 64–84.

[27] N. Kumar, "How Emerging Giants Are Rewriting the Rules of M&A," *Harvard Business Review,* May 2009, pp. 115–21.

[28] H. Rui and G. Yip, "Foreign Acquisitions by Chinese Firms: A Strategic Intent Perspective," *Journal of World Business* 43 (2008), pp. 213–26.

need to be assigned. As in the assignment of weights to industry attractiveness measures, the importance weights must add up to 1.0. Each business unit is then rated on each of the chosen strength measures, using a rating scale of 1 to 10 (where a *high* rating signifies competitive *strength* and a *low* rating signifies competitive *weakness*). In the event that the available information is too skimpy to confidently assign a rating value to a business unit on a particular strength measure, it is usually best to use a score of 5, which avoids biasing the overall score either up or down. Weighted strength ratings are calculated by multiplying the business unit's rating on each strength measure by the assigned weight. For example, a strength score of 6 times a weight of 0.15 gives a weighted strength rating of 0.90. The sum of the weighted ratings across all the strength measures provides a quantitative measure of a business unit's overall market strength and competitive standing. Table 8.2 provides sample calculations of competitive strength ratings for three businesses.

TABLE 8.2   Calculating Weighted Competitive Strength Scores for a Diversified Company's Business Units

Competitive Strength Measures	Importance Weight	Competitive Strength Assessments					
		Business A in Industry A		Business B in Industry B		Business C in Industry C	
		Strength Rating	Weighted Score	Strength Rating	Weighted Score	Strength Rating	Weighted Score
Relative market share	0.15	10	1.50	2	0.30	6	0.90
Costs relative to competitors' costs	0.20	7	1.40	4	0.80	5	1.00
Ability to match or beat rivals on key product attributes	0.05	9	0.45	5	0.25	8	0.40
Ability to benefit from strategic fit with sister businesses	0.20	8	1.60	4	0.80	8	0.80
Bargaining leverage with suppliers/customers	0.05	9	0.45	2	0.10	6	0.30
Brand image and reputation	0.10	9	0.90	4	0.40	7	0.70
Competitively valuable capabilities	0.15	7	1.05	2	0.30	5	0.75
Profitability relative to competitors	0.10	5	0.50	2	0.20	4	0.40
Sum of importance weights	**1.00**						
Weighted overall competitive strength scores			**7.85**		**3.15**		**5.25**

[Rating scale: 1 = Very weak; 10 = Very strong]

Interpreting the Competitive Strength Scores   Business units with competitive strength ratings above 6.7 (on a scale of 1 to 10) are strong market contenders in their industries. Businesses with ratings in the 3.3-to-6.7 range have moderate competitive strength vis-à-vis rivals. Businesses with ratings below 3.3 are in competitively weak market positions. If a diversified company's business units all have competitive strength scores above 5, it is fair to conclude that its business units are all fairly strong market contenders in their respective industries. But as the number of business units with scores below 5 increases, there's reason to question whether the company can perform well with so many businesses in relatively weak competitive positions. This concern takes on even more importance when business units with low scores account for a sizable fraction of the company's revenues.

Using a Nine-Cell Matrix to Simultaneously Portray Industry Attractiveness and Competitive Strength   The industry attractiveness and business strength scores can be used to portray the strategic positions of each business in a diversified company. Industry attractiveness is plotted on the vertical axis and competitive strength on the horizontal axis. A nine-cell grid emerges from dividing the vertical axis into three regions (high, medium, and low attractiveness) and the horizontal axis into three regions (strong, average, and weak competitive strength). *Each business unit is plotted on the nine-cell matrix according to its overall attractiveness score and strength score, and then it is shown as a "bubble."* The size of each bubble is scaled to the percentage of revenues the business generates relative to total corporate revenues. The bubbles in Figure 8.3 were located on the grid using the three industry attractiveness scores from Table 8.1 and the strength scores for the three business units in Table 8.2.

The locations of the business units on the attractiveness–strength matrix provide valuable guidance in deploying corporate resources. In general, *a diversified company's best prospects for good overall performance involve concentrating corporate resources on business units having the greatest competitive strength and industry attractiveness.* Businesses plotted in the three cells in the upper left portion of the attractiveness–strength matrix have both favorable industry attractiveness and competitive strength and should receive a high investment priority. Business units plotted in these three cells (like business A) are referred to as "grow and build" businesses because of their capability to drive future increases in shareholder value.

Next in priority come businesses positioned in the three diagonal cells stretching from the lower left to the upper right (like business C in Figure 8.3). Such businesses usually merit intermediate priority in the parent's resource allocation ranking. However, some businesses in the medium-priority diagonal cells may have brighter or dimmer prospects than others. For example, a small business in the upper right cell of the matrix, despite being in a highly attractive industry, may occupy too weak a competitive position in its industry to justify the investment and resources needed to turn it into a strong market contender.

Businesses in the three cells in the lower right corner of the matrix (like business B in Figure 8.3) have comparatively low industry attractiveness and minimal competitive strength, making them weak performers with little potential for improvement. At best, they have the lowest claim on corporate resources and often are good candidates for being divested (sold to other companies). However, there are occasions when a business located in the three lower-right cells generates sizable positive cash flows. It may make sense to retain such businesses and manage them in a manner calculated to squeeze out the maximum cash flows from operations—the cash flows from

FIGURE 8.3 A Nine-Cell Industry Attractiveness–Competitive Strength Matrix

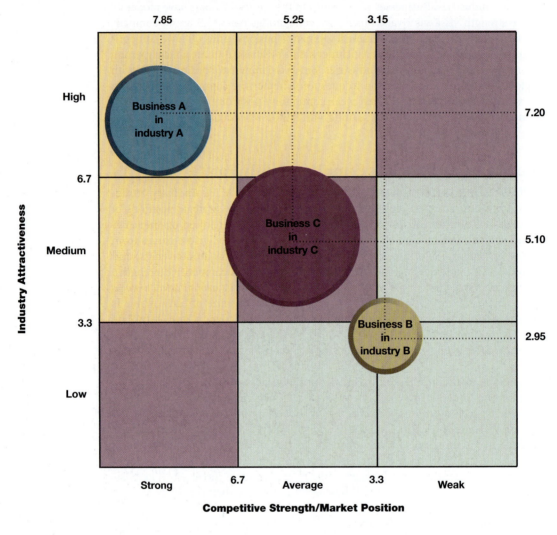

Note: Circle sizes are scaled to reflect the percentage of companywide revenues generated by the business unit.

low-performing/low-potential businesses can then be diverted to financing expansion of business units with greater potential for revenue and profit growth.

The nine-cell attractiveness–strength matrix provides clear, strong logic for why a diversified company needs to consider both industry attractiveness and business strength in allocating resources and investment capital to its different businesses. A good case can be made for concentrating resources in those businesses that enjoy higher degrees of attractiveness and competitive strength, being very selective in making investments in businesses with intermediate positions on the grid, and withdrawing resources from businesses that are lower in attractiveness and strength unless they offer exceptional profit or cash flow potential.

Step 3: Determining the Competitive Value of Strategic Fit in Diversified Companies

While this step can be bypassed for diversified companies whose businesses are all unrelated (since, by design, strategic fit is lacking), assessing the degree of strategic fit across its businesses is central to evaluating a company's related diversification strategy. *But more than just strategic-fit identification is needed. The real test is what competitive value can be generated from strategic fit.* To what extent can cost savings be realized? How much competitive value will come from the cross-business transfer of skills, technology, or intellectual capital? Will transferring a potent brand name to the products of other businesses increase sales significantly? Will cross-business collaboration to create or strengthen competitive capabilities lead to significant gains in the marketplace or in financial performance? Without significant strategic fit and dedicated company efforts to capture the benefits, one has to be skeptical about the potential for a diversified company's businesses to perform better together than apart.

Figure 8.4 illustrates the process of comparing the value chains of a company's businesses and identifying opportunities to exploit competitively valuable cross-business strategic fit.

> The greater the value of cross-business strategic fit in enhancing a company's performance in the marketplace or on the bottom line, the more competitively powerful is its strategy of related diversification.

FIGURE 8.4 Identifying the Competitive Advantage Potential of Cross-Business Strategic Fit

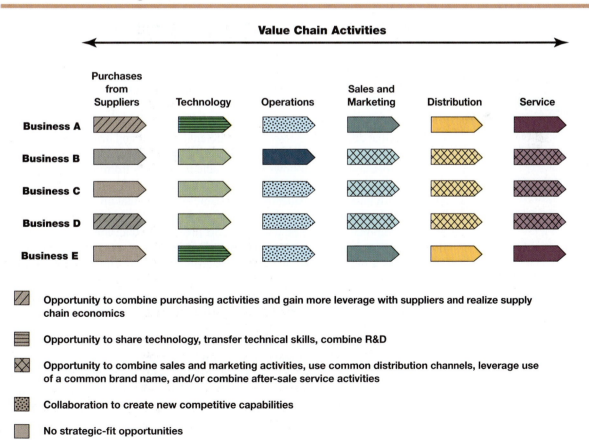

Value Chain Activities

Purchases from Suppliers · Technology · Operations · Sales and Marketing · Distribution · Service

Business A · Business B · Business C · Business D · Business E

- ▨ Opportunity to combine purchasing activities and gain more leverage with suppliers and realize supply chain economics
- ▤ Opportunity to share technology, transfer technical skills, combine R&D
- ▩ Opportunity to combine sales and marketing activities, use common distribution channels, leverage use of a common brand name, and/or combine after-sale service activities
- ▦ Collaboration to create new competitive capabilities
- ▢ No strategic-fit opportunities

Step 4: Checking for Resource Fit

The businesses in a diversified company's lineup need to exhibit good **resource fit**. In firms with a related diversification strategy, resource fit exists *when the firm's businesses have matching resource requirements at points along their value chains* that are critical for the businesses' market success. Matching resource requirements are important in related diversification because they facilitate resource sharing and low-cost transfer. In companies pursuing unrelated diversification, resource fit exists when the company has solid *parenting capabilities or resources of a general nature that it can share or transfer to its component businesses.* Firms pursuing related diversification and firms with combination related-unrelated diversification strategies can also benefit from leveraging corporate parenting capabilities and other general resources. Another dimension of resource fit that concerns all types of multibusiness firms is whether they have resources sufficient to support their group of businesses without being spread too thin.

Financial Resource Fit   One dimension of resource fit concerns whether a diversified company can generate the internal cash flows sufficient to fund the capital requirements of its businesses, pay its dividends, meet its debt obligations, and otherwise remain financially healthy. (Financial resources, including the firm's ability to borrow or otherwise raise funds, are a generalized type of resource.) While additional capital can usually be raised in financial markets, it is important for a diversified firm to have a healthy **internal capital market** that can support the financial requirements of its business lineup. The greater the extent to which a diversified company is able to fund investment in its businesses through internally generated cash flows rather than from equity issues or borrowing, the more powerful its financial resource fit and the less dependent the firm is on external financial resources. This can provide a competitive advantage over single business rivals when credit market conditions are tight, as they have been in the United States and abroad in recent years.

A **portfolio approach** to ensuring financial fit among a firm's businesses is based on the fact that different businesses have different cash flow and investment characteristics. For example, business units in rapidly growing industries are often **cash hogs**—so labeled because the cash flows they are able to generate from internal operations aren't big enough to fund their expansion. To keep pace with rising buyer demand, rapid-growth businesses frequently need sizable annual capital investments—for new facilities and equipment, for new product development or technology improvements, and for additional working capital to support inventory expansion and a larger base of operations. A business in a fast-growing industry becomes an even bigger cash hog when it has a relatively low market share and is pursuing a strategy to become an industry leader.

In contrast, business units with leading market positions in mature industries are frequently **cash cows**—businesses that generate substantial cash surpluses over what is needed to adequately fund their operations. Market leaders in slow-growth industries often generate sizable positive cash flows *over and above what is needed for growth and reinvestment* because their industry-leading positions tend to generate attractive earnings and because the slow-growth nature of their industry often entails relatively modest annual investment requirements. Cash cows, although not always attractive from a growth standpoint, are valuable businesses from a financial resource perspective. The surplus cash flows they generate can be used to pay corporate dividends, finance acquisitions, and provide funds for investing in the company's promising cash hogs. It

---

CORE CONCEPT

A diversified company exhibits **resource fit** when its businesses add to a company's overall resource strengths and have matching resource requirements and/or when the parent company has adequate corporate resources to support its businesses' needs and add value.

CORE CONCEPT

A strong **internal capital market** allows a diversified company to add value by shifting capital from business units generating *free cash flow* to those needing additional capital to expand and realize their growth potential.

CORE CONCEPT

A **portfolio approach** to ensuring financial fit among a firm's businesses is based on the fact that different businesses have different cash flow and investment characteristics.

CORE CONCEPT

A **cash hog** business generates cash flows that are too small to fully fund its operations and growth and requires cash infusions to provide additional working capital and finance new capital investment.

makes good financial and strategic sense for diversified companies to keep cash cows in a healthy condition, fortifying and defending their market position so as to preserve their cash-generating capability and have an ongoing source of financial resources to deploy elsewhere. General Electric considers its advanced materials, equipment services, and appliance and lighting businesses to be cash cow businesses.

Viewing a diversified group of businesses as a collection of cash flows and cash requirements (present and future) is a major step forward in understanding what the financial ramifications of diversification are and why having businesses with good financial resource fit can be important. For instance, *a diversified company's businesses exhibit good financial resource fit when the excess cash generated by its cash cow businesses is sufficient to fund the investment requirements of promising cash hog businesses.* Ideally, investing in promising cash hog businesses over time results in growing the hogs into self-supporting *star businesses* that have strong or market-leading competitive positions in attractive, high-growth markets and high levels of profitability. Star businesses are often the cash cows of the future. When the markets of star businesses begin to mature and their growth slows, their competitive strength should produce self-generated cash flows that are more than sufficient to cover their investment needs. The "success sequence" is thus cash hog to young star (but perhaps still a cash hog) to self-supporting star to cash cow. While the practice of viewing a diversified company in terms of cash cows and cash hogs has declined in popularity, it illustrates one approach to analyzing financial resource fit and allocating financial resources across a portfolio of different businesses.

Aside from cash flow considerations, there are two other factors to consider in assessing whether a diversified company's businesses exhibit good financial fit:

- *Do each of the individual businesses adequately contribute to achieving companywide performance targets?* A business exhibits poor financial fit if it soaks up a disproportionate share of the company's financial resources, while making subpar or insignificant contributions to the bottom line. Too many underperforming businesses reduce the company's overall performance and ultimately limit growth in shareholder value.

- *Does the corporation have adequate financial strength to fund its different businesses and maintain a healthy credit rating?* A diversified company's strategy fails the resource fit test when the resource needs of its portfolio unduly stretch the company's financial health and threaten to impair its credit rating. Many of the world's largest banks (e.g., Royal Bank of Scotland, Citigroup, HSBC) recently found themselves so undercapitalized and financially overextended that they were forced to sell off some of their business assets to meet regulatory requirements and restore public confidence in their solvency.

Nonfinancial Resource Fit   Just as a diversified company must have adequate financial resources to support its various individual businesses, it must also have a big enough and deep enough pool of managerial, administrative, and competitive capabilities to support all of its different businesses. The following two questions help reveal whether a diversified company has sufficient nonfinancial resources:

- *Does the company have (or can it develop) the specific resources and capabilities needed to be successful in each of its businesses?*[23] Sometimes a diversified company's resources and capabilities are poorly matched to the resource requirements of one or more businesses it has diversified into. For instance, BTR, a multibusiness company in Great Britain, discovered that the company's resources and managerial skills were quite well suited for parenting its industrial manufacturing businesses but not for parenting its distribution businesses (National Tyre Services and Texas-based Summers Group). As a result, BTR decided to divest its distribution businesses and focus exclusively on diversifying around small industrial manufacturing.[24] For companies pursuing related diversification strategies, a mismatch between the company's competitive assets and the key success factors of an industry can be serious enough to warrant divesting businesses in that industry or not acquiring a new business. In contrast, when a company's resources and capabilities are a good match with the key success factors of industries it is not presently in, it makes sense to take a hard look at acquiring companies in these industries and expanding the company's business lineup.

- *Are the company's resources being stretched too thinly by the resource requirements of one or more of its businesses?* A diversified company must guard against overtaxing its resources and capabilities, a condition that can arise when (1) it goes on an acquisition spree and management is called on to assimilate and oversee many new businesses very quickly or (2) it lacks sufficient resource depth to do a creditable job of transferring skills and competencies from one of its businesses to another. The broader the diversification, the greater the concern about whether the company has sufficient managerial depth to cope with the diverse range of operating problems its wide business lineup presents. Plus, the more a company's diversification strategy is tied to transferring its existing know-how or technologies to new businesses, the more it has to develop a big-enough and deep-enough resource pool to supply these businesses with sufficient capability to create competitive advantage.[25] Otherwise, its competitive assets end up being thinly spread across many businesses, and the opportunity for competitive advantage slips through the cracks.

Step 5: Ranking Business Units and Assigning a Priority for Resource Allocation

Once a diversified company's strategy has been evaluated from the perspective of industry attractiveness, competitive strength, strategic fit, and resource fit, the next step is to use this information to rank the performance prospects of the businesses from best to worst. Such ranking helps top-level executives assign each business a priority for resource support and capital investment.

The locations of the different businesses in the nine-cell industry attractiveness/competitive strength matrix provide a solid basis for identifying high-opportunity businesses and low-opportunity businesses. Normally, competitively strong businesses in attractive industries have significantly better performance prospects than competitively weak businesses in unattractive industries. Also, the revenue and earnings outlook for businesses in fast-growing businesses is normally better than for businesses in slow-growing businesses. As a rule, *business subsidiaries with the brightest profit and growth prospects, attractive positions in the nine-cell matrix, and solid strategic and resource fit should receive top priority for allocation of corporate resources.* However, in ranking the prospects of the different businesses from best to worst, it is usually wise to also take into account each business's past performance as concerns sales growth, profit growth, contribution to company earnings, return on capital invested in the business, and cash flow from operations. While past performance is not always a reliable predictor of future performance, it does signal whether a business already has good to excellent performance or has problems to overcome.

Allocating Financial Resources   Figure 8.5 shows the chief strategic and financial options for allocating a diversified company's financial resources. Divesting

FIGURE 8.5 The Chief Strategic and Financial Options for Allocating a Diversified Company's Financial Resources

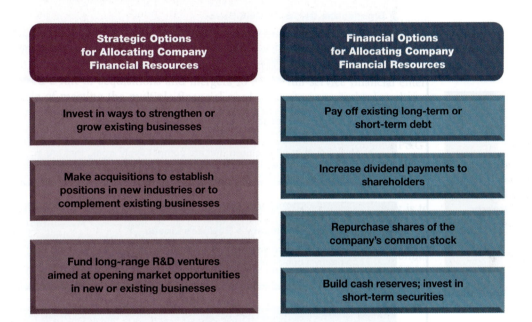

businesses with the weakest future prospects and businesses that lack adequate strategic fit and/or resource fit is one of the best ways of generating additional funds for redeployment to businesses with better opportunities and better strategic and resource fit. Free cash flows from cash cow businesses also add to the pool of funds that can be usefully redeployed. *Ideally,* a diversified company will have sufficient financial resources to strengthen or grow its existing businesses, make any new acquisitions that are desirable, fund other promising business opportunities, pay off existing debt, and periodically increase dividend payments to shareholders and/or repurchase shares of stock. But, as a practical matter, a company's financial resources are limited. Thus for top executives to make the best use of the available funds, they must steer resources to those businesses with the best opportunities and performance prospects and allocate little if any resources to businesses with marginal or dim prospects—this is why ranking the performance prospects of the various businesses from best to worst is so crucial. Strategic uses of corporate financial resources (see Figure 8.5) should usually take precedence unless there is a compelling reason to strengthen the firm's balance sheet or better reward shareholders.

Step 6: Crafting New Strategic Moves to Improve Overall Corporate Performance

LO 5

Understand a diversified company's four main corporate strategy options for solidifying its diversification strategy and improving company performance.

The conclusions flowing from the five preceding analytical steps set the agenda for crafting strategic moves to improve a diversified company's overall performance. The strategic options boil down to four broad categories of actions (see Figure 8.6):

1. Sticking closely with the existing business lineup and pursuing the opportunities these businesses present.
2. Broadening the company's business scope by making new acquisitions in new industries.

cross-cultural differences in ethical standards, it is appropriate for *local ethical standards to take precedence over what the ethical standards may be in a company's home market.*[4] In a world of ethical relativism, there are few absolutes when it comes to business ethics, and thus few ethical absolutes for consistently judging the ethical correctness of a company's conduct in various countries and markets.

While the ethical relativism rule of "When in Rome, do as the Romans do" appears reasonable, it leads to the conclusion that what prevails as local morality is an adequate and definitive guide to ethical behavior. But this poses some challenging ethical dilemmas. Consider the following two examples.

The Use of Underage Labor

In industrialized nations, the use of underage workers is considered taboo. Social activists are adamant that child labor is unethical and that companies should neither employ children under the age of 18 as full-time employees nor source any products from foreign suppliers that employ underage workers. Many countries have passed legislation forbidding the use of underage labor or, at a minimum, regulating the employment of people under the age of 18. However, in India, Bangladesh, Botswana, Sri Lanka, Ghana, Somalia, Turkey, and more than 50 other countries, it is customary to view children as potential, even necessary, workers.[5] As of 2012, the International Labor Organization estimated that 215 million children, from age 5 to 14, were working around the world.[6]

While exposing children to hazardous work and long work hours is unquestionably deplorable, the fact remains that poverty-stricken families in many poor countries cannot subsist without the work efforts of young family members; sending their children to school instead of having them work is not a realistic option. If such children are not permitted to work (especially those in the 12–17 age group)—due to pressures imposed by activist groups in industrialized nations—they may be forced to go out on the streets begging or to seek work in parts of the "underground" economy such as drug trafficking and prostitution.[7] So if all businesses in countries where employing underage workers is common succumb to the pressures to stop employing underage labor, then have they served the best interests of the underage workers, their families, and society in general?

The Payment of Bribes and Kickbacks

A particularly thorny area facing multinational companies is the degree of cross-country variability in paying bribes.[8] In many countries in eastern Europe, Africa, Latin America, and Asia, it is customary to pay bribes to government officials in order to win a government contract, obtain a license or permit, or facilitate an administrative ruling.[9] In some developing nations, it is difficult for any company, foreign or domestic, to move goods through customs without paying off low-level officials.[10] Senior managers in China often use their power to obtain kickbacks when they purchase materials or other products for their companies.[11] Likewise, in many countries it is normal to make payments to prospective customers in order to win or retain their business. In some developing nations, it is difficult for any company, foreign or domestic, to move goods through customs without paying off low-level officials. A *Wall Street Journal* article reported that 30 to 60 percent of all business transactions in eastern Europe involved paying bribes and the costs of bribe payments averaged 2 to 8 percent of revenues.[12] Some people stretch to justify the payment of bribes and kickbacks on grounds that bribing government officials to get goods through customs or giving kickbacks to customers to retain their business or win new orders is simply a payment for services rendered, in the same way that people tip for service at restaurants.[13] But while this is a clever rationalization, it rests on moral quicksand.

Companies that forbid the payment of bribes and kickbacks in their codes of ethical conduct and that are serious about enforcing this prohibition face a particularly vexing problem in countries where bribery and kickback payments are an entrenched local custom. Complying with the company's code of ethical conduct in these countries is very often tantamount to losing business to competitors that have no such scruples—an outcome that penalizes ethical companies and ethical company personnel (who may suffer lost sales commissions or bonuses). On the other hand, the payment of bribes or kickbacks not only undercuts the company's code of ethics but also risks breaking the law. U.S. companies are prohibited by the Foreign Corrupt Practices Act (FCPA) from paying bribes to government officials, political parties, political candidates, or others in all countries where they do business. The Organization for Economic Cooperation and Development (OECD) has anti-bribery standards that criminalize the bribery of foreign public officials in international business transactions—as of 2009, the 30 OECD members and 8 nonmember countries had adopted these standards.[14]

Despite laws forbidding bribery to secure sales and contracts, the practice persists. In 2010, there were some 345 cases in various stages of investigation for bribery and corruption. In 2010, Hewlett-Packard (HP) agreed to pay $16.25 million to settle allegations that it bribed Texas school officials with expensive gifts in exchange for federally funded contracts that paid for Internet connections for schools and libraries. In 2011, Daimler AG, the maker of Mercedes-Benz vehicles, paid $185 million in fines to settle charges that it used secret bank accounts to make 200 illicit payments totaling more than $56 million to foreign officials in 22 countries between 1998 and 2008. Daimler's kickback scheme of cash and gifts enabled it to secure sales of about 6,300 commercial vehicles and 500 passenger cars worth $1.9 billion and earn an estimated $91.4 million in profits. In recognition of such problems, penalizing companies for overseas bribes is becoming more widespread internationally.

Basing Ethical Standards on Ethical Relativism Is Problematic for Multinational Companies

From a global markets perspective, ethical relativism results in a maze of conflicting ethical standards for multinational companies wanting to address the very real issue of which ethical standards to enforce companywide. It is a slippery slope indeed to resolve such ethical diversity without any kind of higher-order moral compass. Consider, for example, the ethical inconsistency of a multinational company that, in the name of ethical relativism, declares it impermissible to engage in bribery and kickbacks, unless such payments are customary and generally overlooked by legal authorities. It is likewise problematic for a multinational company to declare it ethically acceptable to use underage labor in its plants in those countries where child labor is allowed but ethically inappropriate to employ underage labor at its plants elsewhere. If a country's culture is accepting of environmental degradation or exposing workers to dangerous conditions (toxic chemicals or bodily harm), then should a multinational company lower its ethical bar in that country and deem such actions within ethical bounds but raise the ethical bar and rule the very same actions to be ethically wrong in other countries?

Company managers who rely upon the principle of ethical relativism to justify conflicting ethical standards for operating in different countries have little moral basis for establishing or enforcing ethical standards companywide. Rather, when a company's ethical standards vary from country to country, the clear message being sent to employees is that the company has no ethical standards or convictions of its own and prefers to let its standards of ethically right and wrong be governed by the customs and practices of the countries in which it operates. Applying multiple sets of ethical standards without some kind of higher-order moral compass is scarcely a basis for holding company personnel to high standards of ethical behavior.

Under ethical relativism, there can be no one-size-fits-all set of authentic ethical norms against which to gauge the conduct of company personnel.

Codes of conduct based on ethical relativism can be *ethically dangerous* for multinational companies by creating a maze of conflicting ethical standards.

Ethics and Integrative Social Contracts Theory

Integrative social contracts theory provides a middle position between the opposing views of universalism and relativism.[15] According to this theory, the ethical standards a company should try to uphold are governed by both (1) a limited number of universal ethical principles that are widely recognized as putting legitimate ethical boundaries on behaviors in *all* situations and (2) the circumstances of local cultures, traditions, and values that further prescribe what constitutes ethically permissible behavior. The universal ethical principles are based on the collective views of multiple cultures and societies and combine to form a "social contract" that all individuals, groups, organizations, and businesses in all situations have a duty to observe. *Within the boundaries of this social contract,* local cultures or groups can specify what other actions may or may not be ethically permissible. While this system leaves some "moral free space" for the people in a particular country (or local culture, or profession, or even a company) to make specific interpretations of what other actions may or may not be permissible, *universal ethical norms always take precedence.* Thus, local ethical standards can be *more* stringent than the universal ethical standards, but never less so. For example, both the legal and medical professions have standards regarding what kinds of advertising are ethically permissible that extend beyond the universal norm that advertising not be false or misleading.

The strength of integrated social contracts theory is that it accommodates the best parts of ethical universalism and ethical relativism. Moreover, integrative social contracts theory offers managers in multinational companies clear guidance in resolving cross-country ethical differences: Those parts of the company's code of ethics that involve universal ethical norms must be enforced worldwide, but within these boundaries there is room for ethical diversity and the opportunity for host country cultures to exert *some* influence over the moral and ethical standards of business units operating in that country. Such an approach avoids the discomforting case of a self-righteous multinational company trying to operate as the standard bearer of moral truth and imposing its interpretation of its code of ethics worldwide no matter what. And it avoids the equally disturbing case for a company's ethical conduct to be no higher than local ethical norms in situations where local ethical norms permit practices that are generally considered immoral or when local norms clearly conflict with a company's code of ethical conduct.

A good example of the application of integrative social contracts theory to business involves the payment of bribes and kickbacks. Yes, bribes and kickbacks seem to be common in some countries, but does this justify paying them? Just because bribery flourishes in a country does not mean it is an authentic or legitimate ethical norm. Virtually all of the world's major religions (e.g., Buddhism, Christianity, Confucianism, Hinduism, Islam, Judaism, Sikhism, and Taoism) and all moral schools of thought condemn bribery and corruption.[16] Therefore, a multinational company might reasonably conclude that there is a universal ethical principle to be observed in this case—one of refusing to condone bribery and kickbacks on the part of company personnel no matter what the local custom is and no matter what the sales consequences are.

HOW AND WHY ETHICAL STANDARDS IMPACT THE TASKS OF CRAFTING AND EXECUTING STRATEGY

Many companies have acknowledged their ethical obligations in official codes of ethical conduct. In the United States, for example, the Sarbanes–Oxley Act, passed in 2002, requires that companies whose stock is publicly traded have a code of ethics or else explain in writing to the Securities and Exchange Commission (SEC) why they do not. But there's a big difference between having a code of ethics because it is mandated and having ethical standards that truly provide guidance for a company's strategy and business conduct.[17] *The litmus test of whether a company's code of ethics is cosmetic is the extent to which it is embraced in crafting strategy and in operating the business day to day.*

It is up to senior executives to lead the way on compliance with the company's ethical code of conduct. They can do so by making a point to consider three sets of questions whenever a new strategic initiative is under review:

- Is what we are proposing to do fully compliant with our code of ethical conduct? Are there any areas of ambiguity that may be of concern?
- Is it apparent that this proposed action is in harmony with our code? Are any conflicts or potential problems evident?
- Is there anything in the proposed action that could be considered ethically objectionable? Would our customers, employees, suppliers, stockholders, competitors, communities, the SEC, or the media view this action as ethically objectionable?

Unless questions of this nature are posed—either in open discussion or by force of habit in the minds of strategy makers—there's room for strategic initiatives to become disconnected from the company's code of ethics. If a company's executives believe strongly in living up to the company's ethical standards, they will unhesitatingly reject strategic initiatives and operating approaches that don't measure up. However, in companies with a cosmetic approach to ethics, any strategy–ethics linkage stems mainly from a desire to avoid the risk of embarrassment and possible disciplinary action for approving a strategic initiative that is deemed by society to be unethical and perhaps illegal.

While most company managers are careful to ensure that a company's strategy is within the bounds of what is legal, evidence indicates they are not always so careful to ensure that all elements of their strategies and operating activities are within the bounds of what is considered ethical. In recent years, there have been revelations of ethical misconduct on the part of managers at such companies as Goldman Sachs, Halliburton, Fannie Mae, Freddie Mac, BP, Deepwater Horizon, Royal Dutch/Shell, Rite Aid, Mexican oil giant Pemex, AIG, several leading brokerage houses, mutual fund companies, investment banking firms, and a host of mortgage lenders. The consequences of crafting strategies that cannot pass the test of moral scrutiny are manifested in sizable fines, devastating public relations hits, sharp drops in stock prices that cost shareholders billions of dollars, and criminal indictments and convictions of company executives. The fallout from all these scandals has resulted in heightened management attention to legal and ethical considerations in crafting strategy.

WHAT ARE THE DRIVERS OF UNETHICAL STRATEGIES AND BUSINESS BEHAVIOR?

Apart from "the business of business is business, not ethics" kind of thinking apparent in recent high-profile business scandals, three other main drivers of unethical business behavior also stand out:[18]

LO 2

Recognize conditions that can give rise to unethical business strategies and behavior.

- Faulty oversight, enabling the unscrupulous pursuit of personal gain and self-interest.
- Heavy pressures on company managers to meet or beat short-term performance targets.
- A company culture that puts profitability and business performance ahead of ethical behavior.

Faulty Oversight, Enabling the Unscrupulous Pursuit of Personal Gain and Self-Interest

People who are obsessed with wealth accumulation, power, status, and their own self-interest often push ethical principles aside in their quest for personal gain. Driven by greed and ambition, they exhibit few qualms in skirting the rules or doing whatever is necessary to achieve their goals. A general disregard for business ethics can prompt all kinds of unethical strategic maneuvers and behaviors at companies. The U.S. government has been conducting a multiyear investigation of "inside trading," the illegal practice of exchanging confidential information to gain an advantage in the stock market. Focusing on the hedge fund industry and nicknamed "Operation Perfect Hedge," the investigation has brought to light scores of violations and led to more than 60 guilty pleas or convictions by early 2012. Among the most prominent of those convicted was Raj Rajarathnam, the former head of Galleon Group, who was sentenced to 11 years in prison and fined $10 million. In January 2012, seven hedge fund managers, described as a "circle of friends who formed a criminal club" were charged with reaping nearly $62 million in illegal profits on trades of Dell Inc.[19]

Responsible corporate governance and oversight by the company's corporate board is necessary to guard against self-dealing and the manipulation of information to disguise such actions by a company's managers. **Self-dealing** occurs when managers take advantage of their position to further their own private interests rather than those of the firm. As discussed in Chapter 2, the duty of the corporate board (and its compensation and audit committees in particular) is to guard against such actions. A strong, independent board is necessary to have proper oversight of the company's financial practices and to hold top managers accountable for their actions.

> **CORE CONCEPT**
>
> **Self-dealing** occurs when managers take advantage of their position to further their own private interests rather than those of the firm.

A particularly egregious example of the lack of proper oversight is the scandal over mortgage lending and banking practices that resulted in a crisis for the U.S. residential real estate market and heartrending consequences for many home buyers. This scandal stemmed from consciously unethical strategies at many banks and mortgage companies to boost the fees they earned on home mortgages by deliberately lowering lending standards to approve so-called "subprime loans" for home buyers whose incomes were insufficient to make their monthly mortgage payments. Once these lenders earned their fees on these loans, they repackaged the loans to hide their true nature and auctioned them off to unsuspecting investors, who later suffered huge losses when the high-risk borrowers began to default on their loan payments. (Government authorities later forced some of the firms that auctioned off these packaged loans to repurchase them at the auction price and bear the losses themselves.) A lawsuit by the attorneys general of 49 states charging widespread and systematic fraud ultimately resulted in a $26 billion settlement by the five largest U.S. banks (Bank of America, Citigroup, JPMorgan Chase, Wells Fargo, and Ally Financial). Included in the settlement were new rules designed to increase oversight and reform policies and practices among the mortgage companies. The settlement includes what are believed to be a set of robust monitoring and enforcement mechanisms that should help prevent such abuses in the future.[20]

Illustration Capsule 9.2 discusses the high-profile multibillion-dollar Ponzi schemes perpetrated at Bernard L. Madoff Investment Securities and alleged at Stanford Financial Group.

Heavy Pressures on Company Managers to Meet Short-Term Earnings Targets

When key personnel find themselves scrambling to meet the quarterly and annual sales and profit expectations of investors and financial analysts, they often feel enormous pressure to *do whatever it takes* to protect their reputation for delivering good results. Executives at high-performing companies know that investors will see the slightest sign of a slowdown in earnings growth as a red flag and drive down the

Investment Fraud at Bernard L. Madoff Investment Securities and Stanford Financial Group

Bernard Madoff engineered the largest investment scam in history to accumulate a net worth of more than $820 million and build a reputation as one of Wall Street's most savvy investors. Madoff deceived investors with a simple Ponzi scheme that promised returns that would beat the market by 400 to 500 percent. The hedge funds, banks, and wealthy individuals that sent Bernard L. Madoff Investment Securities billions to invest on their behalf were quite pleased when their statements arrived showing annual returns as high as 45 percent. But, in fact, the portfolio gains shown on these statements were fictitious. Funds placed with Bernard Madoff were seldom, if ever, actually invested in any type of security—the money went to cover losses in his legitimate stock-trading business, fund periodic withdrawals of investors' funds, and support Madoff's lifestyle (including three vacation homes and a $7 million Manhattan condominium.

For decades, the Ponzi scheme was never in danger of collapse because most Madoff investors were so impressed with the reported returns that they seldom made withdrawals from their accounts, and when they did withdraw funds Madoff used new investors' deposits to cover the payments. Madoff's deception came to an end in late 2008 when the dramatic drop in world stock prices caused so many of Madoff's investors to request withdrawals of their balances that there was not nearly enough new money coming in to cover the amounts being withdrawn. As with any Ponzi scheme, the first

investors to ask Madoff for their funds were paid, but those asking later were left empty-handed. All told, more than 1,300 account holders lost about $65 billion when Bernard Madoff admitted to the scam in December 2008. As of October 2011, investigators had located assets of only about $9 billion to return to Madoff account holders. Madoff was sentenced to 150 years in prison for his crimes.

Increased oversight at the Securities and Exchange Commission after the December 2008 Madoff confession led to the indictment of R. Allen Stanford and five others who were accused of running an investment scheme similar to that perpetrated by Bernard Madoff. Stanford was alleged to have defrauded more than 30,000 Stanford Financial Group account holders out of $7.2 billion through the sale of spurious certificates of deposit (CDs). Federal prosecutors alleged that deposits of at least $1.6 billion were diverted into undisclosed personal loans to Allen Stanford.

At the time of Stanford's indictment, he ranked 605th on *Forbes* magazine's list of the world's wealthiest persons, with an estimated net worth of $2.2 billion. He was also a notable sports enthusiast and philanthropist, having contributed millions to the St. Jude Children's Research Hospital and museums in Houston and Miami. After his indictment, he was denied bail and sent to jail to await trial, where he was badly beaten by prison inmates. In March 2012, he was convicted of money laundering and fraud in a Ponzi scheme.

Sources: James Bandler, Nicholas Varchaver, and Doris Burke, "How Bernie Did It," *Fortune Online,* April 30, 2009 (accessed July 7, 2009); Alyssa Abkowitz, "The Investment Scam-Artist's Playbook," *Fortune Online,* February 25, 2009 (accessed July 9, 2009); Jane J. Kim, "The Madoff Fraud: SIPC Sets Payouts in Madoff Scandal," *The Wall Street Journal* (Eastern Edition), October 29, 2009, p. C4; http://www.dailymail.co.uk/, accessed March 3, 2012; D. Gilbert, "Stanford Guilty in Ponzi Scheme," *WSJ online,* Markets, March 6, 2012.

company's stock price. In addition, slowing growth or declining profits could lead to a downgrade of the company's credit rating if it has used lots of debt to finance its growth. The pressure to "never miss a quarter"—so as not to upset the expectations of analysts, investors, and creditors—prompts nearsighted managers to engage in short-term maneuvers to make the numbers, regardless of whether these moves are really in the best long-term interests of the company. Sometimes the pressure induces company personnel to continue to stretch the rules until the limits of ethical conduct are overlooked.[21] Once ethical boundaries are crossed in efforts to "meet or beat their numbers," the threshold for making more extreme ethical compromises becomes lower.

In 2010, ATM maker Diebold, Inc. agreed to pay $25 million to settle a case brought by the Securities and Exchange Commission alleging that Diebold engaged in a fraudulent accounting scheme to inflate the company's earnings. Three of Diebold's former financial executives were also charged with manipulating the company's books to meet earnings forecasts. As Robert Khuzami, Director of the SEC's Division of Enforcement noted, "When executives disregard their professional obligations to investors, both they and their companies face significant legal consequences.[22] More recently, an investigation into a decade-long cover-up of investment losses by the Japanese camera maker Olympus resulted in the 2012 arrest of seven executives on suspicion of violation of Japanese securities laws. The share price of Olympus collapsed when the scandal broke, and the company now faces a daunting battle to regain its credibility along with its financial footing.

Company executives often feel pressured to hit financial performance targets because their compensation depends heavily on the company's performance. Over the last two decades, it has become fashionable for boards of directors to grant lavish bonuses, stock option awards, and other compensation benefits to executives for meeting specified performance targets. So outlandishly large were these rewards that executives had strong personal incentives to bend the rules and engage in behaviors that allowed the targets to be met. Much of the accounting manipulation at the root of recent corporate scandals has entailed situations in which executives benefited enormously from misleading accounting or other shady activities that allowed them to hit the numbers and receive incentive awards ranging from $10 million to more than $1 billion dollars for hedge fund managers.

> **CORE CONCEPT**
>
> **Short-termism** is the tendency for managers to focus excessively on short-term performance objectives at the expense of longer-term strategic objectives. It has negative implications for the likelihood of ethical lapses as well as company performance in the longer run.

The fundamental problem with **short-termism**—the tendency for managers to focus excessive attention on short-term performance objectives—is that it doesn't create value for customers or improve the firm's competitiveness in the marketplace; that is, it sacrifices the activities that are the most reliable drivers of higher profits and added shareholder value in the long run. Cutting ethical corners in the name of profits carries exceptionally high risk for shareholders—the steep stock price decline and tarnished brand image that accompany the discovery of scurrilous behavior leave shareholders with a company worth much less than before—and the rebuilding task can be arduous, taking both considerable time and resources.

A Company Culture that Puts Profitability and Business Performance Ahead of Ethical Behavior

When a company's culture spawns an ethically corrupt or amoral work climate, people have a company-approved license to ignore "what's right" and employ any strategy they think they can get away with. Such cultural norms as "everyone else does it" and "it is okay to bend the rules to get the job done" permeate the work environment. At such companies, ethically immoral people are certain to play down observance of ethical strategic actions and business conduct. Moreover, cultural pressures to utilize unethical means if circumstances become challenging can prompt otherwise honorable people to behave unethically. A perfect example of a company culture gone awry on ethics is Enron, a now-defunct company found guilty of one of the most sprawling business frauds in U.S. history.[23]

Enron's leaders encouraged company personnel to focus on the current bottom line and to be innovative and aggressive in figuring out how to grow current earnings—regardless of the methods. Enron's annual "rank and yank" performance evaluation process, in which the lowest-ranking 15 to 20 percent of employees were let go, made it abundantly clear that bottom-line results were what mattered most. The name of the game at Enron became devising clever ways to boost revenues and earnings, even if this sometimes meant operating outside established policies. In fact, outside-the-lines behavior was celebrated if it generated profitable new business.

A high-performance/high-rewards climate came to pervade the Enron culture, as the best workers (determined by who produced the best bottom-line results) received

How Novo Nordisk Puts Its Ethical Principles into Practice

Novo Nordisk is a $12B global pharmaceutical company, known for its innovation and leadership in diabetes treatments. It is also known for its dedication to ethical business practices. In 2009, Novo Nordisk was declared one of the world's most ethical companies by the U.S. business ethics think tank *Ethicsphere*. In 2012, the company was listed as the global leader in business ethics by *Corporate Knights*, a corporate social responsibility advisory firm.

Novo Nordisk's company policies are explicit in their attention to both bioethics and business ethics. In the realm of bioethics, the company is committed to conducting its research involving people, animals, and gene technology in accordance with the highest global ethical standards. Moreover, the company requires that all of their suppliers and other external partners also adhere to Novo Nordisk's bioethical standards. In the realm of business ethics, the policies dictate: (1) that high ethical standards be applied consistently across the company's value chain, (2) that all ethical dilemmas encountered be addressed transparently, and (3) that company officers and employees be held accountable for complying with all laws, regulations, and company rules.

Novo Nordisk's strong culture of responsibility helps to translate the company's policies into practice. At Novo Nordisk, every employee pledges to conduct themselves according to the Novo Nordisk Way, a set of behavioral norms that has come to define the company's culture. It's a culture that promotes teamwork, cooperation, respect for others, and fairness. The commitment to business ethics grew out of those values, which are promoted throughout the company by hiring practices, management leadership, and employee mobility to foster a global one-company culture.

As part of this process, Novo Nordisk has set up a business ethics board, composed of senior management. The board identifies key ethical challenges for the company, drafting guidelines and developing training programs. Those training programs are rigorous: all Novo Nordisk employees are trained annually in business ethics. The board is also responsible for ensuring

compliance. It has set up an anonymous hotline and conducts ethics audits. During 2011, 43 audits were conducted. The goal of these audits is to maintain a culture that promotes the principles of the Novo Nordisk Way.

Implementing a code of ethics across an organization of 26,000 employees is very difficult and lapses do occur. But such incidents are exceptional and are swiftly addressed by the company. For example, when insider trading allegations came to light against a corporate executive in 2008, the company immediately suspended and subsequently fired the employee.

Developed with Dennis L. Huggins.

Sources: Jim Edwards, "Novo Nordisk Exec Charged with Insider Trading; Cash Stashed in Caribbean," *CBS News,* September 2008 (accessed at www.cbsnews.com on February 19, 2012); company website, accessed February 19, 2012; Corporate Knights, "The 8th Annual Global 100," (accessed at http://global100.org/ on February 20, 2012).

TABLE 9.1   A Selection of Companies Recognized for Their Triple-Bottom-Line Performance in 2011

Name	Market Sector	Country
Air France-KLM	Travel & Leisure	France
BMW AG	Automobiles & Parts	Germany
Enagas S.A.	Utilities	Spain
Hyundai Engineering & Construction Co. Ltd.	Construction & Materials	Korea
Itausa-Investimentos Itau S/A	Financial Services	Brazil
Koninklijke DSM N.V.	Chemicals	Netherlands
Koninklijke Philips Electronics N.V.	Personal & Household Goods	Netherlands
KT Corp.	Telecommunications	Korea
Lotte Shopping Co. Ltd.	Retail	Korea
Pearson PLC	Media	UK
PepsiCo Inc.	Food & Beverage	United States
PostNL N.V.	Industrial Goods & Services	Netherlands
Repsol YPF S.A.	Oil & Gas	Spain
Roche Holding AG	Health Care	Switzerland
Samsung Electronics Co. Ltd.	Technology	Korea
Stockland	Real Estate	Australia
Swiss Re Limited	Insurance	UK
Westpac Banking Corp.	Banks	Australia
Xstrata PLC	Basic Resources	Switzerland

Sources: Dow Jones indexes, STOXX Limited, and SAM Group, http://www.sustainability-index.com/djsi_pdf/news/PressReleases/110908-djsi-review-2011-e-vdef.pdf (accessed February 13, 2012).

systems, guards against outcomes that will ultimately endanger the planet, and is therefore sustainable for centuries.[34] One aspect of environmental sustainability is keeping use of the Earth's natural resources within levels that can be replenished via the use of sustainable business practices. In the case of some resources (like crude oil, fresh water, and the harvesting of edible fish from the oceans), scientists say that use levels either are already unsustainable or will be soon, given the world's growing population and propensity to consume additional resources as incomes and living standards rise. Another aspect of sustainability concerns containing the adverse effects of greenhouse gases and other forms of air pollution so as to reduce their impact on undesirable climate and atmospheric changes. Other aspects of sustainability include greater reliance on sustainable energy sources, greater use of recyclable materials, the use of sustainable methods of growing foods (so as to reduce topsoil depletion and the use of pesticides, herbicides, fertilizers, and other chemicals that may be harmful to human health or ecological systems), habitat protection, environmentally sound waste management practices, and increased attempts to decouple environmental degradation and economic growth (according to many scientists, economic growth has historically been accompanied by declines in the well-being of the environment).

Unilever, a diversified producer of processed foods, personal care, and home cleaning products, is among the many committed corporations pursuing sustainable business practices. The company tracks 11 sustainable agricultural indicators in its processed-foods business and has launched a variety of programs to improve the environmental performance of its suppliers. Examples of such programs include special low-rate financing for tomato suppliers choosing to switch to water-conserving irrigation systems and training programs in India that have allowed contract cucumber growers to reduce pesticide use by 90 percent while improving yields by 78 percent. Unilever has also reengineered many internal processes to improve the company's overall performance on sustainability measures. For example, the company's factories have reduced water usage by 63 percent and total waste by 67 percent since 1995 through the implementation of sustainability initiatives. Unilever has also redesigned packaging for many of its products to conserve natural resources and reduce the volume of consumer waste. For example, the company's Suave shampoo bottles were reshaped to save almost 150 tons of plastic resin per year, which is the equivalent of 15 million fewer empty bottles making it to landfills annually. As the producer of Lipton Tea, Unilever is the world's largest purchaser of tea leaves; the company has committed to sourcing all of its tea from Rainforest Alliance Certified farms by 2015, due to their comprehensive triple-bottom-line approach toward sustainable farm management.

Crafting Corporate Social Responsibility and Sustainability Strategies

While CSR and environmental sustainability strategies take many forms, those that both provide valuable social benefits *and* fulfill customer needs in a superior fashion may also contribute to a company's competitive advantage.[35] For example, while carbon emissions may be a generic social concern for financial institutions such as Wells Fargo, Toyota's sustainability strategy for reducing carbon emissions has produced both competitive advantage and environmental benefits. Its Prius hybrid electric/gasoline-powered automobile is not only among the least polluting automobiles but is also the best-selling hybrid vehicle in the United States; it has earned the company the loyalty of fuel-conscious buyers and given Toyota a green image. Green Mountain Coffee Roasters' commitment to protect the welfare of coffee growers and their families (in particular, making sure they receive a fair price) also meets its customers' wants and needs. In its dealings with suppliers at small farmer cooperatives in Peru, Mexico, and Sumatra, Green Mountain pays "fair-trade" prices for coffee beans (in 2011, the fair-trade prices were a minimum of $1.26 per pound for conventional coffee versus market prices of $0.70 per pound). Green Mountain also purchases about 29 percent of its coffee directly from farmers so as to cut out intermediaries and see that farmers realize a higher price for their efforts—coffee is the world's second most heavily traded commodity after oil, requiring the labor of some 20 million people, most of whom live at the poverty level.[36] Its consumers are aware of these efforts and purchase Green Mountain coffee, in part, to encourage such practices.

CSR strategies and environmental sustainability strategies are more likely to contribute to a company's competitive advantage if they are linked to a company's competitively important resources and capabilities or value chain activities. Thus, it is common for companies engaged in natural resource extraction, electric power production, forestry

> CSR strategies and environmental sustainability strategies that both provide valuable social benefits *and* fulfill customer needs in a superior fashion can lead to competitive advantage. Corporate social agendas that address only social issues may help boost a company's reputation for corporate citizenship but are unlikely to improve its competitive strength in the marketplace.

and paper products, motor vehicles, and chemical production to place more emphasis on addressing environmental concerns than, say, software and electronics firms or apparel manufacturers. Companies whose business success is heavily dependent on high employee morale or attracting and retaining the best and brightest employees are somewhat more prone to stress the well-being of their employees and foster a positive, high-energy workplace environment that elicits the dedication and enthusiastic commitment of employees, thus putting real meaning behind the claim "Our people are our greatest asset." Ernst & Young, one of the four largest global accounting firms, stresses its "People First" workforce diversity strategy that is all about respecting differences, fostering individuality, and promoting inclusiveness so that its more than 152,000 employees in 140 countries can feel valued, engaged, and empowered in developing creative ways to serve the firm's clients. As a service business, Marriot's most competitively important resource is also people. Thus its social agenda includes providing 180 hours of paid classroom and on-the-job training to the chronically unemployed. Ninety percent of the graduates from the job training program take jobs with Marriott, and about two-thirds of those remain with Marriott for more than a year. At Whole Foods Market, an $11.1 billion supermarket chain specializing in organic and natural foods, its environmental sustainability strategy is evident in almost every segment of its company value chain and is a big part of its differentiation strategy. The company's procurement policies encourage stores to purchase fresh fruits and vegetables from local farmers and screen processed-food items for more than 400 common ingredients that the company considers unhealthy or environmentally unsound. Spoiled food items are sent to regional composting centers rather than landfills, and all cleaning products used in its stores are biodegradable. The company also has created the Animal Compassion Foundation to develop natural and humane ways of raising farm animals and has converted all of its vehicles to run on biofuels.

Not all companies choose to link their corporate environmental or social agendas to their value chain, their business model, or their industry. For example, Chick-Fil-A, an Atlanta-based fast-food chain with over 1,500 outlets in 39 states, has a charitable foundation that funds two scholarship programs and supports 14 foster homes as well as a summer camp for some 1,900 campers.[37] However, unless a company's social responsibility initiatives become part of the way it operates its business every day, the initiatives are unlikely to catch fire and be fully effective. As an executive at Royal Dutch/Shell put it, corporate social responsibility "is not a cosmetic; it must be rooted in our values. It must make a difference to the way we do business."[38] The same is true for environmental sustainability initiatives.

The Moral Case for Corporate Social Responsibility and Environmentally Sustainable Business Practices

The moral case for why businesses should act in a manner that benefits all of the company's stakeholders—not just shareholders—boils down to "It's the right thing to do." Ordinary decency, civic-mindedness, and contributions to the well-being of society should be expected of any business.[39] In today's social and political climate, most business leaders can be expected to acknowledge that socially responsible actions are important and that businesses have a duty to be good corporate citizens. But there is a complementary school of thought that business operates on the basis of an implied social contract with the members of society. According to this contract, society grants a business the right to conduct its business affairs and agrees not to unreasonably restrain its pursuit of a fair profit for the goods or services it sells. In return for this "license to

Every action a company takes can be interpreted as a statement of what it stands for.

operate," a business is obligated to act as a responsible citizen, do its fair share to promote the general welfare, and avoid doing any harm. Such a view clearly puts a moral burden on a company to take corporate citizenship into consideration and do what's best for shareholders within the confines of discharging its duties to operate honorably, provide good working conditions to employees, be a good environmental steward, and display good corporate citizenship.

The Business Case for Corporate Social Responsibility and Environmentally Sustainable Business Practices

Whatever the moral arguments for socially responsible business behavior and environmentally sustainable business practices, there are definitely good business reasons why companies should be public-spirited and devote time and resources to social responsibility initiatives, environmental sustainability, and good corporate citizenship:

- *Such actions can lead to increased buyer patronage.* A strong visible social responsibility or environmental sustainability strategy gives a company an edge in appealing to consumers who prefer to do business with companies that are good corporate citizens. Ben & Jerry's, Whole Foods Market, Stonyfield Farm, and The Body Shop have definitely expanded their customer bases because of their visible and well-publicized activities as socially conscious companies. More and more companies are also recognizing the cash register payoff of social responsibility strategies that reach out to people of all cultures and demographics (women, retirees, and ethnic groups).

- *A strong commitment to socially responsible behavior reduces the risk of reputation-damaging incidents.* Companies that place little importance on operating in a socially responsible manner are more prone to scandal and embarrassment. Consumer, environmental, and human rights activist groups are quick to criticize businesses whose behavior they consider to be out of line, and they are adept at getting their message into the media and onto the Internet. Pressure groups can generate widespread adverse publicity, promote boycotts, and influence like-minded or sympathetic buyers to avoid an offender's products. Research has shown that product boycott announcements are associated with a decline in a company's stock price.[40] When a major oil company suffered damage to its reputation on environmental and social grounds, the CEO repeatedly said that the most negative impact the company suffered—and the one that made him fear for the future of the company—was that bright young graduates were no longer attracted to working for the company. For many years, Nike received stinging criticism for not policing sweatshop conditions in the Asian factories that produced Nike footwear, causing Nike cofounder and former CEO Phil Knight to observe that "Nike has become synonymous with slave wages, forced overtime, and arbitrary abuse."[41] In 1997, Nike began an extensive effort to monitor conditions in the 800 factories of the contract manufacturers that produced Nike shoes. As Knight said, "Good shoes come from good factories and good factories have good labor relations." Nonetheless, Nike has continually been plagued by complaints from human rights activists that its monitoring procedures are flawed and that it is not doing enough to correct the plight of factory workers. As this suggests, a damaged reputation is not easily repaired.

- *Socially responsible actions and sustainable business practices can lower costs and enhance employee recruiting and workforce retention.* Companies with deservedly good

> The higher the public profile of a company or its brand, the greater the scrutiny of its activities and the higher the potential for it to become a target for pressure group action.

reputations for social responsibility and sustainable business practices are better able to attract and retain employees, compared to companies with tarnished reputations. Some employees just feel better about working for a company committed to improving society.[42] This can contribute to lower turnover and better worker productivity. Other direct and indirect economic benefits include lower costs for staff recruitment and training. For example, Starbucks is said to enjoy much lower rates of employee turnover because of its full benefits package for both full-time and part-time employees, management efforts to make Starbucks a great place to work, and the company's socially responsible practices. Sustainable business practices are often concomitant with greater operational efficiencies. For example, when a U.S. manufacturer of recycled paper, taking eco-efficiency to heart, discovered how to increase its fiber recovery rate, it saved the equivalent of 20,000 tons of waste paper—a factor that helped the company become the industry's lowest-cost producer. By helping two-thirds of its employees stop smoking and investing in a number of wellness programs for employees, Johnson & Johnson has saved $250 million on its health care costs over the past decade.[43]

- *Opportunities for revenue enhancement may also come from CSR and environmental sustainability strategies.* The drive for sustainability and social responsibility can spur innovative efforts that in turn lead to new products and opportunities for revenue enhancement. Electric cars such as the Chevy Volt and the Tesla Roadster are one example. In many cases, the revenue opportunities are tied to a company's core products. PepsiCo and Coca-Cola, for example, have expanded into the juice business to offer a healthier alternative to their carbonated beverages. GE has created a profitable new business in wind turbines. In other cases, revenue enhancement opportunities come from innovative ways to reduce waste and use the by-products of a company's production. Tyson Foods now produces jet fuel for B52 bombers from the vast amount of animal waste resulting from its meat product business. Staples has become one of the largest nonutility corporate producers of renewable energy in the United States due to its installation of solar power panels in all of its outlets (and the sale of what it does not consume in renewable energy credit markets).

- *Well-conceived CSR strategies and sustainable business practices are in the best long-term interest of shareholders.* When CSR and sustainability strategies increase buyer patronage, offer revenue-enhancing opportunities, lower costs, increase productivity, and reduce the risk of reputation-damaging incidents, they contribute to the total value created by a company and improve its profitability. A two-year study of leading companies found that improving environmental compliance and developing environmentally friendly products can enhance earnings per share, profitability, and the likelihood of winning contracts. The stock prices of companies that rate high on social and environmental performance criteria have been found to perform 35 to 45 percent better than the average of the 2,500 companies comprising the Dow Jones Global Index.[44] A review of 135 studies indicated there is a positive, but small, correlation between good corporate behavior and good financial performance; only 2 percent of the studies showed that dedicating corporate resources to social responsibility harmed the interests of shareholders.[45] Furthermore, socially responsible business behavior helps avoid or preempt legal and regulatory actions that could prove costly and otherwise burdensome. In some cases, it is possible to craft corporate social responsibility strategies that contribute to competitive advantage and, at the same time, deliver greater value to society. For instance, Walmart, by working with its suppliers to reduce the use of packaging materials and revamping the routes of its delivery trucks to cut out 100 million miles of travel, saved $200 million in costs

Socially responsible strategies that create value for customers and lower costs can improve company profits and shareholder value at the same time that they address other stakeholder interests.

in 2009 (which enhanced its cost competitiveness vis-à-vis rivals) and lowered carbon emissions.[46] Thus, a social responsibility strategy that packs some punch and is more than rhetorical flourish can produce outcomes that are in the best interest of shareholders.

In sum, companies that take social responsibility and environmental sustainability seriously can improve their business reputations and operational efficiency while also reducing their risk exposure and encouraging loyalty and innovation. Overall, companies that take special pains to protect the environment (beyond what is required by law), are active in community affairs, and are generous supporters of charitable causes and projects that benefit society are more likely to be seen as good investments and as good companies to work for or do business with. Shareholders are likely to view the business case for social responsibility as a strong one, particularly when it results in the creation of more customer value, greater productivity, lower operating costs, and lower business risk—all of which should increase firm profitability and enhance shareholder value even as the company's actions address broader stakeholder interests.

Companies are, of course, sometimes rewarded for bad behavior—a company that is able to shift environmental and other social costs associated with its activities onto society as a whole can reap large short-term profits. The major cigarette producers for many years were able to earn greatly inflated profits by shifting the health-related costs of smoking onto others and escaping any responsibility for the harm their products caused to consumers and the general public. Only recently have they been facing the prospect of having to pay high punitive damages for their actions. Unfortunately, the cigarette makers are not alone in trying to evade paying for the social harms of their operations for as long as they can. Calling a halt to such actions usually hinges on (1) the effectiveness of activist social groups in publicizing the adverse consequences of a company's social irresponsibility and marshaling public opinion for something to be done, (2) the enactment of legislation or regulations to correct the inequity, and (3) decisions on the part of socially conscious buyers to take their business elsewhere.

> There's little hard evidence indicating shareholders are disadvantaged in any meaningful way by a company's actions to be socially responsible.

KEY POINTS

1. Ethics concerns standards of right and wrong. Business ethics concerns the application of ethical principles to the actions and decisions of business organizations and the conduct of their personnel. Ethical principles in business are not materially different from ethical principles in general.

2. There are three schools of thought about ethical standards for companies with international operations:

    -   According to the *school of ethical universalism,* common understandings across multiple cultures and countries about what constitutes right and wrong behaviors give rise to universal ethical standards that apply to members of all societies, all companies, and all businesspeople.

    -   According to the *school of ethical relativism,* different societal cultures and customs have divergent values and standards of right and wrong. Thus, what is ethical or unethical must be judged in the light of local customs and social mores and can vary from one culture or nation to another.

- According to the *integrated social contracts theory,* universal ethical principles based on the collective views of multiple cultures and societies combine to form a "social contract" that all individuals in all situations have a duty to observe. Within the boundaries of this social contract, local cultures or groups can specify what additional actions are not ethically permissible. However, universal norms always take precedence over local ethical norms.

3. Apart from "the business of business is business, not ethics" kind of thinking, three other factors contribute to unethical business behavior: (1) faulty oversight that enables the unscrupulous pursuit of personal gain, (2) heavy pressures on company managers to meet or beat short-term earnings targets, and (3) a company culture that puts profitability and good business performance ahead of ethical behavior. In contrast, culture can function as a powerful mechanism for promoting ethical business conduct when high ethical principles are deeply ingrained in the corporate culture of a company.

4. Business ethics failures can result in three types of costs: (1) visible costs, such as fines, penalties, and lower stock prices, (2) internal administrative costs, such as legal costs and costs of taking corrective action, and (3) intangible costs, such as customer defections and damage to the company's reputation.

5. The term *corporate social responsibility* concerns a company's *duty* to operate in an honorable manner, provide good working conditions for employees, encourage workforce diversity, be a good steward of the environment, and support philanthropic endeavors in local communities where it operates and in society at large. The particular combination of socially responsible endeavors a company elects to pursue defines its corporate social responsibility (CSR) strategy.

6. The triple bottom line refers to company performance in three realms: economic, social, environmental. Increasingly, companies are reporting their performance with respect to all three performance dimensions.

7. *Sustainability* is a term that is used in various ways, but most often it concerns a firm's relationship to the environment and its use of natural resources. Sustainable business practices are those capable of meeting the needs of the present without compromising the world's ability to meet future needs. A company's environmental sustainability strategy consists of its deliberate actions to protect the environment, provide for the longevity of natural resources, maintain ecological support systems for future generations, and guard against ultimate endangerment of the planet.

8. CSR strategies and environmental sustainability strategies that both provide valuable social benefits *and* fulfill customer needs in a superior fashion can lead to competitive advantage.

9. The moral case for corporate social responsibility and environmental sustainability boils down to a simple concept: It's the right thing to do. There are also solid reasons why CSR and environmental sustainability strategies may be good business—they can be conducive to greater buyer patronage, reduce the risk of reputation-damaging incidents, provide opportunities for revenue enhancement, and lower costs. Well-crafted CSR and environmental sustainability strategies are in the best long-term interest of shareholders, for the reasons just mentioned and because they can avoid or preempt costly legal or regulatory actions.

ASSURANCE OF LEARNING EXERCISES

1. Ikea is widely known for its commitment to business ethics and environmental sustainability. After reviewing its About Ikea section of its website (http://www.ikea.com/ms/en_US/about_ikea/index.html), prepare a list of 10 specific policies and programs that help the company achieve its vision of creating a better everyday life for people around the world.

   LO 1, LO 4

2. Prepare a one- to two-page analysis of a recent ethics scandal using your university library's access to Lexis-Nexis or other Internet resources. Your report should (1) discuss the conditions that gave rise to unethical business strategies and behavior and (2) provide an overview of the costs resulting from the company's business ethics failure.

   LO 2, LO 3

3. Based on information provided in Illustration Capsule 9.3, discuss the actions taken by top management at Novo Nordisk that have allowed the company to be considered a global leader in business ethics. Also, explain how the company's values encourage employees to act in an ethical manner. What role does the company's culture have in promoting ethical business behavior? Explain.

   connect

   LO 2

4. Review Microsoft's statements about its corporate citizenship programs at www.microsoft.com/about/corporatecitizenship. How does the company's commitment to CSR provide positive benefits for its stakeholders?

   LO 4

5. Go to www.nestle.com and read the company's latest sustainability report. What are Nestlé's key environmental sustainable environmental policies? How do these initiatives relate to the company's principles, values, and culture and its approach to competing in the food industry?

   connect

   LO 4

EXERCISES FOR SIMULATION PARTICIPANTS

1. Is your company's strategy ethical? Why or why not? Is there anything that your company has done or is now doing that could legitimately be considered as "shady" by your competitiors?

   LO 1

2. In what ways, if any, is your company exercising corporate social responsibility? What are the elements of your company's CSR strategy? Are there any changes to this strategy that you would suggest?

   LO 4

3. If some shareholders complained that you and your co-managers have been spending too little or too much on corporate social responsibility, what would you tell them?

   LO 3, LO 4

4. Is your company striving to conduct its business in an environmentally sustainable manner? What specific *additional* actions could your company take that would make an even greater contribution to environmental sustainability?

   LO 4

5. In what ways is your company's environmental sustainability strategy in the best long-term interest of shareholders? Does it contribute to your company's competitive advantage or profitability?

   LO 4

activities that must be attended to, the many ways to put new strategic initiatives in place and keep things moving, and the number of bedeviling issues that always crop up and have to be resolved. It takes first-rate "managerial smarts" to zero in on what exactly needs to be done to put new strategic initiatives in place and, further, how to get good results in a timely manner. Excellent people-management skills and perseverance are required to get a variety of initiatives launched and to integrate the efforts of many different work groups into a smoothly functioning whole. Depending on how much consensus building and organizational change is involved, the process of implementing strategy changes can take several months to several years. To achieve *real proficiency* in executing the strategy can take even longer.

Like crafting strategy, *executing strategy is a job for a company's whole management team—not just a few senior managers.* While the chief executive officer and the heads of major units (business divisions, functional departments, and key operating units) are ultimately responsible for seeing that strategy is executed successfully, the process typically affects every part of the firm—all value chain activities and all work groups. Top-level managers must rely on the active support of middle and lower managers to institute whatever new operating practices are needed in the various operating units to achieve the desired results. Middle and lower-level managers must ensure that frontline employees perform strategy-critical value chain activities well and produce operating results that allow companywide performance targets to be met. In consequence, *all company personnel are actively involved in the strategy execution process in one way or another.*

A FRAMEWORK FOR EXECUTING STRATEGY

CORE CONCEPT

Good strategy execution requires a *team effort*. All managers have strategy-executing responsibility in their areas of authority, and all employees are active participants in the strategy execution process.

Executing strategy entails figuring out the specific actions, and behaviors that are needed to get things done and deliver good results. The exact items that need to be placed on management's action agenda always have to be customized to fit the particulars of a company's situation. The techniques for successfully executing a low-cost provider strategy are different from those for executing a high-end differentiation strategy. Implementing a new strategy for a struggling company in the midst of a financial crisis is a different job from that of making minor improvements to strategy execution in a company that is doing relatively well. Moreover, some managers are more adept than others at using particular approaches to achieving the desired kinds of organizational changes. Hence, there's no definitive managerial recipe for successful strategy execution that cuts across all company situations and all types of strategies or that works for all types of managers. Rather, the specific actions required to execute a strategy—the "to-do list" that constitutes management's action agenda—always represent management's judgment about how best to proceed in light of prevailing circumstances.

LO 1

Gain command of what managers must do to execute strategy successfully.

The Principal Components of the Strategy Execution Process

Despite the need to tailor a company's strategy-executing approaches to the particulars of its situation, certain managerial bases must be covered no matter what the circumstances. These include ten basic managerial tasks (see Figure 10.1):

1. Staff the organization with managers and employees capable of executing the strategy well.
2. Build the organizational capabilities required for successful strategy execution.
3. Create a strategy-supportive organizational structure.

FIGURE 10.1   The 10 Basic Tasks of the Strategy Execution Process

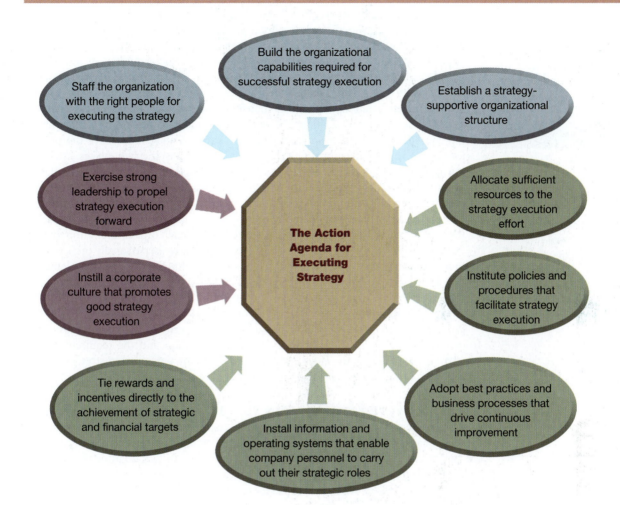

4. Allocate sufficient resources (budgetary and otherwise) to the strategy execution effort.

5. Institute policies and procedures that facilitate strategy execution.

6. Adopt best practices and business processes that drive continuous improvement in strategy execution activities.

7. Install information and operating systems that enable company personnel to carry out their strategic roles proficiently.

8. Tie rewards and incentives directly to the achievement of strategic and financial targets.

9. Instill a corporate culture that promotes good strategy execution.

10. Exercise the internal leadership needed to propel strategy implementation forward.

How well managers perform these 10 tasks has a decisive impact on whether the outcome of the strategy execution effort is a spectacular success, a colossal failure, or something in between.

When strategies fail, it is often because of poor execution. Strategy execution is therefore a critical managerial endeavor.

In devising an action agenda for executing strategy, the place for managers to start is with *a probing assessment of what the organization must do differently to carry out the strategy successfully.* Each manager needs to ask the question "What needs to be done in my area of responsibility to implement our part of the company's strategy and what should I do to get these things accomplished?" It is then incumbent on every manager to determine *precisely how to make the necessary internal changes.* Successful strategy implementers are masters in promoting results-oriented behaviors on the part of company personnel and following through on making the right things happen in a timely fashion.[3]

The two best signs of good strategy execution are whether a company is meeting or beating its performance targets and whether they are performing value chain activities in a manner that is conducive to companywide operating excellence.

In big organizations with geographically scattered operating units, the action agenda of senior executives mostly involves communicating the case for change, building consensus for how to proceed, installing strong managers to move the process forward in key organizational units, directing resources to the right places, establishing deadlines and measures of progress, rewarding those who achieve implementation milestones, and personally leading the strategic change process. Thus, the bigger the organization, the more that successful strategy execution depends on the cooperation and implementing skills of operating managers who can promote needed changes at the lowest organizational levels and deliver results. In small organizations, top managers can deal directly with frontline managers and employees, personally orchestrating the action steps and implementation sequence, observing firsthand how implementation is progressing, and deciding how hard and how fast to push the process along. Regardless of the organization's size and whether strategy implementation involves sweeping or minor changes, the most important leadership trait is a strong, confident sense of what to do and how to do it. Having a strong grip on these two things comes from understanding the circumstances of the organization and the requirements for effective strategy execution. Then it remains for company personnel in strategy-critical areas to step up to the plate and produce the desired results.

What's Covered in Chapters 10, 11, and 12   In the remainder of this chapter and in the next two chapters, we will discuss what is involved in performing the 10 key managerial tasks that shape the process of executing strategy. This chapter explores the first three of these tasks (highlighted in blue in Figure 10.1): (1) staffing the organization with people capable of executing the strategy well, (2) building the organizational capabilities needed for successful strategy execution, and (3) creating an organizational structure supportive of the strategy execution process. Chapter 11 concerns the tasks of allocating resources, instituting strategy-facilitating policies and procedures, employing business process management tools and best practices, installing operating and information systems, and tying rewards to the achievement of good results (highlighted in green in Figure 10.1). Chapter 12 deals with the two remaining tasks: creating a strategy-supportive corporate culture and exercising the leadership needed to drive the execution process forward (highlighted in purple).

BUILDING AN ORGANIZATION CAPABLE OF GOOD STRATEGY EXECUTION: THREE KEY ACTIONS

Proficient strategy execution depends foremost on having in place an organization capable of the tasks demanded of it. Building an execution-capable organization is thus always a top priority. As shown in Figure 10.2, three types of organization-building actions are paramount:

1. *Staffing the organization*—Putting together a strong management team, and recruiting and retaining employees with the needed experience, technical skills, and intellectual capital.

2. *Acquiring, developing, and strengthening strategy-supportive resources and capabilities*—Accumulating the required resources, developing proficiencies in performing strategy-critical value chain activities, and updating the company's capabilities to match changing market conditions and customer expectations.

3. *Structuring the organization and work effort*—Organizing value chain activities and business processes, establishing lines of authority and reporting relationships, and deciding how much decision-making authority to delegate to lower-level managers and frontline employees.

Implementing a strategy depends critically on ensuring that strategy-supportive resources and capabilities are in place, ready to be deployed. These include the skills, talents, experience, and knowledge of the company's human resources (managerial and otherwise)—see Figure 10.2. Proficient strategy execution depends heavily on competent personnel of

FIGURE 10.2 Building an Organization Capable of Proficient Strategy Execution: Three Key Actions

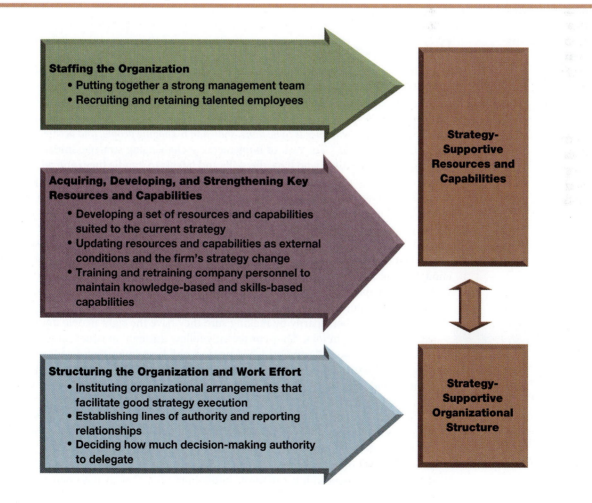

all types, but because of the many managerial tasks involved and the role of leadership in strategy execution, assembling a strong management team is especially important.

If the strategy being implemented is a new strategy, the company may need to add to its resource and capability mix in other respects as well. But renewing, upgrading, and revising the organization's resources and capabilities is a part of the strategy execution process even if the strategy is fundamentally the same, since resources depreciate and conditions are always changing. Thus, augmenting and strengthening the firm's core competencies and seeing that they are suited to the current strategy are also top priorities.

Structuring the organization and work effort is another critical aspect of building an organization capable of good strategy execution. An organization structure that is well matched to the strategy can help facilitate its implementation; one that is not well suited can lead to higher bureaucratic costs and communication or coordination breakdowns.

STAFFING THE ORGANIZATION

LO 2

Learn why hiring, training, and retaining the right people constitute a key component of the strategy execution process.

No company can hope to perform the activities required for successful strategy execution without attracting and retaining talented managers and employees with suitable skills and intellectual capital.

Putting Together a Strong Management Team

Assembling a capable management team is a cornerstone of the organization-building task.[4] While different strategies and company circumstances sometimes call for different mixes of backgrounds, experiences, management styles, and know-how, *the most important consideration is to fill key managerial slots with smart people who are clear thinkers, good at figuring out what needs to be done, skilled in managing people, and accomplished in delivering good results.*[5] The task of implementing challenging strategic initiatives must be assigned to executives who have the skills and talents to handle them and who can be counted on to get the job done well. Without a capable, results-oriented management team, the implementation process is likely to be hampered by missed deadlines, misdirected or wasteful efforts, and managerial ineptness. Weak executives are serious impediments to getting optimal results because they are unable to differentiate between ideas that have merit and those that are misguided. In contrast, managers with strong strategy-implementation capabilities have a talent for asking tough, incisive questions. They know enough about the details of the business to be able to ensure the soundness of the decisions of the people around them, and they can discern whether the resources people are asking for to put the strategy in place make sense. They are good at getting things done through others, partly by making sure they have the right people under them, assigned to the right jobs. They consistently follow through on issues, monitor progress carefully, make adjustments when needed, and keep important details from slipping through the cracks. In short, they understand how to drive organizational change, and they have the managerial discipline requisite for first-rate strategy execution.

Putting together a talented management team with the right mix of experiences, skills, and abilities to get things done is one of the first steps to take in launching the strategy-executing process.

Sometimes a company's existing management team is up to the task. At other times it may need to be strengthened by promoting qualified people from within or by bringing in outsiders whose experiences, talents, and leadership styles better suit the situation. In turnaround and rapid-growth situations, and in instances when a company doesn't have insiders with the requisite know-how, filling key management slots from the outside is a fairly standard organization-building approach. In addition, it is important to identify and replace managers who are incapable, for whatever reason, of making the required changes in a timely and cost-effective manner. For a management team to be truly effective at strategy execution, it must be composed of managers who recognize that organizational changes are needed and who are ready to get on with the process.

The overriding aim in building a management team should be to assemble a *critical mass* of talented managers who can function as agents of change and oversee top-notch strategy execution. Every manager's success is enhanced (or limited) by the quality of his or her managerial colleagues and the degree to which they freely exchange ideas, debate ways to make operating improvements, and join forces to tackle issues and solve problems. When a first-rate manager enjoys the help and support of other first-rate managers, it's possible to create a managerial whole that is greater than the sum of individual efforts—talented managers who work well together as a team can produce organizational results that are dramatically better than what one or two star managers acting individually can achieve.[6]

Illustration Capsule 10.1 describes Procter & Gamble's widely acclaimed approach to developing a top-caliber management team.

Recruiting, Training, and Retaining Capable Employees

Assembling a capable management team is not enough. Staffing the organization with the right kinds of people must go much deeper than managerial jobs in order for strategy-critical value chain activities to be performed competently. *The quality of an organization's people is always an essential ingredient of successful strategy execution—knowledgeable, engaged employees are a company's best source of creative ideas for the nuts-and-bolts operating improvements that lead to operating excellence.* Companies like Google, Edward Jones, Mercedes-Benz, Intuit, McKinsey & Company, REI, Goldman Sachs, DreamWorks Animation, and Boston Consulting Group make a concerted effort to recruit the best and brightest people they can find and then retain them with excellent compensation packages, opportunities for rapid advancement and professional growth, and interesting assignments. Having a pool of "A players" with strong skill sets and lots of brainpower is essential to their business.

Facebook makes a point of hiring the very brightest and most talented programmers it can find and motivating them with both good monetary incentives and the challenge of working on cutting-edge technology projects. McKinsey & Company, one of the world's premier management consulting firms, recruits only cream-of-the-crop MBAs at the nation's top-10 business schools; such talent is essential to McKinsey's strategy of performing high-level consulting for the world's top corporations. The leading global accounting firms screen candidates not only on the basis of their accounting expertise but also on whether they possess the people skills needed to relate well with clients and colleagues. Southwest Airlines goes to considerable lengths to hire people who can have fun and be fun on the job; it uses special interviewing and screening methods to gauge whether applicants for customer-contact jobs have outgoing personality traits that match its strategy of creating a high-spirited, fun-loving, in-flight atmosphere for passengers. Southwest Airlines is so selective that only about 3 percent of the people who apply are offered jobs.

In high-tech companies, the challenge is to staff work groups with gifted, imaginative, and energetic people who can bring life to new ideas quickly and inject into the organization what one Dell executive calls "hum."[7] The saying "People are our most

> In many industries, adding to a company's talent base and building intellectual capital are more important to good strategy execution than additional investments in capital projects.

"Build From Within": P&G's Approach to Management Development

Procter and Gamble takes a systematic approach to management development with its "Build From Within" program—a mutually reinforcing set of policies and practices designed to nurture home-grown managerial talent. Ninety-five percent of P&G's managers (including its 12 past and present CEOs) first joined the company at the entry level. The promote-from-within approach has paid off: P&G regularly tops lists of "Best Companies for Leaders" and is a well-known breeding ground for future general managers. To ensure a pipeline of committed, high-quality leaders, P&G invests in each stage of the management development life cycle:

- **Rigorous recruiting process.** P&G hires less than 1 percent of applicants each year. The recruiting process includes multiple rounds of tests that assess leadership, logical and numerical abilities, as well as interviews to test candidates' intellectual, interpersonal, and executional fit.

- **Extensive on-the-job and formal training opportunities.** P&G rotates employees through a series of challenging 18-24 month "Accelerator Experiences" that build collaborative, project management, and customer-facing skills. The company has also developed a world-class training curriculum; each employee logs nearly 70 hours per year in required courses and seminars.

- **Detailed development and career planning.** The company's Work and Development Planning (W&DP) system tracks each employee's development in terms of: (1) previous year's plan versus results; (2) areas for further growth; (3) near- and long-term career goals; (4) development targets for the coming year. Monthly, quarterly, and annual talent reviews serve as a consistent mechanism for identifying and investing in top talent.

- **Clear path to leadership.** P&G was the first consumer packaged goods company to develop and implement the Brand Manager (BM) position, a role requiring cross-functional relationships, deep business knowledge, and an ability to synthesize complex data into pithy recommendations. Though the path is demanding (requiring, on average, two to three rotations in an entry level role), it is the only track to company leadership.

- **Actively managed succession planning.** At P&G, developing future leaders is everyone's responsibility: managers seek feedback from cross-functional partners in making promotion and compensation decisions. Most importantly, senior leaders play an active role, meeting regularly to review P&G's talent pipeline. As a result, the company always has replacement candidates lined up for key managerial positions.

Developed with Divya A. Mani.

Sources: company websites; *Winning with the P&G 99,* Charles L. Decker, 1998; "100 Best Companies to Work For," Fortune, 2007; "Some Firms' Fertile Soil Grows Crop of Future CEOs," *USA Today,* January 9, 2008; "P&G's Leadership Machine," *Fortune,* May 20, 2009; "How Companies Develop Great Leaders," *Bloomberg Businessweek,* February 16, 2010; "25 Top Companies for Leaders," *Fortune,* November 4, 2011.

important asset" may seem trite, but it fits high-technology companies precisely. Besides checking closely for functional and technical skills, Dell tests applicants for their tolerance of ambiguity and change, their capacity to work in teams, and their ability to learn on-the-fly. Companies like **Amazon.com**, Google, and Cisco Systems have broken new ground in recruiting, hiring, cultivating, developing, and retaining talented employees—almost all of whom are in their 20s and 30s. Cisco goes after the top 10 percent, raiding other companies and endeavoring to retain key people at the companies it acquires. Cisco executives believe that a cadre of star engineers, programmers, managers, salespeople, and support personnel is the backbone of the company's efforts to execute its strategy and remain the world's leading provider of Internet infrastructure products and technology.

The practices listed next are common among companies dedicated to staffing jobs with the most capable people they can find:

1. Putting forth considerable effort on screening and evaluating job applicants—selecting only those with suitable skill sets, energy, initiative, judgment, aptitude for learning, and personality traits that mesh well with the company's work environment and culture.

2. Providing employees with training programs that continue throughout their careers.

3. Offering promising employees challenging, interesting, and skill-stretching assignments.

4. Rotating people through jobs that span functional and geographic boundaries. Providing people with opportunities to gain experience in a variety of international settings is increasingly considered an essential part of career development in multinational companies.

5. Making the work environment stimulating and engaging so that employees will consider the company a great place to work.

6. Encouraging employees to challenge existing ways of doing things, to be creative and innovative in proposing better ways of operating, and to push their ideas for new products or businesses. Progressive companies work hard at creating an environment in which employees are made to feel that their views and suggestions count.

7. Striving to retain talented, high-performing employees via promotions, salary increases, performance bonuses, stock options and equity ownership, fringe-benefit packages, and other perks.

8. Coaching average performers to improve their skills and capabilities, while weeding out underperformers and benchwarmers.

> The best companies make a point of recruiting and retaining talented employees—the objective is to make the company's entire workforce (managers and rank-and-file employees) a genuine competitive asset.

ACQUIRING, DEVELOPING, AND STRENGTHENING KEY RESOURCES AND CAPABILITIES

High among the organization-building priorities in the strategy execution process is the need to build and strengthen competitively valuable resources and capabilities. As explained in Chapter 4, a company's ability to perform value-creating activities and realize its strategic objectives depends upon its resources and capabilities. In the course of crafting strategy, it is important for managers to identify the resources and capabilities that will enable the firm's strategy to succeed. Good strategy execution requires putting those resources and capabilities into place, strengthening them as needed, and then modifying them as market conditions evolve.

If the strategy being implemented is new, company managers may have to acquire new resources, significantly broaden or deepen certain capabilities, or even add entirely new competencies in order to put the strategic initiatives in place and execute them proficiently. But even if the strategy has not changed materially, good strategy execution involves refreshing and strengthening the firm's resources and capabilities to keep them in top form.

LO 3

Understand that good strategy execution requires continuously building and upgrading the organization's resources and capabilities.

Three Approaches to Building and Strengthening Capabilities

Building core competencies and competitive capabilities is a time-consuming, managerially challenging exercise. While some assist can be gotten from discovering how best-in-industry or best-in-world companies perform a particular activity, trying to replicate and then improve on the capabilities of others is, however, much easier said than done—for the same reasons that one is unlikely to ever become a world-class moguls skier just by studying what Olympic gold medal winner Hannah Kearney does.

With deliberate effort, well-orchestrated organizational actions, and continued practice, however, it is possible for a firm to become proficient at capability building despite the difficulty. Indeed, by making capability-building activities a routine part of their strategy execution endeavors, some firms are able to develop *dynamic capabilities* that assist them in managing resource and capability change, as discussed in Chapter 4. The most common approaches to capability building include (1) internal development, (2) acquiring capabilities through mergers and acquisitions, and (3) accessing capabilities via collaborative partnerships.[8]

Developing Capabilities Internally   Capabilities develop incrementally along an evolutionary development path as organizations search for solutions to their problems. The process is a complex one, since capabilities are the product of bundles of skills and know-how that are integrated into organizational routines and deployed within activity systems through the combined efforts of teams that are often cross-functional in nature, spanning a variety of departments and locations. For instance, the capability of speeding new products to market involves the collaborative efforts of personnel in R&D, engineering and design, purchasing, production, marketing, and distribution. Similarly, the capability to provide superior customer service is a team effort among people in customer call centers (where orders are taken and inquiries are answered), shipping and delivery, billing and accounts receivable, and after-sale support. The process of building a capability begins when managers set an objective of developing a particular capability and organize activity around that objective.[9] Managers can ignite the process by having high aspirations and setting "stretch objectives" for the organization, as described in Chapter 2.[10]

Because the process is incremental, the first step is to develop the *ability* to do something, however imperfectly or inefficiently. This entails selecting people with the requisite skills and experience, upgrading or expanding individual abilities as needed, and then molding the efforts of individuals into a collaborative effort to create an organizational ability. At this stage, progress can be fitful since it depends on experimentation, active search for alternative solutions, and learning through trial and error.[11]

As experience grows and company personnel learn how to perform the activities consistently well and at an acceptable cost, the ability evolves into a tried-and-true competence. Getting to this point requires a continual investment of resources and systematic efforts to improve processes and solve problems creatively as they arise. Improvements in the functioning of a capability come from task repetition and the resulting learning by doing of individuals and teams. But the process can be accelerated by making learning a more deliberate endeavor and providing the incentives that will motivate company personnel to achieve the desired ends.[12] This can be critical to successful strategy execution when market conditions are changing rapidly.

It is generally much easier and less time-consuming to update and remodel a company's existing capabilities as external conditions and company strategy change than it is to create them from scratch. Maintaining capabilities in top form may simply require exercising them continually and fine-tuning them as necessary. Refreshing and updating capabilities require only a limited set of modifications to a set of routines that is otherwise in place. Phasing out an existing capability takes significantly less effort than adding a brand new one. Replicating a company capability, while not an easy process, still begins with an established template.[13] Even the process of augmenting a capability may require less effort if it involves the recombination of well-established company capabilities and draws on existing company resources.[14] Companies like Cray in large computers and Honda in gasoline engines, for example, have leveraged the expertise of their talent pool by frequently re-forming high-intensity teams and reusing key people on special projects designed to augment their capabilities. Canon combined miniaturization capabilities that it developed in producing calculators with its existing capabilities in precision optics to revolutionize the 35-mm camera market.[15] Toyota, en route to overtaking General Motors as the global leader in motor vehicles, aggressively upgraded its capabilities in fuel-efficient hybrid engine technology and constantly fine-tuned its famed Toyota Production System to enhance its already proficient capabilities in manufacturing top-quality vehicles at relatively low costs—see Illustration Capsule 10.2.

Managerial actions to develop core competencies and competitive capabilities generally take one of two forms: either strengthening the company's base of skills, knowledge, and experience or coordinating and integrating the efforts of the various work groups and departments. Actions of the first sort can be undertaken at all managerial levels, but actions of the second sort are best orchestrated by senior managers who not only appreciate the strategy-executing significance of strong capabilities but also have the clout to enforce the necessary cooperation and coordination among individuals, groups, and departments.[16]

Acquiring Capabilities through Mergers and Acquisitions

Sometimes a company can refresh and strengthen its competencies by acquiring another company with attractive resources and capabilities.[17] An acquisition aimed at building a stronger portfolio of resources and capabilities can be every bit as valuable as an acquisition aimed at adding new products or services to the company's lineup of offerings. The advantage of this mode of acquiring new capabilities is primarily one of speed, since developing new capabilities internally can take many years of effort. Capabilities-motivated acquisitions are essential (1) when a market opportunity can slip by faster than a needed capability can be created internally and (2) when industry conditions, technology, or competitors are moving at such a rapid clip, that time is of the essence.

At the same time, acquiring capabilities in this way is not without difficulty. Capabilities involve tacit knowledge and complex routines that cannot be transferred readily from one organizational unit to another. This may limit the extent to which the new capability can be utilized. For example, the Newell Company acquired Rubbermaid in part for its famed product innovation capabilities. Transferring these capabilities to other parts of the Newell organization proved easier said than done, however, contributing to a slump in the firm's stock prices that lasted for some time. Integrating the capabilities of two firms involved in a merger or acquisition may pose an additional challenge, particularly if there are underlying incompatibilities in their supporting systems or processes.

Toyota's Legendary Production System: A Capability that Translates into Competitive Advantage

The heart of Toyota's strategy in motor vehicles is to out-compete rivals by manufacturing world-class, quality vehicles at lower costs and selling them at competitive price levels. To achieve this result, Toyota began efforts to improve its manufacturing competence over 50 years ago. Through tireless trial and error, the company gradually took what started as a loose collection of techniques and practices and integrated them into a full-fledged process now known as the Toyota Production System (TPS). TPS is grounded in the following principles, practices, and techniques:

- *Use just-in-time delivery of parts and components to the point of vehicle assembly.* The idea here is to stop transferring materials from place to place and to discontinue all activities on the part of workers that don't add value.

- *Develop people who can come up with unique ideas for production improvements.* Toyota encourages employees at all levels to question existing ways of doing things—even if this means challenging a boss on the soundness of a directive. Also, Toyota gives workers training to become better problem solvers.

- *Emphasize continuous improvement.* Workers are expected to develop better ways of doing things. Toyota managers tout messages such as "Never be satisfied." Another mantra is that the *T* in TPS also stands for "Thinking."

- *Empower workers to stop the assembly line when there's a problem or a defect is spotted.* Toyota views worker efforts to purge defects and sort out the problem immediately as critical to the whole concept of building quality into the production process.

- *Deal with defects only when they occur.* TPS philosophy holds that when things are running smoothly, they should not be subject to control; if attention is directed to fixing problems that are found, quality control can be handled with fewer personnel.

- *Ask yourself "Why?" five times.* The value of asking "Why?" five times enables identifying the root cause of the error and correcting it so that the error won't recur.

- *Organize all jobs around human motion to create a production/assembly system with no wasted effort.* Work organized in this fashion is called "standardized work" and people are trained to observe standardized work procedures so workers can do their jobs continuously in a set sequence of subprocesses.

- *Find where a part is made cheaply, and use that price as a benchmark.*

There's widespread agreement that Toyota's ongoing effort to refine and improve on its renowned TPS gives it manufacturing capabilities that others envy. Not only have auto manufacturers attempted to emulate key elements of TPS, but elements of Toyota's production philosophy have been adopted by hospitals and postal services.

Sources: Information posted at www.toyotageorgetown.com; Hirotaka Takeuchi, Emi Osono, and Norihiko Shimizu, "The Contradictions That Drive Toyota's Success," *Harvard Business Review* 86, no. 6 (June 2008), pp. 96–104; Taiichi Ohno, *Toyota Production System: Beyond Large-Scale Production* (New York: Sheridan, 1988).

Moreover, since internal fit is important, there is always the risk that under new management the acquired capabilities may not be as productive as they had been. In a worst-case scenario, the acquisition process may end up damaging or destroying the very capabilities that were the object of the acquisition in the first place.

Accessing Capabilities through Collaborative Partnerships

Another method of acquiring capabilities from an external source is to access them via collaborative partnerships with suppliers, competitors, or other companies having the cutting-edge expertise. There are three basic ways to pursue this course of action:

1. *Outsource the function requiring the capabilities to a key supplier or another provider.* Whether this is a wise move depends on what can be safely delegated to outside suppliers or allies and which internal capabilities are key to the company's long-term success. As discussed in Chapter 6, outsourcing has the advantage of conserving resources so that the firm can focus its energies on those activities most central to its strategy. It may be a good choice for firms that are too small and resource-constrained to execute all the parts of their strategy internally.

2. *Collaborate with a firm that has complementary resources and capabilities in a joint venture, strategic alliance, or other type of partnership established for the purpose of achieving a shared strategic objective.* This requires launching initiatives to identify the most attractive potential partners and to establish collaborative working relationships. Since the success of the venture will depend on how well the partners work together, potential partners should be selected as much for their management style, culture, and goals as for their resources and capabilities.

3. *Engage in a collaborative partnership for the purpose of learning how the partner does things, internalizing its methods and thereby acquiring its capabilities.* This may be a viable method when each partner has something to learn from the other. But in other cases, it involves an abuse of trust. In consequence, it not only puts the cooperative venture at risk but also encourages the firm's partner to treat the firm similarly or refuse further dealings with the firm.

The Strategic Role of Employee Training

Training and retraining are important when a company shifts to a strategy requiring different skills, competitive capabilities, and operating methods. Training is also strategically important in organizational efforts to build skills-based competencies. And it is a key activity in businesses where technical know-how is changing so rapidly that a company loses its ability to compete unless its employees have cutting-edge knowledge and expertise. Successful strategy implementers see to it that the training function is both adequately funded and effective. If the chosen strategy calls for new skills, deeper technological capability, or the building and using of new capabilities, training efforts need to be placed near the top of the action agenda.

The strategic importance of training has not gone unnoticed. Over 600 companies have established internal "universities" to lead the training effort, facilitate continuous organizational learning, and upgrade their company's knowledge resources. Many companies conduct orientation sessions for new employees, fund an assortment of competence-building training programs, and reimburse employees for tuition and other expenses associated with obtaining additional college education, attending professional development courses, and earning professional certification of one kind or another. A number of companies offer online, just-in-time training courses to employees around the clock. Increasingly, employees at all levels are expected to take an active role in their own professional development and assume responsibility for keeping their skills up to date and in sync with the company's needs.

Strategy Execution Capabilities and Competitive Advantage

> Superior strategy execution capabilities are the only source of sustainable competitive advantage when strategies are easy for rivals to copy.

As firms get better at executing their strategies, they develop capabilities in the domain of strategy execution much as they build other organizational capabilities. Superior strategy execution capabilities allow companies to get the most from their organizational resources and competitive capabilities. In this way they contribute to the success of a firm's business model. But excellence in strategy execution can also be a more direct source of competitive advantage, since more efficient and effective strategy execution can lower costs and permit firms to deliver more value to customers. Superior strategy execution capabilities may also enable a company to react more quickly to market changes and beat other firms to the market with new products and services. This can allow a company to profit from a period of uncontested market dominance.

Because strategy execution capabilities are socially complex capabilities that develop with experience over long periods of time, they are hard to imitate. And there is no substitute for good strategy execution. (Recall the tests of resource advantage from Chapter 4.) As such, they may be as important a source of sustained competitive advantage as the capabilities that drive a firm's strategies. Indeed, they may be a far more important avenue for securing a competitive edge over rivals in situations where it is relatively easy for rivals to copy promising strategies. In such cases, the only way for firms to achieve lasting competitive advantage is to outexecute their competitors.

MATCHING ORGANIZATIONAL STRUCTURE TO THE STRATEGY

LO 4

Recognize what issues to consider in establishing a strategy-supportive organizational structure and organizing the work effort.

While there are few hard-and-fast rules for organizing the work effort to support good strategy execution, there is one: a firm's organizational structure should be matched to the particular requirements of implementing the firm's strategy. Every company's strategy is grounded in its own set of organizational capabilities and value chain activities. Moreover, every firm's organization chart is partly a product of its particular situation, reflecting prior organizational patterns, varying internal circumstances, executive judgments about reporting relationships, and the politics of who gets which assignments. Thus, the determinants of the fine details of each firm's organizational structure are unique. But some considerations in organizing the work effort are common to all companies. These are summarized in Figure 10.3 and discussed in the following sections.

Deciding Which Value Chain Activities to Perform Internally and Which to Outsource

Aside from the fact that an outsider may be able to perform certain value chain activities better or cheaper than a company can perform them internally (as discussed in Chapter 6), outsourcing can also sometimes make a positive contribution to strategy execution. Outsourcing the performance of selected value chain activities to outside vendors enables a company to heighten its strategic focus and *concentrate its full energies on performing those value chain activities that are at the core of its strategy, where it can create unique value.* For example, E. & J. Gallo Winery outsources 95 percent of its grape production, letting farmers take on weather-related and other grape-growing risks while it concentrates its full energies on wine production and sales.[18] Broadcom, a global leader in chips for broadband communication systems, outsources the manufacture of its chips to Taiwan

FIGURE 10.3   Structuring the Work Effort to Promote Successful Strategy Execution

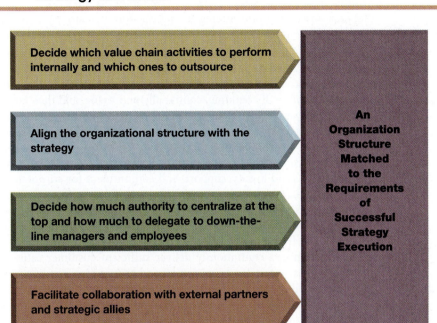

Semiconductor, thus freeing company personnel to focus their efforts on R&D, new chip design, and marketing. Nike concentrates on design, marketing, and distribution while outsourcing virtually all production of its shoes and sporting apparel. Illustration Capsule 10.3 describes Apple's decisions about which activities to outsource and which to perform in-house.

Such heightened focus on performing strategy-critical activities can yield three important execution-related benefits:

- *The company improves its chances for outclassing rivals in the performance of strategy-critical activities and turning a competence into a distinctive competence.* At the very least, the heightened focus on performing a select few value chain activities should promote more effective performance of those activities. This could materially enhance competitive capabilities by either lowering costs or improving quality. Whirlpool, ING Insurance, Hugo Boss, Japan Airlines, and Chevron have outsourced their data processing activities to computer service firms, believing that outside specialists can perform the needed services at lower costs and equal or better quality. A relatively large number of companies outsource the operation of their websites to web design and hosting enterprises. Many businesses that get a lot of inquiries from customers or that have to provide 24/7 technical support to users of their products around the world have found that it is considerably less expensive to outsource these functions to specialists (often located in foreign countries where skilled personnel are readily available and worker compensation costs are much lower) than to operate their own call centers.

- *The streamlining of internal operations that flows from outsourcing often acts to decrease internal bureaucracies, flatten the organizational structure, speed internal decision making, and shorten the time it takes to respond to changing market conditions.*[19] In consumer electronics, where advancing technology drives new product

Wisely choosing which activities to perform internally and which to outsource can lead to several strategy-executing advantages—lower costs, heightened strategic focus, less internal bureaucracy, speedier decision making, and a better arsenal of organizational capabilities.

innovation, organizing the work effort in a manner that expedites getting next-generation products to market ahead of rivals is a critical competitive capability. The world's motor vehicle manufacturers have found that they can shorten the cycle time for new models by outsourcing the production of many parts and components to independent suppliers. They then work closely with the suppliers to swiftly incorporate new technology and to better integrate individual parts and components to form engine cooling systems, transmission systems, and electrical systems.

- *Partnerships can add to a company's arsenal of capabilities and contribute to better strategy execution.* By building, continually improving, and then leveraging partnerships, a company enhances its overall organizational capabilities and strengthens its competitive assets—assets that deliver more value to customers and consequently pave the way for competitive success. Soft-drink and beer manufacturers cultivate their relationships with their bottlers and distributors to strengthen access to local markets and build loyalty, support, and commitment for corporate marketing programs, without which their own sales and growth are weakened. Similarly, fast-food enterprises like Wendy's and Burger King find it essential to work hand in hand with franchisees on outlet cleanliness, consistency of product quality, in-store ambience, courtesy and friendliness of store personnel, and other aspects of store operations. Unless franchisees continuously deliver sufficient customer satisfaction to attract repeat business, a fast-food chain's sales and competitive standing will suffer quickly. Companies like Boeing, Aerospatiale, Verizon Communications, and Dell have learned that their central R&D groups cannot begin to match the innovative capabilities of a well-managed network of supply chain partners.

However, as emphasized in Chapter 6, a company must guard against going overboard on outsourcing and becoming overly dependent on outside suppliers. A company cannot be the master of its own destiny unless it maintains expertise and resource depth in performing those value chain activities that underpin its long-term competitive success.[20] As a general rule, therefore, it is the strategically less important activities—like handling customer inquiries and providing technical support, doing the payroll, administering employee benefit programs, providing corporate security, maintaining fleet vehicles, operating the company's website, conducting employee training, and managing an assortment of information and data processing functions—where outsourcing is likely to make the most strategic sense.

Aligning the Firm's Organizational Structure with Its Strategy

The design of the firm's **organizational structure** is a critical aspect of the strategy execution process. The organizational structure comprises the formal and informal arrangement of tasks, responsibilities, and lines of authority and communication by which the firm is administered.[21] It specifies the linkages among parts of the organization, the reporting relationships, the direction of information flows, and the decision-making processes. It is a key factor in strategy implementation since it exerts a strong influence on how well managers can coordinate and control the complex set of activities involved.[22]

A well-designed organizational structure is one in which the various parts (e.g., decision-making rights, communication patterns) are aligned with one another and also matched to the requirements of the strategy. With the right structure in place, managers can orchestrate the various aspects of the implementation process with an even hand and a light touch. Without a supportive structure, strategy execution is more likely to become bogged down by administrative confusion, political maneuvering, and bureaucratic waste.

Which Value Chain Activities Does Apple Outsource and Why?

Innovation and design are core competencies for Apple and the drivers behind the creation of winning products such as the iPod, iPhone, and iPad. In consequence, all activities directly related to new product development and product design are performed internally. For example, Apple's Industrial Design Group is responsible for creating the look and feel of all Apple products—from the Mac mini to the iPad Touch.

Producing a continuing stream of great new products and product versions is key to the success of Apple's strategy. But executing this strategy takes more than innovation and design capabilities. Manufacturing flexibility and speed are imperative in the production of Apple products to ensure that the latest ideas are reflected in the products and that the company meets the high demand for their products—especially around launch.

For these capabilities, Apple turns to outsourcing, like the majority of its competitors in the consumer electronics space. Apple outsources the manufacturing of products like its iPhone to Asia, where Contract Manufacturing Organizations (CMOs) create value through their vast scale, high flexibility, and low cost. Perhaps no company better epitomizes the Asian CMO value proposition than FoxConn, a company that assembles not only for Apple, but for Hewlett-Packard,

Motorola, Amazon, and Samsung as well. FoxConn's scale is incredible, with their largest facility (FoxConn City in Shenzhen, China) employing over 230,000 workers. Such scale offers companies a significant degree of flexibility as FoxConn has the ability to hire 3,000 employees on practically a moment's notice. Apple, more so than their competitors, is able to capture CMO value creation by leveraging their immense sales volume and strong cash position to receive preferred treatment.

Developed with Margaret W. Macauley.

Sources: Company website; Charles Duhigg, "How the U.S. Lost Out on iPhone Work," *The New York Times,* January 22, 2012. Web: February 19, 2012, accessed March 5, 2012.

Good organizational design may even contribute to the firm's ability to create value for customers and realize a profit. By enabling lower bureaucratic costs and facilitating operational efficiency, it can lower a firm's operating costs. By facilitating the coordination of activities within the firm, it can improve the capability-building process, leading to greater differentiation and/or lower costs. Moreover, by improving the speed with which information is communicated and activities are coordinated, it can enable the firm to beat rivals to the market and profit from a period of unrivaled advantage.

Making Strategy-Critical Activities the Main Building Blocks of the Organizational Structure
In any business, some activities in the value chain are always more critical to successful strategy execution than others. For instance, a ski apparel company like Spyder must be good at styling and design, low-cost manufacturing, distribution (convincing an attractively large number of dealers to stock and promote the company's brand), and marketing and advertising (building a brand

image that generates buzz and appeal among ski enthusiasts). For discount stock brokers, like Scottrade and TDAmeritrade, the strategy-critical activities are fast access to information, accurate order execution, efficient record keeping and transactions processing, and good customer service. Where such is the case, it is important for management to build its organizational structure around proficient performance of these activities, making them the centerpieces or main building blocks in the enterprise's organizational structure.

The rationale for making strategy-critical activities the main building blocks in structuring a business is compelling: If activities crucial to strategic success are to have the resources, decision-making influence, and organizational impact they need, they have to be centerpieces in the organizational scheme. Making them the focus of structuring efforts will also facilitate their coordination and promote good internal fit—an essential attribute of a winning strategy, as summarized in Chapter 1 and elaborated in Chapter 4. To the extent that implementing a new strategy entails new or altered key activities or capabilities, different organizational arrangements may be required.

Matching Type of Organizational Structure to Strategy Execution Requirements

Organizational structures can be classified into a limited number of standard types. The type that is most suitable for a given firm will depend on the firm's size and complexity as well as its strategy. As firms grow and their needs for structure evolve, their structural form is likely to evolve from one type to another. The four basic types are the *simple structure,* the *functional structure,* the *multidivisional structure,* and the *matrix structure,* as described next.

1. Simple Structure   A **simple structure** is one in which a central executive (often the owner-manager) handles all major decisions and oversees the operations of the organization with the help of a small staff.[23] Simple structures are also known as *line-and-staff structures,* since a central administrative staff supervises line employees who conduct the operations of the firm, or *flat structures,* since there are few levels of hierarchy. It is characterized by limited task specialization; few rules; informal relationships; minimal use of training, planning, and liaison devices; and a lack of sophisticated support systems. It has all the advantages of simplicity, including low administrative costs, ease of coordination, flexibility, quick decision making, adaptability, and responsiveness to change. Its informality and lack of rules may foster creativity and heightened individual responsibility.

Simple organizational structures are typically employed by small firms and entrepreneurial startups. The simple structure is the most common type of organizational structure since small firms are the most prevalent type of business. As an organization grows, however, this structural form becomes inadequate to the demands that come with size and complexity. In response, growing firms tend to alter their organizational structure from a simple structure to a *functional structure.*

2. Functional Structure   A **functional structure** is one that is organized along functional lines, where a function represents a major component of the firm's value chain, such as R&D, engineering and design, manufacturing, sales and marketing, logistics, and customer service. Each functional unit is supervised by functional line managers who report to the chief executive officer and a corporate staff. This arrangement allows functional managers to focus on their area of responsibility, leaving it to the CEO and headquarters to provide direction and ensure that their activities are coordinated and integrated. Functional structures are also known as *departmental structures,* since the functional units are commonly called departments, and *unitary structures* or *U-forms,* since a single unit is responsible for each function.

In large organizations, functional structures lighten the load on top management, relative to simple structures, and make for a more efficient use of managerial resources. Their primary advantage, however, is due to greater task specialization, which promotes learning, enables the realization of scale economies, and offers productivity advantages not otherwise available. Their chief disadvantage is that the departmental boundaries can inhibit the flow of information and limit the opportunities for cross-functional cooperation and coordination.

It is generally agreed that some type of functional structure is the best organizational arrangement when a company is in just one particular business (irrespective of which of the five generic competitive strategies it opts to pursue). For instance, a technical instruments manufacturer may be organized around research and development, engineering, supply chain management, assembly, quality control, marketing, and technical services. A discount retailer, such as Dollar General or Kmart, may organize around such functional units as purchasing, warehousing, distribution logistics, store operations, advertising, merchandising and promotion, and customer service. Functional structures can also be appropriate for firms with high-volume production, products that are closely related, and a limited degree of vertical integration. For example, General Motors now manages all of its brands (e.g., Cadillac, GMC, Chevrolet, Buick) under a common functional structure designed to promote technical transfer and capture economies of scale.

As firms continue to grow, they often become more diversified and complex, placing a greater burden on top management. At some point, the centralized control that characterizes the functional structure becomes a liability, and the advantages of functional specialization begin to break down. To resolve these problems and address a growing need for coordination across functions, firms generally turn to the *multidivisional structure*.

3. *Multidivisional Structure*   A **multidivisional structure** is a decentralized structure consisting of a set of operating divisions organized along market, customer, product, or geographic lines, along with a central corporate headquarters, which monitors divisional activities, allocates resources, performs assorted support functions, and exercises overall control. Since each division is essentially a business (often called *single business units* or *SBUs*), the divisions typically operate as independent profit centers (i.e., with profit/loss responsibility) and are organized internally along functional lines. Division managers oversee day-to-day operations and the development of business-level strategy, while corporate executives attend to overall performance and corporate strategy, the elements of which were described in Chapter 8. Multidivisional structures are also called *divisional structures* or *M-forms*, in contrast with U-form (functional) structures.

Multidivisional structures are common among companies pursuing some form of diversification strategy or multinational strategy, with operations in a number of businesses or countries. When the strategy is one of unrelated diversification, as in a conglomerate or holding company, the divisions generally represent businesses in separate industries. When the strategy is based on related diversification, the divisions may be organized according to markets, customer groups, product lines, geographic regions, or technologies. In this arrangement, the decision about where to draw the divisional lines depends foremost on the nature of the relatedness and the strategy-critical building blocks, in terms of which businesses have key value chain activities in common. For example, a company selling closely related products to business customers as well as two types of end consumers—online buyers and in-store buyers—may organize its divisions according to customer groups since the value chains involved in serving the three groups differ. Another company may organize by product line due to commonalities in product development and production within each product line. Multidivisional structures are also common among vertically integrated firms. There the major building blocks are often divisional units performing one or more of the major processing steps along the value chain (e.g., raw-material production, components manufacture, assembly, wholesale distribution, retail store operations).

Multidivisional structures offer significant advantages over functional structures in terms of facilitating the management of a complex and diverse set of operations.[24] Putting business-level strategy in the hands of division managers while leaving corporate strategy to top executives reduces the potential for information overload and improves the quality of decision making in each domain. This also minimizes the costs of coordinating divisionwide activities while enhancing top management's ability to control a diverse and complex operation. Moreover, multidivisional structures can help align individual incentives with the goals of the corporation and spur productivity by encouraging competition for resources among the different divisions.

But a divisional business-unit structure can also present some problems to a company pursuing related diversification, because having independent business units—each running its own business in its own way—inhibits cross-business collaboration and the capture of cross-business synergies. To solve this type of problem, firms turn to more complex structures, such as the matrix structure.

CORE CONCEPT

A **matrix structure** is a structure that combines two or more organizational forms, with multiple reporting relationships. It is used to foster cross-unit collaboration. Matrix structures are also called *composite* structures or *combination* structures.

4. *Matrix Structure*   A **matrix structure** is a combination structure in which the organization is organized along two or more dimensions at once (e.g., business, geographic area, value chain function) for the purpose of enhancing cross-unit communication, collaboration, and coordination. In essence, it overlays one type of structure onto another type. Matrix structures are managed through multiple reporting relationships, so a middle manager may report to several bosses. For instance, in a matrix structure based on product line, region, and function, a sales manager for plastic containers in Georgia might report to the manager of the plastics division, the head of the southeast sales region, and the head of marketing.

Matrix organizational structures have evolved from the complex, overformalized structures that were popular in the 1960s, '70s, and '80s but often produced inefficient, unwieldy bureaucracies. The modern incarnation of the matrix structure is generally a more flexible arrangement, with a single primary reporting relationship that can be overlaid with a temporary secondary reporting relationship as need arises. For example, a software company that is organized into functional departments (software design, quality control, customer relations) may assign employees from those departments to different projects on a temporary basis, so an employee reports to a project manager as well as to his or her primary boss (the functional department head) for the duration of a project.

Matrix structures are also called *composite structures* or *combination structures*. They are often used for project-based, process-based, or team-based management. Such approaches are common in businesses involving projects of limited duration, such as consulting, architecture, and engineering services. The type of close cross-unit collaboration that a flexible matrix structure supports is also needed to build competitive capabilities in strategically important activities, such as speeding new products to market, that involve employees scattered across several organizational units.[25] Capabilities-based matrix structures that combine process departments (like new product development) with more traditional functional departments provide a solution.

An advantage of matrix structures is that they facilitate the sharing of plant and equipment, specialized knowledge, and other key resources. Thus, they lower costs by enabling the realization of economies of scope. They also have the advantage of flexibility in form and may allow for better oversight since supervision is provided from more than one perspective. A disadvantage is that they add an additional layer of management, thereby increasing bureaucratic costs and possibly decreasing response time to new situations.[26] In addition, there is a potential for confusion among employees due to dual reporting relationships and divided loyalties. While there is some controversy over the utility of matrix structures, the modern approach to matrix structures does much to minimize their disadvantages.[27]

Determining How Much Authority to Delegate

Under any organizational structure, there is room for considerable variation in how much authority top managers retain and how much is delegated to down-the-line managers and employees. In executing strategy, companies must decide how much authority to delegate to the managers of each organizational unit—especially the heads of divisions, functional departments, and other operating units—and how much decision-making latitude to give individual employees in performing their jobs. The two extremes are to *centralize decision making* at the top or to *decentralize decision making* by giving middle managers and front-line employees considerable decision-making latitude in their areas of responsibility. As shown in Table 10.1, the two approaches are based on sharply different underlying principles and beliefs, with each having its pros and cons.

LO 5

Become aware of the pros and cons of centralized and decentralized decision making in implementing the chosen strategy.

Centralized Decision Making: Pros and Cons
In a highly centralized organizational structure, *top executives retain authority for most strategic and operating decisions* and keep a tight rein on business-unit heads, department heads, and the managers of key operating units. Comparatively little discretionary authority is granted to frontline supervisors and rank-and-file employees. The command-and-control paradigm of centralized structures is based on the underlying assumptions that frontline personnel have neither the time nor the inclination to direct and properly control the work they are performing and that they lack the knowledge and judgment to make wise decisions about how best to do it—hence the need for managerially prescribed policies and procedures, close supervision, and tight control. The thesis underlying centralized structures is that strict enforcement of detailed procedures backed by rigorous managerial oversight is the most reliable way to keep the daily execution of strategy on track.

One advantage of a centralized structure is tight control by the manager in charge—it is easy to know who is accountable when things do not go well. This structure can also reduce the potential for conflicting decisions and actions among lower-level managers who may have differing perspectives and ideas about how to tackle certain tasks or resolve particular issues. For example, a manager in charge of an engineering department may be more interested in pursuing a new technology than is a marketing manager who doubts that customers will value the technology as highly. Another advantage of a command-and-control structure is that it can enable a more uniform and swift response to a crisis situation that affects the organization as a whole.

But there are some serious disadvantages as well. Hierarchical command-and-control structures can make a large organization with a complex structure sluggish in responding to changing market conditions because of the time it takes for the review/approval process to run up all the layers of the management bureaucracy. Furthermore, to work well centralized decision making requires top-level managers to gather and process whatever information is relevant to the decision. When the relevant knowledge resides at lower organizational levels (or is technical, detailed, or hard to express in words), it is difficult and time-consuming to get all the facts and nuances in front of a high-level executive located far from the scene of the action—full understanding of the situation cannot be readily copied from one mind to another. Hence, centralized decision making is often impractical—the larger the company and the more scattered its operations, the more that decision-making authority must be delegated to managers closer to the scene of the action.

TABLE 10.1 Advantages and Disadvantages of Centralized versus Decentralized Decision Making

Centralized Organizational Structures	Decentralized Organizational Structures
Basic Tenets • Decisions on most matters of importance should be in the hands of top-level managers who have the experience, expertise, and judgment to decide what is the best course of action • Lower-level personnel have neither the knowledge, the time, nor the inclination to properly manage the tasks they are performing • Strong control from the top is a more effective means for coordinating company actions	**Basic Tenets** • Decision-making authority should be put in the hands of the people closest to, and most familiar with, the situation • Those with decision-making authority should be trained to exercise good judgment • A company that draws on the combined intellectual capital of all its employees can outperform a command-and-control company
Chief Advantages • Fixes accountability through tight control from the top • Eliminates potential for conflicting goals and actions on the part of lower-level managers • Facilitates quick decision making and strong leadership under crisis situations	**Chief Advantages** • Encourages company employees to exercise initiative and act responsibly • Promotes greater motivation and involvement in the business on the part of more company personnel • Spurs new ideas and creative thinking • Allows for fast response to market change • Entails fewer layers of management
Primary Disadvantages • Lengthens response times by those closest to the market conditions because they must seek approval for their actions • Does not encourage responsibility among lower-level managers and rank-and-file employees • Discourages lower-level managers and rank-and-file employees from exercising any initiative	**Primary Disadvantages** • Higher-level managers may be unaware of actions taken by empowered personnel under their supervision • Puts the organization at risk if empowered employees happen to make "bad" decisions • Can impair cross-unit collaboration

The ultimate goal of decentralized decision making is to put authority in the hands of those persons closest to and most knowledgeable about the situation.

Decentralized Decision Making: Pros and Cons

In a highly decentralized organization, *decision-making authority is pushed down to the lowest organizational level capable of making timely, informed, competent decisions.* The objective is to put adequate decision-making authority in the hands of the people closest to and most familiar with the situation and train them to weigh all the factors and exercise good judgment. Decentralized decision making means that the managers of each organizational unit are delegated lead responsibility for deciding how best to execute strategy. At Starbucks, for example, employees are encouraged to exercise initiative in promoting customer satisfaction—there's the oft-repeated story of a store employee who, when the computerized cash register system went offline, enthusiastically offered free coffee to waiting customers.[28]

The case for empowering down-the-line managers and employees to make decisions related to daily operations and strategy execution is based on the belief that a company that draws on the combined intellectual capital of all its employees can outperform a command-and-control company.[29] The challenge in a decentralized system is in maintaining adequate control. With decentralized decision making, top management maintains control by placing limits on the authority granted to company personnel, installing companywide strategic control systems, holding people accountable for their decisions, instituting compensation incentives that reward people for doing their jobs well, and creating a corporate culture where there's strong peer pressure on individuals to act responsibly.[30]

Decentralized organization structures have much to recommend them. Delegating authority to lower-level managers and rank-and-file employees encourages them to take responsibility and exercise initiative. It shortens organizational response times to market changes and spurs new ideas, creative thinking, innovation, and greater involvement on the part of all company personnel. In worker-empowered structures, jobs can be defined more broadly, several tasks can be integrated into a single job, and people can direct their own work. Fewer layers of managers are needed because deciding how to do things becomes part of each person's or team's job. Further, today's online communication systems and smart phones make it easy and relatively inexpensive for people at all organizational levels to have direct access to data, other employees, managers, suppliers, and customers. They can access information quickly (via the Internet or company network), readily check with superiors or whomever else as needed, and take responsible action. Typically, there are genuine gains in morale and productivity when people are provided with the tools and information they need to operate in a self-directed way.

But decentralization also has some disadvantages. Top managers lose an element of control over what goes on and may thus be unaware of actions being taken by personnel under their supervision. Such lack of control can put a company at risk in the event that empowered employees happen to make unwise decisions. Moreover, because decentralization gives organizational units the authority to act independently, there is risk of too little collaboration and coordination between different organizational units.

Many companies have concluded that the advantages of decentralization outweigh the disadvantages. Over the past 15 to 20 years, there's been a decided shift from centralized, hierarchical structures to flatter, more decentralized structures that stress employee empowerment. This shift reflects a strong and growing consensus that authoritarian, hierarchical organizational structures are not well suited to implementing and executing strategies in an era when extensive information and instant communication are the norm and when a big fraction of the organization's most valuable assets consists of intellectual capital and resides in the knowledge and capabilities of its employees.

Capturing Cross-Business Strategic Fit in a Decentralized Structure   Diversified companies striving to capture the benefits of synergy between separate businesses have to beware of giving business-unit heads full rein to operate independently. Cross-business strategic fit typically must be captured either by enforcing close cross-business collaboration or by centralizing performance of functions requiring close coordination at the corporate level.[31] For example, if businesses with overlapping process and product technologies have their own independent R&D departments— each pursuing its own priorities, projects, and strategic agendas—it's hard for the corporate parent to prevent duplication of effort, capture either economies of scale or economies of scope, or encourage more collaborative R&D efforts. Where cross-business strategic fit with respect to R&D is important, the best solution is usually to centralize the R&D function and have a coordinated corporate R&D effort that serves both the interests of individual businesses and the company as a whole. Likewise, centralizing the related

activities of separate businesses makes sense when there are opportunities to share a common sales force, use common distribution channels, rely on a common field service organization, use common e-commerce systems, and so on.

Facilitating Collaboration with External Partners and Strategic Allies

Organizational mechanisms—whether formal or informal—are also required to ensure effective working relationships with each major outside constituency involved in strategy execution. Strategic alliances, outsourcing arrangements, joint ventures, and cooperative partnerships can contribute little of value without active management of the relationship. Unless top management sees that constructive organizational bridge-building with external partners occurs and that productive working relationships emerge, the potential value of cooperative relationships is lost and the company's power to execute its strategy is weakened. For example, if close working relationships with suppliers are crucial, then supply chain management must enter into considerations regarding how to create an effective organizational structure. If distributor/dealer/franchisee relationships are important, then someone must be assigned the task of nurturing the relationships with forward channel allies.

Building organizational bridges with external partners and strategic allies can be accomplished by appointing "relationship managers" with responsibility for making particular strategic partnerships generate the intended benefits. Relationship managers have many roles and functions: getting the right people together, promoting good rapport, facilitating the flow of information, nurturing interpersonal communication and cooperation, and ensuring effective coordination.[32] Multiple cross-organization ties have to be established and kept open to ensure proper communication and coordination. There has to be enough information sharing to make the relationship work and periodic frank discussions of conflicts, trouble spots, and changing situations.

Organizing and managing a network structure provides another mechanism for encouraging more effective collaboration and cooperation among external partners. A **network structure** is the arrangement linking a number of independent organizations involved in some common undertaking. A well-managed network structure typically includes one firm in a more central role, with the responsibility of ensuring that the right partners are included and the activities across the network are coordinated. The high-end Italian motorcycle company Ducati operates in this manner, assembling its motorcycles from parts obtained from a hand-picked integrated network of parts suppliers.

Further Perspectives on Structuring the Work Effort

All organization designs have their strategy-related strengths and weaknesses. To do a good job of matching structure to strategy, strategy implementers first have to pick a basic organizational design and modify it as needed to fit the company's particular business lineup. They must then (1) supplement the design with appropriate coordinating mechanisms (cross-functional task forces, special project teams, self-contained work teams, and so on) and (2) institute whatever networking and communications arrangements it takes to support effective execution of the firm's strategy. Some companies may avoid setting up "ideal" organizational arrangements because they do not want to disturb existing reporting relationships or because they need to accommodate other situational idiosyncrasies, yet they must still work toward the goal of building a competitively capable organization.

What can be said unequivocally is that building a capable organization entails a process of consciously knitting together the efforts of individuals and groups. Organizational capabilities emerge from establishing and nurturing cooperative working relationships among people and groups to perform activities in a more efficient, value-creating fashion. While an appropriate organizational structure can facilitate this, organization building is a task in which senior management must be deeply involved. Indeed, effectively managing both internal organization processes and external collaboration to create and develop competitively valuable organizational capabilities remains a top challenge for senior executives in today's companies.

KEY POINTS

1. Executing strategy is an action-oriented, operations-driven activity revolving around the management of people and business processes. In devising an action agenda for executing strategy, the place for managers to start is with a probing assessment of what the organization must do differently to carry out the strategy successfully. They should then consider precisely *how* to make the necessary internal changes.

2. Good strategy execution requires a *team effort.* All managers have strategy-executing responsibility in their areas of authority, and all employees are active participants in the strategy execution process.

3. Ten managerial tasks are part of every company effort to execute strategy: (1) staffing the organization with the right people, (2) building the necessary organizational capabilities, (3) creating a supportive organizational structure, (4) allocating sufficient resources, (5) instituting supportive policies and procedures, (6) adopting processes for continuous improvement, (7) installing systems that enable proficient company operations, (8) tying incentives to the achievement of desired targets, (9) instilling the right corporate culture, and (10) exercising internal leadership to propel strategy execution forward.

4. The two best signs of good strategy execution are whether a company is meeting or beating its performance targets and performing value chain activities in a manner that is conducive to companywide operating excellence. *Shortfalls in performance signal weak strategy, weak execution, or both.*

5. Building an organization capable of good strategy execution entails three types of actions: (1) *staffing the organization*—assembling a talented management team, and recruiting and retaining employees with the needed experience, technical skills, and intellectual capital; (2) a*cquiring, developing, and strengthening strategy-supportive resources and capabilities*—accumulating the required resources, developing proficiencies in performing strategy-critical value chain activities, and updating the company's capabilities to match changing market conditions and customer expectations; and (3) *structuring the organization and work effort*—instituting organizational arrangements that facilitate good strategy execution, deciding how much decision-making authority to delegate, and managing external relationships.

6. Building core competencies and competitive capabilities is a time-consuming, managerially challenging exercise that can be approached in three ways: (1) developing capabilities internally, (2) acquiring capabilities through mergers and acquisitions, and (3) accessing capabilities via collaborative partnerships.

7. In building capabilities internally, the first step is to develop the *ability* to do something, through experimentation, active searches for alternative solutions, and

FIGURE 11.1 How Policies and Procedures Facilitate Good Strategy Execution

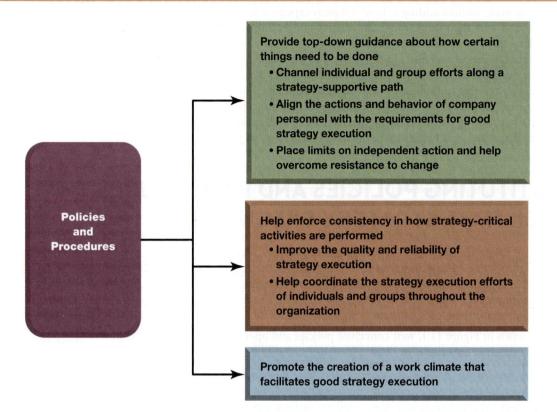

Policies and Procedures

Provide top-down guidance about how certain things need to be done
- Channel individual and group efforts along a strategy-supportive path
- Align the actions and behavior of company personnel with the requirements for good strategy execution
- Place limits on independent action and help overcome resistance to change

Help enforce consistency in how strategy-critical activities are performed
- Improve the quality and reliability of strategy execution
- Help coordinate the strategy execution efforts of individuals and groups throughout the organization

Promote the creation of a work climate that facilitates good strategy execution

centers, or the individual outlets in a chain operation helps a company deliver consistent product quality and service to customers. Good strategy execution nearly always entails an ability to replicate product quality and the caliber of customer service at every location where the company does business—anything less blurs the company's image and lowers customer satisfaction.

3. *They promote the creation of a work climate that facilitates good strategy execution.* A company's policies and procedures help to set the tone of a company's work climate and contribute to a common understanding of "how we do things around here." Because abandoning old policies and procedures in favor of new ones invariably alters the internal work climate, managers can use the policy-changing process as a powerful lever for changing the corporate culture in ways that produce a stronger fit with the new strategy. The trick here, obviously, is to come up with new policies or procedures that catch the immediate attention of company personnel and which quickly shift their actions and behavior—eventually becoming embedded in how things are done.

To ensure consistency in product quality and service behavior patterns, McDonald's policy manual spells out detailed procedures that personnel in each McDonald's unit are expected to observe. For example, "Cooks must turn, never flip, hamburgers. If they haven't been purchased, Big Macs must be discarded in 10 minutes after being cooked and French fries in 7 minutes. Cashiers must make eye contact with and smile at every customer."

Nordstrom has a company policy of promoting only those people whose personnel records contain evidence of "heroic acts" to please customers—especially customers who may have made "unreasonable requests" that require special efforts. This induces store personnel to dedicate themselves to outstanding customer service, consistent with the requirements of executing a strategy based on exceptionally high service quality. To ensure that its R&D activities are responsive to customer needs and expectations, Hewlett-Packard requires its R&D people to make regular visits to customers to learn about their problems and learn their reactions to HP's latest new products.

One of the big policy-making issues concerns what activities need to be rigidly prescribed and what activities ought to allow room for independent action on the part of empowered personnel. Few companies need thick policy manuals to direct the strategy execution process or prescribe exactly how daily operations are to be conducted. Too much policy can be as obstructive as wrong policy and as confusing as no policy. There is wisdom in a middle approach: *Prescribe enough policies to give organization members clear direction and to place reasonable boundaries on their actions; then empower them to act within these boundaries in pursuit of company goals.* Allowing company personnel to act with some degree of freedom is especially appropriate when individual creativity and initiative are more essential to good strategy execution than standardization and strict conformity. Instituting policies that facilitate strategy execution can therefore mean policies that require things be done according to a strictly defined standard or policies that give employees substantial leeway to do activities the way they think best.

INSTITUTING BEST PRACTICES AND EMPLOYING PROCESS MANAGEMENT TOOLS

Company managers can significantly advance the cause of superior strategy execution by employing best practices and process management tools to drive continuous improvement in how internal operations are conducted. One of the most widely used methods for gauging how well a company is executing its strategy entails benchmarking the company's performance of particular activities and business processes against "best-in-industry" and "best-in-world" performers.[1] It can also be useful to look at "best-in-company" performers of an activity if a company has a number of different organizational units performing much the same function at different locations. Identifying, analyzing, and understanding how top-performing companies or organizational units conduct particular value chain activities and business processes provides useful yardsticks for judging the effectiveness and efficiency of internal operations and setting performance standards for organizational units to meet or beat.

How the Process of Identifying and Incorporating Best Practices Works

A **best practice** is a method of performing an activity or business process that consistently delivers superior results compared to other approaches.[2] To qualify as a legitimate best practice, the method must have been employed by at least one enterprise and shown to be *unusually effective* in lowering costs, improving quality or performance, shortening time requirements, enhancing safety, or achieving some other highly positive operating outcome. Best practices thus identify a path to operating excellence.

As discussed in Chapter 4, *benchmarking* is the backbone of the process of identifying, studying, and implementing best practices. The role of benchmarking is to look outward to find best practices and then to develop the data for measuring how well a company's own performance of an activity stacks up against the best-practice standard. However, benchmarking is more complicated than simply identifying which companies are the best performers of an activity and then trying to imitate their approaches—especially if these companies are in other industries. Normally, the best practices of other organizations must be *adapted* to fit the specific circumstances of a company's own business, strategy, and operating requirements. Since each organization is unique, the telling part of any best-practice initiative is how well the company puts its own version of the best practice into place and makes it work. Indeed, a best practice remains little more than another company's interesting success story unless company personnel buy into the task of translating what can be learned from other companies into real action and results. The agents of change must be frontline employees who are convinced of the need to abandon the old ways of doing things and switch to a best-practice mindset.

As shown in Figure 11.2, to the extent that a company is able to successfully adapt a best practice pioneered elsewhere to fit its circumstances, it is likely to improve its performance of the activity, perhaps dramatically—an outcome that promotes better strategy execution. It follows that a company can make giant strides toward excellent strategy execution by adopting a best-practices mindset and successfully *implementing the use of best practices across more of its value chain activities*. The more that organizational units use best practices in performing their work, the closer a company moves toward performing its value chain activities more effectively and efficiently. This is what operational excellence in strategy execution is all about. Employing best practices to improve internal operations has powerful appeal—legions of companies across the world are now making concerted efforts to employ best practices in performing many value chain activities, and they regularly benchmark their performance of these activities against best-in industry or best-in-world performers.

> The more that organizational units use best practices in performing their work, the closer a company comes to achieving effective and efficient strategy execution.

FIGURE 11.2   From Benchmarking and Best-Practice Implementation to Operational Excellence in Strategy Execution

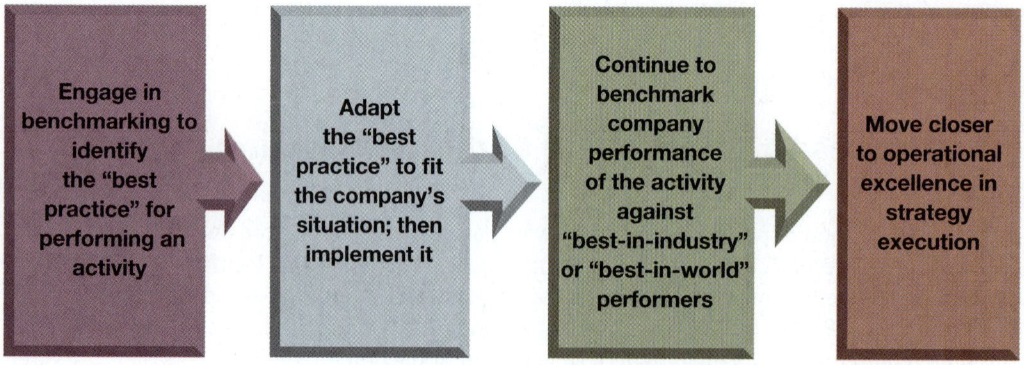

Business Process Reengineering, Total Quality Management, and Six Sigma Quality Programs: Tools for Promoting Operating Excellence

Three other potent management tools for promoting operating excellence and better strategy execution are business process reengineering, total quality management (TQM) programs, and Six Sigma quality control techniques. Each of these merits discussion because, in recent years, many companies around the world have begun using them to help execute strategies keyed to cost reduction, defect-free manufacture, superior product quality, superior customer service, and total customer satisfaction.

Business Process Reengineering   Companies searching for ways to improve their operations have sometimes discovered that the execution of strategy-critical activities is hampered by a disconnected organizational arrangement whereby pieces of an activity are performed in several different functional departments, with no one manager or group being accountable for optimal performance of the entire activity. This can easily occur in such inherently cross-functional activities as customer service (which can involve personnel in order filling, warehousing and shipping, invoicing, accounts receivable, after-sale repair, and technical support), particularly for companies with a functional organizational structure.

To address the suboptimal performance problems that can arise from this type of situation, a company can *reengineer the work effort,* pulling the pieces of an activity out of different departments and creating a single department or cross-functional work group to take charge of the whole process. The use of cross-functional teams has been popularized by the practice of **business process reengineering**, which involves radically redesigning and streamlining the workflow (often enabled by cutting-edge use of online technology and information systems), with the goal of achieving quantum gains in performance of the activity.[3]

The reengineering of value chain activities has been undertaken at many companies in many industries all over the world, with excellent results being achieved at some firms.[4] Hallmark reengineered its process for developing new greeting cards, creating teams of mixed-occupation personnel (artists, writers, lithographers, merchandisers, and administrators) to work on a single holiday or greeting card theme. The reengineered process speeded development times for new lines of greeting cards by up to 24 months, was more cost-efficient, and increased customer satisfaction.[5] In the order-processing section of General Electric's circuit breaker division, elapsed time from order receipt to delivery was cut from three weeks to three days by consolidating six production units into one, reducing a variety of former inventory and handling steps, automating the design system to replace a human custom-design process, and cutting the organizational layers between managers and workers from three to one. Productivity rose 20 percent in one year, and unit manufacturing costs dropped 30 percent. Northwest Water, a British utility, used process reengineering to eliminate 45 work depots that served as home bases to crews who installed and repaired water and sewage lines and equipment. Under the reengineered arrangement, crews worked directly from their vehicles, receiving assignments and reporting work completion from computer terminals in their trucks. Crew members became contractors to Northwest Water rather than employees, a move that not only eliminated the need for the work depots but also allowed Northwest Water to eliminate a big percentage of the bureaucratic personnel and supervisory organization that managed the crews.[6]

CORE CONCEPT

Business process reengineering involves radically redesigning and streamlining how an activity is performed, with the intent of achieving quantum improvements in performance.

Nucor Corporation: Tying Incentives Directly to Strategy Execution

The strategy at Nucor Corporation, one of the three largest steel producers in the United States, is to be *the* low-cost producer of steel products. Because labor costs are a significant fraction of total cost in the steel business, successful implementation of Nucor's low-cost leadership strategy entails achieving lower labor costs per ton of steel than competitors' costs. Nucor management uses an incentive system to promote high worker productivity and drive labor costs per ton below rivals'. Each plant's workforce is organized into production teams (each assigned to perform particular functions), and weekly production targets are established for each team. Base-pay scales are set at levels comparable to wages for similar manufacturing jobs in the local areas where Nucor has plants, but workers can earn a 1 percent bonus for each 1 percent that their output exceeds target levels. If a production team exceeds its weekly production target by 10 percent, team members receive a 10 percent bonus in their next paycheck; if a team exceeds its quota by 20 percent, team members earn a 20 percent bonus. Bonuses, paid every two weeks, are based on the prior two weeks' actual production levels measured against the targets.

Nucor's piece-rate incentive plan has produced impressive results. The production teams put forth exceptional effort; it is not uncommon for most teams to beat their weekly production targets anywhere from 20 to 50 percent. When added to their base pay, the bonuses earned by Nucor workers make Nucor's workforce among the highest-paid in the U.S. steel industry. From a management perspective, the incentive system has resulted in Nucor having labor productivity levels 10 to 20 percent above the average of the unionized

workforces at several of its largest rivals, which in turn has given Nucor a significant labor cost advantage over most rivals.

After years of record-setting profits, Nucor struggled in the economic downturn of 2008–2010, along with the manufacturers and builders who buy its steel. But while bonuses have dwindled, Nucor showed remarkable loyalty to its production workers, avoiding layoffs by having employees get ahead on maintenance, perform work formerly done by contractors, and search for cost savings. Morale at the company has remained high and Nucor's CEO Daniel DiMicco has been inducted into *IndustryWeek* magazine's Manufacturing Hall of Fame because of his no-layoff policies. As industry growth resumes, Nucor will have a well-trained workforce still in place, more committed than ever to achieving the kind of productivity for which Nucor is justifiably famous. When the turnaround comes, DiMicco has good reason to expect Nucor to be "first out of the box."

Sources: Company website (accessed March 2012); N. Byrnes, "Pain, but No Layoffs at Nucor," *Bloomberg Businessweek,* March 26, 2009.

- *Keep the time between achieving the performance target and receiving the reward as short as possible.* Nucor, a leading producer of steel products, has achieved high labor productivity by paying its workers weekly bonuses based on prior-week production levels. To limit the problem of late-arriving flights, Continental pays employees a bonus whenever actual on-time flight performance meets or beats the monthly on-time target. Annual bonus payouts work best for higher-level managers and for situations where the outcome target relates to overall company profitability.

- *Avoid rewarding effort rather than results.* While it is tempting to reward people who have tried hard, gone the extra mile, and yet fallen short of achieving performance targets because of circumstances beyond their control, it is ill advised to do so. The problem with making exceptions for unknowable, uncontrollable, or unforeseeable circumstances is that once "good excuses" start to creep into justifying rewards for subpar results, the door opens to all kinds of reasons as to why actual performance has failed to match targeted performance. A "no excuses" standard is more even-handed, easier to administer, and more conducive to creating a results-oriented work climate.

For an organization's incentive system to work well, the details of the reward structure must be communicated and explained. Everybody needs to understand how their incentive compensation is calculated and how individual/group performance targets contribute to organizational performance targets. The pressure to achieve the specified financial and strategic performance objectives and continuously improve on strategy execution should be unrelenting. People at all levels must be held accountable for carrying out their assigned parts of the strategic plan, and they must understand that their rewards are based on the caliber of results achieved. But with the pressure to perform should come meaningful rewards. Without an ample payoff, the system breaks down, and managers are left with the less workable options of issuing orders, trying to enforce compliance, and depending on the goodwill of employees.

> The unwavering standard for judging whether individuals, teams, and organizational units have done a good job must be whether they meet or beat performance targets that reflect good strategy execution.

KEY POINTS

1. Implementing a new or different strategy calls for managers to identify the resource requirements of each new strategic initiative and then consider whether the current pattern of resource allocation and the budgets of the various subunits are suitable.

2. Company policies and procedures facilitate strategy execution when they are designed to fit the strategy and its objectives. Anytime a company alters its strategy, managers should review existing policies and operating procedures and replace those that are out of sync. Well-conceived policies and procedures aid the task of strategy execution by (1) providing top-down guidance to company personnel regarding how certain things need to be done and what the limits are on independent actions, (2) enforcing consistency in the performance of strategy-critical activities, thereby improving the quality of the strategy execution effort and coordinating the efforts of company personnel, however widely dispersed, and (3) promoting the creation of a work climate conducive to good strategy execution.

3. Competent strategy execution entails visible unyielding managerial commitment to best practices and continuous improvement. Benchmarking, best-practice adoption, business process reengineering, total quality management (TQM), and Six Sigma programs are important process management tools for promoting better strategy execution.

4. Company strategies can't be implemented or executed well without a number of support systems to carry on business operations. Real-time information systems and control systems further aid the cause of good strategy execution.

5. Strategy-supportive motivational practices and reward systems are powerful management tools for gaining employee commitment and focusing their attention on the strategy execution goals. The key to creating a reward system that promotes good strategy execution is to make measures of good business performance and good strategy execution the *dominating basis* for designing incentives, evaluating individual and group efforts, and handing out rewards. Positive motivational practices generally

CHAPTER 12

CORPORATE CULTURE AND LEADERSHIP

Keys to Good Strategy Execution

Learning Objectives

LO 1   Be able to identify the key features of a company's corporate culture and appreciate the role of a company's core values and ethical standards in building corporate culture.

LO 2   Gain an understanding of how and why a company's culture can aid the drive for proficient strategy execution.

LO 3   Learn the kinds of actions management can take to change a problem corporate culture.

LO 4   Understand what constitutes effective managerial leadership in achieving superior strategy execution.

The thing I have learned at IBM is that culture is everything.

> Louis V. Gerstner, Jr. – *Former CEO of IBM*

Management is doing things right; leadership is doing the right things.

> Peter Drucker – *Author and management consultant*

If your actions inspire others to dream more, learn more, do more and become more, you are a leader.

> John Quincy Adams – *6th President of the United States*

In the previous two chapters, we examined eight of the managerial tasks that drive good strategy execution: staffing the organization, acquiring the needed resources and capabilities, designing the organizational structure, allocating resources, establishing policies and procedures, employing process management tools, installing operating systems, and providing the right incentives. In this chapter, we explore the two remaining managerial tasks that contribute to good strategy execution: creating a strategy-supportive corporate culture and exerting the internal leadership needed to drive the implementation of strategic initiatives forward.

INSTILLING A CORPORATE CULTURE CONDUCIVE TO GOOD STRATEGY EXECUTION

Every company has its own **corporate culture**—the shared values, ingrained attitudes, and company traditions that determine norms of behavior, accepted work practices, and styles of operating.[1] The character of a company's culture is a product of the core values and beliefs that executives espouse, the standards of what is ethically acceptable and what is not, the "chemistry" and the "personality" that permeates the work environment, the company's traditions, and the stories that get told over and over to illustrate and reinforce the company's shared values, business practices, and traditions. In a very real sense, the culture is the company's automatic, self-replicating "operating system" that defines "how we do things around here."[2] It can be thought of as the company's psyche or *organizational DNA*.[3] A company's culture is important because it influences the organization's actions and approaches to conducting business. As such, it plays an important role in strategy execution and may have an appreciable effect on business performance as well.

Corporate cultures vary widely. For instance, the bedrock of Walmart's culture is dedication to the zealous pursuit of low costs and frugal operating practices, a strong work ethic, ritualistic headquarters meetings to exchange ideas and review problems, and company executives' commitment to visiting stores, listening to customers, and soliciting suggestions from employees. General Electric's culture is founded on a hard-driving, results-oriented atmosphere; extensive cross-business sharing of ideas, best practices, and learning; reliance on "workout sessions" to identify, debate, and resolve burning issues; a commitment to Six Sigma quality; and a globalized approach to operations. At Nordstrom, the corporate culture is centered on delivering exceptional service to customers, where the company's motto is "Respond to unreasonable customer requests," and each out-of-the-ordinary request is seen as an opportunity for a "heroic" act by an employee that can further the company's reputation for unparalleled customer service. Nordstrom makes a point of promoting employees noted for their heroic acts and dedication to outstanding service. The company motivates its salespeople with a commission-based compensation system that enables Nordstrom's best salespeople to earn more than double what other department stores pay. Illustration Capsule 12.1 describes the corporate culture at W. L. Gore & Associates—the inventor of GORE-TEX.

Identifying the Key Features of a Company's Corporate Culture

LO 1

Be able to identify the key features of a company's corporate culture and appreciate the role of a company's core values and ethical standards in building corporate culture.

A company's corporate culture is mirrored in the character or "personality" of its work environment—the features that describe how the company goes about its business and the workplace behaviors that are held in high esteem. Some of these features are readily apparent, and others operate quite subtly. The chief things to look for include the following:

- The values, business principles, and ethical standards that management preaches and *practices*—these are the key to a company's culture, but actions speak much louder than words here.
- The company's approach to people management and the official policies, procedures, and operating practices that provide guidelines for the behavior of company personnel.
- The atmosphere and spirit that pervades the work climate—whether competitive and political, vibrant and fun, methodical and all business, and the like.
- The way managers and employees interact and relate to one another—the reliance on teamwork and open communication, the extent to which there is good camaraderie, whether people are called by their first names, whether co-workers spend little or lots of time together outside the workplace, and the dress code.
- The strength of peer pressure to do things in particular ways and conform to expected norms.
- The actions and behaviors that are explicitly encouraged and rewarded by management in the form of compensation and promotion.
- The company's revered traditions and oft-repeated stories about "heroic acts" and "how we do things around here."
- The manner in which the company deals with external stakeholders—whether it treats suppliers as business partners or prefers hard-nosed, arm's-length business arrangements, and the strength and genuineness of the commitment to corporate citizenship and environmental sustainability.

The values, beliefs, and practices that undergird a company's culture can come from anywhere in the organizational hierarchy, most often representing the business philosophy and managerial style of influential executives but also resulting from exemplary actions

The Culture that Drives Innovation at W. L. Gore & Associates

W. L. Gore & Associates is best known for GORE-TEX, the waterproof/breathable fabric so highly prized by outdoor enthusiasts. But the company has developed a wide variety of other revolutionary products, including Elixir guitar strings, Ride-On bike cables, and a host of medical devices such as cardiovascular patches and synthetic blood vessels. As a result, it is now one of the largest privately held companies in the United States, with roughly $3B in revenue and more than 9,500 employees in 30 countries worldwide.

When Gore developed the core technology on which most of its more than 2,000 worldwide patents is based, the company's unique culture played a crucial role in allowing it to pursue multiple end-market applications simultaneously, enabling rapid growth from a niche business into a diversified multinational company. The company's culture is team-based and designed to foster personal initiative. It is described on the company's website as follows:

> There are no traditional organizational charts, no chains of command, nor predetermined channels of communication. Instead, we communicate directly with each other and are accountable to fellow members of our multi-discipline teams. We encourage hands-on innovation, involving those closest to a project in decision making. Teams organize around opportunities and leaders emerge.

Personal stories posted on the website describe the discovery process behind a number of breakthrough products developed by particular teams at W. L. Gore & Associates. Employees are encouraged to use 10 percent of their time to tinker with new ideas and to take the long view regarding the idea's development. Promising ideas

attract more people who are willing to work on them without orders from higher-ups. Instead, self-managing associates operating in self-developed teams are simply encouraged to pursue novel applications of Gore technology until these applications are fully commercialized or have had their potential exhausted. The encouragement comes from both the culture (norms and practices) of the organization and from a profit-sharing arrangement that allows employees to benefit directly from their successes.

This approach makes Gore a great place to work and has helped it attract, retain, and motivate top talent globally. Gore has been on *Fortune* magazine's list of the "100 Best Companies to Work For" in the United States for the last 14 years. Gore places similarly on the lists of other countries in which it operates, such as the United Kingdom, Germany, France, Italy, and Sweden.

Developed with Kenneth P. Fraser.

Sources: Company websites; http://www.gore.com/en_xx/news/FORTUNE-2011.html; http://www.director.co.uk/magazine/2010/2_Feb/ WLGore_63_06.html; http://www.fastcompany.com/magazine/89/open_gore.html; accessed March 10, 2012.

on the part of company personnel and consensus agreement about appropriate norms of behavior.[4] Typically, key elements of the culture originate with a founder or certain strong leaders who articulated them as a set of business principles, company policies, operating approaches, and ways of dealing with employees, customers, vendors, shareholders, and local communities where the company has operations. Over time, these cultural underpinnings take root, become embedded in how the company conducts its business, come to be accepted by company managers and employees alike, and then persist as new employees are encouraged to embrace the company values and adopt the implied attitudes, behaviors, and work practices.

The Role of Core Values and Ethics   The foundation of a company's corporate culture nearly always resides in its dedication to certain core values and the bar it sets for ethical behavior. The culture-shaping significance of core values and ethical behaviors accounts for one reason why so many companies have developed a formal values statement and a code of ethics. Of course, sometimes a company's stated core values and code of ethics are cosmetic, existing mainly to impress outsiders and help create a positive company image. But more usually they have been developed to mold the culture and communicate what kinds of actions and behavior are expected of all company personnel. Many executives want the work climate at their companies to mirror certain values and ethical standards, not only because of personal convictions, but also because they are convinced that adherence to such principles will promote better strategy execution, make the company a better performer, and improve its image.[5] Not incidentally, strongly ingrained values and ethical standards reduce the likelihood of lapses in ethical and socially approved behavior that mar a company's reputation and put its financial performance and market standing at risk.

> A company's culture is grounded in and shaped by its core values and ethical standards.

As depicted in Figure 12.1, a company's stated core values and ethical principles have two roles in the culture-building process. First, a company that works hard at putting its stated core values and ethical principles into practice fosters a work climate in which company personnel share strongly held convictions about how the company's business is to be conducted. Second, the stated values and ethical principles provide company personnel with guidance about the manner in which they are to do their jobs—which behaviors and ways of doing things are approved (and expected) and which are out-of-bounds. These values-based and ethics-based cultural norms serve as yardsticks for gauging the appropriateness of particular actions, decisions, and behaviors, thus helping steer company personnel toward both doing things right and doing the right thing.

FIGURE 12.1   The Two Culture-Building Roles of a Company's Core Values and Ethical Standards

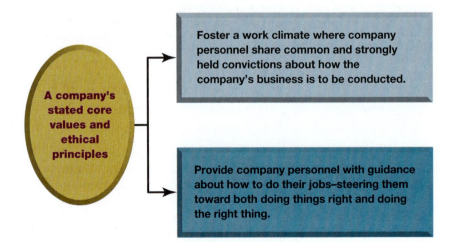

Transforming Core Values and Ethical Standards into Cultural Norms
Once values and ethical standards have been formally adopted, they must be institutionalized in the company's policies and practices and embedded in the conduct of company personnel. This can be done in a number of different ways.[6] Tradition-steeped companies with a rich folklore rely heavily on word-of-mouth indoctrination and the power of tradition to instill values and enforce ethical conduct. But most companies employ a variety of techniques, drawing on some or all of the following:

> A company's values statement and code of ethics communicate expectations of how employees should conduct themselves in the workplace.

1. Giving explicit attention to values and ethics in recruiting and hiring to screen out applicants who do not exhibit compatible character traits.

2. Incorporating a discussion of the company's values and code of ethics into orientation programs for new employees and training courses for managers and employees.

3. Having senior executives frequently reiterate the importance and role of company values and ethical principles at company events and in internal communications to employees.

4. Using values statements and codes of ethical conduct as benchmarks for judging the appropriateness of company policies and operating practices.

5. Making the display of core values and ethical principles a factor in evaluating each person's job performance.

6. Making sure that managers from the CEO down to front-line supervisors stress the importance of ethical conduct and that line managers at all levels give serious and continuous attention to the task of explaining how the values and ethical code apply in their areas.

7. Encouraging everyone to use his or her influence in helping enforce observance of core values and ethical standards.

8. Periodically having ceremonial occasions to recognize individuals and groups who display the company values and ethical principles.

9. Instituting ethics monitoring and enforcement procedures.

To deeply ingrain the stated core values and high ethical standards, companies must turn them into *strictly enforced cultural norms*. They must make it unequivocally clear that living up to the company's values and ethical standards has to be "a way of life" at the company and that there will be little toleration for errant behavior.

The Role of Stories
Frequently, a significant part of a company's culture is captured in the stories that get told over and over again to illustrate to newcomers the importance of certain values and the depth of commitment that various company personnel have displayed. One of the folktales at FedEx, world renowned for the reliability of its next-day package delivery guarantee, is about a deliveryman who had been given the wrong key to a FedEx drop box. Rather than leave the packages in the drop box until the next day when the right key was available, the deliveryman unbolted the drop box from its base, loaded it into the truck, and took it back to the station. There, the box was pried open and the contents removed and sped on their way to their destination the next day. Nordstrom keeps a scrapbook commemorating the heroic acts of its employees and uses it as a regular reminder of the above-and-beyond-the-call-of-duty behaviors that employees are encouraged to display. When a customer was unable to find a shoe she was looking for at Nordstrom, a salesman found the shoe at a competing store and had

it shipped to her, at Nordstrom's expense. At Frito-Lay, there are dozens of stories about truck drivers who went to extraordinary lengths in overcoming adverse weather conditions in order to make scheduled deliveries to retail customers and keep store shelves stocked with Frito-Lay products. Such stories serve the valuable purpose of illustrating the kinds of behavior the company reveres and inspiring company personnel to perform similarly. Moreover, each retelling of a legendary story puts a bit more peer pressure on company personnel to display core values and do their part in keeping the company's traditions alive.

Forces that Cause a Company's Culture to Evolve   Despite the role of time-honored stories and long-standing traditions in perpetuating a company's culture, cultures are far from static—just like strategy and organization structure, they evolve. New challenges in the marketplace, revolutionary technologies, and shifting internal conditions—especially an internal crisis, a change in company direction, or top executive turnover—tend to breed new ways of doing things and, in turn, drive cultural evolution. An incoming CEO who decides to shake up the existing business and take it in new directions often triggers a cultural shift, perhaps one of major proportions. Likewise, diversification into new businesses, expansion into foreign countries, rapid growth that brings an influx of new employees, and the merger with or acquisition of another company can all precipitate significant cultural change.

Strong vs. Weak Cultures

Company cultures vary widely in strength and influence. Some are strongly embedded and have a big influence on a company's operating practices and the behavior of company personnel. Others are weakly ingrained and have little effect on behaviors and how company activities are conducted.

> **CORE CONCEPT**
>
> In a **strong-culture company,** deeply rooted values and norms of behavior are widely shared and regulate the conduct of the company's business.

Strong-Culture Companies   The hallmark of a **strong-culture company** is the dominating presence of certain deeply rooted values and behavioral norms that "regulate" the conduct of company personnel as they go about the company's business.[7] Strong cultures enable a company to operate like a well-oiled machine, smoothly operating without a lot of intervention from management. Senior managers in strong-culture companies embody the cultural norms in their own actions and expect the same of others within the company. An unequivocal expectation that company personnel will act and behave in accordance with the adopted values and ways of doing business leads to two important outcomes: (1) Over time, the values come to be widely shared by rank-and-file employees—people who dislike the culture tend to leave—and (2) individuals encounter strong peer pressure from co-workers to observe the culturally approved norms and behaviors. Hence, a strongly implanted corporate culture ends up having a powerful influence on behavior because so many company personnel are accepting of cultural traditions and because this acceptance is reinforced by both management expectations and co-worker peer pressure to conform to cultural norms.

Strong cultures emerge over a period of years (sometimes decades) and are never an overnight phenomenon. Two factors contribute to the development of strong cultures: (1) a founder or strong leader who established core values, principles, and practices that are viewed as having contributed to the success of the company, and (2) a sincere, long-standing company commitment to operating the business according to these established traditions and values. Continuity of leadership, low workforce turnover, geographic concentration, and considerable organizational success all contribute to the emergence and sustainability of a strong culture.[8]

In strong-culture companies, values and behavioral norms are so ingrained that they can endure leadership changes at the top—although their strength can erode over time if new CEOs cease to nurture them or move aggressively to institute cultural adjustments. The cultural norms in a strong-culture company typically do not change much as strategy evolves, either because the culture constrains the choice of new strategies or because the dominant traits of the culture are somewhat strategy-neutral and compatible with evolving versions of the company's strategy. As a consequence, *strongly implanted cultures provide a huge assist in executing strategy* because company managers can use the traditions, beliefs, values, common bonds, or behavioral norms as levers to mobilize commitment to executing the chosen strategy.

Weak-Culture Companies   In direct contrast to strong-culture companies, weak-culture companies lack widely shared and strongly held values and principles. As a result, they also lack cultural mechanisms for aligning, constraining, and regulating the actions, decisions, and behaviors of company personnel. In weak-culture companies, few widely revered traditions and few culture-induced norms are evident in employee behavior or operating practices. Because top executives at a weak-culture company don't repeatedly espouse any particular business philosophy or exhibit long-standing commitment to particular values or behavioral norms, individuals encounter little pressure to do things in particular ways. A weak company culture breeds no strong employee allegiance to what the company stands for or to operating the business in well-defined ways. While individual employees may well have some bonds of identification with and loyalty toward their department, their colleagues, their union, or their immediate boss, there's neither passion about the company nor emotional commitment to what it is trying to accomplish—a condition that often results in many employees viewing their company as just a place to work and their job as just a way to make a living.

As a consequence, *weak cultures provide little or no assistance in executing strategy* because there are no traditions, beliefs, values, common bonds, or behavioral norms that management can use as levers to mobilize commitment to executing the chosen strategy. Without a work climate that channels organizational energy in the direction of good strategy execution, managers are left with the options of either using compensation incentives and other motivational devices to mobilize employee commitment, supervising and monitoring employee actions more closely, or trying to establish cultural roots that will in time start to nurture the strategy execution process.

Why Corporate Cultures Matter to the Strategy Execution Process

Even if a company has a strong culture, the culture and work climate may or may not be compatible with what is needed for effective implementation of the chosen strategy. When a company's present culture promotes attitudes, behaviors, and ways of doing things that are *in sync with the chosen strategy* and conducive to first-rate strategy execution, the culture functions as a valuable ally in the strategy execution process. For example, a corporate culture characterized by frugality and thrift prompts employee actions to identify cost-saving opportunities—the very behavior needed for successful execution of a low-cost leadership strategy. A culture which celebrates taking initiative, exhibiting creativity, taking risks, and embracing change is conducive to successful execution of product innovation and technological leadership strategies.[9]

LO 2

Gain an understanding of how and why a company's culture can aid the drive for proficient strategy execution.

A culture that is grounded in actions, behaviors, and work practices that are conducive to good strategy implementation assists the strategy execution effort in three ways:

1. *A culture that is well matched to the chosen strategy and the requirements of the strategy execution effort focuses the attention of employees on what is most important to this effort.* Moreover, it directs their behavior and serves as a guide to their decision making. In this manner, it can align the efforts and decisions of employees throughout the firm and minimize the need for direct supervision.

2. *Culture-induced peer pressure further induces company personnel to do things in a manner that aids the cause of good strategy execution.* The stronger the culture (the more widely shared and deeply held the values), the more effective peer pressure is in shaping and supporting the strategy execution effort. Research has shown that strong group norms can shape employee behavior even more powerfully than can financial incentives.

3. *A company culture that is consistent with the requirements for good strategy execution can energize employees, deepen their commitment to execute the strategy flawlessly, and enhance worker productivity in the process.* When a company's culture is grounded in many of the needed strategy-executing behaviors, employees feel genuinely better about their jobs, the company they work for, and the merits of what the company is trying to accomplish. As a consequence, greater numbers of company personnel exhibit passion in their work and exert their best efforts to execute the strategy and achieve performance targets.

In sharp contrast, when a culture is in conflict with the chosen strategy or what is required to execute the company's strategy well, the culture becomes a stumbling block.[10] Some of the very behaviors needed to execute the strategy successfully run contrary to the attitudes, behaviors, and operating practices embedded in the prevailing culture. Such a clash poses a real dilemma for company personnel. Should they be loyal to the culture and company traditions (to which they are likely to be emotionally attached) and thus resist or be indifferent to actions that will promote better strategy execution—a choice that will certainly weaken the drive for good strategy execution? Alternatively, should they go along with the strategy execution effort and engage in actions that run counter to the culture—a choice that will likely impair morale and lead to a less-than-wholehearted commitment to management's strategy execution efforts? Neither choice leads to desirable outcomes. Culture-bred resistance to the actions and behaviors needed for good strategy execution, particularly if strong and widespread, poses a formidable hurdle that must be cleared for a strategy's execution to get very far.

This says something important about the task of managing the strategy execution process: *Closely aligning corporate culture with the requirements for proficient strategy execution merits the full attention of senior executives.* The culture-building objective is to create a work climate and style of operating that mobilize the energy of company personnel squarely behind efforts to execute strategy competently. The more deeply management can embed execution-supportive ways of doing things, the more management can rely on the culture to automatically steer company personnel toward behaviors and work practices that aid good strategy execution and veer from doing things that impede it. Moreover, culturally astute managers understand that nourishing the right cultural environment not only adds power to their push for proficient strategy execution but also promotes strong employee identification with, and commitment to, the company's vision, performance targets, and strategy.

Healthy Cultures that Aid Good Strategy Execution

A strong culture, provided it fits the chosen strategy and embraces execution-supportive attitudes, behaviors, and work practices, is definitely a healthy culture. Two other types of cultures exist that tend to be healthy and largely supportive of good strategy execution: high-performance cultures and adaptive cultures.

High-Performance Cultures   Some companies have so-called high-performance cultures where the standout traits are a "can-do" spirit, pride in doing things right, no-excuses accountability, and a pervasive results-oriented work climate in which people go all out to meet or beat stretch objectives.[11] In high-performance cultures, there's a strong sense of involvement on the part of company personnel and emphasis on individual initiative and effort. Performance expectations are clearly delineated for the company as a whole, for each organizational unit, and for each individual. Issues and problems are promptly addressed; there's a razor-sharp focus on what needs to be done. The clear and unyielding expectation is that all company personnel, from senior executives to frontline employees, will display high-performance behaviors and a passion for making the company successful. Such a culture—permeated by a spirit of achievement and constructive pressure to meet or beat performance targets—is a valuable contributor to good strategy execution and operating excellence.[12]

The challenge in creating a high-performance culture is to inspire high loyalty and dedication on the part of employees, such that they are energized to put forth their very best efforts. Managers have to take pains to reinforce constructive behavior, reward top performers, and purge habits and behaviors that stand in the way of high productivity and good results. They must work at knowing the strengths and weaknesses of their subordinates, so as to better match talent with task and enable people to make meaningful contributions by doing what they do best. They have to stress learning from mistakes and must put an unrelenting emphasis on moving forward and making good progress—in effect, there has to be a disciplined, performance-focused approach to managing the organization.

Adaptive Cultures   The hallmark of adaptive corporate cultures is a willingness on the part of organization members to accept change and take on the challenge of introducing and executing new strategies. Company personnel share a feeling of confidence that the organization can deal with whatever threats and opportunities arise; they are receptive to risk taking, experimentation, innovation, and changing strategies and practices. The work climate is supportive of managers and employees who propose or initiate useful change. Internal entrepreneurship on the part of individuals and groups is encouraged and rewarded. Senior executives seek out, support, and promote individuals who exercise initiative, spot opportunities for improvement, and display the skills to implement them. Managers openly evaluate ideas and suggestions, fund initiatives to develop new or better products, and take prudent risks to pursue emerging market opportunities. As in high-performance cultures, the company exhibits a proactive approach to identifying issues, evaluating the implications and options, and moving ahead quickly with workable solutions. Strategies and traditional operating practices are modified as needed to adjust to, or take advantage of, changes in the business environment.

But why is change so willingly embraced in an adaptive culture? Why are organization members not fearful of how change will affect them? Why does an adaptive culture not break down from the force of ongoing changes in strategy, operating practices, and approaches to strategy execution? The answers lie in two distinctive and dominant

> As a company's strategy evolves, an adaptive culture is a definite ally in the strategy-implementing, strategy-executing process as compared to cultures that are resistant to change.

traits of an adaptive culture: (1) Any changes in operating practices and behaviors must *not* compromise core values and long-standing business principles (since they are at the root of the culture), and (2) the changes that are instituted must satisfy the legitimate interests of stakeholders—customers, employees, shareowners, suppliers, and the communities where the company operates. In other words, what sustains an adaptive culture is that organization members perceive the changes that management is trying to institute as *legitimate,* in keeping with the core values, and in the overall best interests of key constituencies.[13] Not surprisingly, company personnel are usually more receptive to change when their employment security is not threatened and when they view new duties or job assignments as part of the process of adapting to new conditions. Should workforce downsizing be necessary, it is important that layoffs be handled humanely and employee departures be made as painless as possible.

Technology companies, software companies, and Internet-based companies are good illustrations of organizations with adaptive cultures. Such companies thrive on change—driving it, leading it, and capitalizing on it. Companies like Facebook, Twitter, Groupon, LinkedIn, Apple, Google, and Intel cultivate the capability to act and react rapidly. They are avid practitioners of entrepreneurship and innovation, with a demonstrated willingness to take bold risks to create altogether new products, new businesses, and new industries. To create and nurture a culture that can adapt rapidly to shifting business conditions, they make a point of staffing their organizations with people who are flexible, who rise to the challenge of change, and who have an aptitude for adapting well to new circumstances.

In fast-changing business environments, a corporate culture that is receptive to altering organizational practices and behaviors is a virtual necessity. However, adaptive cultures work to the advantage of all companies, not just those in rapid-change environments. Every company operates in a market and business climate that is changing to one degree or another and that, in turn, requires internal operating responses and new behaviors on the part of organization members.

Unhealthy Cultures that Impede Good Strategy Execution

The distinctive characteristic of an unhealthy corporate culture is the presence of counterproductive cultural traits that adversely impact the work climate and company performance. Five particularly unhealthy cultural traits are hostility to change, heavily politicized decision making, insular thinking, unethical and greed-driven behaviors, and the presence of incompatible, clashing subcultures.

Change-Resistant Cultures

Change-Resistant Cultures   Change-resistant cultures—where skepticism about the importance of new developments and a fear of change are the norm—place a premium on not making mistakes, prompting managers to lean toward safe, conservative options intended to maintain the status quo, protect their power base, and guard their immediate interests. When such companies encounter business environments with accelerating change, going slow on altering traditional ways of doing things can be a serious liability. Under these conditions, change-resistant cultures encourage a number of unhealthy behaviors—avoiding risks, not capitalizing on emerging opportunities, taking a lax approach to both product innovation and continuous improvement in performing value chain activities, and responding more slowly than is warranted to market change. In change-resistant cultures, word quickly gets around that proposals to do things differently face an uphill battle and that people who champion them may be seen as something of a nuisance or a troublemaker. Executives who don't value managers or employees with initiative and new ideas put a damper on product innovation, experimentation, and efforts to improve.

Hostility to change is most often found in companies with stodgy bureaucracies that have enjoyed considerable market success in years past and that are wedded to the "We have done it this way for years" syndrome. General Motors, IBM, Sears, and Eastman Kodak are classic examples of companies whose change-resistant bureaucracies have damaged their market standings and financial performance; clinging to what made them successful, they were reluctant to alter operating practices and modify their business approaches when signals of market change first sounded. As strategies of gradual change won out over bold innovation, all four lost market share to rivals that quickly moved to institute changes more in tune with evolving market conditions and buyer preferences. While IBM has made strides in building a culture needed for market success, Sears, GM, and Kodak are still struggling to recoup lost ground.

Politicized Cultures

What makes a politicized internal environment so unhealthy is that political infighting consumes a great deal of organizational energy, often with the result that what's best for the company takes a backseat to political maneuvering. In companies where internal politics pervades the work climate, empire-building managers pursue their own agendas and operate the work units under their supervision as autonomous "fiefdoms." The positions they take on issues are usually aimed at protecting or expanding their own turf. Collaboration with other organizational units is viewed with suspicion, and cross-unit cooperation occurs grudgingly. The support or opposition of politically influential executives or coalitions among departments with vested interests in a particular outcome tends to shape what actions the company takes. All this political maneuvering takes away from efforts to execute strategy with real proficiency and frustrates company personnel who are less political and more inclined to do what is in the company's best interests.

Insular, Inwardly Focused Cultures

Sometimes a company reigns as an industry leader or enjoys great market success for so long that its personnel start to believe they have all the answers or can develop them on their own. There is a strong tendency to neglect what customers are saying and how their needs and expectations are changing. Such confidence in the correctness of how it does things and an unflinching belief in the company's competitive superiority breeds arrogance, prompting company personnel to discount the merits of what outsiders are doing and to see little payoff from studying best-in-class performers. Insular thinking, internally driven solutions, and a must-be-invented-here mindset come to permeate the corporate culture. An inwardly focused corporate culture gives rise to managerial inbreeding and a failure to recruit people who can offer fresh thinking and outside perspectives. The big risk of insular cultural thinking is that the company can underestimate the capabilities and accomplishments of rival companies and overestimate its own progress—all of which diminishes a company's competitiveness over time.

Unethical and Greed-Driven Cultures

Companies that have little regard for ethical standards or that are run by executives driven by greed and ego gratification are scandals waiting to happen. Executives exude the negatives of arrogance, ego, greed, and an "ends-justify-the-means" mentality in pursuing overambitious revenue and profitability targets.[14] Senior managers wink at unethical behavior and may cross over the line to unethical (and sometimes criminal) behavior themselves. They are prone to adopt accounting principles that make financial performance look better than it really is. Legions of companies have fallen prey to unethical behavior and greed, most notably WorldCom, Enron, Quest, HealthSouth, Adelphia, Tyco, Parmalat, Rite Aid, Hollinger International, Refco, Marsh & McLennan, Siemens, Countrywide Financial, and Stanford Financial Group, with executives being indicted and/or convicted of criminal behavior.

Incompatible Subcultures   Although it is common to speak about corporate culture in the singular, it is not unusual for companies to have multiple cultures (or subcultures). Values, beliefs, and practices within a company sometimes vary significantly by department, geographic location, division, or business unit. As long as the subcultures are compatible with the overarching corporate culture and are supportive of the strategy execution efforts, this is not problematic. Multiple cultures pose an unhealthy situation when they are composed of incompatible subcultures that embrace conflicting business philosophies, support inconsistent approaches to strategy execution, and encourage incompatible methods of people management. Clashing subcultures can prevent a company from coordinating its efforts to craft and execute strategy and can distract company personnel from the business of business. Internal jockeying among the subcultures for cultural dominance impedes teamwork among the company's various organizational units and blocks the emergence of a collaborative approach to strategy execution. Such a lack of consensus about how to proceed is likely to result in fragmented or inconsistent approaches to implementing new strategic initiatives and limited success in executing the company's overall strategy.

Changing a Problem Culture

LO 3

Learn the kinds of actions management can take to change a problem corporate culture.

When a strong culture is unhealthy or otherwise out of sync with the actions and behaviors needed to execute the strategy successfully, the culture must be changed as rapidly as can be managed. This means eliminating any unhealthy or dysfunctional cultural traits as fast as possible and aggressively striving to ingrain new behaviors and work practices that will enable first-rate strategy execution. The more entrenched the mismatched or unhealthy aspects of a company culture, the more likely the culture will impede strategy execution and the greater the need for change.

Changing a problem culture is among the toughest management tasks because of the heavy anchor of ingrained behaviors and attitudes. It is natural for company personnel to cling to familiar practices and to be wary, if not hostile, to new approaches of how things are to be done. Consequently, it takes concerted management action over a period of time to root out certain unwanted behaviors and replace an out-of-sync culture with more effective ways of doing things. *The single most visible factor that distinguishes successful culture-change efforts from failed attempts is competent leadership at the top.* Great power is needed to force major cultural change and overcome the "springback" resistance of entrenched cultures—and great power is possessed only by the most senior executives, especially the CEO. However, while top management must be out front leading the effort, the tasks of marshaling support for a new culture and instilling the desired cultural behaviors must involve the whole management team. Middle managers and frontline supervisors play a key role in implementing the new work practices and operating approaches, helping win rank-and-file acceptance of and support for changes, and instilling the desired behavioral norms.

As shown in Figure 12.2, the first step in fixing a problem culture is for top management to identify those facets of the present culture that pose obstacles to executing

FIGURE 12.2   Changing a Problem Culture

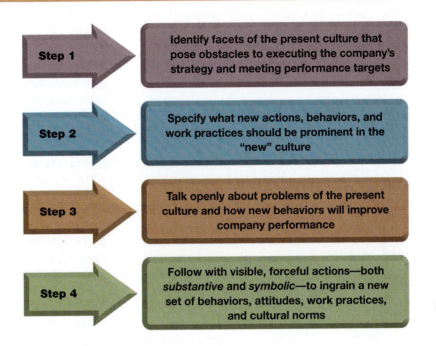

new strategic initiatives and meeting company performance targets. Second, managers must clearly define the desired new behaviors and features of the culture they want to create. Third, managers have to convince company personnel of why the present culture poses problems and why and how new behaviors and operating approaches will improve company performance—the case for cultural reform has to be persuasive. Fourth, and most important, all the talk about remodeling the present culture has to be followed swiftly by visible, forceful actions to promote the desired new behaviors and work practices—actions that company personnel will interpret as a determined top management commitment to bringing about a different work climate and new ways of operating. The actions to implant the new culture must be both substantive and symbolic.

Making a Compelling Case for Culture Change   The way for management to begin a major remodeling of the corporate culture is by selling company personnel on the need for new-style behaviors and work practices. This means making a compelling case for why the culture-remodeling efforts are in the organization's best interests and why company personnel should wholeheartedly join the effort to doing things somewhat differently. This can be done by:

- Explaining why and how certain behaviors and work practices in the current culture pose obstacles to good strategy execution.
- Explaining how new behaviors and work practices will be more advantageous and produce better results. Effective culture-change leaders are good at telling stories to describe the new values and desired behaviors and connect them to everyday practices.

- Citing reasons why the current strategy has to be modified, if the need for cultural change is due to a change in strategy. This includes explaining why the new strategic initiatives will bolster the company's competitiveness and performance and how a change in culture can help in executing the new strategy.

It is essential for the CEO and other top executives to talk personally to company personnel all across the company about the reasons for modifying work practices and culture-related behaviors. Senior officers and department heads have to play a lead role in explaining the need for a change in behavioral norms to those they manage—and the explanations will likely have to be repeated many times. For the culture-change effort to be successful, frontline supervisors and employee opinion leaders must be won over to the cause, which means convincing them of the merits of *practicing* and *enforcing* cultural norms at every level of the organization, from the highest to the lowest. Arguments for new ways of doing things and new work practices tend to be embraced more readily if employees understand how they will benefit company stakeholders (particularly customers, employees, and shareholders). Until a large majority of employees accept the need for a new culture and agree that different work practices and behaviors are called for, there's more work to be done in selling company personnel on the whys and wherefores of culture change. Building widespread organizational support requires taking every opportunity to repeat the message of why the new work practices, operating approaches, and behaviors are good for company stakeholders.

Substantive Culture-Changing Actions

No culture change effort can get very far with just talk about the need for different actions, behaviors, and work practices. Company executives must give the culture-change effort some teeth by initiating *a series of actions* that company personnel will see as credible and unmistakably indicative of the seriousness of management's commitment to cultural change. The strongest signs that management is truly committed to instilling a new culture include:

- Replacing key executives who are resisting and obstructing needed organizational and cultural changes.
- Promoting individuals who have stepped forward to spearhead the shift to a different culture and who can serve as role models for the desired cultural behavior.
- Appointing outsiders with the desired cultural attributes to high-profile positions—bringing in new-breed managers sends an unmistakable message that a new era is dawning.
- Screening all candidates for new positions carefully, hiring only those who appear to fit in with the new culture.
- Mandating that all company personnel attend culture-training programs to better understand the culture-related actions and behaviors that are expected.
- Designing compensation incentives that boost the pay of teams and individuals who display the desired cultural behaviors. Company personnel are much more inclined to exhibit the desired kinds of actions and behaviors when it is in their financial best interest to do so.
- Revising policies and procedures in ways that will help drive cultural change.

Executives must take care to launch enough companywide culture-change actions at the outset so as to leave no room for doubt that management is dead serious about changing the present culture and that a cultural transformation is inevitable. The series of actions initiated by top management must create lots of hallway talk across the whole company, get the change process off to a fast start, and be followed by unrelenting efforts to firmly establish the new work practices, desired behaviors, and style of operating as "standard."

Symbolic Culture-Changing Actions There's also an important place for symbolic managerial actions to alter a problem culture and tighten the strategy-culture fit. The most important symbolic actions are those that top executives take to *lead by example.* For instance, if the organization's strategy involves a drive to become the industry's low-cost producer, senior managers must display frugality in their own actions and decisions: inexpensive decorations in the executive suite, conservative expense accounts and entertainment allowances, a lean staff in the corporate office, scrutiny of budget requests, few executive perks, and so on. At Walmart, all the executive offices are simply decorated; executives are habitually frugal in their own actions, and they are zealous in their efforts to control costs and promote greater efficiency. At Nucor, one of the world's low-cost producers of steel products, executives fly coach class and use taxis at airports rather than limousines. Top executives must be alert to the fact that company personnel will be watching their behavior to see if their actions match their rhetoric. Hence, they need to make sure their current decisions and actions will be construed as consistent with the new-culture values and norms.[15]

Another category of symbolic actions includes holding ceremonial events to single out and honor people whose actions and performance exemplify what is called for in the new culture. In addition, each culture-change success needs to be celebrated. Executives sensitive to their role in promoting strategy-culture fit make a habit of appearing at ceremonial functions to praise individuals and groups that exemplify the desired behaviors. They show up at employee training programs to stress strategic priorities, values, ethical principles, and cultural norms. Every group gathering is seen as an opportunity to repeat and ingrain values, praise good deeds, expound on the merits of the new culture, and cite instances of how the new work practices and operating approaches have worked to good advantage.

The use of symbols in culture building is widespread. Numerous businesses have employee-of-the-month awards. The military has a long-standing custom of awarding ribbons and medals for exemplary actions. Mary Kay Cosmetics awards an array of prizes ceremoniously to its beauty consultants for reaching various sales plateaus.

How Long Does It Take to Change a Problem Culture? Planting and growing the seeds of a new culture require a determined effort by the chief executive and other senior managers. It demands a sustained and persistent effort to reinforce the culture at every opportunity through both word and deed. Changing a problem culture is never a short-term exercise. It takes time for a new culture to emerge and prevail; overnight transformations simply don't occur. And it takes even longer for a new culture to become deeply embedded. The bigger the organization and the greater the cultural shift needed to produce an execution-supportive fit, the longer it takes. In large companies, fixing a problem culture and instilling a new set of attitudes and behaviors can take two to five years. In fact, it is usually tougher to reform an entrenched problematic culture than it is to instill a strategy-supportive culture from scratch in a brand new organization.

Illustration Capsule 12.2 discusses the approaches used at Chrysler in 2009–2010 to change a culture that was grounded in a 1970s view of the automobile industry.

Changing the "Old Detroit" Culture at Chrysler

When Chrysler Group LLC emerged from bankruptcy in June 2009, its road to recovery was far from certain. "It was questionable whether they'd survive 2010," said Michelle Krebs, an analyst with auto information provider Edmunds.com. One thing that was holding Chrysler back was its culture—a legacy of "the Old Detroit," which was characterized by finger-pointing and blame shifting whenever problems arose.[a]

Chrysler's management had long been aware of its culture problem. In 2008, Robert Nardelli, Chrysler's autocratic new CEO, placed himself in charge of a wide-ranging culture-change program designed to break the ingrained behaviors that had damaged the company's reputation for quality. Chrysler's slide into bankruptcy was hardly the comeback that the controversial Nardelli envisioned when he was hired for the job by private-equity firm Cerberus Capital Management (which controlled Chrysler from 2007 until 2009).

A strategic partnership ceding management control to Italian automaker Fiat SpA was part of the deal for Chrysler's bankruptcy reorganization, with Fiat's CEO, Sergio Marchionne, becoming Chrysler's CEO as well. In discussing his five-year plan for Chrysler, Marchionne remarked, "What I've learned as a CEO is that culture is not part of the game—it is the game!"[b]

Marchionne put Doug Betts, a veteran of Toyota Motor Corp. and Nissan Motor Co., in charge of a systematic overhaul of Chrysler quality, with cultural change as the fundamental driver. Betts began by creating new

cross-functional teams designed to break down Chrysler's balkanized silos of manufacturing and engineering. Whereas problems were formerly handed off from one department to another, delaying action for an average of 71 days, quality teams are now encouraged to take ownership of solutions. Betts has also taken aim at the climate of fear, replacing concerns over recrimination and retribution with a positive focus on team empowerment and problem solving. By the end of 2009, Betts was saying, "It's different now. People are talking openly about problems now and how to fix [them]."[d] By August 2011, confidence in Chrysler had increased and U.S. sales were up by 42 percent over the same period in the previous year, resulting in the best August sales since 2007. This marked the 17th month of year-over-year gains for Chrysler.

[a] Jerry Hirsch, "Chrysler Performance Exceeds Expectations: The Fiat-Managed Company Cut Its Losses to $197 Million and Recorded a $143-Million Operating Profit in the First Quarter of the Year," Los Angeles Times, April 22, 2010, http://articles.latimes.com/2010/apr/22/business/la-fi-chrysler-20100422.

[b] Daniel Howes, "Chrysler's Last Chance to Get It Right," Detroit News, Business section, 1-dot edition, p. 4B.

[d] Alisa Priddle, "'Different' Chrysler Zeroes In on Quality," Detroit News, Business section, 2-dot edition, p. 1A. Developed with Amy Florentino.

Sources: Company website, accessed April 3, 2012; http://topics.nytimes.com/top/reference/timestopics/people/n/robert_l_nardelli/index.html, updated May 1, 2009; Neal E. Boudette, "Nardelli Tries to Shift Chrysler's Culture," The Wall Street Journal, June 18, 2008, p. B1.

LEADING THE STRATEGY EXECUTION PROCESS

LO 4

Understand what constitutes effective managerial leadership in achieving superior strategy execution.

For an enterprise to execute its strategy in truly proficient fashion and approach operating excellence, top executives have to take the lead in the strategy implementation process and personally drive the pace of progress. They have to be out in the field, seeing for themselves how well operations are going, gathering information firsthand, and gauging the progress being made. Proficient strategy execution requires company managers to be diligent and adept in spotting problems, learning what obstacles lay in the path of good execution, and then clearing the way for progress—the goal must be to produce better results speedily and productively. There must be constructive, but unrelenting, pressure on organizational units to (1) demonstrate excellence in all dimensions of strategy execution and (2) do so on a consistent basis—ultimately, that's what will enable a well-crafted strategy to achieve the desired performance results.

For the most part, leading the strategy execution process must be done top-down and be driven by mandates to get things on the right track and show good results. The specifics of how to implement a strategy and deliver the intended results must start with understanding the requirements for good strategy execution. Afterward comes a diagnosis of the organization's preparedness to execute the strategic initiatives and decisions as to how to move forward and achieve the targeted results.[16] In general, leading the drive for good strategy execution and operating excellence calls for three actions on the part of the manager-in-charge:

- Staying on top of what is happening and closely monitoring progress.
- Putting constructive pressure on the organization to execute the strategy well and achieve operating excellence.
- Initiating corrective actions to improve strategy execution and achieve the targeted performance results.

Staying on Top of How Well Things Are Going

To stay on top of how well the strategy execution process is going, senior executives have to tap into information from a wide range of sources. In addition to communicating regularly with key subordinates and reviewing the latest operating results, watching the competitive reactions of rival firms, and visiting with key customers and suppliers to get their perspectives, they usually visit various company facilities and talk with many different company personnel at many different organization levels—a technique often labeled **managing by walking around (MBWA).** Most managers attach great importance to spending time with people at company facilities, asking questions, listening to their opinions and concerns, and gathering firsthand information about how well aspects of the strategy execution process are going. Facilities tours and face-to-face contacts with operating-level employees give executives a good grasp of what progress is being made, what problems are being encountered, and whether additional resources or different approaches may be needed. Just as important, MBWA provides opportunities to give encouragement, lift spirits, shift attention from the old to the new priorities, and create some excitement—all of which generate positive energy and help boost strategy execution efforts.

Jeff Bezos, Amazon.com's CEO, is noted for his practice of MBWA, firing off a battery of questions when he tours facilities and insisting that Amazon managers spend time in the trenches with their people to prevent getting disconnected from the reality of what's happening.[17] Walmart executives have had a long-standing practice of spending two to three days every week visiting Walmart's stores and talking with store managers and employees. Sam Walton, Walmart's founder, insisted, "The key is to get out into the store and listen to what the associates have to say." Jack Welch, the highly effective CEO of General Electric (GE) from 1980 to 2001, not only spent several days each month personally visiting GE operations and talking with major customers but also arranged his schedule so that he could spend time exchanging information and ideas with GE managers from all over the world who were attending classes at the company's leadership development center near GE's headquarters.

Many manufacturing executives make a point of strolling the factory floor to talk with workers and meeting regularly with union officials. Some managers operate out of open cubicles in big spaces populated with open cubicles for other personnel so that they can interact easily and frequently with co-workers. Managers at some companies host weekly get-togethers (often on Friday afternoons) to create a regular opportunity for information to flow freely between executives and down-the-line employees.

Mobilizing the Effort for Excellence in Strategy Execution

Managers have to be out front in mobilizing the effort for good strategy execution and operating excellence. Part of the leadership task entails nurturing a results-oriented work climate, where performance standards are high and a spirit of achievement is pervasive. Successfully leading the effort to foster a results-oriented, high-performance culture generally entails such leadership actions and managerial practices as:

- *Treating employees as valued partners.* Some companies symbolize the value of individual employees and the importance of their contributions by referring to them as cast members (Disney), crew members (McDonald's), job owners (Graniterock), partners (Starbucks), or associates (Walmart, LensCrafters, W. L. Gore, Edward Jones, Publix Supermarkets, and Marriott International). Very often, there is a strong company commitment to training each employee thoroughly, offering attractive compensation and career opportunities, emphasizing promotion from within, providing a high degree of job security, and otherwise making employees feel well treated and valued.

- *Fostering an esprit de corps that energizes organization members.* The task here is to skillfully use people-management practices calculated to build morale, foster pride in doing things right, promote teamwork, create a strong sense of involvement on the part of company personnel, win their emotional commitment, and inspire them to do their best.[18]

- *Using empowerment to help create a fully engaged workforce.* Top executives—and, to some degree, the enterprise's entire management team—must seek to engage the full organization in the strategy execution effort. A fully engaged workforce, one where individuals bring their best to work every day, is necessary to produce great results.[19] So is having a group of dedicated managers committed to making a difference in their organization. The two best things top-level executives can do to create a fully engaged organization are (1) delegate authority to middle and lower-level managers to get the strategy execution process moving and (2) empower rank-and-file employees to act on their own initiative. Operating excellence requires that everybody contribute ideas, exercise initiative and creativity in performing his or her work, and have a desire to do things in the best possible manner.

- *Setting stretch objectives and clearly communicating an expectation that company personnel are to give their best in achieving performance targets.* Stretch objectives—those beyond an organization's current capacities—can sometimes spur organization members to increase their resolve and redouble their efforts to execute the strategy flawlessly and ultimately reach the stretch objectives. When stretch objectives are met, the satisfaction of achievement and boost to employee morale can result in an even higher level of organizational drive.

- *Using the tools of benchmarking best practices, business process reengineering, TQM, and Six Sigma to focus attention on continuous improvement.* These are proven approaches to getting better operating results and facilitating better strategy execution.

- *Using the full range of motivational techniques and compensation incentives to inspire company personnel, nurture a results-oriented work climate, and reward high-performance.* Managers cannot mandate innovative improvements by simply exhorting people to "be creative," nor can they make continuous progress toward operating excellence with directives to "try harder." Rather, they must foster a culture where innovative ideas and experimentation with new ways of doing things can blossom and thrive. Individuals and groups should be strongly encouraged to brainstorm, let their imaginations fly in all directions, and come up with proposals for improving how things are done. This means giving company personnel enough autonomy to stand out, excel, and contribute. And it means that the rewards for successful champions of new ideas and operating improvements should be large and visible.

- *Celebrating individual, group, and company successes.* Top management should miss no opportunity to express respect for individual employees and appreciation of extraordinary individual and group effort.[20] Companies like Mary Kay Cosmetics, Tupperware, and McDonald's actively seek out reasons and opportunities to give pins, ribbons, buttons, badges, and medals for good showings by average performers—the idea being to express appreciation and give a motivational boost to people who stand out in doing ordinary jobs. General Electric and 3M Corporation make a point of ceremoniously honoring individuals who believe so strongly in their ideas that they take it on themselves to hurdle the bureaucracy, maneuver their projects through the system, and turn them into improved services, new products, or even new businesses.

While leadership efforts to instill a results-oriented, high-performance culture usually accentuate the positive, negative consequences for poor performance must be in play as well. Managers whose units consistently perform poorly must be replaced. Low-performing workers and people who reject the results-oriented cultural emphasis must be weeded out or at least employed differently. Average performers should be candidly counseled that they have limited career potential unless they show more progress in the form of additional effort, better skills, and improved ability to execute the strategy well and deliver good results.

Leading the Process of Making Corrective Adjustments

There comes a time at every company when managers have to fine-tune or overhaul the approaches to strategy execution since no action plan for executing strategy can foresee all the problems that will arise. Clearly, when a company's strategy execution effort is not delivering good results, it is the leader's responsibility to step forward and initiate corrective actions, although sometimes it must be recognized that unsatisfactory performance may be due as much or more to flawed strategy as weak strategy execution.[21]

Success in making corrective actions hinges on (1) a thorough analysis of the situation, (2) the exercise of good business judgment in deciding what actions to take, and (3) good implementation of the corrective actions that are initiated. Successful managers are skilled in getting an organization back on track rather quickly. They (and their staffs) are good at discerning what actions to take and in bringing them to a successful conclusion. Managers who struggle to show measurable progress in implementing corrective actions in a timely fashion are often candidates for being replaced.

The process of making corrective adjustments in strategy execution varies according to the situation. In a crisis, taking remedial action fairly quickly is of the essence. But it still takes time to review the situation, examine the available data, identify and evaluate options (crunching whatever numbers may be appropriate to determine which options are likely to generate the best outcomes), and decide what to do. When the situation allows managers to proceed more deliberately in deciding when to make changes and what changes to make, most managers seem to prefer a process of incrementally solidifying commitment to a particular course of action.[22] The process that managers go through in deciding on corrective adjustments is essentially the same for both proactive and reactive changes: They sense needs, gather information, broaden and deepen their understanding of the situation, develop options and explore their pros and cons, put forth action proposals, strive for a consensus, and finally formally adopt an agreed-on course of action. The time frame for deciding what corrective changes to initiate can be a few hours, a few days, a few weeks, or even a few months if the situation is particularly complicated.

The challenges of making the right corrective adjustments and leading a successful strategy execution effort are, without question, substantial.[23] Because each instance of executing strategy occurs under different organizational circumstances, the managerial agenda for executing strategy always needs to be situation-specific—there's no generic procedure to follow. But the job is definitely doable. Although there is no prescriptive answer to the question of exactly what to do, any of several courses of action may produce good results. And, as we said at the beginning of Chapter 10, executing strategy is an action-oriented, make-the-right-things-happen task that challenges a manager's ability to lead and direct organizational change, create or reinvent business processes, manage and motivate people, and achieve performance targets. If you now better understand what the challenges are, what tasks are involved, what tools can be used to aid the managerial process of executing strategy, and why the action agenda for implementing and executing strategy sweeps across so many aspects of administrative and managerial work, then the discussions in Chapters 10, 11, and 12 have been a success.

A FINAL WORD ON LEADING THE PROCESS OF CRAFTING AND EXECUTING STRATEGY

In practice, it is hard to separate leading the process of executing strategy from leading the other pieces of the strategy process. As we emphasized in Chapter 2, the job of crafting, implementing, and executing strategy consists of five interrelated and linked stages, with much looping and recycling to fine-tune and adjust the strategic vision, objectives, strategy, and implementation approaches to fit one another and to fit changing circumstances. The process is continuous, and the conceptually separate acts of crafting and executing strategy blur together in real-world situations. The best tests of good strategic leadership are whether the company has a good strategy and business model, whether the strategy is being competently executed, and whether the enterprise is meeting or beating its performance targets. If these three conditions exist, then there is every reason to conclude that the company has good strategic leadership and is a well-managed enterprise.

KEY POINTS

1. Corporate culture is the character of a company's internal work climate—the shared values, ingrained attitudes, core beliefs and company traditions that determine norms of behavior, accepted work practices, and styles of operating. A company's culture is important because it influences the organization's actions and approaches to conducting business. It can be thought of as the company's organizational DNA.

2. The key features of a company's culture include the company's values and ethical standards, its approach to people management, its work atmosphere and company spirit, how its personnel interact, the strength of peer pressure to conform to norms, the behaviors awarded through incentives (both financial and symbolic), the traditions and oft-repeated "myths," and its manner of dealing with stakeholders.

3. A company's culture is grounded in and shaped by its core values and ethical standards. Core values and ethical principles serve two roles in the culture-building process: (1) They foster a work climate in which employees share common and strongly held convictions about how company business is to be conducted, and (2) they provide company personnel with guidance about the manner in which they are to do their jobs—which behaviors and ways of doing things are approved (and expected) and which are out-of-bounds. They serve as yardsticks for gauging the appropriateness of particular actions, decisions, and behaviors.

4. Company cultures vary widely in strength and influence. Some cultures are strong and have a big impact on a company's practices and behavioral norms. Others are weak and have comparatively little influence on company operations.

5. Strong company cultures can have either positive or negative effects on strategy execution. When they are in sync with the chosen strategy and well matched to the behavioral requirements of the company's strategy implementation plan, they can be a powerful aid to strategy execution. A culture that is grounded in the types of actions and behaviors that are conducive to good strategy execution assists the effort in three ways:

    - By focusing employee attention on the actions that are most important in the strategy execution effort.
    - Through culture-induced peer pressure for employees to contribute to the success of the strategy execution effort.
    - By energizing employees, deepening their commitment to the strategy execution effort, and increasing the productivity of their efforts

    It is thus in management's best interest to dedicate considerable effort to establishing a strongly implanted corporate culture that encourages behaviors and work practices conducive to good strategy execution.

6. Strong corporate cultures that are conducive to good strategy execution are healthy cultures. So are high-performance cultures and adaptive cultures. The latter are particularly important in dynamic environments. Strong cultures can also be unhealthy. The five types of unhealthy cultures are those that are (1) change-resistant, (2) heavily politicized, (3) insular and inwardly focused, (4) ethically unprincipled and infused with greed, and (5) composed of incompatible subcultures. All five impede good strategy execution.

7. Changing a company's culture, especially a strong one with traits that don't fit a new strategy's requirements, is a tough and often time-consuming challenge. Changing a culture requires competent leadership at the top. It requires making a compelling case for cultural change and employing both symbolic actions and substantive actions that unmistakably indicate serious commitment on the part of top management. The more that culture-driven actions and behaviors fit what's needed for good strategy execution, the less managers must depend on policies, rules, procedures, and supervision to enforce what people should and should not do.

8. Leading the drive for good strategy execution and operating excellence calls for three actions on the part of the manager in charge:

- Staying on top of what is happening and closely monitoring progress. This is often accomplished through managing by walking around (MBWA).
- Mobilizing the effort for excellence in strategy execution by putting constructive pressure on the organization to execute the strategy well.
- Initiating corrective actions to improve strategy execution and achieve the targeted performance results.

ASSURANCE OF LEARNING EXERCISES

LO 1

1. Go to the company page for John Deere at http://www.deere.com/wps/dcom/en_US/corporate/our_company/our_company.page?
   Click through several of the tabs provided there (about us, citizenship, careers, etc.) to see what they reveal about the company's culture. What do you think are the key features of their culture and why? How do they link to the company's core values and ethical standards?

LO 2

2. Based on what you learned about John Deere from answering the previous question, how do you think their culture affects their ability to execute strategy and operate with excellence?

LO 3

3. Using Google Scholar or your university library's access to EBSCO, Lexis-Nexis, or other databases, search for recent articles in business publications on "culture change." Give examples of two companies that have recently undergone culture-change initiatives. What are the key features of each company's culture-change program? What results did management achieve at each company?

LO 1

4. Go to www.jnj.com, the website of Johnson & Johnson, and read the J&J Credo, which sets forth the company's responsibilities to customers, employees, the community, and shareholders. Then read the "Our Company" section. Why do you think the credo has resulted in numerous awards and accolades that recognize the company as a good corporate citizen?

LO 4

5. In recent years, Liz Claiborne, Inc., has been engaged in efforts to turn around its faltering Mexx chain. Use your favorite browser to search for information on the turnaround plan at Mexx, and read at least two articles or reports on this subject. Describe in one to two pages the approach being taken to turn around the Mexx chain. In your opinion, have the managers involved been demonstrating the kind of internal leadership needed for superior strategy execution at Mexx? Explain your answer.

6. Illustration Capsule 12.1 discusses W. L. Gore's strategy-supportive corporate culture. What are the standout features of Gore's corporate culture? How does W. L. Gore's culture contribute to innovation and creativity at the company? How does the company's culture make W. L. Gore a good place to work?

LO 1, LO 2

EXERCISE FOR SIMULATION PARTICIPANTS

1. If you were making a speech to company personnel, what would you tell them about the kind of corporate culture you would like to have at your company? What specific cultural traits would you like your company to exhibit? Explain.

LO 1, LO 2

2. What core values would you want to ingrain in your company's culture? Why?

LO 1

3. Following each decision round, do you and your co-managers make corrective adjustments in either your company's strategy or how well the strategy is being executed? List at least three such adjustments you made in the most recent decision round. What hard evidence (in the form of results relating to your company's performance in the most recent year) can you cite that indicates the various corrective adjustments you made either succeeded or failed to improve your company's performance?

LO 3, LO 4

4. What would happen to your company's performance if you and your co-managers stick with the status quo and fail to make any corrective adjustments after each decision round?

LO 4

ENDNOTES

[1] Jennifer A. Chatham and Sandra E. Cha, "Leading by Leveraging Culture," *California Management Review* 45, no. 4 (Summer 2003), pp. 20–34; Edgar Shein, *Organizational Culture and Leadership: A Dynamic View* (San Francisco, CA: Jossey-Bass, 1992).

[2] T. E. Deal and A. A. Kennedy, *Corporate Cultures: The Rites and Rituals of Corporate Life* (Harmondsworth, UK: Penguin Books, 1982).

[3] Joanne Reid and Victoria Hubbell, "Creating a Performance Culture," *Ivey Business Journal* 69, no. 4 (March–April 2005), p. 1.

[4] John P. Kotter and James L. Heskett, *Corporate Culture and Performance* (New York: Free Press, 1992); Robert Goffee and Gareth Jones, *The Character of a Corporation* (New York: HarperCollins, 1998).

[5] Joseph L. Badaracco, *Defining Moments: When Managers Must Choose between Right and Wrong* (Boston: Harvard Business School Press, 1997); Joe Badaracco and Allen P. Webb. "Business Ethics: A View from the Trenches," *California Management Review* 37, no. 2 (Winter 1995), pp. 8–28; Patrick E. Murphy, "Corporate Ethics Statements: Current Status and Future Prospects," *Journal of Business Ethics* 14 (1995), pp. 727–40; Lynn Sharp Paine, "Managing for Organizational Integrity,"

Harvard Business Review 72, no. 2 (March–April 1994), pp. 106–17.

[6] Emily F. Carasco and Jang B. Singh, "The Content and Focus of the Codes of Ethics of the World's Largest Transnational Corporations," *Business and Society Review* 108, no. 1 (January 2003), pp. 71–94; Patrick E. Murphy, "Corporate Ethics Statements: Current Status and Future Prospects," *Journal of Business Ethics* 14 (1995), pp. 727–40; John Humble, David Jackson, and Alan Thomson, "The Strategic Power of Corporate Values," *Long Range Planning* 27, no. 6 (December 1994), pp. 28–42; Mark S. Schwartz, "A Code of Ethics for Corporate Codes of Ethics," *Journal of Business Ethics* 41, nos. 1–2 (November–December 2002), pp. 27–43.

[7] Terrence E. Deal and Allen A. Kennedy, *Corporate Cultures* (Reading, MA: Addison-Wesley, 1982); Terrence E. Deal and Allen A. Kennedy, *The New Corporate Cultures: Revitalizing the Workplace after Downsizing, Mergers, and Reengineering* (Cambridge, MA: Perseus Publishing, 1999).

[8] Vijay Sathe, *Culture and Related Corporate Realities* (Homewood, IL: Irwin, 1985).

[9] Avan R. Jassawalla and Hemant C. Sashittal, "Cultures That Support Product-Innovation Processes," *Academy of Management*

Executive 16, no. 3 (August 2002), pp. 42–54.

[10] Kotter and Heskett, *Corporate Culture and Performance*, p. 5.

[11] Joanne Reid and Victoria Hubbell, "Creating a Performance Culture," *Ivey Business Journal* 69, no. 4 (March/April 2005), pp. 1–5.

[12] Jay B. Barney and Delwyn N. Clark, *Resource-Based Theory: Creating and Sustaining Competitive Advantage* (New York: Oxford University Press, 2007), ch. 4.

[13] Rosabeth Moss Kanter, "Transforming Giants," *Harvard Business Review* 86, no. 1 (January 2008), pp. 43–52.

[14] Kurt Eichenwald, *Conspiracy of Fools: A True Story* (New York: Broadway Books, 2005).

[15] Judy D. Olian and Sara L. Rynes, "Making Total Quality Work: Aligning Organizational Processes, Performance Measures, and Stakeholders," *Human Resource Management* 30, no. 3 (Fall 1991), p. 324.

[16] Larry Bossidy and Ram Charan, *Confronting Reality: Doing What Matters to Get Things Right* (New York: Crown Business, 2004); Larry Bossidy and Ram Charan, *Execution: The Discipline of Getting Things Done* (New York: Crown Business, 2002); John P. Kotter, "Leading Change: Why Transformation Efforts Fail," *Harvard*

Business Review 73, no. 2 (March–April 1995), pp. 59–67; Thomas M. Hout and John C. Carter, "Getting It Done: New Roles for Senior Executives," *Harvard Business Review* 73, no. 6 (November–December 1995), pp. 133–45; Sumantra Ghoshal and Christopher A. Bartlett, "Changing the Role of Top Management: Beyond Structure to Processes," *Harvard Business Review* 73, no. 1 (January–February 1995), pp. 86–96.

[17] Fred Vogelstein, "Winning the Amazon Way," *Fortune,* May 26, 2003, p. 64.

[18] Benjamin Schneider, Sarah K. Gunnarson, and Kathryn Niles-Jolly, "Creating the Climate and Culture of Success" *Organizational Dynamics,* Summer 1994, pp. 17–29.

[19] Michael T. Kanazawa and Robert H. Miles, *Big Ideas to Big Results* (Upper Saddle River, NJ: FT Press, 2008).

[20] Jeffrey Pfeffer, "Producing Sustainable Competitive Advantage through the Effective Management of People," *Academy of Management Executive* 9, no.1 (February 1995), pp. 55–69.

[21] Cynthia A. Montgomery, "Putting Leadership Back into Strategy," *Harvard Business Review* 86, no. 1 (January 2008), pp. 54–60.

[22] James Brian Quinn, *Strategies for Change: Logical Incrementalism* (Homewood, IL: Richard D. Irwin, 1980).

[23] Daniel Goleman, "What Makes a Leader," *Harvard Business Review* 76, no. 6 (November–December 1998), pp. 92–102; Ronald A. Heifetz and Donald L. Laurie, "The Work of Leadership," *Harvard Business Review* 75, no. 1 (January–February 1997), pp. 124–34; Charles M. Farkas and Suzy Wetlaufer, "The Ways Chief Executive Officers Lead," *Harvard Business Review* 74, no. 3 (May–June 1996), pp. 110–22; Michael E. Porter, Jay W. Lorsch, and Nitin Nohria, "Seven Surprises for New CEOs," *Harvard Business Review* 82, no. 10 (October 2004), pp. 62–72.

PART 2

Readings in Crafting and Executing Strategy

The reference to "pushing until we get there" triggered in my mind an association with the great pushes of 1915–17 during World War I, which led to the deaths of a generation of European youths. Maybe that's why motivational speakers are not the staple on the European management-lecture circuit that they are in the United States. For the slaughtered troops did not suffer from a lack of motivation. They suffered from a lack of competent strategic leadership. A leader may justly ask for "one last push," but the leader's job is more than that. The job of the leader—the strategist—is also to create the conditions that will make the push effective, to have a strategy worthy of the effort called upon.

Bad Strategic Objectives

Another sign of bad strategy is fuzzy strategic objectives. One form this problem can take is a scrambled mess of things to accomplish—a dog's dinner of goals. A long list of things to do, often mislabeled as strategies or objectives, is not a strategy. It is just a list of things to do. Such lists usually grow out of planning meetings in which a wide variety of stakeholders suggest things they would like to see accomplished. Rather than focus on a few important items, the group sweeps the whole day's collection into the strategic plan. Then, in recognition that it is a dog's dinner, the label "long term" is added, implying that none of these things need be done today. As a vivid example, I recently had the chance to discuss strategy with the mayor of a small city in the Pacific Northwest. His planning committee's strategic plan contained 47 strategies and 178 action items. Action item number 122 was "create a strategic plan."

A second type of weak strategic objective is one that is "blue sky"—typically a simple restatement of the desired state of affairs or of the challenge. It skips over the annoying fact that no one has a clue as to how to get there. A leader may successfully identify the key challenge and propose an overall approach to dealing with the challenge. But if the consequent strategic objectives are just as difficult to meet as the original challenge, the strategy has added little value.

Good strategy, in contrast, works by focusing energy and resources on one, or a very few, pivotal objectives whose accomplishment will lead to a cascade of favorable outcomes. It also builds a bridge between the critical challenge at the heart of the strategy and action—between desire and immediate objectives that lie within grasp. Thus, the objectives that a good strategy sets stand a good chance of being accomplished, given existing resources and competencies.

Fluff

A final hallmark of mediocrity and bad strategy is superficial abstraction—a flurry of fluff—designed to mask the absence of thought.

Fluff is a restatement of the obvious, combined with a generous sprinkling of buzzwords that masquerade as expertise. Here is a quote from a major retail bank's internal strategy memoranda: "Our fundamental strategy is one of customer-centric intermediation." Intermediation means that the company accepts deposits and then lends out the money. In other words, it is a bank. The buzzphrase "customer centric" could mean that the bank competes by offering better terms and service, but an examination of its policies does not reveal any distinction in this regard. The phrase "customer-centric intermediation" is pure fluff. Remove the fluff and you learn that the bank's fundamental strategy is being a bank.

WHY SO MUCH BAD STRATEGY?

Bad strategy has many roots, but I'll focus on two here: the inability to choose and template-style planning—filling in the blanks with "vision, mission, values, strategies."

The Inability to Choose

Strategy involves focus and, therefore, choice. And choice means setting aside some goals in favor of others. When this hard work is not done, weak strategy is the result. In 1992, I sat in on a strategy discussion among senior executives at Digital Equipment Corporation (DEC). A leader of the minicomputer revolution of the 1960s and 1970s, DEC had been losing ground for several years to the newer 32-bit personal computers. There were serious doubts that the company could survive for long without dramatic changes.

To simplify matters, I will pretend that only three executives were present. "Alec" argued that DEC had always been a computer company and should continue integrating hardware and software into usable systems, "Beverly" felt that the only distinctive resource DEC had to build on was its customer relationships. Hence, she derided Alec's "Boxes" strategy and argued in favor of a "Solutions" strategy that solved customer problems. "Craig" held that the heart of the computer industry was semiconductor technology and that the company should focus its resources on designing and building better "Chips."

Choice was necessary: both the Chips and Solutions strategies represented dramatic transformations of the firm, and each would require wholly new skills and work practices. One wouldn't choose either risky alternative unless the status quo Boxes strategy was likely to fail. And one wouldn't choose to do both Chips and Solutions at the same time, because there was little common ground between them. It is not feasible to do two separate, deep transformations of a company's core at once.

With equally powerful executives arguing for each of the three conflicting strategies, the meeting was intense. DEC's chief executive, Ken Olsen, had made the mistake of asking the group to reach a consensus. It was unable to do that, because a majority preferred Solutions to Boxes, a majority preferred Boxes to Chips, and a majority also preferred Chips to Solutions. No matter which of the three paths was chosen, a majority preferred something else. This dilemma wasn't unique to the stand-off at DEC. The French philosopher Nicolas de Condorcet achieved immortality by first pointing out the possibility of such a paradox arising, and economist Kenneth Arrow won a Nobel Prize for showing that "Condorcet's paradox" cannot be resolved through cleverer voting schemes.

Not surprisingly, the group compromised on a statement: "DEC is committed to providing high-quality products and services and being a leader in data processing." This fluffy, amorphous statement was, of course, not a strategy. It was a political outcome reached by individuals who, forced to reach a consensus, could not agree on which interests and concepts to forego.

Ken Olsen was replaced, in June 1992, by Robert Palmer, who had headed the company's semiconductor engineering. Palmer made it clear that the strategy would be Chips. One point of view had finally won. But by then it was five years too late. Palmer stopped the losses for a while but could not stem the tide of ever more powerful personal computers that were overtaking the firm. In 1998, DEC was acquired by Compaq, which, in turn, was acquired by Hewlett-Packard three years later.

Template-Style Strategy

The Jack Welch quote about "reaching for what appears to be the impossible" is fairly standard motivational fare, available from literally hundreds of motivational speakers, books, calendars, memo pads, and websites. This fascination with positive thinking has helped inspire ideas about charismatic leadership and the power of a shared vision, reducing them to something of a formula. The general outline goes like this: the transformational leader (1) develops or has a vision, (2) inspires people to sacrifice (change) for the good of the organization, and (3) empowers people to accomplish the vision.

By the early 2000s, the juxtaposition of vision-led leadership and strategy work had produced a template-style system of strategic planning. (Type "vision mission strategy" into a search engine and you'll find thousands of examples of this kind of template for sale and in use.) The template looks like this:

The Vision   Fill in your vision of what the school/business/nation will be like in the future. Currently popular visions are to be the best or the leading or the best known.

The Mission   Fill in a high-sounding, politically correct statement of the purpose of the school/business/nation. Innovation, human progress, and sustainable solutions are popular elements of a mission statement.

The Values   Fill in a statement that describes the company's values. Make sure they are noncontroversial. Key words include "integrity," "respect," and "excellence."

The Strategies   Fill in some aspirations/goals but call them strategies. For example, "to invest in a portfolio of performance businesses that create value for our shareholders and growth for our customers."

This template-style planning has been enthusiastically adopted by corporations, school boards, university presidents, and government agencies. Scan through such documents and you will find pious statements of the obvious presented as if they were decisive insights. The enormous problem all this creates is that someone who actually wishes to conceive and implement an effective strategy is surrounded by empty rhetoric and bad examples.

The approach to business model experimentation presented in this article stems from over four years of field work carried out with more than 20 companies—including Kennametal, Infineum, Johnson & Johnson, P&G and Medtronic—in an array of industries, including consumer packaged goods, chemicals, medical devices, pharmaceuticals, and financial services. This work entailed in-depth, interview-based primary market research with existing and potential customers; extensive working team idea formulation and prioritization activities, and in-market assumption testing and business piloting. Our purpose was to understand the range of alternatives available for companies to optimize the value captured through commercialization of their innovative offerings. The specific company examples presented in this article highlight two distinct approaches to employing the proposed business model innovation process. These two cases represent starting points at opposite ends of the value chain—one driven by an understanding of unsatisfied customer needs, the other driven by the pursuit of applications for a set of technical solutions. This demonstrates the broad applicability of the approach.

WHAT IS A BUSINESS MODEL?

At a conceptual level, a business model includes all aspects of a company's approach to developing a profitable offering and delivering it to its target customers. A review of the relevant literature reveals that more than 40 different components—such as target customer, type of offering and pricing approach—have been included in various definitions of business models put forward over the past few decades, with much of the variation stemming from differences between the industries and circumstances in which a definition has been applied.[3]

For our purposes, we will explore the concept of a business model by addressing several core questions that the majority of business model researchers deal within their models:

- Who is the target customer?
- What need is met for the customer?
- What offering will we provide to address that need?
- How does the customer gain access to that offering?
- What role will our business play in providing the offering?
- How will our business earn a profit?

In any working business model, the answers to these questions are fixed. But what if they weren't? What if you considered each of them as a variable? What new opportunities could you capture that you can't address with your current business model? The answers to these questions form the essence of business model experimentation.

STARTING THE PROCESS

The first step in the business model exploration process is to create a template to examine possible alternative answers to the questions above. (See the chart "A Business Model Development Template," later in this reading.) The questions that help to shape a business model represent a series of decisions, each of which has a set of possible outcomes. Our template lays out various possible outcomes within the business model structure. Selecting one possibility from each category and then linking them together forms one potential new way to proceed. And, of course, selecting different combinations creates other possible outcomes.

To see how this works, consider how an airline might use the template to generate alternative business models. Currently, airlines serve a range of customers with the same basic model. For example, regardless of whether the customer is going on vacation with her family, traveling on business or responding to an emergency, airlines use the standard pay-per-seat model with which we are all familiar. Minor levels of customization exist—for example, larger seats and priority boarding for those who pay for them—but the core model is the same for all.

To explore business model innovation, an airline could start by picking a specific customer group and then beginning to explore potential options other than its current model. Answers to the question "How does the customer gain access to the offering?" (which is essentially the same as asking "How will we sell it?") could include "Through travel agents" or "Through online websites" or "Through self-service kiosks" or

"As part of partnerships." As for where on the value chain the airline might operate, it could be the service provider, but it might also be a wholesaler selling off excess capacity to reduce unprofitable flights. Various profit models would likely start with the traditional pay-per-seat but might expand to include subscription models. The offering itself might be a premium seat, a low-cost seat or maybe even fractional ownership of a plane or chartered use of an aircraft. We experimented with "What we sell" for an airline to show how changing just one variable can result in a substantially different business. (See the chart "Generating New Business Models by Changing One Variable," later in this reading.)

Working out what elements should be in a business model—and then examining different combinations of them—can be a rapid and robust way to explore the possibilities of business model innovation. This process has the potential, for instance, to uncover combinations that are common in other industries but not in your own. In fact, deliberately applying analogies from other industries (for example, what if a company became the NetJets of agricultural equipment or the Dell of automobiles?) can be highly fruitful. It may also highlight links that create a "systemic" level of competitive advantage in the business concept—much as Apple did with the agreements it made with record labels to distribute songs through its iTunes online music site. Alternatively, the business model innovation process can uncover opportunities to more comprehensively fulfill a customer need than any current competitors do.

A quick run-through of simple combinations of high-level strategic questions can produce a wide range of potential business models. But each of the questions could be examined in more detail in a systematic way to yield deeper insight into some specific aspect of the business. For example, rather than brainstorming various alternatives for the "What we sell" category, a company could break the category down into its constituent parts and ask a series of additional questions such as:

- Should we sell a product or a service?
- Should it be standard or customizable?
- Will its benefits be tangible or intangible?
- Will we sell a generic or branded offering?
- Should it be a durable or a consumable?

We have often found it useful to visualize such choices as switches, or levers, which can be flipped one way or the other. (See the chart "Exploring Offering Options in More Depth.") You could engage in a similar exercise to systematically explore potential variations in the way a customer might gain access to an offering or the way a customer might pay for it.

NARROWING THE CHOICES

Despite what one might think, these choices are not infinite. In working through possible combinations of variables, it becomes clear that some are inherently interrelated. For example, if the offering is a durable good like a car, it is unlikely that the consumer will need to purchase new ones frequently. Such realizations dramatically reduce the number of options that must be explored.

What's more, there are likely only a handful of ways that any of these questions can be practically addressed while remaining consistent with the mission of the organization and its "goals and bounds"[4]—that is, what the organization is willing, and not willing, to do. Some answers form a more natural path to making the business more efficient or better able to deliver the existing value proposition. Some will lead to models that are more feasible to implement than others, given the company's existing competencies and its ability to develop new ones.

In fact, it is possible to use this approach to deliberately align the exploration of alternative business models with wider corporate goals by "locking in" one or more variables as you go about your experimentation. To see how this might work, let's take a look at two cases in more depth. In the first, a tool manufacturer explores opportunities to enter new lines of business spurred by market trends; in the second, a maker of petroleum additives seeks to identify new ways to employ its core competencies.

EXPLORING NEW CUSTOMER NEEDS

Kennametal is a tool manufacturer based in Latrobe, Pennsylvania. Faced with an evolving manufacturing environment, a changing customer base and increasing global competition, Kennametal embarked on a business model experimentation initiative to diversify its revenue stream by identifying two to three new businesses in adjacent markets that would leverage core assets. A small team kicked off the initiative with a research effort focused on developing a more

A Business Model Development Template

The questions that help to shape a business model represent a series of decisions, each of which has a set of possible outcomes. This template lays out various possible outcomes within the business model structure.

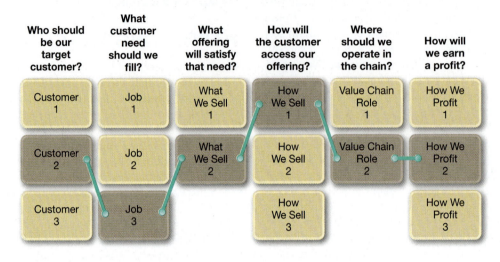

Generating New Business Models by Changing One Variable

Changing even just one variable—in this case, "What is sold" for an airline business—can result in a substantially different business model.

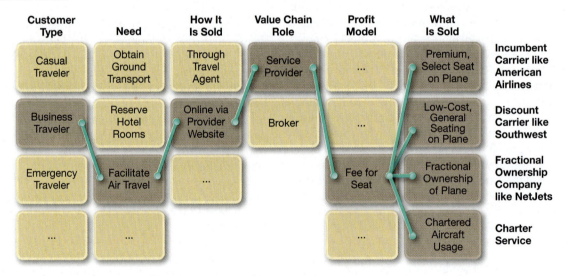

comprehensive understanding of potential customers' frustrations, desires and challenges, in order to populate both the target customer and possible needs categories of the business model template. The research involved a combination of qualitative, quantitative and observational activities.[5]

Since the goal was to create diversified revenue streams, Kennametal chose to prioritize needs based on the classic measures of their profit potential: importance to the customer, the customer's level of dissatisfaction with the offerings currently on the market and the degree to which the need had not already been targeted

Exploring Offering Options in More Depth

Rather than just brainstorming various alternatives for the "What we sell" question that is part of a business model, a company could more systematically examine its options by asking a series of additional questions, such as whether what it sells is a product or service, whether that product or service is standard or customizable, etc.

What We Sell				
Type	**Features**	**Benefit**	**Brand**	**Lifetime**
Product	Custom	Tangible	Generic	Consumable
Service	Off-the-Shelf	Intangible	Branded	Durable

by other internal efforts. The company then identified three high-potential combinations. For example, one was small "job shops" that had unmet training needs. The next step was to focus on developing the offering and determine how the company would deliver it.

For each possibility, the team methodically reviewed a list of levers for the remaining business model components—for example, "What we sell" and "How we profit"—and articulated multiple options for each lever. By examining more than 30 different levers in multiple combinations, they systematically generated an expansive list of possible business model options. Conceptualizing the different components of a business model as levers forced the team to consider new combinations they likely would have otherwise overlooked. For example, Kennametal has traditionally been a product-centered company that provides service as part of product sales. However, by looking at its service capabilities and examining the options for some "How we profit" levers, the company was able to consider a number of interesting fee-for-service business models. In doing so, Kennametal was essentially exploring ways to monetize the latent wealth of knowledge contained in the organization's experience, people, and knowledge-management systems.

With more than 30 levers, there were literally thousands of possible permutations and, therefore, the last step in the process was to identify the most attractive ones. The team focused on the possibilities that would generate the greatest customer satisfaction, would be the hardest for competitors to copy, and were the most feasible to pilot. This process ensured not only that a wide range of options were considered

but that the opportunities selected were well matched to customers' needs, were competitively robust, and leveraged existing resources appropriately.

The initiative required a minimal amount of time from a small, multifunctional team over an eight-week period—truly a low-risk way to home in on new growth options. In this way, Kennametal used the business model innovation process to move beyond incremental improvements in its businesses and generate three new opportunities to pursue in adjacent markets. In particular, two of these initiatives formed the foundation of new service-based offerings for Kennametal.

USING CORE COMPETENCIES TO CREATE NEW BUSINESSES AT INFINEUM

Infineum, an enterprise based in Oxfordshire, United Kingdom, with about 1,600 employees that conducts business in more than 70 countries, is another organization that has used the business model experimentation process. Infineum is one of the leading formulators, manufacturers, and marketers of petroleum additives for the fuel and lubricant industry, and its customers are oil and fuel marketers. Infineum's goal in the business model experimentation process was to leverage its product technology and know-how and create a list of profitable new opportunities that fit with its core competencies.

Since Infineum wished to hold to a strong interpersonal sales model in any initiative it pursued, we locked down the "How we sell" switch making. We try to simplify the highly complex strategy making process for application at all levels.

THE RESEARCH PROCESS

We conducted 20 semi-structured interviews with CEOs (informants) from South African organizations to establish the dominant approaches to strategy making in their organizations. Combining this information with an extensive literature scrutiny, we formulated a questionnaire that was completed by managers (respondents) from the companies where the CEOs were interviewed. Data was subjected to several analyses to make sense from it leading to the framework elements discussed next.

THE STRATEGY-MAKING APPROACH FRAMEWORK WITH ITS ELEMENTS

From the analysis it was found that strategy making has three main elements (each with its own variables critical to the approach) to consider when measuring strategy making (see also Exhibit 2). The three elements that respondents identified were:

1. Performance consensus that explains agreement among managers and organizational members on effectiveness of and satisfaction with the organizational strategy-making approaches and consequent strategies as well as organizational performance. For example, if consensus is linked to performance then one may argue that some competitive strategies lend themselves to greater agreement among managers (Baum and Wally, 2003, p, 1108). For this reason, consensus may be high among segment controllers where everyone seems to understand the niche being targeted by the business, but be low among first movers where the essence of the strategy is not always well understood (Parnell, 2000, p. 33).

2. Ends and means specificity which explains the specificity of organizational ends as well as the specificity of organizational means (Box 2).

3. Ends and means flexibility which explains the flexibility of planning structures, tolerance for change and flexibility of planning time frame as opposed to organizational rigidity.

Looking at these elements, instinctively one would associate the deliberate strategy approach with high ends and means specificity, low ends and means flexibility, and high performance consensus compared to the emergent strategy approach with low ends and means specificity, high ends and means flexibility, and low performance consensus (Wooldridge and Floyd, 1994, p. 47). However, this does not show in practice.

EXHIBIT 2   Strategy-Making Elements and Their Relative Position Associated with Each Approach

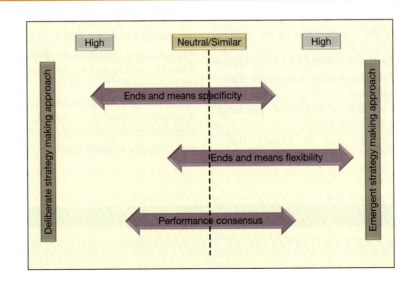

Source: Own compilation.

The findings suggest that ends and means specificity as well as ends and means flexibility correspond with the continuum extremes but not performance consensus (as shown in Exhibit 2). Performance consensus remains a neutral element and can be either high or low regardless of the strategy-making approach followed. It may be influenced by any of the moderators discussed in the next section.

Generally informants were not able to clearly state their strategy-making approach at the start of the interviews. After discussion of the elements they were able to determine their dominant approaches to strategy making. Eventually the questionnaire contained many single variables that respondents evaluated individually to meaningfully judge the approach elements.

DOMINANT APPROACH TO STRATEGY MAKING

We hypothesized that the sample firms would lean more towards a deliberate strategy-making approach. Underlying this assumption was partly the idea that most academic learning of strategy focuses on the rational process approach to strategy formation (i.e. the deliberate approach), and partly the consulting experience of the researchers showing the opposite. The sample averages and modes for the elements across all respondents' feedback showed that;

1. Ends and means specificity had a high value in line with a more deliberate approach.
2. Ends and means flexibility had a high value. This showed that organizations had more flexible planning structures and time frames in line with a more emergent approach.
3. Performance consensus showed high values on average.

Based on the above statistics the dominant approach to strategy making can therefore be described as:

- rational with high ends and means specificity; but
- high flexibility of planning structures and tolerance for change; as well as

- high performances consensus on strategy effectiveness and general satisfaction with strategy.

It was also clear that there were absolute positions on the strategy-making continuum. Several respondent firms appeared to have components of both, which rather increased than reduced the complexity of their strategy-making process.

The approach to strategy making was furthermore enlightened through three observations in the data showing significant differences between opposing approach characteristics, namely:

1. *Degree of risk taking preferred.* Performance consensus is significantly different between respondents selecting low versus high degree of risk taking, The analysis showed that agreement on effectiveness of strategy (performance consensus) leads organizations to be more tolerant towards high risk taking. In other words, if organizational members agree on the effectiveness of their strategies and if they are satisfied with and agree on strategy-making approaches followed, they tend to take greater risks.

2. *Comfort with stability and predictability.* Ends and means specificity and ends and means flexibility were found significantly different for respondents selecting "comfort with stability and predictability" versus those selecting "comfort with ambiguity and instability". Thus comfort with stability and predictability leads organizations to determine highly specific ends and means and be less flexible (hence following a rational approach to strategy making). This finding is hardly surprising since the predictability is associated with the rational planning approach (described by high specificity and low flexibility). As such this finding corresponds with the literature on rational planning.

3. *Primarily autonomous or individual behavior preferred.* Ends and means specificity is significantly different for respondents selecting "primarily autonomous or individual behavior" versus those selecting "primarily cooperative, interdependent behavior." The analysis showed that organizations where primarily autonomous or individual

---

Box 2

"Ends" can be defined as "the major, higher-level purposes, mission, goals, or objectives set by organizations, each of which (should there be more than one) significantly influences the overall direction and viability of the firm concerned"; and "means" can be defined as "the patterns of action which marshal/allocate organizational resources into postures that once implemented, increase the probability of attaining organizational ends".

behavior is favored determine less specific ends and means. This is a surprising finding since cooperative and interdependent behavior is associated with the emergent approach in literature (Wooldridge and Floyd, 1994, p. 50). However, it could be argued that higher levels of cooperation and interdependent behavior require a more coordinated and more specific approach to strategy making, such as the rational approach. Specific ends and means are then required to coordinate cooperation among organizational members.

The following relevant conclusion can be drawn from the results of the informant interviews.

The majority of informants (67 percent) indicated that an emergent approach to strategy was followed where emergence of strategies are encouraged, but with discipline typically built into strategy making through deliberate ends and means. In the interviews informants indicated certain types of practices employed in their organizations. These practices focus mainly on operations, marketing, and product innovation and as such correspond with emergent strategies (see also Box 3).

MODERATORS OF THE STRATEGY-MAKING APPROACH

Exhibit 1 also shows several moderators to the strategy-making approach eventually used by the firm. While exhaustive discussion is not possible, we briefly point out those moderators that were relevant in this research:

- *Size of the firm.* Was the only moderating factor impacting the strategy-making approach and that could be successfully measured. The larger the organization, the more its approach leaned towards deliberate strategy making. This makes sense as larger organizations suffer more from communication, control, complexity, and rigidity issues. There is higher demand for ends and means specificity,

less potential for ends and means flexibility and mostly some performance consensus problems. Smaller organizations are much more flexible in their ends and means, and as long as performance consensus is fairly high, the emergent strategy making approach would be more relevant.

- *CEO influence.* Refers to the individual's philosophy, risk propensity, drive, and more. Many studies report relationships between strategy making and the CEO, but this study did not confirm any.

- *Environmental uncertainty.* The more stable the environment the more strategy making will lean towards the deliberate approach. In fact, emergent strategy making develops in response to this environmental change. The environment referred to can include elements such as industry maturity, speed of change, stability of technology, and information availability.

Other factors such as industry (type), planning time frame, market orientation, and munificence of resources may also moderate the strategy-making approach selected.

MANAGEMENT IMPLICATIONS AND GUIDELINES

This study has some important guidelines for managers and practitioners, namely:

- Do not discard one approach for the other—rather be aware of the benefits of both and use appropriately or in synthesis—each has advantages and disadvantages.

- The demand for the emergent strategy-making approach is increasing due to rapid environmental changes over which firms have little control.

- Emergent strategy making may demand higher performance consensus due to its inherent flexibility and lower specificity of ends and means. With low performance consensus, strategic intent and directi on can be jeopardized and organizational performance ultimately influenced.

- Self-analysis of the strategy team for degree of risk taking, comfort with stability and predictability, and whether primarily autonomous and individual behavior is preferred, is critical as this might influence the team's choice of strategy-making approach.

The study therefore showed that reflecting only on one aspect or extreme of strategy making to the exclusion of other views when conducting strategy research or training, distorts the truth and reality of strategy making and cripples the application of strategy in general.

STUDY LIMITATIONS AND FUTURE RESEARCH

Limitations of one study serve as challenges for future research. Firstly, the search for averages and composite description may be irrelevant or even harmful. Individual firms should be investigated as such. Despite this an interesting picture was discovered, illustrating the status of strategy making. Secondly, no empirical data is presented in this paper but it is being reported to an academic journal for that purpose.

The study also explored the relationship between organizational dynamics such as managerial level and perceptions on strategy-making mode, the influence of certain factors on the selection of a strategy-making approach as well as the link between organizational performance and profitability and strategy-making approaches. These findings and conclusions will be presented in future articles.

REFERENCES

Baum, J,R, and Wally, S. (2003), "Strategic decision speed and firm performance", *Strategic Management Journal,* Vol. 24. pp. 1107–29.

Harrington R.J., Lemak. D.J., Reed, R. and Kendall, K.W. (2004), "A question of fit the links among environment, strategy formulation, and performance", *Journal of Business and Management,* Vol. 10 No. 1, pp. 15–38,

Maritz R. (2009), "Strategy-making approaches in South African organizations",

D Com unpublished thesis, University of Pretoria, Pretoria.

Parnell J.A. (2000), "Refraining the combination strategy debate: defining forms of combination", *Journal of Applied Management studies,* Vol. 9 No. 1, pp. 33–54.

Parnell J.A. and Lester, D.L. (2003). "Towards a philosophy of strategy: reassessing five critical dilemmas in strategy formulation and change", *Strategic Change,* Vol. 12 No. 6, pp. 291–303.

Wooldridge B. and Floyd, S.W. (1994), "Dinosaurs or dynamos? Recognizing middle management's strategic role", *Academy of Management Executive,* Vol. 8 No. 4. pp. 47–57.

bottom line, the company prioritized its complementor strategy once it decided to pursue an ecosystem approach (as witnessed, for example, by developers' prominence at Apple product launches and in its advertising).

Nokia still makes great phones, but in the mobile phone market hardware is no longer enough. Their phones remain remarkable as products, but they are impoverished as solutions. As the competition shifted from products to ecosystems, the very essence of the game changed under Nokia's feet. Its recent tie-up with Microsoft is an attempt to reposition itself in a world of joint value creation. While the wisdom of this specific choice has yet to be revealed (I have my doubts), the need to make a new choice was long overdue.

Success in an innovation ecosystem is rooted in the same principles of competitive advantage and value creation that have always been at the heart of strategy. But the way in which these principles are applied has changed. When we depend on others for our success, the ways in which we prioritize opportunities and threats, how we think about market timing and positioning, indeed the very ways in which we measure and reward success all need to change to explicitly account for this dependence.

The message is clear: The collaborative advantage at the heart of ecosystem-based strategies comes with added peril and promise. Leaders and organizations that go down this path must do so with eyes wide open, not only to the potential benefits of a well-executed ecosystem strategy but also to the risks involved. For the next wave of industry leaders, confronting the new paradigms brought about by innovation ecosystems will not be an option. It will be mandatory.

Adaptability: The New Competitive Advantage

Martin Reeves
Boston Consulting Group

Mike Deimler
Boston Consulting Group

WE LIVE IN AN ERA OF RISK AND INSTABILITY

Globalization, new technologies, and greater transparency have combined to upend the business environment and give many CEOs a deep sense of unease. Just look at the numbers. Since 1980 the volatility of business operating margins, largely static since the 1950s, has more than doubled, as has the size of the gap between winners (companies with high operating margins) and losers (those with low ones).

Market leadership is even more precarious. The percentage of companies falling out of the top three rankings in their industry increased from 2% in 1960 to 14% in 2008. What's more, market leadership is proving to be an increasingly dubious prize: The once strong correlation between profitability and industry share is now almost nonexistent in some sectors. According to our calculation, the probability that the market share leader is also the profitability leader declined from 34% in 1950 to just 7% in 2007. And it has become virtually impossible for some executives even to clearly identify in what industry and with which companies they're competing.

All this uncertainty poses a tremendous challenge for strategy making. That's because traditional approaches to strategy—though often seen as the answer to change and uncertainty—actually assume a relatively stable and predictable world.

Think about it. The goal of most strategies is to build an enduring (and implicitly static) competitive advantage by establishing clever market positioning (dominant scale or an attractive niche) or assembling the right capabilities and competencies for making or delivering an offering (doing what the company does

well). Companies undertake periodic strategy reviews and set direction and organizational structure on the basis of an analysis of their industry and some forecast of how it will evolve.

But given the new level of uncertainty, many companies are starting to ask:

- How can we apply frameworks that are based on scale or position when we can go from market leader one year to follower the next?
- When it's nuclear where one industry ends and another begins, how do we even measure position?
- When the environment is so unpredictable, how can we apply the traditional forecasting and analysis that are at the heart of strategic planning?
- When we're overwhelmed with changing information, how can our managers pick up the right signals to understand and harness change?
- When change is so rapid, how can a one-year—or, worse, five-year—planning cycle stay relevant?

The answers these companies are coming up with point in a consistent direction. Sustainable competitive advantage no longer arises exclusively from position, scale, and first-order capabilities in producing or delivering an offering. All those are essentially static. So where does it come from? Increasingly, managers are finding that it stems from the "second-order" organizational capabilities that foster rapid adaptation. Instead of being really good at doing some particular thing, companies must be really good at learning how to do new things.

THE ABILITY TO MANAGE COMPLEX MULTICOMPANY SYSTEMS

Signal detection and experimentation require a company to think beyond its own boundaries and perhaps to work more closely and smartly with customers and suppliers. This flies somewhat in the face of the unspoken assumption that the unit of analysis for strategy is a single company or business unit.

With an increasing amount of economic activity occurring beyond corporate boundaries—through outsourcing, offshoring, value nets, value ecosystems, peer production, and the like—we need to think about strategies not only for individual companies but also for dynamic business systems. Increasingly, industry structure is better characterized as competing webs or ecosystems of codependent companies than as a handful of competitors producing similar goods and services and working on a stable, distant, and transactional basis with their suppliers and customers.

In such an environment, advantage will flow to those companies that can create effective strategies at the network or system level. Adaptive companies are therefore learning how to push activities outside the company without benefiting competitors and how to design and evolve strategies for networks without necessarily being able to rely on strong control mechanisms.

Typically, adaptive companies manage their ecosystems by using common standards to foster interaction with minimal barriers. They generate trust among participants—for example, by enabling people to interact frequently and by providing transparency and rating systems that serve as "reputational currency." Toyota's automotive supply pyramids, with their *kanban* and *kaizen* feedback mechanisms, are early examples of adaptive systems. EBay's complex network of sellers and buyers is another; the company relies on seller ratings and online payment systems to support the online marketplace.

If the experience curve and the scale curve were the key indicators of success, Nokia would still be leading the smartphone market; it had the advantage of being an early mover and the market share leader with a strong cost position. But Nokia was attacked by an entirely different kind of competitor: Apple's adaptive system of suppliers, telecom partnerships, and numerous independent application developers, created to support the iPhone. Google's Android operating system, too, capitalized on a broad array of hardware partners and application developers. The ability to bring together the assets and capabilities of so many entities allowed these smartphone entrants to leapfrog the experience curve and become new market leaders in record time. As Stephen Elop, Nokia's CEO, wrote in a memo to his staff, "Our competitors aren't taking out market share with devices; they are taking out market share with an entire ecosystem." Through broader signal detection, parallel innovation, superior flexibility, and rapid mobilization, multicompany systems can enhance the adaptiveness of individual companies.

THE ABILITY TO MOBILIZE

Adaptation is necessarily local in nature—somebody experiments first at a particular place and time. It is also necessarily global in nature, because if the experiment succeeds, it will be communicated, selected, amplified, and refined. Organizations therefore need to create environments that encourage the knowledge flow, diversity, autonomy, risk taking, sharing, and flexibility on which adaptation thrives. Contrary to classical strategic thinking, strategy follows organization in adaptive companies.

A flexible structure and the dispersal of decision rights are powerful levers for increasing adaptability. Typically, adaptive companies have replaced permanent silos and functions with modular units that freely communicate and recombine according to the situation at hand. To reinforce this framework, it is helpful to have weak or competing power structures and a culture of constructive conflict and dissent. Cisco is one company that has made this transformation. Early on, it relied on a hierarchical, customer-centric organization to become a leader in the market for network switches and routers. More recently the CEO, John Chambers, has created a novel management structure of cross-functional councils and boards to facilitate moves into developing countries and 30 adjacent and diverse markets (ranging from health care to sports) with greater agility than would previously have been possible.

As they create more-fluid structures, adaptive companies drive decision making down to the front lines, allowing the people most likely to detect changes in the environment to respond quickly and proactively. For example, at Whole Foods the basic organizational unit is the team, and each store has about eight teams. Team leaders—not national buyers—decide what to stock. Teams have veto power over new hires. They are encouraged to buy from local powers that meet the company's quality and sustainability standards. And they are rewarded for their performance with bonuses based on store profitability over the previous four weeks.

Creating decentralized, fluid, and even competing organizational structures destroys the big advantage of a rigid hierarchy, which is that everyone knows precisely what he or she should be doing. An adaptive organization can't expect to succeed unless it provides people with some substitute for that certainty. What's needed are some simple, generative rules to facilitate interaction, help people make trade-offs, and set the boundaries within which they can make decisions.

For example, Netflix values nine core behaviors and skills in its employees: judgment, communication, impact, curiosity, innovation, courage, passion, honesty, and selflessness. The company's executives believe that a great workplace is full of "stunning colleagues" who embody these qualities; thus the Netflix model is to "increase employee freedom as we grow, rather than limit it, to continue to attract and nourish innovative people, so we have a better chance of long-term continued success." Consistent with this philosophy, Netflix has only two types of rules: those designed to prevent irrevocable disaster and those designed to prevent moral, ethical, and legal issues. It has no vacation policy and does no tracking of time—the company's focus is on what needs to get done, not how many hours or days are worked. As the Netflix "Reference Guide on Our Freedom & Responsibility Culture" puts it, "Avoid Chaos as you grow with Ever More High Performance People—not with Rules."

THE CHALLENGE FOR BIG BUSINESS

Becoming an adaptive competitor can be difficult, especially for large, established organizations. Typically, these companies are oriented toward managing scale and efficiency, and their hierarchical structures and fixed routines lack the diversity and flexibility needed for rapid learning and change. Such management paradigms die hard, especially when they have historically been the basis for success.

However, several tactics have proved effective at fostering adaptive advantage even in established companies. To the managers involved, they may look like nothing more than an extension of business as usual, but in fact they create a context in which adaptive capabilities can thrive. If you are the CEO of a large company that wants to be more adaptive, challenge your managers to:

Look at the Mavericks   Fast-changing industries are characterized by the presence of disruptive mavericks—often entirely new players, sometimes from other sectors. Ask your managers to shift their focus from traditional competitors' moves to what the new players are doing and to think of ways to insure your company against this new competition or neutralize its effect. They should also look at what's happening in adjacent or analogous industries and markets and ask, "What if this happened in mine?" Although pattern recognition is harder in an uncertain environment and can easily be obstructed by entrenched beliefs and narrow industry definitions, it has tremendous competitive value.

Identify and Address the Uncertainties Get your managers to put aside the traditional single-business forecast and instead examine the risks and uncertainties that could significantly affect the company. This simple extension of the familiar long-range strategy exercise can force people to realize what they don't yet know and to address it. Your organization needs to distinguish "false knowns" (questionable but firmly held assumptions) from "underexploited knowns" (megatrends you may recognize and perhaps have even acted on, but without sufficient speed or emphasis) and "unknown unknowns" (intrinsic uncertainties that you can prepare for only by hedging your bets).

Put an Initiative on Every Risk   Most companies have a portfolio of strategic initiatives. It should become the engine that drives your organization into adaptability—and it can, with a couple of simple enhancements. First, every significant source of uncertainty should be addressed with an initiative. Depending on the nature of the uncertainty, the goal of the initiative may be responding to a neglected business trend, creating options for responding to it down the line, or simply learning more about it. In managing these initiatives, your company should be as disciplined with metrics, time frames, and responsibilities as it would be for the product portfolio or the operating plan.

Examine Multiple Alternatives   In a stable environment it is sufficient to improve what already exists or to examine single change proposals. The simple step of requiring that every change proposal be

When Will Increased Scale Lower Costs?

If fixed costs represent a large percentage of your total costs, you can reap substantial savings by increasing scale. But if your costs are more variable than fixed, scale increases may require new overhead investments and so deliver minimal savings.

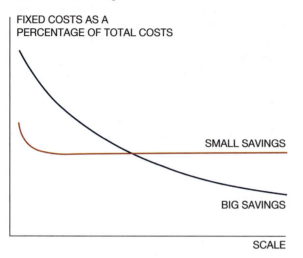

a single source for all of them holds no advantage. Cross-selling in circumstances like these will complicate and confuse, and will rarely reduce sales costs.

REINVENTING YOUR BUSINESS MODEL

The second fundamental task of a general manager is to lay the groundwork for long-term growth by creating new ways of doing business, since the value of existing business models fades as competition and technological progress erode their profit potential. RBM acquisitions help managers tackle that task.

Investors' expectations give executives a strong incentive to embrace the work of reinvention. As Alfred Rappaport and Michael Mauboussin point out in their book *Expectations Investing* (Harvard Business Review Press, 2003), managers quickly learn that it is not earnings growth per se that determines growth in their company's share price—it's growth relative to investors' expectations. A firm's share price represents myriad pieces of information about its predicted performance, synthesized into a single number and discounted into its present value. If managers grow cash flows at the rate the market expects, the firm's share price will grow only at its cost of capital, because those expectations have already been factored into its current share price. To persistently create shareholder value at a greater rate, managers must do something that investors haven't already taken into account—and they must do it again and again.

Acquiring a Disruptive Business Model

The most reliable sources of unexpected growth in revenues and margins are disruptive products and business models. Disruptive companies are those whose initial products are simpler and more affordable than the established players' offerings. They secure their foothold in the low end of the market and then move to higher-performance, higher-margin products, market tier by market tier. Although investment analysts can see a company's potential in the market tier where it's currently positioned, they fail to foresee how a disruptor will move upmarket as its offerings improve. So they persistently underestimate the growth potential of disruptive companies.

To understand how that works, consider Nucor, an operator of steel minimills. which back in the 1970s developed a radically simpler and less costly way to make steel than the big integrated steelmakers of the day. Initially, Nucor made only concrete reinforcing bar (rebar), the simplest and lowest-margin of all steel products. Analysts valued Nucor according to the size of the rebar market and the profits Nucor could earn in it. But the pursuit of profit drove Nucor to develop further capabilities, and as it invaded subsequent product tiers, commanding higher and higher margins from its low-cost manufacturing technique, analysts kept having to revisit their estimates of the company's addressable market—and hence its growth.

As a result, Nucor's share price fairly exploded, as the exhibit "Why Disruptive Businesses Are Worth So Much" demonstrates. From 1983 to 1994, Nucor's stock appreciated at a 27% compounded annual rate, as analysts continually realized that they had underestimated the markets the company could address. By 1994, Nucor was in the top market tier, and analysts caught up with its growth potential. Even though sales continued to increase handsomely, that accurate understanding, or "discountability," caused Nucor's share price to level off. If executives had wanted the company's share price to keep appreciating at rates in excess of analysts' expectations, they would have had to continue to create or acquire disruptive businesses.

A company that acquires a disruptive business model can achieve spectacular results. Take, for

Why Disruptive Businesses Are Worth So Much

What produces a dramatic increase in a company's share price? Growth that investors weren't predicting. As Nucor developed revolutionary approaches to steel making, the company was able to enter increasingly larger segments of the steel market—each time prompting investors to reconsider Nucor's share price. Once there were no new markets to conquer, the company's share price leveled off.

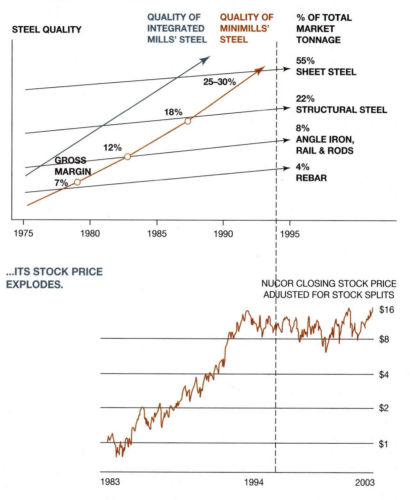

Source: Bloomberg.

example, information technology giant EMC's acquisition of VMware, whose software enabled IT departments to run multiple "virtual servers" on a single machine, replacing server vendors' pricey hardware solution with a lower-cost software one. Although this offering was disruptive to server vendors, it was complementary to EMC, giving the storage hardware vendor greater reach into its customers' data rooms. When EMC acquired VMware, for $635 million in cash, VMware's revenues were just $218 million. With a disruptive wind at its back, VMware's growth exploded: Annual revenues reached $2.6 billion in 2010. Currently, EMC's stake in VMware is worth more than $28 billion, a stunning 44-fold increase of its initial investment.

Johnson & Johnson's Medical Devices & Diagnostics division provides another example of how reinventing a business model through acquisition

How the Market Rewards Disruptors

High price/earnings ratios (which indicate a high share price relative to net income or profits) in a sample of 37 disruptive companies led analysts to believe their shares were overpriced at the time of their IPOS. The extraordinary performance of these companies in the market, however, suggests that their shares were in fact persistently underpriced.

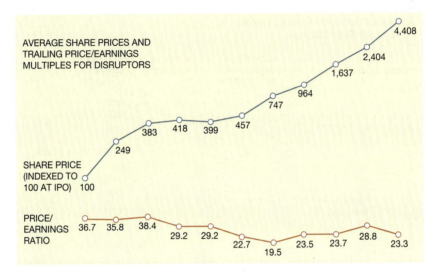

AVERAGE SHARE PRICES AND
TRAILING PRICE/EARNINGS
MULTIPLES FOR DISRUPTORS

4,408
2,404
1,637
964
747
457
383   418   399
249
SHARE PRICE
(INDEXED TO
100 AT IPO) 100

PRICE/
EARNINGS   36.7   35.8   38.4
RATIO   29.2   29.2
                                    22.7   23.5   23.7   28.8
                                         19.5   23.3

Sources: Compustat, Thompson Reuters, Bloomberg.

can boost growth from average to exceptional. From 1992 through 2001, the division's portfolio of products performed adequately, growing revenues at an annual rate of 3%. But during the same period, the division acquired four small but disruptive business models that ignited outsize growth. Together these RBM acquisitions grew 41% annually over this period, fundamentally changing the division's growth trajectory.

Acquiring to Decommoditize   One of the most effective ways to use RBM acquisitions is as a defense against commoditization. As we have described previously in this magazine, the dynamics of commoditization tend to follow a predictable pattern (see Clayton M. Christensen, Michael Raynor, and Matt Verlinden, "Skate to Where the Money Will Be," HBR, November 2001). Over time, the most profitable point in the value chain shifts as proprietary, integrated offerings metamorphose into modular, undifferentiated ones. The innovative companies supplying the components start to capture the most attractive margins in the chain.

If a firm finds itself being commoditized in this way, acquisitions won't improve the output of its profit formula. In fact, nothing will. Firms in this situation should instead migrate to "where the profits will be"— the point in the value chain that will capture the best margins in the future. Right now, the business models of major pharmaceutical companies are floundering for a host of reasons, including their inability to fill new-product pipelines and the obsolescence of the direct-to-doctor sales model. Industry leaders like Pfizer, GSK, and Merck have tried to boost the output of their troubled business models by buying and integrating the products and pipeline resources of competing drugmakers. But in the wake of such acquisitions, Pfizer's share price plummeted 40%. A far better strategy would be to focus on the place in the value chain that is becoming decommoditized: the management of clinical trials, which are now an integral part of the drug research process and so a critical capability for pharmaceutical companies. Despite this, most drugmakers have been outsourcing their clinical trials to contract research organizations such as Covance and Quintiles, better positioning those companies in the value chain. Acquiring those organizations, or a disruptive drugmaker like Dr. Reddy's Laboratories, would help reinvent big pharma's collapsing business model.

PAYING THE RIGHT PRICE

Given our assertion that RBM acquisitions most effectively raise the rate of value creation for share-holders, it's ironic that acquirers typically underpay for those acquisitions and overpay for LBM ones.

The stacks of M&A literature are littered with warnings about paying too much, and for good reason. Many an executive has been caught up in deal fever and paid more for an LBM deal than could be justified by cost synergies. For that kind of deal, it's crucial to determine the target's worth by calculating the impact on profits from the acquisition. If an acquirer pays less than that, the stock price will increase, but only to a slightly higher plateau, with a gentle upward slope representing the company's weighted-average cost of capital, which for most firms is about 8%. In contrast, consider the exhibit "How the Market Rewards Disruptors," which charts the average earnings multiple of 37 companies we've determined to be disruptive in the 10 years after they went public. Annual P/E ratios for this group are far higher than historical levels, leading analysts to believe their shares were overpriced. Yet investors who purchased at the time of the IPO and held the stock for 10 years realized an astounding 46% annual return, indicating that the shares were persistently underpriced, even at these "high" multiples.

Analysts charged with determining the right price for a company's shares work hard to find appropriate comparables. For LBM acquisitions, the correct comparables are companies that make similar products in similar industries. For RBM acquisitions, however, such comparables make disruptive companies seem overpriced, deterring companies from pursuing the very acquisitions they need for reinvention. In reality, the right comparables for disruptive companies are other disruptors, regardless of industry.

Ultimately, the "right" price for an acquisition is not something that can be set by the seller, far less by an investment banker looking to sell to the highest bidder. The right price can be determined only by the buyer, since it depends on what purpose the acquisition will serve.

AVOIDING INTEGRATION MISTAKES

Your approach to integration should be determined almost entirely by the type of acquisition you've made. If you buy another company for the purpose of improving your current business model's effectiveness, you should generally dissolve the acquired model as its resources are folded into your operations. That's what Cisco does with the great majority of its technology acquisitions. (There are certainly exceptions: An acquired process, for instance, is sometimes so valuable or distinct that it substitutes for or is added to the acquirer's.) But if you buy a company for its business model, it's important to keep the model intact, most commonly by operating it separately. That's what Best Buy did with Geek Squad, running its high-touch, higher-cost service model as a separate business alongside its low-margin, low-touch retail operation. Likewise, VMware's server-focused business model was distinct enough from EMC's storage model that EMC chose not to integrate VMware very closely. EMC's original business model continued to perform well, but the addition of VMware's disruptive business model allowed EMC to grow at an exceptional rate.

Failing to understand where the value resides in what's been bought, and therefore integrating incorrectly, has caused some of the biggest disasters in acquisitions history. Daimler's 1998 acquisition of Chrysler for $36 billion is a quintessential example. Although the purchase of one car company by another looks like a classic resource acquisition, that was a fatal way to look at it. From about 1988 to 1998, Chrysler had aggressively modularized its products, outsourcing the subsystems from which its cars could be assembled to its tier-one suppliers. This so simplified its design processes that Chrysler could cut its design cycle from five years to two (compared with about six years at Daimler) and could design a car at one-fifth the overhead cost that Daimler required. As a result, during this period Chrysler introduced a series of very popular models and gained nearly a point of market share every year.

When Daimler's acquisition of Chrysler was announced, analysts began the "synergies" drumbeat—and Daimler responded that integrating the companies would strip out $8 billion in "redundant" costs. But when Daimler folded Chrysler's resources (brands, dealers, factories, and technology) into its operations, the real value of the acquisition (Chrysler's speedy processes and lean profit formula) disappeared, and with it the basis for Chrysler's success. Daimler would have done far better to preserve Chrysler's business model as a separate entity.

Companies rightly turn to acquisitions to meet goals they can't achieve internally. But there is no magic in buying another company. Companies can make acquisitions that allow them to command higher prices, but only in the same way they could have raised prices all along—by improving products that are not yet good enough for the majority of their customers. Similarly, they can make acquisitions to cut costs by using excess capacity in their resources and processes to serve new customers—but again, only in the same way they could have by finding new customers on their own. And companies can acquire new business models to serve as platforms for transformative growth—just as they could if they developed new business models in-house. At the end of the day, the decision to acquire is a question of whether it is faster and more economical to buy something that you could, given enough time and resources, make yourself.

Every day, the wrong companies are purchased for the wrong purpose, the wrong measures of value are applied in pricing the deals, and the wrong elements are integrated into the wrong business models. Sounds like a mess—and it has been a mess. But it need not be. We hope that the next time an investment banker knocks on your door with a guaranteed fee for himself and the acquisition of a lifetime for you, you'll be able to predict with greater accuracy whether the company on offer is a dream deal or a debacle.

Adding Value through Offshoring

Joan Enric Ricart
IESE, University of Navarra, Spain

Pablo Agnese
Pompeu Fabra University, Spain

EXECUTIVE SUMMARY

For decades, offshoring involved little more than moving call centers to countries with lower labor costs. But things have changed. Today's new generation of offshoring increasingly features value-added services, such as highly complex software projects or specific R&D functions. These changes are forcing companies to rethink their internationalization strategies in order to incorporate more of these kinds of value-added offshoring processes.

In this article, the authors discuss the risks and opportunities that managers must consider when offshoring, and they propose six steps aimed at creating value rather than simply reducing costs.

The U.S. sitcom *Outsourced* is based on an all-too-real premise: An American manager named Todd suddenly finds his departmental functions being outsourced to a call center in Mumbai.

"Todd, we decided to restructure Order Fulfillment."

"Restructure how?"

"Offshore the whole department."

(Laughs.) "Good one."

"I'm not kidding. Check out this spreadsheet. Any American job that's done on the phone or online is going overseas. The savings are incredible."

"You can't outsource Order Fulfillment. Our catalog is patriotic knick-knack. If a factory worker from Wisconsin calls the 800 number to buy this and gets a person from another country, he will flip out. You expect me to walk in there and tell everyone, 'I'm sorry, your job has been outsourced?'"

"I'll do it."

"So I'm fired, too?"

"No, not at all. We need you in India. Someone has to train the new guy."

"What does this new guy get paid?"

"Half a million . . . rupees. That's $11,000 a year to do your job. As in, eight for the price of one."

In real life, as in fiction, the arguments made by numerous companies to offshore services in the 90s usually followed this same script. Those years saw offshoring as little more than simply moving call centers to countries with lower labor costs.

But things have changed. Today's new generation of offshoring increasingly features value-added services, such as highly complex software projects or specific R&D functions. Gone are the days of simple cost reduction, which favored the routine use of call centers and overseas software developers for minor projects.

Two of Spain's biggest banking groups, BBVA and Santander, exemplify the new and improved offshoring trend.

Less than a decade ago, BBVA was running its entire back office out of Madrid. Five years later, it had relocated these operations, first to the southern Spanish city of Malaga, before outsourcing two-thirds of its operations to low-cost destinations such as Buenos Aires, Mexico City, and Lima. BBVA is currently doing the same with its remaining administrative activities in the other geographic areas where it operates.

Santander has taken a much more radical approach. Since 2000, the banking group has progressively transferred software development, computer centers, and business operations to three subsidiaries. These, in turn, were given the freedom to concentrate, outsource,

Joan Enric Ricart and Pablo Agnese. "Adding Value through Offshoring." *IESE Insight*, no. 10 (2011), pp. 60–66. Copyright © IESE Publishing. Reprinted with permission.

or transfer part of those activities as they saw fit, but always under the supervision of the banks. At the same time, Santander has developed a single, shared technology platform and common processes, among which offshoring is just one facet of an overall operating strategy.

This article is based on studies conducted by the Offshoring Research Network, which is associated with IESE's Center for Globalization and Strategy. For companies interested in moving operations overseas, our research shows that offshoring has become a critical component of a business strategy aimed at creating value.

For those who have not yet made the leap, an understanding of the current state of offshoring is essential. First, we explain the factors that have contributed to transforming this business practice. Then, we weigh up the benefits and risks, before sharing some of the tools that will help you to define a successful international offshoring strategy suited to your organization.

THE IT IMPETUS

How did offshoring get to be so popular? Undoubtedly, the development of information technology, fuelled by the Internet, gave rise to a certain set of functions that could be relocated more easily, and influenced which business relationships could be maintained through offshore destinations.

Information and communications technology (ICT), such as Voice Over IP and telepresence, became not only much cheaper, but also, with the advent of more collaborative applications and cloud computing phenomena, more comprehensive. This enabled companies to carry out high value-added activities far from home with the maximum degree of reliability and efficiency. With digitization, distance ceased to be a problem and, in many ways, disappeared.

The Telemedicine Clinic is a good case in point. What began life in 2003 as a means to centralize

diagnostic services performed by hospitals in Sweden has since expanded to become a full radiology solutions provider to where public hospitals across the European Union are able to subcontract their diagnostic services. A specialist based in Barcelona, for example, can have immediate access to X-rays taken in Sweden, and on-call specialists in Sydney make sure that quality readings are provided day or night.

Eventually, offshoring evolved beyond providing technical support services, to actually being a source of new professional expertise in the form of research and development. Such was the path taken by General Electric, IBM, and Cisco. This went hand in hand with the proliferation of professional services firms and management consultancies, which specialized in offshoring and facilitated these tendencies even further.

FROM COST SAVINGS TO HEAD-HUNTING

In 2009, the Offshoring Research Network surveyed senior executives representing more than 2,000 companies and 4,300 offshore projects in four continents. While these executives continued to cite "labor cost savings" as the top advantage of offshoring, the survey also turned up significant numbers of executives who valued, for instance, the benefits of access to qualified personnel or greater organizational flexibility (see Exhibit 1).

There are two main reasons behind this. First, many have come to the realization that "labor cost savings" cannot serve as the only source of competitive advantage, as there will always be someone who can do it cheaper.

Also, what's happening is that, thanks to better education, the supply of skilled labor in offshore

EXHIBIT 1   More than Cost Savings

Companies increasingly value offshoring from the viewpoint of access to talent and improved flexibility.

	Finance & Insurance	High Tech	Manufacturing	Professional Services	Consumer Goods	Software
Labor costs	92	84	78	82	78	86
Other costs	74	68	70	66	74	56
Access to talent	67	65	61	55	53	63
Growth strategy	56	69	69	64	74	62
Organizational flexibility	70	53	77	70	85	64

Source: "Taking Offshoring to the Next Level." The 2009 Offshoring Research Network Corporate Client Survey Report.

destinations has improved significantly over the years. This means that these workers are able to take on and carry out new business tasks requiring high levels of knowledge.

Our research corroborates the development of talent and knowledge as a critical element in offshoring strategies—a development that reinforces the association of offshoring with value creation processes. As our analysis shows, improving the quality of skilled workers worldwide will encourage product development offshoring, as opposed to just offshoring lower value activities.

This shift has been partly driven by emerging countries making a firm commitment to invest in education and infrastructure. Several studies, including the one by the Offshoring Research Network, reveal explosive growth in the number of engineering and computer science graduates, especially in the two major offshoring destinations of India and China. No wonder the U.S. administration is concerned, as reflected by President Obama's pledge in 2010 for the United States to "produce eight million more college graduates by 2020, because America has to have the highest share of graduates compared to every other nation."

This growth in the availability of skilled labor has led to the emergence of clusters specialized in offshoring activities, like investment banks in Mumbai or call centers in Bangalore. The phenomenon is not restricted to the Asian giants. There are now IT-associated clusters in Latin America, too, from Guadalajara, Mexico, to Recife, Brazil, and Córdoba, Argentina.

Having clusters concentrated together in one area makes it easier for companies and universities to exchange ideas and people, with universities tending to become the main recruitment centers. Clusters can also generate pools of talent with specific capabilities, making these offshore destinations even more attractive.

But the picture is not entirely perfect. Some of these regions have suffered significant inflation as well as high turnover of labor.

BENEFITS NOT WITHOUT RISKS

The positive effects of offshoring on the productivity of companies and—by extension—the economy, are well-documented (see the box "An Argument Blown Out of Proportion").

One study of 450 U.S. industries found that, between 1992 and 2000, offshoring succeeded in boosting productivity by as much as 10 percent. Another study, of 35,000 British production plants over a three-year period, estimated that increasing offshoring activities by 10 percent saw a corresponding 0.37 percent rise in total-factor productivity. Meanwhile, a study of 83 Japanese industries found that, between 1980 and 2005, a 1 percent rise in offshoring resulted in an improvement in total-factor productivity of between 0.5 percent and 2 percent.

Other studies, however, underscore the risks of offshoring, such as the problems associated with limiting the number of offshore destinations. A 2009 McKinsey survey found that 70 percent of offshore centers, whether company-owned or outsourced, were concentrated in just three countries: India, China, and the Philippines.

The risks of such concentration include unstable currencies and wages, intense competition for employees and regulatory limits—none of which compensate for the lower labor cost advantage. Certainly, the emergence of clusters in other parts of the world will undoubtedly help to mitigate such risks through a wider geographic distribution of activities.

The Offshoring Research Network study highlights the primary risks perceived by senior management, and how their perceptions changed from 2007 to 2009 (see Exhibit 2). Of particular note are the changes in how managers rank data security and the quality of the services provided. This should come as little surprise, since the financial crisis that erupted during this period made these issues of paramount importance for company survival.

DESTINATIONS Á LA CARTE

Most services offshoring used to go primarily to India (Hyderabad, Bangalore, Delhi, and Mumbai), Eastern Europe (Prague and Budapest) and Russia (mainly Moscow). In recent years, however, some of these cities have become less attractive in terms of labor costs and infrastructure, as they have been inundated with demand. New offshoring destinations have emerged, with unique selling points of their own.

Dubai and the United Arab Emirates, for example, have focused on internationality, state-of-the-art infrastructure, a stable and qualified workforce, low taxes, and five-star attractions. Cape Town, South Africa, stresses its highly qualified workforce, strong

The Impact of Offshoring on Employment in Countries of Origin Is Neither as Significant nor as Lasting as Some Would Portray

The argument that offshoring leads to serious job losses has found sympathizers in the media and certain political spheres. There is no shortage of voices advocating a return to tighter regulation and protectionism. But many of these fears are unfounded, and taking the measures some call for would bring results diametrically opposed to the desired ones.

HIGHER PRODUCTIVITY, MORE DEMAND

The greater efficiency and productivity obtained through offshoring exerts downward pressure on domestic prices, which, over time, raises demand for goods and services, and thus, for labor. How? By being more productive, companies can offer lower prices, which stimulates demand for their products and services, thereby boosting domestic job demand. This line of reasoning is supported by Mary Amiti and Shang-Jin Wei, who, in a 2006 study of U.S. industries, noted sufficient consequent growth in demand to offset any negative effects. More recent research by Pablo Agnese on the offshoring experiences of Japan found very probable gains in employment and productivity for local firms.

IMPACT ON EMPLOYMENT LESS THAN BELIEVED

The impact of offshoring on labor markets in the economies of origin is neither significant nor lasting. With few exceptions, the research agrees that any negative consequences are nil or negligible. Despite the recent crisis, Forrester stands by its estimates that, by 2015, the United States will have exported about 3.3 million service jobs—far from the alarming 40 million predicted in other reports.

RELEASED RESOURCES BRING LONG-TERM GAINS

Alarmist figures pale further against employment projections of the U.S. Bureau of Labor Statistics, which foresees the creation of 160 million jobs for the same year, 2015. While some workers may be affected in the short term, as jobs they used to perform go overseas, the new resources that are freed as a result of offshoring opens up new opportunities for employees and employers alike. In the long run, labor markets in the economies of origin find themselves performing new activities or entering whole new sectors.

insurance and professional services sectors, alongside its well-developed telecommunications network. Morocco specializes in customer service and back-office functions for many French and Spanish companies, since many of its workers speak both languages. Vietnam boasts a large number of math graduates who also speak English, French, German, or Russian.

Given the expanding choice of destinations, managers who consider offshoring will need to compile lists of locations and weigh their suitability based on the following criteria: costs, availability of skilled labor, local or regional market potential, quality of infrastructure, the country's risk profile, and the political and business environment.

FINDING THE RIGHT STRATEGY

Are managers fully aware of what they face in implementing offshoring strategies? Until now, services offshoring has followed the traditional strategy applied to industrial processes—that is, identifying any repetitive and nonstrategic processes that can be relocated to geographic areas with lower labor costs.

Experience shows that this approach is not enough. To make offshoring decisions, one must have a clear strategy of activity assignment for different locations. This requires a systemic view of the changes in the business model.

EXHIBIT 2   Risks to Consider

MANAGERS PERCEIVE SERVICE QUALITY AND DATA SECURITY AS THE PRIMARY RISKS ASSOCIATED WITH OFFSHORING.

	Finance & Insurance	High Tech	Manufacturing	Professional Services	Consumer Goods	Software	Average 2007/2008	Average 2009
Service quality	70	56	54	53	35	46	51	65
Data security	72	47	43	36	33	31	43	59
Loss of control	45	44	44	42	34	33	43	44
High turnover	42	42	47	33	17	42	41	39
Cultural differences	37	50	47	32	28	26	32	40

Source: "Taking Offshoring to the Next Level." The 2009 Offshoring Research Network Corporate Client Survey Report.

In line with IESE Prof. Pankaj Ghemawat's globalization theories, we consider three types of strategies that yield different business models: aggregation, adaptation, and arbitrage. They usually come two at a time; rarely all three at once.

Aggregation means exploiting economies of scale through the use of regional business units offering a standardized product or service. Here, the purpose of offshoring is to centralize the activities in a specific geographic region to gain efficiencies through economies of scale.

Adaptation, on the other hand, seeks to compete through personalized dealings with customers at the local level. Unless the locations share many traits, it is very hard to think of offshoring processes designed according to the framework of this type of global strategy.

Arbitrage involves exploiting the differences that may arise between countries where the different business units are located. Most off-shoring processes are associated with this last strategy. The goal is to take advantage of other economies with lower wages and, as recent research indicates, the possibility of competing for talent at a global level.

What happens when your existing strategy is incompatible with offshoring—that is, when your business model is not flexible enough to integrate it? This is a question that should make managers reconsider the pros and cons of the drive toward offshoring at all costs.

CHOOSE YOUR STRATEGY WISELY

Implementing all three of the previously mentioned strategies often results in friction or imbalances between them, or between the business models involved. Sometimes offshoring strategies will force changes in the current orientation that can be very hard to assume, especially if the process involves changes to the long-term business model.

The experience of the companies studied shows that it isn't necessary to "go all out" when embarking on a strategy of global scale. Instead, it's enough to focus on one or two strategies, at most. It should be remembered that the optimal strategy depends not only on conditions in the market or sector, but also on the company's position relative to its competitors.

Managers also need to consider whether a strategy based on activity offshoring is the most appropriate when it comes time to take action. Other options might be more suitable to the company's situation and market conditions. Productive resources—labor services, know-how, raw materials—allotted to arbitrage, for example, could be used for other purposes, such as tasks related to adaptation or aggregation strategies.

Thus, the final decision of whether or not to go for offshoring must take into account the company's comparative advantages.

AN ADVANCED OFFSHORING MODEL

The case of Santander illustrates some of the salient aspects of offshoring processes.

The banking group has concentrated most of its software development activities in its subsidiary, Isban. With this centralization in a single unit, and all banks sharing the same technology platform, the group reaps enormous benefits from aggregation.

Meanwhile, Santander leaves control of the management of these processes to those banks that have a manager for operations and technology. This enables total adaptation to the idiosyncrasies of each context.

Furthermore, by operating this way in all the countries where the group is present, Santander can move its software factories to locations that provide the maximum benefits of arbitrage.

Ultimately, with this model, Santander obtains benefits from each of the key aspects of its international strategy. It gains flexibility and resilience, making the group better able to react to adverse conditions, as well as better able to challenge its main competitors.

Admittedly, this three-pronged strategy is rare and seems to work only in companies with large infrastructure and vast experience. Even then, implementation is not easy and requires three critical elements.

First, there needs to be a common transaction platform flexible enough to serve the needs of each bank, while at the same time being uniform enough to achieve the benefits of aggregation.

Second, there needs to be a complex system of governance that balances efficiency improvements, acceptable risks, and the quality of services.

Third, there needs to be an unequivocal desire to serve the client banks.

Yet if the functioning and coordination of these tasks is correct, the results are extremely positive, as has been the case for Santander.

SIX STEPS TO FOLLOW

Formulating an appropriate strategy is tricky, and following generic advice can lead to disaster. Instead, we offer you a sequence of specific steps that can help to guide managers.

1. Think big picture, not item by item. Offshoring that's not linked to the overall strategy can be a one-way ticket to failure. In the search for the best capabilities at the best price, a company must adapt both its global strategy and its organization.

2. Decide what you want to outsource and how. Defining a global strategy requires deciding which activities or processes are suitable for offshoring, how—through subsidiaries or outsourcing —and where. Study the complexity or simplicity of your processes and services, and the interdependencies between them, to identity the most outsourceable. You should also take into consideration issues such as whether these processes require some sort of presence or physical proximity, or specific company expertise. You will need to review this analysis from time to time, since studies show that these situations are changeable.

3. Examine destinations carefully. You should take into account variables such as labor costs, availability of talent, market potential, quality of infrastructure, acceptable risks, and the environment of each destination.

4. Adapt your organization to the new reality. According to our studies, in most companies, adapting business processes to the new reality entails a long learning curve. Therefore, it pays to make the transition with the help of a specialized company.

5. Develop local talent. Another organizational difficulty is learning how to attract, manage and develop talent in the destination countries. Again, this task is easier if you hire the services of an experienced, specialized provider in the chosen country, as BBVA did. If you opt for full outsourcing, it is important that you create some way of incorporating their know-how, otherwise you run the risk of these operations being held hostage by the local talent.

6. Govern your offshored business. Finally, the company needs to develop management mechanisms to oversee activities in different parts of the world, often with different suppliers. The development of sound governance capabilities is vital.

Activity offshoring is evolving rapidly toward ever-higher levels of complexity. The sequence from labor costs to skilled personnel to value creation illustrates the continuous evolution and adaptation of firms to the technological revolution. But companies shouldn't underestimate the risks. Prudence may be the most useful tool in your approach to offshoring—even more so in times of crisis.

framework, firms erect barriers to entry that keep rivals out and confer the market power to set prices. A firm that successfully erects barriers to entry can prevent rivals from entering and leveraging its monopoly power to pay suppliers less, charge customers more, and squash would-be rivals.

Seen through the resource-based view, firms create and sustain value to the extent they control resources or competencies that share three characteristics: First, a resource or competency must create value by cutting costs—think Wal-Mart's logistics—or increase willingness to pay—Coca-Cola charging twice what a store-brand cola costs. Second, a resource or competency must be rare—if every car included BMW's technology, the German automaker could command no premium. Finally, it must be difficult to substitute an alternative resource or competency—Saudi Aramco's oil stockpiles will remain valuable until mass-market automobiles can run on alternative fuels. Power, in this view, arises from dependence. Coca-Cola exercises power over its bottlers, to the extent these distributors depend on Coca-Cola. Owning a resource, in this case one of the most valuable brands in the world, is the source of both the bottlers' dependence and Coke's power.

The conventional strategic wisdom, therefore, views power as a good thing for the firm that wields it. Powerful firms—think Coca-Cola, Royal Dutch Shell, Microsoft, Roche, or Wal-Mart—can capture more economic value by squeezing their suppliers and distributors or charging customers a premium. Strategic power helps firms sustain profits into the future by fending off established rivals or new entrants that might compete away profits. No wonder powerful firms are so attractive to investors, such as Warren Buffett, who described his ideal company as an economic castle protected by an unbreachable moat.

Executives crave strategic power as much or more than investors do, because it makes their life much easier. First, managers can get things done by the raw exercise of power over employees, distributors, suppliers, and even customers who are dependent on the firm. Second, strategic power provides greater certainty about future revenues and profits. Finally, strategic power allows firms to weather changes in the marketplace without having to respond immediately. General Motors' market power in the 1950s allowed the automaker to survive decades of changes in technology, regulations, competition, and consumer preferences before finally succumbing to bankruptcy.

The GM example hints that strategic power is not an absolute good. The obvious risk of overreliance on strategic power is that no positional or resource advantage lasts forever. The personal computer disrupted IBM's stranglehold on mainframes, just as the tablet threatens Microsoft's dominance in PC operating systems. But we all know that. The more insidious risk is that the very market power that companies use to protect their established business hinders them from seizing new opportunities.

Over time, strategic power tends to pervade a company's culture and not in a good way. When speaking to customers with high switching costs, company representatives often lecture customers on what they should want rather than listening to what they do want. Sony lost to the iPod, in part, because it forced users of its digital music players to use its proprietary ATRAC software rather than the MP3 standard that customers wanted. In selecting partners to work with, power-drunk executives prefer vassal organisations whose dependency renders them easy to control. Leaders who can exert hierarchal control to get things done within their own company often apply the same heavy-handed tactics to corporate partners.

To grow revenues, companies must often enter new market segments in which they lack power, as Microsoft discovered in the game box, mobile phone and Internet search segments. To seize an emerging opportunity, these companies must also assemble a new set of resources or competencies that they do not already control. The iPod's success depended not on hardware and software alone, but on the cooperation of record labels and producers of complementary products such as speakers and carrying cases. Owning its own record label hampered Sony from striking a deal with other music companies.

There is another way. Strategic orchestration describes a time when a firm pursues an opportunity not by leveraging strategic power, but by assembling and managing a network of partners. This is not about pursuing partnerships for their own sake—the corporate equivalent of having 1,000 connections on LinkedIn. These networks are strategic in the sense that they serve to create, capture, and sustain economic value. Strategic orchestration flips traditional strategy on its head. Rather than start with what you control and look for ways to leverage it, managers begin with the opportunity and then assemble the required resources in its wake. (See the box for problems that strategic orchestration can help solve.)

Strategic orchestration requires a shift in orientation. Existing strategy theory is egocentric—its starting point is the individual firm that exists to create, capture and sustain economic value. The firm focuses on opportunities that it can seize by leveraging its strategic power. The allocentric orientation, by contrast, takes a broader perspective and incorporates the various partners in the network as the unit of analysis. Apple's renaissance began when the newly returned Steve Jobs reframed the company as the hub of a digital lifestyle, rather than a computer maker that had to do everything important itself. An allocentric view allows executives to recognise and, more importantly, seize a whole range of opportunities that could only be pursued by a network rather than an individual firm, no matter how powerful. An allocentric orientation does not imply that managers ignore the interests of their own company. Rather, they recognise that the value lies in the network, which they cannot own.

PUT YOURSELF IN YOUR CUSTOMERS' (AND PARTNERS') SHOES

When executives in powerful companies want to grow revenues, they often start with the same basic question: How can we sell more software, pizza, cement, insurance, coffee? Asking the same question leads to the same tired answers—use better raw materials and hope the customer will notice, cut prices to steal share, boost advertising, add features, or simply give up and focus on cost reduction. These stale answers are often attributed to a lack of imagination, and they indeed share a tiresome lack of creativity. But that is not all they share. These responses are all actions that are under the company's exclusive control. In taking these actions, companies avoid the difficulties of probing customers' unmet needs or collaborating with partners to provide an integrated solution. How else can one explain the mindless proliferation of features that no one understands (let alone uses) that clutter consumer electronics, other than employees' desire to rely exclusively on actions under their control?

To break out of the arrogance of power, it helps to start with a different set of questions. *What really matters to our customers? What emotional need, beyond the purely functional, is unmet? What do our customers hope for? What do they fear?* You may think these are absurd questions for an insurance or coffee company to ask. You would be wrong. By asking just these questions, Swiss insurance firm Baloise learned that customers bought insurance but craved safety; while CEMEX discovered that low-income customers bought cement to build a legacy that they could pass on to their children, Armed with these insights, these companies could begin to assemble a network of resources to address customers' deep desires and fears.

Customer empathy is the first step in discovering how a product could resonate with a deep emotional need. Empathy is not the same thing as niceness, which is often used as an excuse to avoid hard discussions, Rather it is the ability to put yourself in someone else's shoes. Strategic power erodes the empathy required to understand customers' deepest hopes and fears. When working with a large European bank, for example, one of the authors sat with the top management team as they discussed how to grow revenues. As they spoke, he jotted down the verbs they used to describe what they would do to (never for or with) the customer. The list included 'cross-sell,' 'leverage,' 'squeeze,' 'exploit,' and 'penetrate,' at which point, he interrupted the proceedings to note that he was not one of their customers and never would be since no one in that room was going to exploit, let alone penetrate, him. A leading technology firm, to give another example, refers to customers as 'sockets,' presumably just waiting to be screwed.

How can managers, whose empathy has been blunted by strategic power, see the world from the customers' point of view? Most companies collect reams of monthly sales data and survey current customers' satisfaction. These quantitative data reveal only those times when a customer is satisfied with a current product but mute on what would delight or surprise a customer or meet his or her deeper needs. Some companies attempt to discover this with focus groups, but this is the equivalent of scientists going to the zoo to study animal behaviour.

To empathise with customers' unmet needs, managers must observe them in the wild, not the zoo. To better understand the needs of Mexico's less affluent customers, CEMEX assembled a cross-functional team of high-potential managers who spent 10 hours each day for a year in an extremely poor neighbourhood in Guadalajara.

This intense observation provided many surprising insights. They noticed, for example, that poorer consumers generally bought less-expensive powdered cement in bags, rather than pricier ready-mixed concrete delivered by trucks. In these neighbourhoods, cement is a consumer product. Their observation led CEMEX to market powdered cement like powdered soap, through consumer advertising and sponsoring local football clubs.

More importantly, the team gleaned insight into the subtle emotional benefits of home extension that supplemented the functional benefits of more room. Home improvements not only added space, they learned, but also conferred an important psychological satisfaction by creating 'patrimonio'—something of enduring value that customers could pass on to their children and grandchildren. The insight that buildings represented more than utility inspired CEMEX to create a programme called 'Patrimonio Hoy' (legacy today) that appeals to consumers' aspirations to create an enduring legacy that their children and grandchildren could enjoy.

To help customers realise their legacy, the CEMEX team had to understand obstacles that prevented consumers from building a legacy. Funding was one. They discovered that poor Mexicans raised capital for building by organising 'tandas,' a lottery in which a collection of families contribute a set sum to a pool each week and one family wins the entire pot at the end of the week (no family can win more than once). Although these funds were intended for building, winnings were often diverted to alternate uses such as celebrating a wedding or birthday. Lack of building equipment and expertise also hindered construction. Although bagged cement represented a significant expenditure, the CEMEX team discovered that 40 percent of all cement went bad, because customers lacked the tools or blueprints to complete their construction project.

GET PARTNERS TO PLAY BALL

Indentifying an unmet customer need is one thing, but meeting that need is quite another, particularly when providing an integrated solution would require resources and competencies that your company doesn't control. CEMEX executives had no desire to run hardware stores or provide financing for construction. To provide their customers with an integrated experience, CEMEX needed to work with partners, including mom and pop retailers and banks, over which the company could exercise more power. The team was also charged with observing local hardware stores first-hand to understand what would induce them to work with CEMEX.

When faced with the need to find partners, managers accustomed to exercising power often look for companies they can easily boss around. When that doesn't work, they look to pay the partners to play, but this is not the only or best approach. In many cases, particularly when dealing with customers at the bottom of the pyramid, there is not enough profit to go around. Second, by linking cooperation exclusively to cash payment, companies risk the winner's curse, paying above the odds to woo partners over their next best offer. Finally, exclusive reliance on financial incentives, rebates, and commissions to attract and retain partners fosters a transactional attitude in which more cooperation requires more cash. Of course, a partnership must work for everyone financially; but cash need not be the only, or even most important, way to attract partners.

Empathy is as important for partners as it is for customers in order to understand what matters to them beyond money and to structure deals that appeal to their values. CEMEX attracted local hardware stores into a network of Construrama solutions providers, in large part by providing them with access to best practices from CEMEX, the opportunity to learn from other leading retailers and the use of the Construrama brand that signalled quality to customers. Apple's commitment to elegant design attracts accessory producers, apps providers, and product reviewers at sites such as iLounge that value aesthetically pleasing products. High-end equipment markers, leading hotel chains, premium airlines, and sommeliers at Michelin Star restaurants are attracted to Nestlé's Nespresso coffee system for its luxury and elegance. Nespresso's elegance likewise attracts customers who sign up to the company's Nespresso Club, which might sound like a marketing gimmick until you realise that half of new customers learn about the system through demonstrations by current club members. These evangelists have helped make Nespresso Nestlé's fastest growing brand with revenues approaching $3 billion.

In some cases, a dominant value such as design or luxury will attract partners. In other cases, however, strategic orchestration requires different deals to induce different partners to play ball. Consider the case of JLT, a British insurance and risk management firm, which was attempting to grow its business in emerging markets. JLT's Peruvian management team knew that the government was concerned about its aging taxi fleet that caused pollution and traffic accidents and also knew that the country had ample supplies of low-cost natural gas. The JLT team saw an opportunity to convince taxi drivers to buy new vehicles that ran on natural gas and to make money selling auto insurance.

It was a great idea in theory, but it faced myriad obstacles in practice. The banks wouldn't lend to taxi drivers with no credit rating; lacking bank accounts, drivers could not pay their bills; without customers gas stations refused to stock natural gas; and car dealers refused to order natural-gas powered cars. Rather than give up, the JLT Peru team figured out a way to get everyone to play ball. JLT added mortgage insurance to the bundle of insurance it sold drivers, agreeing to pay off the loan on the car if the driver defaulted, which induced the banks to make loans.

To stimulate the use of natural gas, the Peruvian government provided low-cost natural gas to filling stations that agreed to invest to distribute the new fuel and also install a billing system that allowed taxi drivers to pay their bank loan and insurance premium when paying for gas. Facing new demand, auto dealers started stocking vehicles that could run on natural gas. JLT Peru also worked with the national taxi drivers' association to identify drivers who would drive the 200 kilometres per day required to cover the financing charges and with two local companies who installed GPS systems to monitor miles driven and locate the cars if they were stolen.

The Peruvian taxi case illustrates that one company has to take the lead in identifying the pieces needed to seize the opportunity, understanding what matters to each player and structuring deals that make it work for everyone. This may seem like a lot of work—and it is. But it offers several advantages. First, the network is simple for the customer to use, thereby stimulating adoption. Demand for the new taxis grew five-fold in its second year as did the number of filling stations carrying natural gas.

Second, while the network is simple to use, it is very difficult to copy because key partners are already locked in. Finally, the company that orchestrates the network is well-positioned to make money. As a trusted partner within the network, JLT has offered a comprehensive insurance package including damage, theft, liability, mortgage, and policies to ensure the bank is paid if the driver is ill or the car is in the shop. The network also provides a platform for offering additional coverage, such as health or life insurance, to existing customers, or expanding the programme to shipping companies or private bus firms.

GUIDE THE NETWORK WITH A LIGHT TOUCH, NOT A HEAVY HAND

Strategic orchestration requires a shift in how executives deal with partners. Executives often brandish their company's strategic power as a stick to threaten partners into compliance with their wishes. But when value creation depends on partners' voluntary participation, firms like Nespresso, CEMEX, or JLT can guide a network, but they cannot dictate what partners do. Guiding without power requires executives to exercise diplomacy rather than raw power in dealing with their partners.

Part of guiding a network is dealing effectively with communities rather than engaging in bilateral agreements in which you can leverage your power. JLT's success in Peru, for example, hinged on the insurance firm's ability to work with the local association of taxi drivers. In selecting growers, Nespresso identifies regions with the potential to deliver exceptional coffee and then works with local farmer cooperatives to secure the high-quality beans the company needs for its espresso. To spark continued innovation in coffee machines and the overall drinking experience, Nespresso taps into the global design community by sponsoring design competitions. This diplomatic orientation to partners permeates the coffee makers' language, which refers to customer-facing employees as 'ambassadors.'

It is not enough to talk the talk of communities, but companies also have to actively treat community members as equals, not vassals. With a global brand and billions of dollars in sales, Nespresso could easily use its strategic power to get things done, but it consistently relies on diplomacy in working with its partners. After identifying attractive growing areas, Nespresso offers local farmers the opportunity to 'opt in' by joining neighbouring farms to participate in the cooperative to supply Nespresso.

The lead partner must also be willing to delegate key decisions to partners. It was not the company but Nespresso Club members, the network of millions of customer advocates, who selected George Clooney as the brand's representative.

Networks rely on trust, and the lead partner in an orchestrated network must go out of its way to build and maintain trust among members. Transparent communication is one powerful way to build trust. Transparency does not mean that all information has to be shared with all partners all the time. Apple,

The challenge for companies is to transform the inherently ad hoc nature of this informal learning into something with more structure and rigor. That's where social networking and collaboration technologies are now beginning to create learning opportunities.

Social media is an inescapable presence today. It would be hard to find a major business that's not asking people to follow it on Facebook, or that isn't tweeting regular news about its products. But it's one thing to leverage the enormous popularity of social networking to reach customers and manage brand awareness. It's quite another to integrate social media into a core capability such as learning. Sound easy? It's not.

What training professionals refer to as "social learning" will be a force in every organization, sooner or later. In the words of Claudia Rodriguez, vice president and head of Motorola Solutions Learning, organizations are at "a major inflection point" when it comes to the use of social media and collaboration tools in business—not just in learning but in everything a business does. "Gradually, social networking is becoming so ingrained in how we live that it will also become ingrained in the way we work," says Rodriguez. "The question is, how do we do it in a way that advances the business and also contains the risks? We are answering that question by providing more robust tools that make collaboration even more accessible and efficient to the broader internal and external ecosystem, while also educating users on how to be effective and more accountable social learners."

Social learning is not without risks—some perceived but some very real: leaked information, learning programs that might be inconsistent and contradictory, productivity losses, and a candor in exchanges that may not always be productive.

Consider the company that established an internal forum akin to a Facebook page. Direct reports to a senior executive were asked to post their vision statements for their organization onto his page. One manager did so, but the executive didn't like it. His response—visible to everyone in the entire company—was that the manager's posting wasn't a true vision statement and would need to be totally reworked before it would be acceptable. Not something that's likely to stimulate learning and the open sharing of ideas again anytime soon.

Properly designed and managed, however, social media tools have great potential to harness the experiential dimension of the workplace to deliver relevant learning experiences that reflect both proven expertise within a function or industry and timely access to an organization's best thinking, wherever it might be.

GLOBAL LEARNING

A social learning solution developed by Microsoft—called Academy Mobile—is an internal platform employees can use to share knowledge by creating and posting audio and video podcasts. The platform has been enormously popular, with download traffic up 115 times in its first two years.

Its value resides largely in how easily employees across Microsoft's global organization can translate interactions, meetings, or timely personal insights into content that can support better learning, performance, and idea generation. For example, using the platform, virtual meetings can be captured, catalogued, indexed, and converted to video or audio. Content is searchable, and learning programs are also organized and catalogued by topic, creating a kind of virtual curriculum. The academy is available on workers' mobile devices as well.

The Academy Mobile platform is especially valuable to employees such as salespeople: It enables them to learn rapidly about particular products, solutions, and sales techniques so they can capitalize on an immediate customer opportunity.

How does a Microsoft employee know what content is more valuable than other content? In part, through a ranking system from the users themselves. The ranking (from one to five stars) becomes a means by which the best ideas rise to the top because of their practical value. Employees can also interact and ask questions of content creators, generating a dialogue that may become as important as the original posting—and offers another indicator of what content is "hot."

The ability to rate content sourced online will become increasingly important to effective enterprise learning. In its totality, the Internet is the world's greatest source of learning but, to use the cliché, that's a bit like saying that a fire hose is the greatest source of drinking water.

A company's knowledge system might well provide a search capability and generate abundant content in response to a query, but then what? Content may be king but context is queen. To provide value to employees and enable faster routes to innovation, a search engine needs to aggregate results from a number of internal and external sources and then, as the

Microsoft solution does, rank those results according to how likely the content is to support someone's needs and intentions.

TECHNOLOGY OPTIONAL

Not every company needs to develop its own social media platform. Many organizations will find that the social networks already in use by consumers have functionality that goes well beyond what they can create in-house.

Rather than trying to introduce competing solutions, companies should think about how to integrate commercially available (and popular) social media technologies into their own learning ecosystem. Using existing platforms like YouTube, companies have ready access to rich sets of tools that deliver learning in a format that has already gained widespread acceptance and popularity.

Social learning doesn't even necessarily require technology-based tools. Coaching and mentoring programs require planning and time from supervisors but little capital investment. They can also support employees who don't fit the typical knowledge worker profile.

For example, at Tiendas Aurgi, a chain of automobile repair shops in Spain, a new informal mentoring system helped to quickly provide employees with new skills. Those whose skill sets were restricted to such tasks as changing tires were able to get the personal coaching, through a master-apprentice model, needed to perform more complex tasks, such as repairing clutches. The program improved overall shop floor productivity by more than 30 percent, which the company believes will potentially lead to a 20 percent increase in revenue.

THE RIGHT BLEND

The point here, however, is not to throw out everything organizations know about learning and supporting their employees' performance and replace it with a user-generated social learning solution. The point is rather to recognize where different media and learning approaches are most appropriate and have the best payoff in terms of performance improvement—then to blend or chain these together for maximum impact.

The statistical evidence suggesting that some types of formal learning are failing to deliver value to employees does not mean that traditional classroom training or e-learning is inherently an out-of-date delivery channel. Rather, it is an indication that it too often delivers learning experiences that are not timely or relevant, and not linked to reinforcing knowledge, and so the program does not ultimately support an employee's ongoing needs. In other words, formal learning isn't failing because it's formal but because it's often poorly conceived and delivered.

It's not uncommon to hear disparaging remarks in the learning field about how, in spite of all the innovations in electronic and web-based learning, as much as 70 percent of corporate training is still delivered in the old-fashioned way: an instructor in front of a classroom. But the fact is, formal channels are still the best way to deliver many forms of training when consistent knowledge and performance behaviors are what's sought.

For example, what Accenture calls an "academy" approach to learning is a way to ensure that specific workforces, such as finance, supply chain, and sales, get high-quality and consistent knowledge to drive common understandings and common approaches to getting things done.

Learning is targeted to jobs and roles, and designed to fill specific needs and skills gaps. There is rigor to the curriculum because, frankly, no one wants different members of the finance workforce analyzing a balance statement in different ways. Formal learning is good at that—building common skills, ensuring shared understanding, and making best practices available to everyone at the same time.

Properly designed, this approach can also be a way to improve relevance. An academy, for example, offers content tightly aligned to functional- and industry-based competency models and job frameworks so that learning is tailored to real and relevant performance needs. Content can be continuously updated by an organization's internal experts as well as by academics and industry specialists.

The formal learning aspects of the academy can also be augmented by social media and collaboration opportunities, and other kinds of follow-on experiences to reinforce initial training. Without that, the learning program can stagnate and lose relevance and credibility.

However, many organizations actually block their employees from external social networking sites; their collaboration platforms may be adequate for internal use, but they are closed systems and offer an inadequate link to outside perspectives. By building social media hooks into formal learning solutions, an organization can leverage the biggest database of all—the collective experience of people both within and outside their own organization.

How can an enterprise harness the best qualities of both formal training and informal, social learning to turn its entire organization into a corporate-wide enterprise learning team?

Inventory Your Skills

Companies rarely manage their workforce capabilities with the same rigor they do their stock inventory—that is, through careful assessments of what they have versus what they need. Only 53 percent of employees responding to the Accenture Skills Gap Study said their employers document their skills. Even those that do skills assessments rarely go beyond a "dump" of basic resume data.

An organization's strategic plans should generate a list of the workforce capabilities needed to execute business strategy, as well as a monetary value for each capability based on how critical it is to generating new revenues or reducing costs. Then, as with a well-managed supply chain, companies should compare the skills and experience they need with the inventory they actually have.

The gap between the ideal and the real can keep learning needs (and budgets) in line because it will sustain a focus on what people really need to be competent and execute strategy.

Identify Interdependencies

A related, but more difficult, task is to identify the interdependencies between competencies. No worker operates in isolation. Everyone depends on one another, and every business function interacts with others, so identifying the most critical dependencies is important. It can also be helpful in developing the most useful social media-based support tools, identifying which parts of the organization—and which learning sources—need to be especially linked.

Locate Pockets of Expertise

The ability to identify particularly valuable content or performance behaviors and then rapidly get those into training vehicles is especially important to delivering on both relevance and timeliness. Several leading companies work to design learning experiences for a particular function based on what top performers are doing, right now, to be successful.

For example, the Eastern European unit of a major consumer products company was looking to improve the performance of its sales force. The company was able to identify specific behaviors of top-performing store executives and field sales supervisors, and rapidly embed those insights and approaches into training activities. Those activities were a blend of social or informal learning such as coaching, as well as e-learning modules and instructor-led workshops and classes.

Create Learning Chains

It is important to leverage many sources and modalities of learning, and to offer a variety of reinforcing experiences linked together over time. This can improve retention, reinforce knowledge, and encourage behaviors that support business goals. This is an excellent way to combine the best of formal learning techniques with social learning as well as with such related areas as communications and coaching.

For example, one company with a supply chain academy combines formal training (both classroom and online) with informal learning that may come from Internet searches, podcasts, YouTube videos, professional research organizations, books and journals, as well as internal resources.

So a search for knowledge and skills in a particular area does not simply turn up a course to enroll in or to take online; it delivers comprehensive results that provide information sources across a wide range of internal and external media. It is important that employees be given a choice in the medium and channel they use to learn, depending on their location and need.

Create Responsibility for Learning Among Employees

Employees need to understand that they cannot be merely passive recipients of training. One of the more positive results from the Accenture Skills Gap Study was the finding that more than two-thirds of workers surveyed believe they bear the primary responsibility for their ongoing skills development. But they also need to understand the current and future demand for their own skills and the value of skills they could develop, and then be proactive participants both in their general career development and in any specific re-skilling they may need or be interested in.

Of course, the organization needs to support employees and harness their energy as they work to upgrade their skills, helping them develop learning plans and providing them with access to expertise, often through the social learning tools discussed here.

For example, global retailer Carrefour has implemented a social learning pilot at a number of its stores, involving about 1,000 employees. The program has enabled workers to identify skills they wish to develop, and then find experts to help them do so. Employees identified a learning gap in a simple database, then shared it with their supervisors for approval. Once approved, the need was posted, and experts volunteered to work with individuals to help them develop new capabilities. Preliminary results have been impressive, with the pilot stores reporting a 267 percent increase in sales of specific product lines.

Keep Learning Continuously Aligned with Business Needs

It is critical that organizations keep an eye on how well learning is aligned with business goals and needs, particularly as these programs grow. This can be especially important when it comes to dealing with social learning and networking, which, because they are still early in the hype cycle, may engender an enthusiasm that needs to be tempered by operational realities.

Jeanne Beliveau-Dunn, vice president and general manager of Learning@ Cisco, which delivers product training and career certifications at Cisco Systems, is adamant on this point. As she wrote in *Chief Learning Officer* magazine, "Business needs come first, social learning second."

To reach Cisco's global audience of employees, partners, and customers with timely information and training, the company created a social learning environment called the Cisco Learning Network. But the idea, as Beliveau-Dunn stresses, wasn't the social learning platform for its own sake; it was about serving the needs of the business. The development team spent considerable time upfront to understand the business needs that the platform was meant to address.

The drive to ensure ongoing alignment with business needs has generated innovative approaches at high-tech company Motorola Solutions. As Claudia Rodriguez explains, the audience for learning at the company is extremely varied—employees, channel partners, and customers. It's also global, but organized into four geographic regions. So in developing innovative learning, Rodriguez has to balance and align with different levels of priorities.

Globally, learning development leaders are joined at the hip with global business leaders to ensure that the training strategy—from new product and solution introductions to service offerings and skills in sales and marketing—stays in lockstep with business objectives. The regional leaders in the learning organization then validate these priorities with their go-to-market colleagues and adapt the scope and delivery timing to best suit each region's specific needs.

Rodriguez and her team have developed tools, processes, and communications plans (formal meetings multiple times a year, plus ongoing engagement) to obtain input, prioritize training development, and drive alignment at those two levels. It's important to have one common vision for training development not only for strategy reasons but also for management efficiencies. Notes Rodriguez: "I develop one list of priorities that my head of design and development can plan against from a capacity planning perspective."

She concludes, "At the end of the day, what we get out of this governance and planning structure is alignment with all the right stakeholders, true visibility to what's going on and then ultimately even the ability to measure the impact of all those key priorities and validate that they are helping to achieve the company's business goals."

Social learning represents a shift, and a major opportunity, for organizations. It enables the exchange and delivery of timely, relevant knowledge and can bring people together—inside and outside the enterprise—to generate fresh thinking and potentially profitable innovations.

At the same time, it's not the answer to everything. The key is to plan the right learning and collaboration solution for the right need, and to blend formal with informal to reinforce knowledge and build new skills.

As they seek to harness brainpower through social media platforms, integrated with formal learning, organizations should bear in mind the same kinds of development rigor and consistent delivery that has brought them success in the past.

The 12 Organization Culture Styles, as Measured by the Organizational Culture Inventory

CONSTRUCTIVE NORMS

Constructive cultures, in which members are encouraged to interact with others and approach tasks in ways that will help them meet their higher order *satisfaction* needs, are characterized by achievement, self-actualizing, humanistic-encouraging, and affiliative norms.

Achievement   An achievement culture characterizes organizations that do things well and value members who set and accomplish their own goals. Members are expected to set challenging but realistic goals, establish plans to reach these goals, and pursue them with enthusiasm (pursuing a standard of excellence).

Self-actualizing   A self-actualizing culture characterizes organizations that value creativity, quality over quantity, and both task accomplishment and individual growth. Members are encouraged to gain enjoyment from their work, develop themselves, and take on new and interesting activities (thinking in unique and independent ways).

Humanistic-encouraging   A humanistic-encouraging culture characterizes organizations that are managed in a participating and person-centered way. Members are expected to be supportive, constructive, and open to influence in their dealings with one another (helping others to grow and develop).

Affiliative   An affiliative culture characterizes organizations that place a high priority on constructive interpersonal relationships. Members are expected to be friendly, open, and sensitive to the satisfaction of their workgroup (dealing with others in a friendly way).

PASSIVE/DEFENSIVE NORMS

Passive-defensive cultures, in which members believe they must interact with *people* in ways that will not threaten their own *security*, are characterized by approval, conventional, dependent, and avoidance norms.

Approval   An approval culture describes organizations in which conflicts are avoided and interpersonal relationships are pleasant—at least superficially. Members feel that they should agree with, gain the approval of, and be liked by others ("going along" with others).

Conventional   A conventional culture is descriptive of organizations that are conservative, traditional, and bureaucratically controlled. Members are expected to conform, follow the rules, and make a good impression (always following policies and practices).

Dependent   A dependent culture is descriptive of organizations that are hierarchically controlled and nonparticipative. Centralized decision making in such organizations leads members to do only what they are told and to clear all decisions with superiors (pleasing those in positions of authority).

Avoidance   An avoidance culture characterizes organizations that fail to reward success but nevertheless punish mistakes. This negative reward system leads members to shift responsibilities to others and avoid any possibility of being blamed for a mistake (waiting for others to act first).

AGGRESSIVE/DEFENSIVE NORMS

Aggressive-defensive cultures, in which members are expected to approach *tasks* in forceful ways to protect their status and *security,* are characterized by "oppositional, power, competitive, and perfectionistic norms" (Cooke and Szumal, 1993, p. 1302).

Oppositional   An oppositional culture describes organizations in which confrontation and negativism are rewarded. Members gain status and influence by being critical and thus are reinforced to oppose the ideas of others (pointing out flaws).

Power

A power culture is descriptive of non-participative organizations structured on the basis of the authority inherent in members' positions. Members believe they will be rewarded for taking charge, controlling subordinates and, at the same time, being responsive to the demands of superiors (building up one's power base).

Competitive

A competitive culture is one in which winning is valued and members are rewarded for outperforming one another. Members operate in a "win-lose" framework and believe they must work against (rather than with) their peers to be noticed (turning the job into a contest).

Perfectionistic

A perfectionistic culture characterizes organizations in which perfectionism, persistence, and hard work are valued. Members feel they must avoid any mistake, keep track of everything, and work long hours to attain narrowly defined objectives (doing things perfectly).

Sources: Cooke and Lafferty (1983, 1986, 1987). © 1987 by Human Synergistics, Inc. Adapted by permission.

PHOTO CREDITS

Chapter 1

page 6: © David Paul Morris/Bloomberg via Getty Images; page 11: © PR NEWSWIRE / AP

Chapter 2

page 26: © 2010, Zappos.com, Inc.; page 30: Joe Raedle/Getty Images; page 39: © Jason Reed/Reuters/Corbis; Jay Mallin/Bloomberg via Getty Images

Chapter 3

page 73: © Bloomberg via Getty Images; © Bloomberg via Getty Images

Chapter 4

page 100: © KP MacLane/Brian Woodcock

Chapter 5

page 127: © Bloomberg via Getty Images; page 137: © Willie Davis/Aravind Eye Foundation; page 138: © Martin Klimek/ZUMApress.com

Chapter 6

page 153: © PRNewsFoto/Gilt Groupe/AP; page 157: © Amazon.com; page 161 © Bloomberg via Getty Images; page 166: © American Apparel

Chapter 7

page 192: © Bloomberg via Getty Images; page 205: © Julie Dermansky/Julie Dermansky/Corbis; page 208: © Bloomberg via Getty Images

Chapter 8

page 248: © AP Photo/Mike Derer; page 250: © Bloomberg via Getty Images

Chapter 9

page 259: © Bloomberg via Getty Images; page 267 © PRNewsFoto/Novo Nordisk/AP; page 273: © Bloomberg via Getty Images

Chapter 10

page 294: © Proctor and Gamble; page 298: © Toyota; page 303 © Apple Inc.

Chapter 11

page 326: © Paulo Fridman/Corbis; page 333: © Bloomberg via Getty Images; page 336: © Bloomberg via Getty Images

Chapter 12

page 345: © PRNewsFoto/W. L. Gore & Associates/AP

COMPANY INDEX

NAME INDEX

SUBJECT INDEX